PRAISE FOR COLD CASE CONFESSION

'This case is like an Agatha Christie whodunit:
abduction, murder and a confession.'
– *Carte Blanche*

'Wonderful, evocative and vivid writing. Eliseev is a
very exciting new talent.'
– Peter James

'This book has become a South African classic.'
– Jenny Crwys Williams

'Johannesburg is often described as a city of
immigrants, and Eliseev and Ketani are two
eloquent examples. One has given voice to another.
It seems pleasingly fitting.'
– Sue Blaine, *Business Day*

'One of the most electric and captivating legal battles
in South African history.'
– *Get It* magazine

'An intriguing and heartfelt read.'
– Patricia McCracken, *Farmers Weekly*

Grateful acknowledgment is made to the Taco Kuiper Fund for Investigative Journalism based at Wits Journalism, University of the Witwatersrand, Johannesburg, for covering some of the costs associated with this book.

COLD CASE CONFESSION

Unravelling the Betty Ketani Murder

With a new final chapter and updated Epilogue added for this edition

Alex Eliseev

For Robin and Kim,
Thank you for keeping this
story alive and for everything
you have done for me.
In deep gratitude,

Alex

MARCH 2019

MACMILLAN

*Proceeds from this book will be shared with Betty Ketani's children
and her brother Mankinki Kula.*

First published in 2016
by Pan Macmillan South Africa

This edition published in 2017
by Pan Macmillan South Africa
Private Bag X19
Northlands
Johannesburg
2116

www.panmacmillan.co.za

ISBN 978-1-77010-554-6
e-ISBN 978-1-77010-555-3

Editing by Sean Fraser
Proofreading by Lisa Compton
Design and typesetting by Triple M Design
Cover design by Anastasya Eliseeva

Printed by **paarlmedia**, a division of Novus Holdings
2428

The role-players

Ndaba Bhebe Relative of a former Cranks waitress. Ndaba was abducted and tortured in 1999. The hidden confession describes this kidnapping.

Vuyani (Ronnie) Bikauri Betty Ketani's brother who reported her missing in 1999.

Ana Bilić One of the state's international DNA experts, based at the ICMP laboratory in Bosnia and Herzegovina.

Claudio Bisso Bones expert called out to the excavation of Betty Ketani's grave.

Teunis Briers Policeman involved in the final excavation of Betty Ketani's grave.

Herman Broodryk Lead prosecutor in the Betty Ketani murder trial. A Senior Counsel, he is one of the most senior state advocates in his jurisdiction.

Blanche Brown Wife of Conway Brown.

Conway Brown Friend of Carrington Laughton. The confession was found at his home, as was the shallow grave in which Betty Ketani's body was buried.

André Coetzer Friend and former business associate of Carrington Laughton. He is mentioned in the confession relating to the 1999 Hillbrow abductions.

Warren Dawson State witness who testified in relation to Carrington Laughton's alibi.

Rachel Dube Former Cranks employee, and the last known person to see Betty Ketani alive.

Mark Eardley Owner of the farm on which Betty Ketani died after being left inside an old bus on a winter's night. Not implicated in the kidnapping and murder.

Sandor Egyed Friend of Carrington Laughton, and the man to whom the confession is addressed. Resides in New Zealand.

Alan Fagan Yeoville police commander who interviewed Carrington Laughton during his arrest.

Keith Green (Doc) Former Scorpions undercover agent who investigated the Betty Ketani murder following the discovery of the confession.

Cecil Greenfield Defence's handwriting expert who testified on behalf of Carrington Laughton.

Karyn Griffin Mark Lister's ex-girlfriend, and state witness who testified in relation to Carrington Laughton's alibi.

Laurence Hodes Senior Counsel and experienced lawyer who was Carrington Laughton's defence advocate.

Betty Tandiwe Ketani Mother of three, kidnapped and murdered in May 1999. Worked as a cook at Cranks restaurant in Johannesburg.

Bulelwa Ketani Betty Ketani's eldest daughter.

Lusanda Ketani Betty Ketani's youngest daughter. She was seven months old when her mother vanished.

Thulani Ketani Betty Ketani's son and the oldest of her three children.

Namika Kowlas Prosecutor in the Betty Ketani trial. Herman Broodryk's junior.

Mankinki Kula Betty Ketani's older brother.

Anel Laughton Third wife of Carrington Laughton.

Candice Laughton First wife of Carrington Laughton. Her attempted suicide in 1999 is mentioned in the confession.

Carrington Laughton Former private investigator and the alleged author of the confession found under the carpet. He denies murdering Betty Ketani.

Jayne Laughton Second wife of Carrington Laughton. She testified against him in relation to an envelope of photographs she was asked to keep safe on his behalf.

Mark Lister Former policeman residing in Australia. Hidden confession mentions him in relation to the Betty Ketani murder and other crimes.

Jabez Loubser (JB) Friend and business partner of Keith Green, and private investigator who investigated the Betty Ketani murder following the discovery of the confession.

Jeffrey Marshall Young man who discovered the hidden confession under a carpet at his parents' house.

Shama Marshall Involved in the discovery of the confession. Jeffrey Marshall's mother. At the time, engaged to Werner Nortjé.

Thabang Mathopo Carrington Laughton's defence advocate and Laurence Hodes's junior.

Ruth Mncube Former Cranks employee, who escaped a kidnapping in June 1999 and is mentioned in the confession.

Malemleli Mpofu Victim named in the confession but never found.

Eric Neeteson-Lemkes Owner of Cranks restaurant and Betty Ketani's former boss. Carrington Laughton claims Eric framed him for murder.

Monique Neeteson-Lemkes Eric Neeteson-Lemkes's daughter. Hidden confession mentions her in relation to the Betty Ketani murder and other crimes. Resides in Australia.

André Neethling Senior policeman who assisted the Yeoville detectives investigating the Betty Ketani murder.

Werner Nortjé Involved in the discovery of the confession. At the time, engaged to Jeffrey Marshall's mother. Family spokesman and representative in court.

Thomas Parsons One of the state's international DNA experts. He works at the ICMP, a world-renowned laboratory in Bosnia and Herzegovina.

Melanie Pienaar Police forensics expert based at the Victim Identification Centre, and involved in the final exhumation of Betty Ketani's grave.

Gerhard Pretorius Senior police detective based in Yeoville, involved in the early stages of the Betty Ketani murder investigation.

Natvarial Ranchod High Court judge who presided over the Betty Ketani murder trial.

Carel Ranger Former policeman implicated in kidnapping Betty Ketani from hospital. Also accused of being involved in a spate of violent Cranks-related abductions in Hillbrow in 1999.

David Ranger Implicated in kidnapping Betty Ketani from hospital, and still serving as a policeman at the time of his arrest.

Leonie Ras Head of the police's Victim Identification Centre. She suggested that the three small bones be sent abroad for DNA tests.

Leon Rehrl Friend of Carrington Laughton, and ex-husband of Carrington's second wife, Jayne. He testified in Carrington Laughton's defence.

Dirk Reinecke Friend of Carrington Laughton, and a crucial link in how Carrington's confession came to be in Conway Brown's possession.

Lufuno Sono Detective at Yeoville police station, and initial investigating officer in the Betty Ketani murder case.

David Swanepoel Defence's DNA expert.

Paul Toft-Nielsen Childhood friend of Carrington Laughton, and implicated in digging up Betty Ketani's grave and disposing of her body.

Themba Tshabalala Married to a former Cranks waitress, and the victim of several 1999 kidnappings linked to the restaurant.

Marco van der Hammen Police handwriting expert who examined the confession.

James van Rooyen Former police detective who investigated the 1999 Hillbrow abductions linked to Cranks restaurant.

Gerhard van Wyk Police detective based at the Hawks, and the second and final investigating officer in the Betty Ketani murder case.

Roelof van Wyk Defence advocate representing Carel and David Ranger.

Warren Williams Hidden confession mentions him in relation to the Betty Ketani murder. He denies any involvement and, due to lack of evidence, was not arrested or prosecuted.

Howard Woolf Carrington Laughton's instructing attorney.

The full confession letter can be found in the Appendix, starting on page 401.

PART ONE

An unfinished life

'When Death comes cloaked in mystery he is terrible indeed.'

— AMBROSE BIERCE, 'MY FAVORITE MURDER'

1.

The truth ... according to Conway Brown

The R59 highway out of Johannesburg enters another gentle bend as Conway spots the blue, red and white glow of the Engen 1-Stop petrol station and the dark outline of the Blockhouse watchtower, a lingering ghost from a forgotten battlefield, once used to guard a railway running across the Highveld.

The city lights are long gone and there's little out here except maize and dairy farms, empty windswept fields and slivers of low-lying hills off in the distance.

Conway Brown is behind the wheel of his wife's second-hand Uno, almost 40 kilometres out of town. He has no idea why Carrington Laughton has called him out this late in the evening.

In the boot, just in case it's a roadside emergency, Conway has packed his toolbox and tow rope. He's also thrown in some jumper cables.

As instructed, Conway drives past the slipway leading into the Blockhouse 1-Stop and pulls over in the emergency lane of the highway near the exit. Carrington is already there. He doesn't wait for the Uno Pacer to reach him; instead he climbs into a dark sedan and fires up the engine. Through his open window, Conway offers a greeting, hoping for an explanation.

'Just follow me,' Carrington replies.

Conway hasn't bothered to change out of his T-shirt, tracksuit pants and sneakers. He had been painting when his phone rang. He figured either someone had broken down or he would need to help out with another one of Carrington's private investigations, a part-time job that occasionally earns him a few hundred bucks. Either way, he'd be home in a few hours.

He lights a cigarette as he follows the car in front of him back onto the highway, turning up the music on the new sound system he installed for his wife.

Another man might have questioned why he was being asked to leave his family at night and drive out of the city. But Conway's entire life has been spent being tossed about in a turbulent stream of adventures and misadventures. He's often landed up in situations, as he puts it, far broader than his IQ. Plus, Carrington has not only thrown some jobs his way, he is someone Conway admires: a businessman, a smart sleuth, the product of a wealthy family who, in his mind, has money, power and friends in all the right places. Conway, on the other hand, is a boilermaker's son and a Grade 8 dropout. The kind of man who once woke up in Durban with a skull-crushing hangover and a tattoo of a bird on his bicep or, on another occasion, in hospital after a punch-up at a pizzeria. He's also battling financially and is in no position to turn down requests from the one person he believes can change his fortune.

So when the call came, Conway packed his things and shouted across the house: 'I've got to go and help someone; they're stuck.' He said nothing about whom he was meeting because he knew his wife would get angry. She has never approved of this particular friendship, convinced it would lead her husband deep into trouble.

Conway hasn't finished his cigarette before the lead car begins to indicate left. He's not familiar with these parts and doesn't recognise the off-ramp. It's the first or second after the Engen petrol station. A moment later, they swing back over the highway and make a sharp left turn onto a sand road.

The smooth tar disappears and the white Uno begins to rattle over the uneven surface, its wheels spitting out loose stones. The two cars kick up a cloud of dust and Conway eases off the accelerator. He doesn't want to damage his wife's car or return it to her 'covered in shit'. He watches every bump, every stone, every pothole, trying to drive as carefully as possible.

The road is dark. There's not a single street lamp and the farms around them appear to be fast asleep. Conway can make out a green fence on the left as he follows the glare of the red tail lights in front of him. Carrington couldn't have picked a quieter spot.

A minor intersection appears in the distance and Conway watches Carrington turn right and then perform a sharp U-turn, driving back down the street. The car's headlights run over the thick bush, sweeping across the darkness like a lighthouse.

As the lead car slows down and stops, Conway drifts over to the right side of the road to meet Carrington head-on. He leaves a gap between the bumpers, kills the headlights, silences the music and switches off the engine before climbing out. The sand and gravel crunch under his feet.

The silent street runs parallel to the R59 Sybrand van Niekerk freeway, separated in parts by tall bluegum trees. The branches catch flashes of light from the highway and shred them into soft flickers. Somewhere in the distance a dog barks.

Carrington climbs out and walks to the back of his car. It looks like he's opening the boot. No, the back door. Suddenly, there are two figures. Two silhouettes that look like friends stumbling out of a bar, one holding up the other.

Carrington says something, but the words are swept away by the panicked thoughts that flood Conway's head. He's now two metres away, close enough to see that it's a woman, her hands bound behind her back and her head covered with some kind of fabric. A black balaclava or a hood of some kind. The moonlight makes it difficult to distinguish. Carrington says something like 'Hold here', and shoves the woman towards him. Suddenly she's in his arms, her hidden face just centimetres from his. Conway fights to regain his balance. He's a strong man and springs back quickly.

He doesn't know who the woman is. He doesn't know whether she's been injured or drugged. He doesn't know why she's been kidnapped and brought here. He can feel her breasts against his chest. She's short and stocky, dressed in dark clothes.

Take away the weather, take away the wind and the cold. It's pitch, pitch black. Leave a black vacuum, so there is nothing, it's just space. You can't hear the cars behind you on the highway. You don't have the smell of the trees. You don't have any of that. Everything is quiet and at that instant your mind is running at a hundred kilometres in all directions.

Conway sees a flash of silver in Carrington's right hand. He can't make out what it is. The steel spike looks like a knitting needle the size of a small radio aerial or a bicycle spoke. In one swift, silent action, Carrington stabs the woman in the right side of her head with the sharp silver weapon. It penetrates somewhere around the ear, with enough force to break through her skull. There's no blood. The woman makes no sound as her legs buckle. For a split second Conway tries to hold her up, but it feels like a 100-kilogram stone has fallen into his arms. He releases his grip and lets her drop to the ground.

> *Carrington just turns around and walks away. He doesn't say anything. I turn around and run towards my car. I get to my car, or I'm climbing into my car, when he pulls up next to me. He looks through the passenger window, looks at me and carries on. I turn the car around and leave. I don't know where he goes. His headlights disappear. There is nothing. There is dust …*

Leaving the woman where she has fallen, Conway tries to catch up to Carrington. As he joins the highway, he realises his friend is gone. He starts to panic. He's trying to gather his thoughts, trying to figure out what just happened. He bursts into tears. He can't undo any of it. The pressure balloons in his chest. He feels sick and scared. It all happened so quickly. In what seems like a split second. Playing out like some silent movie.

Conway is in shock, his hands shaking, the bile rising in his throat, but there's no time to process it all now. His first instinct is to figure out what evidence links him to the crime scene. He's in his wife's car and wonders whether anyone saw the number plate. He is sure no one could have. He thinks about any possible markings on the car. Tyre marks in the sand. Anything to connect the car to the murder.

As he approaches the Blockhouse again, he's replaying the scene in his mind. Did anyone see him? Did he leave anything behind? Footprints. He definitely left footprints. What if the police can use these to identify him as one of the killers? He has seen it done on television. Without stopping, Conway winds down the passenger-side window of the small Uno, wrestles with his sneakers, tosses them out into the darkness and drives home barefoot.

The truth ... according to Carrington Laughton

Alone in his limited-edition Mazda Astina, its windows tinted for covert surveillance, Carrington clocks up thousands of kilometres between Johannesburg and Cape Town. Weekdays are spent working at the coast and the weekends with his wife Candice, who is trying to manage their business in his absence but is not coping. This back and forth between the two cities continues for five full weeks.

Carrington Laughton has his mind set on growing C&C Commercial Services. The company is still new, but already he feels as though things are stagnating. Last year, in the summer, he and Candice flew to England to explore their business options and to network. A few months later, a contact they had made there visited them in South Africa to discuss new technology being used in the world of private investigations: high-tech spy cameras, bugging equipment and the like. They managed to secure a meeting with government officials involved in state security and gave them the sales pitch. It was all looking very promising.

Then came another business opportunity. Candice was working part-time as a waitress at a bar in Hyde Park and met barman Mark Lister. He was considering moving to Cape Town and proposed running the Laughtons' business from there, as a franchise. Mark brought one of his friends, Warren Dawson, into the mix and the four of them began sculpting an agreement.

The first formal negotiation took place six months ago, when Carrington and Candice were in Cape Town. They had gone to visit her aunt and uncle in Newlands and used the time to meet their new business partners.

Mark and Warren are in their early twenties and have no experience in investigation. They have access to a little company called Edenvale Dry Cleaners, which can trade under a different name. Warren lives in a small, messy house in End Street in Swanepoel, near Hermanus, a room of which will serve as their office. He's 21 and this, he feels, is an opportunity to do something with his life. Mark lives in Johannesburg and is dating one of Warren's friends. He's a police reservist who spends his free time exercising horses for the mounted unit at his station. His studies aren't going well so he too is ready for a new adventure.

A month ago, with the help of Carrington's lawyer, a franchise agreement was signed and Mark and Warren were introduced to their first client, a baggage-handling company. Their brief was to find and place a few undercover agents at Cape Town International Airport and then to debrief them, sending the reports to Carrington. It was a pretty standard operation designed to catch out employees pilfering suitcases.

But Mark and Warren are young, have never worked in the field and are tripping over all the basics. For Carrington, this is a crisis. His company's reputation is precious and he can't afford to let the standards drop. He is a proud man and image is important. That's why he decides to help Mark and Warren get their business off the ground. The intention is to teach them how to communicate with clients, write up reports and manage all that happens in between. In order to spend time with them, he's prepared to run his new Astina to Cape Town and back – a thousand kilometres in each direction – every week for more than a month.

> I was there to guide and assist them and to make sure that they were doing the job properly. It was important for me that, as it was my company name and my reputation, that the job was done correctly. So I would be half a step behind them, looking over their shoulders, making sure they were doing things correctly.

The training with Mark and Warren takes place at precisely the same time that Conway says the two of them met on the shoulder of the R59 highway. According to Carrington, on that night, and most others that month, he was on the other side of the country.

Carrington denies every detail of what he calls Conway's 'horror story', from the phone call to the stabbing. He claims that none of it happened. Instead, he describes himself as an ethical man with a personal code, a decorated army lieutenant and devoted family man, envied by those around him. He claims none of his investigations ever turned violent.

Carrington dismisses his friend's version as 'absolute rubbish'. Pure fiction. He says the accusations are so far-fetched, so ridiculous, they wouldn't cut it in a B-grade movie.

The truth ...

Two men know the truth.

There are no other witnesses to what Conway says happened near the Blockhouse. No crime scene. No forensic evidence. No body. Just his word against Carrington's. One man who says he was destroyed by a dark secret and another who claims he is the victim of a sinister conspiracy to frame him for a murder he did not commit.

An unsolvable mystery. A dead end. Or is it just the beginning? One thread of evidence in a fist-like knot loosened by a most unexpected discovery. A discovery which reveals that a better place to start searching for answers about the events Conway describes is back in Johannesburg, a few days earlier, inside the kitchen of one of the city's best-loved and most peculiar restaurants ...

2.

Rachel Dube arrives for her shift at Cranks to find that her colleague, Tandiwe Ketani, has already mixed the next batch of Thai sauces, tossed her blue apron into the wash basket and is preparing some rubbish bags to be thrown out.

Tandiwe greets Rachel – whom she affectionately calls 'Oros' (a private joke based on how much sweet concentrate her friend drank during a recent pregnancy) – and asks Rachel to help her take out the trash.

It's around five o'clock in the evening and Tandiwe is knocking off a day shift at the Rosebank eatery, handing over to Rachel, who, along with Nomsa, will work into the night until the last customers leave. It's late May 1999.

Tandiwe is the head cook and has worked at Cranks for 13 or 14 years, teaching most of the other women how to prepare the exotic Eastern dishes. Over the years, she has become the owner's favourite and most trusted chef.

Cranks is a cultural enigma, a bohemian bubble of a restaurant that started out in Hillbrow in the mid-1980s and has been reborn three times around town, eventually landing up in the wealthy northern suburbs. Its owner, Eric Neeteson-Lemkes, calls himself 'Mad Dog' and is notorious for his volcanic temper. His bakkie, with barbed wire wrapped around the canopy and the words 'Loverboy' and 'Yanky Go Home!' painted across the back, is a curious site at the Rosebank Mall. Even his most loyal admirers call him a 'strange man'.

In its current incarnation, the restaurant's décor is a psychedelic clash of themes, including naked Barbie dolls contorted into all kinds of sexual positions and suspended from the ceiling; wild, colourful lanterns; mannequins wrapped in silver tinfoil; giant metal insect creatures with bright-red lobster claws; mosaics and mirrors; and cheap plastic tablecloths. 'Welcome to Fabulous Cranks Bangkok,' the Las Vegas-style sign above the entrance declares. It's a freak show, but just about everyone in Johannesburg has a Cranks story. Most begin with a description of how bizarre the place is (with a compulsory mention of the mysterious owner) and end with how wonderful or irresistible the food is. It's a hugely popular, gaudy spot with a constant flow of customers. What makes it even more interesting is the mystery that swirls around the establishment. Some suspect it's a cheap brothel. Others are convinced it's a front for a drug den. No one really knows what lies behind Cranks and the rumours only boost its popularity. What most people agree on, though, is that when it opened in Joburg, Cranks was the first of its kind, offering authentic Thai, Vietnamese and Indonesian cuisine.

In Rosebank, Eric attempted to recreate a typical scene from the busy, sweaty streets of Bangkok. He wasn't interested in expensive finishes, choosing instead cheap forks that easily bend out of shape and Corn Flakes boxes for decorations. A shot of schnapps awaits patrons on arrival, followed by hot, oily spring rolls. There is often live entertainment and tables are pushed aside to make room for a dance floor, which only shuts down in the early hours of the morning. It is a portal to a faraway land. A 'wondrous' escape where Eric glides from table to table, sharing tales from abroad and ordering meals (aromatic curries, pungent soups and mussels) for his spellbound customers.

Eric hired Tandiwe to work at Cranks in the eighties, when the restaurant was still a tiny bistro tucked away behind the OK Bazaars in Hillbrow. She was then a single mother in her mid-twenties who had travelled from the Eastern Cape to find work. Like so many others during apartheid, Tandiwe left her family behind in Queenstown to take whatever job she could find in Joburg, the 'city of thieves and dreamers' but also a place of immense wealth. She also began using her Christian name: Betty.

For a few years after school, she worked as a domestic housekeeper; the last stamp in her pass book (a sinister creation of the apartheid state) was signed by a 'Dr BP Rabinowitz'. In her *dompas*, the black-and-white photograph of Betty shows a young woman with short, neat hair and no hint of make-up. Her face seems gentle, with soft, round features. Her eyes are impossible to read. The Betty that will bloom in Johannesburg – falling in love with bright lipstick, parties and shopping – has not yet emerged.

Coincidentally, Eric was born in Tarkastad, about 60 kilometres west of Queenstown and the same tiny Karoo town outside which Betty's father, Wilson, grew up. Betty and Eric travelled very different roads to Johannesburg, but those who worked at Cranks said they always got on well and had grown close.

Probably out of fear, the staff at Cranks called Eric 'indlovu', which in isiZulu means 'elephant'. Betty was the only one who stood up to the elephant and shouted back at him when he went into one of his rages. After all the years, she had another name for him: 'Umlunguwami', which loosely translated means 'my white man'. She was known to always speak her mind and defend her colleagues. In the words of Winnie Mlelo, a waitress who worked there at the time, 'She was one person who didn't take shit from anyone.' In another setting, she may well have become a trade-union shop steward or leader.

Betty was also a mother figure at the restaurant. She cooked chicken wings and rice for the other ladies and walked around calling them 'my children', even though she was only in her late thirties and they were just a few years younger than her. The job kept her in the kitchen but Betty knew the waitresses – Ruth, Mighty, Esther and Winnie – who worked out front. Many, if not most, Cranks employees were unregistered foreigners working without contracts and for cash, which arrived in sealed envelopes.

By 1999, Betty had given birth to three children. Thulani, her firstborn, and Bulelwa, her middle child, were back home in Queenstown. Lusanda, who was only seven months old, was with her mother in Johannesburg. All three children were born to different fathers.

When Thulani and Bulelwa came to visit, they remember being treated like special guests at the restaurant, allowed to eat anything they liked. Eric also slipped a little bit of cash for them into envelopes and handed them out as they left.

The cooking job allowed Betty to send money home every month, which she did without fail. She had a large family to support. Whenever she went back to Queenstown, which was two or three times a year, she arrived with bags of clothes for her children. She took great pleasure in spoiling them and ran up her accounts at clothing stores in the city. Her trips to the Eastern Cape were festive occasions.

But by May 1999 something has gone terribly wrong at Cranks. Allegations of theft are flying around, a staff member has been fired and private detectives are snooping around.

No one knows exactly where it all started, but they suspect it was with the arrival of Eric's family from Australia, in particular his daughter Monique, who now works at the restaurant. There haven't been any dramatic changes. Staff are apparently still being made to work long hours for poor pay. Eric still locks them in the kitchen for hours. He still takes away their tips and hurls abuse at his kitchen workers, using the colours of their aprons or physiques to identify them, not taking the trouble to remember their names. But until now, everyone was still able to make the best of the situation. Betty and the others would sing church hymns in the back of the restaurant and have a few drinks when the doors closed. But by late May, even Betty – the most loyal and well-treated employee – has become embroiled in a fight with her bosses.

As Betty and Rachel take out the trash, Betty talks about taking Eric to the Commission for Conciliation, Mediation and Arbitration (CCMA), an organisation established to settle workplace disputes. The two women are close. Betty was there to comfort Rachel after she lost her baby two weeks ago. Rachel took time off work to grieve and this is her first day back. Seeing Betty emptying the rubbish bins surprises her.

Betty complains that 22-year-old Monique – who grew up in her family's restaurants – has demoted her, ordering her (the head cook and the longest-serving employee) to wash dishes and take out the trash. There's also a dispute over what she calls a 'long-service fee' should she leave. Betty says she's ready to quit but isn't being allowed to. She is angry and bitter. More importantly, she's broke, relying on her boyfriend to help with taxi fare to and from Rosebank as well as money for groceries.

Once they have had a good vent, the women prepare to go their separate ways. Betty asks Rachel to wash her apron and shoes and allow them to dry overnight. She promises to tell her more about her situation when they next meet.

'See you tomorrow,' Betty says, waving goodbye to Rachel.

• • •

The following morning, Betty doesn't arrive at work.

At first, no alarm is raised. Her friends and colleagues figure she drank too much the night before and will arrive later in the day or maybe in time for the next shift. Betty is a hard worker – often the first to arrive in the kitchen – but it's no secret she sometimes drinks at work and loves to spend weekends partying at her friends' houses or drinking beer at the LeRossa pub in Hillbrow. But she doesn't pitch up for work that day. Or the next.

Days pass before people at work begin to worry. Some wonder whether Betty has met a new man and has left the province or even the country. But how could she leave behind an infant daughter? No one believes she is capable of abandoning her children.

Betty is sharing a flat in Berea with her younger sister Nombusela, who, unlike the colleagues at Cranks, begins to worry immediately. Nombusela calls their brother Vuyani Bikauri, who lives in Lenasia, on the other side of the city.

Betty and Vuyani – who is also known as Ronnie – speak often. He uses a public phone near the factory where he works to call the restaurant, hoping to catch her for a few minutes. When he visits, he waits patiently outside Cranks for her to slip out of the kitchen.

Betty has never left town without letting Ronnie know, even if she's going home to the Eastern Cape to be with the rest of their family. She has never gone missing before, not for a day.

Ronnie speaks to Betty's latest boyfriend and Lusanda's father, Small Ndawonde, and establishes that the last time she was with him was on the morning of 20 May. Both Small and Betty live on Olivia Road and are virtually neighbours. That morning, she stopped by his place to fetch some money for food and transport, dashed home to change and went to work.

Ronnie had spoken to his sister a day earlier, on 19 May, and was told that the CCMA had ruled in her favour. It seems to him that on the day she disappeared, Betty was set to have some kind of a confrontation with her employers.

Ronnie calls their elder sister Lilly, who lives in Queenstown, and explains the situation. Lilly arrives in Johannesburg to help with the search. They visit Betty's flat and find her ID book along with all her belongings. Her clothes are all there. She has vanished with nothing but what she was wearing that

Thursday morning. Betty didn't own a passport, so nobody from her family even considers the possibility that she may have left the country.

With the help of her boyfriend, they track down Betty's friends and ask whether any of them have seen her. They start to check hospitals, mortuaries and police stations. They chat to Rachel and are told about her last interaction with Betty. At Cranks, a white man walks out to speak to them, but says he knows nothing about their sister's whereabouts.

Winnie, a waitress, remembers seeing this, saying it was Eric who sent Betty's family on their way after what appeared to be a fight. She says that if he saw staff members speaking to them, he would shout, 'Why are you talking to those people, what do they want, what are they saying?' She adds: 'Eric called me and warned me not to talk to Betty's family ...'

Lilly spends about a week in Johannesburg, but has to go back to the school where she teaches. Ronnie calls their mother, Eunice, who also lives in the Eastern Cape. She tells him to wait and see what happens.

'Only God knows whether she will come back,' the old woman says.

Nine days after Betty was last seen, Ronnie runs out of patience and walks into the Hillbrow police station to open a missing person case. He is assisted in filling out a lengthy SAP55, a dreary government form similar to those at a licensing centre or a home affairs office. Ronnie is told that the details from that form will be loaded onto the police database and circulated, while a station-level detective will be assigned to investigate the case.

He gives as much information as he can but somehow his sister's name and surname are recorded as 'Thandiwe Betty Khethane' instead of the 'Tandiwe Ketani' that appears in her ID book. With Ronnie's guidance, the police officer works through the rest of the pages, filling in blank lines or marking appropriate boxes with an 'X'.

Identity Number: 620219 0081 089
Birthplace: Queenstown
Age Group: Middle Aged
Race: BL
Ethnic Group: Xhosa
Marital Status: Unmarried
Address: Houghton Residence, No. 38, Olivia Road, Berea

Crime Suspected: No
Place Missing: The last time she was seen is when she went to work
on 20-05-99. (The time is given as 7.30am.)
Last Seen By: S Ndawonde
Relationship: Boyfriend
Build: Fat
Height: Approximately 1.6m
Hair Colour: Black. Relaxed. Not very long, on the neck
Forehead: Broad
Nose: Particularly large
Ears: Particularly small
Chin: Round
Teeth: Missing. Three lower front teeth missing and she wears false
teeth
Complexion: Brown coffee
Speech Impairment: Normal

Crude descriptions required by the police. Under 'Occupation/Employer Information', Betty is listed as a 'caterer' working at Cranks restaurant in Rosebank since 1985. Some sections are skipped altogether, like 'Tattoos' and 'Scars'. Under hobbies, the following is noted: 'Sitting at home. To have some drinks with friends.'

Ronnie names the school Betty attended in Queenstown as Nkwanla High School (which is, in fact, Nkwanca Senior Secondary School) but tells the officer he doesn't know how far she got. To be safe, on the following page under 'Qualification', he commits to 'Standard 8' (Grade 10). With families torn apart by distance, even the most basic facts can prove elusive.

As with all missing persons reports, the outfit Betty was wearing when she was last seen is recorded. She left home in a pair of blue jeans, a red jacket, and green, red and yellow shoes.

Just before signing an indemnity form to allow the police to send Betty's photograph to the public broadcaster to be shown on television, and despite answering 'No' to a question about whether a crime has been committed, Ronnie raises a suspicion with the police officer, who writes it down on the final page:

The reporter suspects Thandiwe's boss from Cranks restaurant as they had some quarell [sic] after her boss told her that there was no more work and he does not have money to pay her any more. That is when Thandiwe wanted her money that she worked for.

The SAP55 is fed into the system and carried away to the Missing Persons division at what is now the Sophiatown police station. The unit deals with thousands of missing persons reports each year. Some years 5 000 names cross the desks, other years there are as many as 7 000. On average, a third of all people reported missing are never found.

In 1999, the role of the Missing Persons division is to guide the traffic, so to speak, and to make sure all names are logged, circulated and sent for broadcast on the SABC. When there are lulls in the reports, and inboxes are low, members call to check up on cases. But the physical investigation, the actual tracing, is done by detectives at various stations.

Inspector Johan Reynecke, who joined the unit when it opened in 1994 and who will go on to become its commander, receives the Betty Ketani form on 31 May 1999.

He makes an entry in an A4 notebook, writing Betty's name below a list of other people who have disappeared. There's 67-year-old Dimakatso Monaka, who went missing in Mamelodi, near Pretoria. There are three teenagers: Cynthia Sithole, Eliya Mocamo and Sendrina Mabaso. There's Angelina Mohlala, a 20-year-old from Kagiso, and pages upon pages of other names.

Betty is the last entry for the month of May and Reynecke leaves some blank space in his notebook before drawing a thick line across the double-page spread. He crunches some numbers, scribbling notes as he goes. Reported: 22. Over 18: 14. Under 18: 8. Found: 5.

The month of June will bring new names onto the neat columns of Reynecke's notebook: Kholeka Ngwanya (22, Pretoria Central); Victoria Malinga (38, Etwatwa); Lenah Tsotetsi (34, Letlhabile); Refilwe Mufamane (17, Vaalwater); Sevinhlanhla Nkabinde (4, Alexandra) …

Reynecke flags children as priority cases by circling their ages. Betty is 37 and nothing about her case warrants special attention. She exists as a combination of letters and numbers on a piece of paper.

Betty's case receives a new reference number before being pushed to Pretoria, to be logged into the system. Reynecke notes the police case assigned at Hillbrow: CAS 12/05/1999. By the time her name is sent to head office, her first name has become 'Thanoiwe' and her surname has been butchered. On a conveyor belt carrying thousands of names, dates, ages, addresses and identity numbers, glitches like this are common.

Once Betty's name is circulated, the country's border posts will be alerted not to let her in or out without notifying the police. Theoretically, if she lands up at a hospital or a mortuary, finding out who she is and tracking down her next of kin should be possible – if not through her name, then at least with her identity number.

At Cranks, little is said of Betty's disappearance. There are many theories but these are not discussed in public. Eric will later claim he noticed Betty's disappearance but assumed she had a family problem and left town. To him, this was not unusual and eventually he just 'let it go'. As far as the customers are concerned, it's business as usual.

Lilly returns to Queenstown with a heavy heart. She tells her mother that she has done everything she could to find her sister Tandiwe, whose name means 'the loved one' or 'the loving one'. Thulani, Bulelwa and Lusanda will now live with their grandmother Eunice, who is in her sixties.

Betty's youngest sister, Nomapelo, sends a letter to the television programme *Khumbul'Ekhaya*, which helps reunite broken families or trace lost relatives. The show is full of miraculous stories of long-lost family members appearing after decades of being missing. She tries twice, but nothing comes of it.

3.

In his youth, Betty Ketani's son, Thulani, was a troublemaker. At the age of 13, he was caught shoplifting and his mother sat him down and warned him never to steal again. She told him that with her job in Johannesburg she would provide whatever he needed and asked him to focus on his schoolwork. She threatened to withhold his Christmas gifts, but didn't have the heart to go through with the threat.

Later Thulani and his teenage friends were caught trying to get drunk on a strange concoction of Coca-Cola and Disprin. Betty gave them a case of Black Label beer and locked them in her house, ordering them to drink every last drop. Before long, the liquor overpowered the boys and they slept off the lesson, waking up to regret it. But, being so far away, Betty couldn't keep Thulani off the streets, where he continued to drink, smoke and misbehave.

During the Easter holidays of 1999 – just weeks before she vanished – Betty returned home to visit her family. Lusanda was not yet a year old and the only thing Bulelwa remembers from that occasion was seeing her mother off at the taxi rank. But for Thulani, the visit marked a milestone in his life.

First, he and his mother went to apply for his ID book at the Department of Home Affairs in Queenstown. Betty had never registered Thulani's birth so she had to fill out a special form and submit a signed letter from the headmaster of his school. On 13 April 1999, Betty and her son handed in all the required documents.

Then they sat down to discuss his passage into manhood. It wasn't an easy conversation to have with his mother, but he didn't know his father and the time had arrived. A Xhosa boy must go 'up the mountain' to undergo a traditional circumcision so that he can return a man. Thulani was six months away from turning 18 and asked his mother for permission to take part in the ritual. She agreed.

Later that year, he went through *ulwaluko*, leaving his childhood behind and finding a new status in his community. The circumcision ritual is gruelling and can be dangerous – even fatal – and is followed by a hearty traditional feast. On his return, Thulani celebrated with one of his mother's uncles instead of her. He didn't know why Betty wasn't there to witness his proud moment. He had no idea it would be the first of many missed moments.

For some time, the adults of the family tried to shield Betty's children from what had happened to their mother. Perhaps they hoped she would reappear and all would be well again, and the children could be spared the trauma. But weeks turned into months and months melted into years and eventually CAS 12/05/1999 was filed away as unsolved.

Betty's case became another statistic gathered by one of the country's busiest police stations. The Hillbrow flatlands – or the 'Bronx', as local policemen used to call it – was notorious for swallowing up those who had come in search of a better life.

A policeman who worked in Hillbrow in the late nineties recalls: 'As a duty officer, I had 13 murder scenes in a week, of which 11 were on the weekend. You didn't sleep. And the building hijackings, robberies, drugs … it was like a Christmas tree of crime.'

He says Hillbrow was a 'punishment station', where officers were sent if they misbehaved or annoyed their commanders. 'It was a haven for any corrupt policeman. I mean for taking money off Nigerians, Zimbabweans and Mozambicans. We had a large amount of these cases …'

Betty's file landed on the desk of a randomly selected detective. From the docket diary, it's clear he – or whoever continued with the investigation – made no serious attempt to find out what happened to her.

On 31 May 1999, the same day the SAP55 reached the Missing Persons division, the officer received orders from his commander to interview Betty's family and friends. The diary section in the docket reflects this instruction:

1. *Received for further investigation.*
2. *Entry noted and will be complied with.*

On the same day, a photo of a relaxed Betty posing with a small group of friends was sent to Pretoria to be circulated.

The next entry comes half a month later, on 15 June 1999: 'Person still missing.' The words are followed by a signature.

A month and a half passes before the diary is updated, this time on 27 July 1999: 'Person still missing.'

In late September the investigating officer writes, 'No answer', meaning he can't reach Ronnie Bikauri, who reported his sister missing. Four whole months have lapsed and the police have yet to take a statement from Betty's family.

The last entry in the diary is made on 6 December 1999, as Betty's children prepare to spend their first Christmas without their mother: 'Reporter not available.'

The entire investigation into Betty Ketani's disappearance is summarised in fewer than 20 words in the docket's diary section, which is supposed to be filled with detailed notes. Ronnie had given two landline numbers in the SAP55 and had left his home address.

There's no record of the detective ever visiting Cranks to speak to Betty's bosses. No evidence of interviews with any of her colleagues or friends, or Tracy the neighbour, who was named in Ronnie's report as a potential witness. There's no effort to interview Betty's boyfriend, who eventually leaves town and is never heard from again. The docket is filed away, buried in the cemetery of unsolved cases. This may not have been a high-priority or high-profile case, and there may not have been many leads to follow, but the ones that were available were ignored.

Lilly returned to Johannesburg a second time, still hoping to find her sister. She had to find money to make the 800-kilometre journey past Lesotho, through Bloemfontein and into the City of Gold. After another week of searching, she returned empty-handed.

As the years slide by, Bulelwa finishes school, singing in the choir and spending a little too much time with her friends. This leads to some stern lectures from Aunt Lilly. Bulelwa's most vivid memory of her mother is from a year she can no longer place, but it was during a visit to Johannesburg, when Betty's flat suddenly filled up with smoke. She remembers standing on the balcony, paralysed by panic, and her mother walking up to her and leading her out through the apartment and down to the safety of the ground floor. She could see Betty's face clearly in those manic moments.

'We watched her flat burn down,' she says. 'It was sad.'

Later in life, when she gives birth to her own children – twin girls – Bulelwa will yearn for Betty's steady hand and motherly advice.

Lusanda, the youngest, never knew her real mother and goes about her life as normal. As far as she is concerned, Lilly is her mom. At school, she studies hard and takes an interest in athletics. She is a natural runner and races for her school, bringing home a few medals. Like her biological mother, she takes a liking to netball.

In 2004, five years after Betty disappeared, her mother, Eunice, dies without ever finding out what happened to her daughter. Like everyone else in the family, she lived with a restless hope that Betty would some day return. That she was alive and had left without having the chance to say goodbye.

Betty's older brother, Mankinki Kula, believes grief played a big role in their mother's death. He says her heart eventually just gave up.

Aunt Lilly takes over from their mother and begins to look after Thulani, Bulelwa and Lusanda. Slowly, the world around them changes. Thulani fails matric and lands up taking part-time jobs as a security guard before falling ill and going onto a government grant. Bulelwa matriculates and gets a job at a busy clothing store while trying to figure out her future. Lusanda grows up and becomes a teenager, her eyes constantly glued to a cellphone, her school photographs earning pride of place in Aunt Lilly's modest home.

Lusanda never knew, but her brother and sister found out that their mother was missing after Bulelwa overheard a conversation the adults in the house were having. Bulelwa wondered whether Betty may have been kidnapped. What she knew for certain was that she would never have abandoned them.

A decision was made to protect Lusanda from the truth. Even when she found what she calls a 'clinic card' from her birth, which gave the mother's name as 'Tandiwe', she was told by Aunt Lilly that Tandiwe was a person who had looked after her. The name was later blanked out.

With Betty gone, her youngest sister, Nomapelo, is sent to live with relatives in the tiny town of Barkly East because their mother can no longer afford to put her through school. Without the money Betty had been sending home, Nomapelo's hopes of studying further are crushed and she begins to work at a petrol-station convenience store. Nombusela, the sister who shared a flat with Betty in Johannesburg, dies in 2008.

In 2010, World Cup football fever blows through Queenstown and Betty's children visit fan parks and pose for cameras, the country's colourful national flag painted on their cheeks. Her brother, Mankinki, builds a giant plastic vuvuzela and fixes it to the roof of his car, earning a brief mention in the local newspaper.

During the same World Cup, Carrington Laughton lands a job offering security to a group of Italian journalists covering the event. As usual, he offers some part-time work to his friends.

In Johannesburg, Cranks hits hard times. Eric Neeteson-Lemkes has gone to war with his landlords and the case lands up in court. He owes more than a million rand in rent and is on the verge of being evicted and having the restaurant's assets seized.

By early 2012, Betty has been missing for nearly 13 years.

Thulani is now a man in his thirties, still sick and unable to work. Bulelwa doesn't know it yet, but she will soon become a mother herself, putting her dreams of being a social worker on hold. Of all the children, her face carries the strongest resemblance to Betty, a genetic echo passed down from mother to daughter. Their brown eyes are hauntingly similar. Bulelwa's wide nose and full lips are identical to Betty's, as is her smile. Bulelwa's warm, playful face makes it easy to imagine a young Betty Ketani in those same features, especially when Bulelwa scrunches up her eyebrows or bites down on her bottom lip.

Now grown up, and finally aware of the truth, Lusanda's head is filled with questions about her real mother. But in almost 13 years (virtually Lusanda's entire life), not a single clue about Betty's disappearance has shaken loose. Not a hint of hope for a family suffering the greatest pain: the absence of closure. Presidents have changed, wars have broken out around the world and a new millennium has arrived. On the police system, Betty is still registered as 'missing'. One afternoon she was chatting to her friend at the restaurant, the next morning she was gone.

Then, on the last day of March 2012, something unusual happens. Behind the walls of a house in Kenilworth, a working-class suburb in Johannesburg south, a secret breaks free and changes everything.

4.

Jeffrey Marshall and his girlfriend are about to leave for a movie at the local mall when his cellphone rings. On the line is his mother's fiancé, Werner, who asks Jeffrey to come home immediately. Werner explains that the place next door, which they've been renting out for years, has been trashed and new tenants are planning to move in the following day. The entire house smells like dog piss and the carpets need to be ripped up. Werner says it's an emergency. Jeffrey plummets into a bad mood, knowing his date night is ruined.

It had started out like any other Saturday. He had picked up his girlfriend Shekaila Troskie from her part-time job and had taken her to ballet class, after which they hung out. He made some bad joke about the fact that her family doesn't have satellite TV and they agreed to go to the cinema at Southgate and find something to watch once they got there.

After the call from Werner, Jeffrey jumps into his mother's old Honda Ballade and speeds all the way to the house in Leo Street, Kenilworth. With nothing better to do, Shekaila comes along for the ride. Most of it is a straight run down Rifle Range Road and the trip takes ten minutes. Jeffrey arrives to find Werner Nortjé on the phone in the kitchen, taking down quotations. Having ruled out the option of having the carpet cleaned, Werner is trying to find out what it will cost to have it replaced or the original wooden floor beneath it restored.

Jeffrey is impressed that Werner, a supermarket chef, is able to reach service providers this late at night, on a weekend, even if the figures they are quoting him are way out of their price range. He's also not at all surprised that Werner has decided to start a major renovation late at night. That's just the kind of man he is.

Once off the phone, Werner explains the situation to Jeffrey. The previous tenants had all but moved out of the house next door and arrived earlier that night to grab the last of their belongings. They came to see him and demanded their R900 deposit. Knowing how much it would cost to fix the floors – which their two 'piss-pot' dogs had ruined – he told them they were out of their minds. They parted ways, them without their deposit and him without any idea how to get the house ready in time for the new tenants.

Jeffrey goes next door to see for himself, taking Shekaila with him. The house his father bought half a century ago is subdivided, and the minute they enter the empty half next door, the smell attacks them. By the time they get to the lounge, in the centre of the home, they are almost gagging and escape out the back to get some air.

The young couple are still dressed for a night out, Jeffrey in his black jeans and New Rock boots and Shekaila in her high heels. She's 17 and still at school, and has only recently been allowed to ride as a passenger on his Yamaha motorbike. He's six years older, with short jet-black hair, heavy dark eyebrows and bushy sideburns. He relies on discreet hearing aids and lip-reads when holding a conversation. Two sets of earrings – one gold, one silver – hang from his ears. A little awkwardly, he carries the image of a 1950s rebel.

Once back inside the house, Jeffrey digs into his pocket and pulls out a silver butterfly knife. He pops the safety latch and flicks the handles around a few times, hoping to make it look like a magic trick. He collects knives and has been practising in front of the mirror. Now, with his girlfriend watching, he's not about to let a 'show-off' opportunity slip by.

Jeffrey drives the blade of the butterfly knife under the edge of a dirty old carpet square. The metal slides easily through the carpet's outer layer, which has the texture of a compressed toothbrush. The knife slips under the rubber base and parts it from the floor. The glue, laid down more than 15 years ago, offers little resistance.

The brown carpet blocks were leftovers from a company where Jeffrey's mother, Shama, once worked. They're ugly and belong in an office, but at 50 cents each they were a steal and if the tenants' dogs hadn't spoilt them, they might have been good for a few more years.

Jeffrey is the son of a former Royal Air Force pilot who came to work in South Africa and met an Indian woman half his age. They fell in love and settled down in Kenilworth, which sprang up on top of the city's golden reef at the turn of the twentieth century. The suburb is located next to the historic Turffontein Racecourse, bordering Rosettenville and La Rochelle, or 'Little Portugal'.

Shama's husband, also named Geoffrey, bought the place in the early 1960s. He was 66 when Jeffrey was born, and by the time his son was a teenager, Geoffrey was suffering from ill health. He had spent too many years in his workshop without an extractor fan or protective gear and ended up with emphysema. He spent six years on oxygen and died in 2009.

His father's age and his death, which left Shama and her son on their own, trapped Jeffrey in a strange limbo between boy and man. At the age of six, he was helping his dad lay down the very carpet he would land up removing years later. He went to work as a mechanic when he was just 15 and picked up many of his father's British mannerisms: 'little nipper', 'top-notch bloke' or 'we had a tiff'. He also soaked up the accent. Normally, Jeffrey speaks with a unique blend of posh English and racy Indian, but if he is nervous or guarded the English accent elbows its way to the fore.

After testing out a few more squares, Jeffrey announces that the carpet will be easy to lift. The job can't wait, but neither can his girlfriend's parents, who have set a strict 10pm curfew. His anger about the ruined night is still simmering as Jeffrey begins to stab at the dirty carpet.

• • •

The rented side of the Marshall home is split into a lounge, two bedrooms, a kitchen and a bathroom. Space is not in abundance, but the place doesn't feel cramped either. The old white pressed ceilings are in immaculate condition, a treasure from the past. Yellow with age, the lampshade in the lounge hangs from the ceiling like a frozen teardrop, leading the eye to a kaleidoscope of patterns above. The bedrooms have heavyset doors but the passage between them flows through clean, narrow arches. It's a neat, compact home.

Werner works as a chef at a Spar supermarket up north and met Shama online. Jeffrey jokes that Werner carries a 'keg instead of a six-pack', but sees him as a kind, caring man who takes good care of his mother. Wisps of thin blond hair cling to Werner's head and he talks eagerly about his plans to refurbish and sell some of the clutter stored in their home. Shuffling around in his Crocs, he boasts about everything that's already been renovated or built.

On this night, 31 March 2012, Shama and Werner – still in his chef's uniform – join the kids next door and before long a 'production line' forms. Jeffrey wedges his knife into the carpet to lift the corners while the others finish pulling them up and carry them to the patio outside. Sometimes, if a square comes out easily, Jeffrey just yanks it up and passes it along.

They begin from the back of the house and move quickly through the first bedroom. Jeffrey is disgusted to find that some of the carpet tiles are still damp with dog urine.

The four of them move out into the passage and work towards the lounge. This is a bigger area and it takes longer. The autumn chill hasn't arrived yet, even in the evenings, so before long Jeffrey begins to sweat. Soon he's drenched, the drops falling to the floor. He has a habit of wearing two shirts over each other, which isn't helping.

They carry on towards the front door, scalping the final stretch of the passage. With Jeffrey on the floor, the others are forced to squeeze past each other, stopping, eventually, at the door of the main bedroom, the one closest to the street.

Down on his knees, Jeffrey crawls into the main bedroom, burrowing under the carpet tiles. For a moment he finds himself alone. The others are either stacking carpet tiles outside or are taking a quick break. He's only a metre in – just behind the door – when he rips up a new square and realises something is hidden beneath it. He peels the carpet tile all the way back and finds an A4 sheet of paper folded in half, with other papers sandwiched in between. This is an unexpected discovery.

Jeffrey picks up the package, stands up and leans against the doorway to rest. He is hot and sweaty. The others return and gather around him, curious to see what he is holding. Werner shouts at him to stop dripping sweat on the pages.

On the dusty side looking up at them are the words 'Do not throw away'.

5.

Carefully, Jeffrey unfolds the piece of paper. Trained in a car workshop, he's careful not to let anything fall out.

'When I open things I'm pretty careful to see if there's anything else inside. It's like pulling apart a gearbox ... things are going to fly out,' he explains. 'So I open it up and there are two other pieces of paper inside.'

Whoever folded the outside page may not have cared whether it was done neatly, but went to some trouble to lift a part of the carpet, slip the bundle inside and then push the carpet back down. Jeffrey's first thought is that this is some kind of a tax document or other legal correspondence. So many times before, he and his father had come to prepare the house for new tenants to find old letters and bills gathering dust inside cupboards.

The 'Do not throw away' instruction is handwritten. The last word is underlined with a zigzag, its tail running off into the corner. The cover offers no other clues and is nothing more than an envelope for whatever lies inside.

The first note Jeffrey slips out reveals a handful of names and telephone numbers, scribbled in skew diagonal lines across the page. The handwriting is similar to the 'Do not throw away' and it is likely the same person wrote both.

They read out the first name, 'Monique Naiyana Neeteson-Lemkes', with an identity number given below. A most unusual, unfamiliar name. The name 'Eric' is next, with the telephone number '880 3442'.

A ring-shaped stain made by a coffee cup cuts across the next set of names.

'Ruth Mncube' is, strangely, followed by the word 'Alive'. Then 'Dirk', his cellphone number and 'Dave & Carel Ranger', once again followed by two sets of telephone numbers. The page offers nothing further.

None of this means anything to the Marshalls.

Jeffrey retrieves the third and final page. This one is different.

It is also handwritten but on both sides of a smaller, more delicate sheet of paper. A company's name appears in the top left corner: 'Howson & Straker (Pty) Ltd'. It is accompanied by a logo: a thick nut and bolt with the date '1945' below it. The page was clearly torn out of a corporate notepad.

The author has turned the notepaper upside down to begin the letter at what should be the bottom of the page, working towards the letterhead using a pencil. The handwriting looks different but it's impossible to tell with any certainty whether this is the work of another person or not. What is apparent is that whoever penned the words was trying to keep up with a stampede of thoughts crashing through his or her mind.

Some words are underlined with wavy lines, others are closed off in brackets. Sentences are squashed and arrows snake out to lead the reader to a different section. Some thoughts are boxed in with jagged lines. Others seem to be afterthoughts, squeezed in at random angles. Several words are crossed out and some of the names are followed by question marks, suggesting uncertainty. Parts of the letter are written with a firm hand while others are difficult to make out, having faded over time. In some places, words are inserted into sentences, with little markers showing where they belong. Car models ('Silver Opel Astra') are attached to names with arrows, trying to provide more detail about those mentioned. It's more like a confusing map of thoughts than a letter.

As the lines run, letters change from capitals to lowercase, from print to cursive. The note appears to be the work of a frazzled mind. Both sides of the paper are used. The custodian of the words would probably have no trouble navigating them, the scribbles reigniting memories like secret clues. But to an outsider they seem wild and frantic. As though the author 'didn't know what end of the pencil to hold'.

No one can quite believe the strange treasure that has been unearthed from under the carpet. They wonder if it is some kind of a joke or a hoax. A game perhaps. The warning not to throw away the documents, the cryptic names, the coffee-cup stain and now this labyrinth of words.

Werner takes the letter from Jeffrey, fearing his sweat will damage them. He's fetched his glasses from the kitchen and is scanning the pages.

The first two are useless, at least for now. But the small letter with the blue border is full of clues. It's addressed to someone. Werner reads out the first line: 'To Blanche. This is what happened.'

A chill runs over Shama and her son. The name means nothing to Werner because he arrived in their lives later, but Blanche – a short, petite woman with a slightly dishevelled look and pale skin – was a tenant at this very house for around a decade. The best tenant they have ever had. She used to take the rent discount they offered her each Christmas and buy them little gifts. She would offer to look after the house while they were away. She never fell behind on her payments.

But even though they were close to Blanche – friends even – they had struck up an even stronger bond with her husband: Conway Brown.

6.

In 2004, Jeffrey and his parents went on holiday to Durban. They can't remember exactly when it was but Geoffrey was already on oxygen and his son was on school holidays.

As usual, they asked Blanche and Conway to watch over their half of the subdivided house while they were away. Feed the dogs, bring in the post, turn on the lights, make sure the place is safe ... the usual house-sitting duties.

Shama remembers that it was around this time that she began noticing something strange happening to Conway. The man her husband considered a close friend – a son even – had stopped coming around for coffee on Fridays. It was a ritual that had begun years previously and she couldn't understand why it had stopped.

Geoffrey had – in his own way – taken Conway under his wing. When Conway lost a job and appeared to be floundering, Geoffrey called him into his garage and gave him some of his own tools. He handed him an old cut-off saw and a drill. He told him he didn't care what he did with them, as long as they helped him find work. Conway used them to erect palisade fences and build wooden desks, which helped him earn some money.

Shama knew Conway as a man who would run late for work and delay dropping off his son at school just so he could help her change a flat tyre. Not only that, but he would call later in the day to check whether she was okay. When she was working on her lawn, he would hop over the fence and help. When thieves broke into their garage, he chased them off and sent Shama and her family to bed while he welded a metal box around the lock so that no one could tamper with it again. The welding took place then and there, in the middle of the night, and couldn't wait until sunrise.

That's where he got the nickname 'One Way Conway'. If a door needed to be mounted, and a hinge required four screws, he'd grab three different-sized ones and get to work. It didn't have to be perfect; it just needed to get done.

Jeffrey saw Conway as a father figure who would be summoned by Shama to talk sense into the rebellious teenager. Conway was a lot younger than Geoffrey and connected with her son.

'He would come down to my level and talk to me in my language,' Jeffrey remembers. 'Sugar-coat it a bit, you know, just to get me going, "This is right and this is wrong".'

Once Shama even asked Conway to talk to her son about safe sex and handed him a condom and a banana. Sitting in the boy's room, they had what turned out to be the most awkward discussion the two would ever have. Conway landed up using a deodorant can for the demonstration.

Jeffrey recalls how well Conway could draw and paint. That he had a million different hobbies, ranging from playing guitar to building jigsaw puzzles. He remembers his tattoo: a bird with musical notes floating from its beak. The Conway Jeffrey knew experimented with magic tricks and watched the youngster bungle his. Conway always told him that to pull off a really spectacular trick – to guess a card or make something vanish – he had to practise it over and over. If he failed to do that, he'd be caught out.

The night the Marshalls returned from their beach holiday, Conway's house was quiet. They went to investigate but could see no signs of life. The curtains were gone and the house appeared to be empty, so they fetched a torch and shone it through the windows. Conway and his family were gone.

They certainly hadn't fled to avoid rent. In fact, they had paid up until the last month. Conway swears he told Geoffrey about his plans to leave, having inherited a house in another suburb. He claims there was nothing unusual about the move. But Shama says they could never figure out why there had been so much secrecy around the departure.

Shama is a feisty woman, who works in the complaints department of a pharmaceutical company and is studying part-time. Her retirement dream is to run her own business. She's the kind of landlord who once found out that her tenant was beating his wife and marched over to personally kick him out of the house, three weeks after he had moved in. She threatened to go to the police if he didn't leave.

In the days leading up to the 2004 holiday, Shama noticed that Conway and Blanche had started to reverse their cars into the narrow driveway. She now thinks they must have been packing up the house.

At the same time, something unusual was happening to Conway. The man who dressed neatly and had a well-sculpted body suddenly began looking ill.

When he came over, Shama asked him whether he was eating properly. He insisted he was, but she didn't believe him and started bringing him a slice of cake or some biscuits, even when he jokingly demanded to know whether she was trying to fatten him up.

Eventually, Shama came out with it and asked him why he was losing weight. He told her he was working two jobs and was exhausted.

'It was totally unlike him. He always looked after his body, he always looked after himself, dressed well, smartly – and here was this guy just wasting away to absolutely nothing,' Shama says.

In her memory, this was all just before Conway and his family left.

When Geoffrey died in 2009, Conway appeared at their door at five in the morning. They knew it was him because the dog didn't bark. It was the first time Conway visited them in five years and he was the first to come to pay his respects. He was still dressed in his cycling gear. He rushed over the moment he heard.

'He was totally, totally broken,' Shama remembers. 'I couldn't believe this man was so broken. Instead of him comforting us, we were comforting him. We brought him into the kitchen and made him a cup of coffee.'

As others began to arrive at the Marshalls' home, Jeffrey and Conway took Ash the dog for a walk. They spoke about old times and then Conway slipped away. They never did resolve why he and his family had taken off in such a hurry.

• • •

Setting the puzzling handwritten note aside, Jeffrey gets back to work on the carpet. He still has a room to finish and his girlfriend's curfew is looming.

He's back on the bedroom floor, tearing off the carpet squares, working his way towards a wooden cupboard to the right. A metre or two away from where he found the first bundle of papers, he uncovers another, once again hidden under the carpet. Like the previous bundle, this one has been carefully placed in its hiding spot.

'I found another one,' he yells. The renovation has turned into a treasure hunt. The others are anxious to see what's inside and regroup in the doorway. Jeffrey holds up three neatly typed pages that have been folded in half. On the side facing them, there's a dark brown moisture stain covering the entire surface.

The pages are nothing like the others; they are typed and resemble a legal affidavit or a police statement. The stapled sheets feel worn and fragile.

The paragraphs in the letter are numbered, 1 through to 20, with a line space between them. Each page is signed at the bottom, as though a lawyer hovered over the author, using his finger to direct the signature. No name is discernible from the signature.

Together the family flips through the pages and discovers a date right at the bottom: 30 September 1999. The date takes a moment to sink in. If this letter is authentic, it was written 12 and a half years ago. If it's not some kind of a joke, one of Conway's crazy little pranks or artworks, then it is a message from the past. From another millennium.

When this letter appears to have been written, Jeffrey was ten years old, playing computer games with Conway's son, Sheldon. Nelson Mandela was not only alive, but was still South Africa's president. There was no such thing as Facebook, no iPhones, and the wall around the Marshall home was so low, Jeffrey could clear it in one leap.

Everyone in the room is thinking the same thing: how much this all feels like a movie.

The letter may not have been slipped under the carpet immediately after it was written, but considering the year of Conway's departure, it's been there for at least eight years. Maybe ten. A decade of feet passing over it. New families moving in and out of the house above it. Jeffrey and his father cleaning out shelves, repainting and replastering. And all those years, these letters lay under this cheap, nasty carpet, sheltered from the winds of time, waiting to be discovered.

• • •

Although the typed letter is much easier to read, the family turns its attention back to the handwritten Howson & Straker page. There's a reference there that makes sense. A name – Blanche – that connects it to reality. It makes sense to start there.

The note is about some kind of a house robbery, although it's not clear where or when it happened. It opens with a list of names: 'Carrington/Alex/His Friend/Andrey or Douglas?' and then: 'Leave at 17H00 Return +/-22H00'.

'Carrington's undercover agent has been watching the house for plus minus 10 days,' the note reads. The spelling is atrocious.

> *Plan: Monica gave Carrington keys for the safe in the House (know one knows she had a set of keys and code for safe). Monica stays in Tailand Now, Carrington and his friend (Andrey) intend going their Friday / Monday.*
>
> *Andrey waits in street in rented golf to alert [us] when security company comes. Alex's friend reverses BMW 5 series into garage keeps engin running, in radio contact and cell with Sandor who is in restrant (Kranks) where Monicas mom & dad work, he is to allert Carrington when Monicas dad leaves. Time eight oclock.*

Next to the mention of a BMW, the author scribbled '(Rented) (Avis) YCA registration'.

> *We pull up out side the house and hoot. Maid opens garage door.*

In a box in the corner of the page, there is an additional note: 'This money to be taken is not decalired currancy and will not be reported stollen?'

Flipping over to the other side of the page, the author continues with the robbery and how the domestic worker is restrained:

> *I distract her Carrington and Alex who are already in yard keep her quiet (Peper Spray) Handcuf her and tape around her mouth.*
>
> *I wait with her by the car. Carrington Alex open small safe if keys for big safe are inside then leave the money in small safe and open big safe*

where (a lot of money is kept) take money (forin currancy) Put maid in
boot of BMW lock safe big and small leave through garage go to hotel,
wher Alex, his friend and Douglas or Andrey will count money. I will
drive with Carrington who will drop maide off somewere far so that it
takes her a long time to find out wher she is. Go back to hotel split money.
Carrington and friend (Silver Opel Astra) will go overseas to Tailand,
Alex and friend will go their own way/cells used for this exercise will be
thrown away 1 X with Sandor 1 X Carrington.

Cars will be vallayed and returned to Avis rent a car after GP plates
were removed. I am know as Bob to Alex and friend / Carringtons friend
Andrey knows my real name.

If this robbery did indeed take place, it is not clear whether this letter was written before or after the event. On one hand, it appears to Werner to be a 'mission report'. On the other, phrases such as 'I will drive …' indicate that this is a plan being hatched. But why then does the letter open with 'To Blanche. This is what happened'? And why do some sentences confuse present and future tenses: 'Cars *will* be vallayed … after GP plates *were* removed …'? It makes no sense.

For now, there are no answers. Jeffrey and his family have not been able to establish who wrote it, never mind why. There is also no way to tell when the note was written. There is no date. No signature. The note ends as abruptly as it begins, without any mention of who was robbed.

Only two short sentences offer a clue as to the identity of the author. Back on the first page, scribbled in a corner, are the words: 'PS# Sorry if I let you down. I love you.' The second 'you' is underlined several times.

The letter is addressed to Blanche so the author is likely to be her husband, Conway. But this is not the Conway Shama and Jeffrey know. In fact, they don't make the connection immediately. Their minds are racing through possible scenarios, absorbing all the details of what to them sounds like a Hollywood-style heist. Jeffrey is waiting for a punchline.

'I thought, no way, this is a prank, it's a joke, it's one of Conway's little moments,' he says. And who could blame him? Conway is a man with the strangest hobbies and an artistic mind. Besides, Jeffrey figures, nobody in their right minds would commit a crime – an armed robbery – and then write down every detail in a letter. Surely, no one would be so reckless. So stupid. And then, on top of it all, move out of the house and forget all about the confession.

The Marshalls scan the letter again, searching for names that match those mentioned on the other pages. A 'Monica' is mentioned in the pencilled note, as is the fact that she now lives in Thailand. 'Monique' appears on the other page, the one with all the names and telephone numbers. It's probably a reference to the same person, but that doesn't solve a thing.

The family feels uneasy. The letter is potentially a window into a crime that may still be under investigation. They suspect it was written by Conway but have no way to prove it. There's little else they can do with it right now and so, searching for clarity, they turn their attention back to the three typed pages.

Werner reads out the opening line: 'Sandor if you are reading this then I am dead.'

7.

Conway saw his father, Vincent Charles Brown, as a 'tough old bastard'. A family man who liked things a particular way and who never ran out of chores for his son to do. Whether it was washing the engine of his Toyota Hilux, mowing the lawn or cleaning the workshop, Conway was always busy. And no matter how tedious the work, he always felt a certain pride when his father called on him.

In his eyes, his older sister got all of his mother's attention and his younger sister was her father's 'little angel'. Conway was stuck in the middle. When his father wanted to show him affection, he would call him 'fuck nut'.

Vincent was a boilermaker by trade but later started his own company, building factories and taking on smaller metalwork projects. At his Kempton Park home he kept a double-storey workshop inside a garage.

The workshop was laid out in a practical manner. The floors were covered in metal sheets so that welding could take place anywhere. Vincent had an oxyacetylene machine, angle grinders, a drill press, an air compressor and spanners of every imaginable size. There were large tables with vice grips and anvils. Upstairs, on the mezzanine level, were shelves and shelves of tools: hammers, crowbars, screwdrivers.

Conway was not allowed in the workshop unattended so when he was invited to spend time there, he considered it a great privilege. It was behind those walls that he learned how to grind, drill, weld or bend the perfect 90-degree angle into a steel pipe.

Conway was given little jobs, such as drilling four neat holes into the corners of a base plate. If he rushed it or did it badly, he'd get a smack across the ear. As they worked, his father lectured him on how to cut high beams or plant support poles, calculating the angle to take into account the weight of the roof. Conway watched Vincent assemble a go-cart using old straps from a backpack as a seat belt. In Conway's mind, there was nothing his father couldn't build. Nothing he couldn't fix.

Vincent was a provider. He held his family together, kept all the parts moving exactly as they should. But he also had a temper. Once, according to Conway, he found his son's racing bike lying in the wrong place and snapped it in half, flinging the mangled frame up onto the roof of the house. Conway shares stories of him punching a man right out of a window and hurling a revolver against a wall so hard that the barrel bent.

Conway's two fondest memories of Vincent are both buried in his childhood. In a way, both relate to his father's idea of justice, which was always 'hard but swift', and how the smallest mercy stayed with Conway for a lifetime. The first was when Vincent took him on holiday to Mtunzini, in KwaZulu-Natal. They were staying near a lagoon and there was a rope that had been tied to a tree, which was used as a swing over the water. Vincent warned his son that the rope was about to break. Conway didn't listen. Moments later he had smashed his head open against the tree roots and a doctor was summoned.

> We waited three hours for the doctor to arrive. My dad took his fishing hat, a cheap blue thing that he wiped his hands on while sticking bait on, and put it on my head as he held me. He could have kicked the shit out of me, but he didn't ...

The second memory is similar. This time Conway climbed an old dead tree in the Rietvlei nature reserve. Once again his father warned him against it. And once again he did not listen. As he tumbled out of it, a branch speared him in the side. Vincent snapped the branch off, leaving only the part stuck in through his son's skin. He took him to a doctor so the stick could be removed.

> Usually there was a smack without warning. Now there had been a warning. So you're waiting for the smack. He had all the right in the world. He had warned me. But he just held me and told me I would pass out when the doctor pulled the stick out. And I passed out.

Vincent was born in South Africa but his family had come from Ireland or Wales, Conway was never sure which. He thought there was some German blood mixed in there somewhere as well. He had never taken the time to research it. He didn't even know whether his grandparents had been born abroad. His world didn't stretch that far.

Conway preferred mysteries and legends to real-life history. Like the story of a sword his father passed down to him through his uncle. He treasured the family heirloom, which he had been told once belonged to an English prince who lived in the nineteenth century. Conway half expected some museum to call him up one day and ask for the sword.

It was Vincent who pulled Conway – known as 'Pikkie' at the time, due to his diminutive stature as a child – out of school after he failed Grade 8 (then Standard 6) and was battling to keep up the second time around. There was some kind of an altercation with a teacher and Vincent decided that his son would do better at a technical college.

Being dyslexic, Conway struggled to read and write. He didn't care much for school and considered his father his teacher, discovering the power of his hands early on. Vincent would allow him to miss school to go with him to a job in another province. The boy would be given a shovel and told to join the workers, as another dairy or factory rose up from the ground. He was driving – transporting labourers – well before he was old enough to have a driver's licence. At home, Conway would help his father pack his tools into his prized bakkie, and in the afternoons, he would be there to unload them.

A few weeks after Conway's seventeenth birthday, his father suffered a heart attack. It happened at home and Conway drove Vincent to the hospital, like all those times when it was Vincent rushing him to a doctor with a gash in his head or a branch in his side. Conway called his mother and took the car home to drop off his dad's tools. When he returned to Kempton Park Hospital, Vincent was dead.

• • •

His father's death had a profound impact on Conway's life.

He had grown up in a middle-class part of Kempton Park, in a spacious house with a tall, pitched roof. His father took care of the family. He was the glue that held it together. White South Africa was still defiantly soaking up the sun in the apartheid swamp and would not be pushed out of it for another two decades, so Conway lived a privileged existence.

He spent his young days running around the suburb raiding postboxes or stealing the little plastic rings used in the door-to-door delivery of milk and orange juice. He and his friends would sell these back to the dairies for a few cents and use the money to buy sweets.

Conway was always in trouble. If a group of boys was kicking a soccer ball, he'd land up shooting it over the wall and would have to climb over to fetch it, only to find the angry neighbour standing there.

He was physically small and felt a constant need to act out, to show off, to punch back just a little harder. Growing up in the company of four big cousins only added to the angst and rebellion.

> *Being small, you don't back down because it's like you are already at the bottom of the food chain; you've got nowhere else to go, so you come out swinging, you come out fighting.*

From a young age, he would take the train on his own to visit family, spending weekends away from home. Few people – if any – could control Conway. So when Vincent died, a new chapter began in Conway's life.

He was at technical college, working through his N qualifications, and it soon became very clear that he was battling to process his loss. His mother had already started hauling him off to the police station, asking the burly Afrikaner officers there to drive some fear into the hooligan teenager. But Conway wasn't one to listen.

One day, he says he got his hands on a bottle of brandy and crashed his father's Hilux, smashing the very engine he had spent his childhood cleaning. The car was a write-off and Conway's mother decided it was time for some real discipline. She sent her son to the army.

Conway landed up as one of the cooks but was bored almost instantly. He began sneaking out of the base to visit his girlfriend. She lived in Port Elizabeth and he would be gone for weeks at a time. Over a festive season, he disappeared for a month. His commander knew about this but, Conway claims, could easily be bribed with a few boxes or a carton of smokes and would mark him down as present in all the logbooks.

Conway's tales of sneaking in and out of the army base, sometimes hidden under a duvet in a car, offers an interesting perspective into his relationship with the concept of right and wrong:

They call it AWOL. But if you don't get caught, it's not AWOL.

8.

... if you are reading this then I am dead.

The sentence is bold and italicised for emphasis. It's directed at a person named Sandor. Another strange name.

The Marshalls are now convinced someone or something has flipped a magic switch, teleporting them inside a detective movie. Do real people write these kinds of letters? Messages from beyond the grave. And do they then hide them under a fitted carpet, hoping that one day the letters will be found and they will be avenged? It's just too surreal.

The letter is typed in a regular Times New Roman font. Before the numbered points begin, there are two more sentences:

> *Contained herein is all the information relating to Monique and the investigation that was undertaken, as well as the details of all those concerned and the level of their involvement. Your mission is to bring them all down completely.*

Revenge. The author has not only a message for Sandor but also an instruction. An assignment. The suggestion is that the writer is dead, but this used to be Conway's home and he's still very much alive. They've seen him since he left Leo Street. But if the letter is not from him, who could possibly have written it?

The Marshalls scan the letter for familiar names but the only one they recognise – and only because of the other pieces of paper – is 'Monique'. They don't know any Moniques. Conway's name also catches their eye, confirming that unless he wrote about himself in the third person, he's not the author. But he, or someone he knew, must have hidden the letter.

Werner and Shama go next door to read the letters properly. Jeffrey and Shekaila stay behind to finish the room. This doesn't take long and no more surprises await under any of the carpet tiles. The treasure hunt is over. The two letters and a few scraps of paper are all they have. Whatever secrets this old house held have been released.

In the kitchen, the family reconvenes to go through the three typed pages. They wonder if the robbery described in the 'Howson & Straker' letter has something to do with this. If the two letters are somehow connected?

Your mission is to bring them all down completely.

The first point reveals the letter is also designed to be a confession:

1. During the course of the investigation several people were abducted and tortured namely; THEMBA TSHABALALA, BETTY KETANI & NDABA BHEBE.

The words 'abducted' and 'tortured' leap off the page. Who are Themba, Betty and Ndaba? What investigation? Why were they kidnapped? They read on.

2. In the case of THEMBA the people involved in his three abductions were myself, Monique, Mark Lister (and Dirk who must be left out of this). Andre Coetzer and Carel Ranger also picked him up once, but did not harm him. Their involvement is being investigated by Internal Affairs (Hillbrow Office) by an Insp. Van Rooyen. The first time THEMBA was abducted was from his home, where he was taken to the place where we played the night paint ball game. We slapped him around for a while and eventually released him – involved were me, Mark, Monique and Dirk. The second time was from his work at the Carnivore restaurant where Mark and I posed as army officers and took him to the broken house near Eardley's place in the bush (the one closest to Eardley and not the one that we first walked to when we checked out that area of bush for the night game). Again the same four of us were involved. I can't remember the details of the third. Insp. Van Rooyen will be most interested to know that Monique, Carel and Andre know each other.

The Marshalls are horrified. A man was taken and tortured on three separate occasions. Taken to an abandoned house to be interrogated. 'Slapped around'. The words make it seem like a twisted game.

None of the names – Mark Lister, Dirk, Eardley, André Coetzer and Carel Ranger – mean anything. Some appear on the piece of paper with the coffee stain, but that's about it. The letter continues:

> 3. BETTY KETANI was "arrested" by Mark and his friend Warren
> Williams in Rosebank. Mark was in army uniform. She was taken to the
> same little house where she was slapped around for a few hours. After
> this Monique, Mark and Warren left her in my care at the house where
> Conway met me, we drove her about 10 minutes further down the high-
> way and "killed her", this was I think on 25 May 1999. However we did
> not do a brilliant job and three weeks later she surfaced and regained con-
> sciousness in the Kopanong Hospital in Vereeniging suffering from mild
> brain damage and severe mental trauma. Dave Ranger, Carel Ranger and
> myself posing as medical transfer service staff uplifted her for the hospital
> and using a hired Kombi took her to the bus on Eardley's farm where we
> locked her up for the night. Dave pushed the wheelchair out of the hospi-
> tal. Mark and Monique followed in my car. However during the night she
> died (I think from shock). On the morning that Candice shot herself (12
> June 1999?) Mark, Monique and Conway fetched the body and buried it
> in about a cubic meter of cement in Conway's garden behind his garage.
> For obvious reasons Conway cannot be involved in this. Her clothing and
> other shit was burned by Mark, Monique and I next to Alexander. For
> this we hired a wheel chair from a medical supply company off Louis
> Botha Ave in Corlett City. This was done in the name of C. Anderson, 25
> Rathmines Road. Both Dave and Carel Ranger are policemen (sergeants)
> who are based at Douglasdale station.

The words stun them. The level of detail is extraordinary. There are telephone numbers next to names, dates and exact addresses. But take all that away and you have a woman who was beaten for hours and then killed on the side of a highway. Only she wasn't. She survived and landed up in hospital – where she was snatched by a gang of criminals posing as medical transfer staff. And then she was taken to some bus, locked up and left to die. They imagine the terror this woman, Betty, must have felt.

The Marshalls wonder what kind of people – what kind of monsters – can commit this kind of an act. What kind of planning must have gone into kidnapping her a second time from the hospital. This is not some crime of passion, followed by a confession riddled with guilt. Real or not, this is a description of a cold and calculated murder.

The last line says the police are involved in the crime. Policemen who are paid to protect people like Betty.

Each paragraph seems to add more horror to the plot. And more characters. This time it's 'Warren Williams'. Again, the Marshalls aren't familiar with the name. The last few lines of that paragraph bring a frightening realisation:

Mark, Monique and Conway fetched the body and buried it in about a cubic meter of cement in Conway's garden behind his garage.

The author is talking about a grave just metres from where they sit. Where Conway started that vegetable patch shortly before he packed up and left. The part of the garden he called his 'special place', where he grew beautiful flowers like lilies and begonias. The letter claims the man they let into their homes – into their lives – was involved in this murder and in concealing it. It dawns on them that there is a body buried in their yard.

Shama whispers a prayer.

9.

When Betty began working at Cranks she was little more than an invisible pair of hands in the kitchen. Her confidence grew over the years and saw her become the head cook, working with clanking woks, burning gas stoves and buckets filled with Thai fish, soy and peanut-butter sauces. She would train and manage the women in the kitchen, cook for them and lead them in song during the quieter times. But her journey began by chopping up ingredients, stirring pots, washing dishes and cleaning counters as Cranks was transformed from a gay bistro in a dingy alleyway to a magnet for rich and influential creative types craving a taste of the exotic.

For Wayne Smith and Keith de la Chaumette, Hillbrow in the late 1980s was as close as they could get to New York City. They had met in the army and felt suffocated by the suburbs, deciding to rent a small apartment downtown and explore the scene. Keith would go on to change his name to Ulla, inspired by a character from *The Producers* movie. In that film, Ulla was a tall, blonde Swedish woman who jumped onto tables and danced while performing 'When You Got It, Flaunt It'.

For them, Hillbrow was fabulous. It was cosmopolitan. It was non-stop 'go go go'. A melting pot of cultures and races, a so-called grey area where apartheid laws were defied and the party never seemed to wind down. The streets were packed with restaurants, bars, cafés, liberal book and music stores, as well as cinema houses that allowed mixed-race audiences. Making your way through shopping malls meant being accosted by the Hare Krishnas, Jehovah's Witnesses or evangelical Christians.

Wayne and Keith went clubbing from Wednesday to Sunday. There was the Bella Napoli, the Summit Club, Mandy's, Anaconda and 2001. They warmed up at gay bars that lined the streets or at Café Wien and Café de Paris.

Wayne was working three jobs: in the morning it was the hippie leather shoe shop, during lunchtime he waited on tables at the Three Sisters Greek restaurant and at night he was at Cranks.

'Hillbrow was an incredible space to be in. It was insane. The pace was incredible, it was crazy,' Wayne remembers. 'In the suburbs you knew black people as domestic workers who were only there during the day, but in Hillbrow it was different.'

The inner city, as a magazine once described it, was 'teeming with the sophisticated, the disaffected and the mad. Ex-cons, metalheads, meatheads, hippies, gays, intellectual revolutionaries who all found a home at Cranks.'

Wayne loved that while the government was feeding them fear about the communists, he could go to the Estoril bookstore on the corner of Pretoria and Abel and buy international magazines that opened up an entire new perspective. It was a liberation. Apartheid was crumbling but the various laws – such as the Group Areas Act – were still in place. The state was implementing a state of emergency, but Hillbrow was changing faster than the country around it.

In about 1986, Eric Neeteson-Lemkes bought a tiny bistro tucked away behind a major Hillbrow supermarket. It had a largely gay clientele, a handful of tables and ambient lighting. Its signature meal was a sandwich called the Chicken Strut, toasted both inside and outside and jam-packed with filling. There were also chicken wings in sweet chilli sauce.

Keith stumbled upon Cranks first and got Wayne a job there. They were waiters working the night shift, peddling plates from the kitchen to the tables. But they were so much more than that. They were performers.

As Eric began changing the menu, introducing Oriental cuisine to a country unfamiliar with it at the time, Keith and Wayne realised they were free to do exactly as they pleased. So while the kitchen staff slaved away in the back and Eric chatted with the regulars, they pushed the boundaries.

'We would wear really outrageous clothing,' Wayne explains. 'I remember going to work in tights and a ballet tutu or long socks and a massive big bamboo grass skirt.' Keith sometimes wore Carmen Miranda-style fruit hats or fruit-shaped earrings. He also had a colourful safari suit. On many nights the pair settled for brightly coloured sarongs, flip-flops and vests. It was comfortable and the place was always hot and overbooked.

'It was a very small restaurant. You couldn't really move in it. Frequently we'd pass food over tables because you just couldn't reach a table. It was always packed,' Wayne said.

Keith remembers even more madness: 'It was packed, packed, packed to capacity every single night. It was crazy mental. There was no way of getting around except falling over people, pushing people, pouring food over people, messing over people – it was insane. Whoever arrived there in their designer gear stank of fish sauce by the end of the night.'

The music was always too loud for a restaurant. The soulful voices of Phyllis Hyman or Patti LaBelle pouring through the speakers. And there was always Anita Baker, caught up in the rapture of love.

Wayne and Keith were rude and bossy. They would watch new clients fumble through the menu – which contained dishes they had never heard of – and then tell them what they were eating. They would make a dramatic, exhausted gesture and say something like 'You're never going to get it', and then disappear into the kitchen to fetch whatever they thought the table needed. Somehow, they always got away with it.

'Eric enjoyed that aspect of it. He got off on the craziness. The more outrageous we were, the more he encouraged us. There were no restrictions.'

One night, by accident, Wayne dropped an entire salad on the head of a blonde wearing a leopard-print boob tube. He remembers watching the dressing slither down her face and into her cleavage. The woman shrieked. Wayne ran back to the kitchen and collapsed in a fit of laughter. Keith had to pick up his tables.

'Eric thought it was the funniest thing ever. In a normal restaurant I would have lost my job,' Wayne says. 'But Eric loved the outrageous. He loved pushing the edge.'

Once, a client asked Wayne for a joint. Wayne wrapped some dried-up basil leaves in Rizla paper, gave it to the gullible man and watched him smoke it. Again, Eric was amused and didn't intervene.

Wayne and Keith wonder if the restaurant wasn't some kind of a fantasy world to Eric. A world of colours, chaos, cigarette smoke and interesting people from the hidden layers of society. Eric even ran an adjacent room to the restaurant called 'The Annex'. It was a room for private parties where the door could be locked and nothing was forbidden. A room where performances were staged and where there was no need to slip away to the toilet to do a line of cocaine.

The kitchen, where Betty and the others worked, was a tornado thrashing around a tiny sauna-of-a-room. Wayne remembers how fights used to erupt because of the immense pressure.

'It was mayhem. A tiny space with a big stove, buckets of ingredients, just woks and women tossing shit everywhere; a spoon of sugar, a spoon of fish sauce, a spoon of coriander, some chicken, stirring it all up, throwing it on a plate. The nature of Thai food is that it has to be in and out really quickly. There were amazing salads and a lot of really hot chilli. There were always ladles flying.'

To Wayne and Keith, who were the stars of the Cranks show, Betty was a 'nice', 'sweet' woman who always held the respect of the other kitchen staff. They remember her as a 'hard worker' who was excellent at her job. Wayne recalls that he would hug her in greeting. He always thought she had a minor lisp in her speech or just battled with certain letters (possibly explained by the missing teeth). But nothing more than that. He and Keith were too busy being outrageous, feeding Eric's appetite and earning what were then great salaries to take much more notice of the ladies in the kitchen. They knew Eric was tough on his kitchen staff and had a fiery temper, but to this day they have nothing but fond memories of the 'strange man' who was their boss.

Eric was also part of the show. He was a tall, enigmatic man who wore floral or long saffron silk shirts and sarongs and spoke with a Dutch accent. He was striking: good-looking and mysterious. He went out of his way to make sure that his customers had a memorable experience, which kept him perpetually busy.

But Eric also seemed to keep secrets and revealed little of his personal life. He would walk around saying his catchphrase: 'It's top secret, top secret.' He was in complete control of every aspect of the restaurant, allowing no one but family to open or close the establishment. And those who knew him say he remained guarded and secretive.

Once, a man walked into Cranks and asked for Eric. He was probably delivering something. A staff member pointed to Eric, who was sitting at the bar counter, and the delivery man made his way over and introduced himself. 'Are you Eric?' Eric looked him square in the eyes and said, 'No,' before adding, 'I'm sorry, there's no Eric here.' The man left embarrassed and confused, and Eric stormed up to the staff member who had given him away, shouting at him to never do that again. Nobody at Cranks ever really understood what had happened.

'I work with people now and know more about them in six months than I knew about Eric in 11 years,' Wayne says.

'With Eric, you never knew where the truth ended or started,' Keith adds. 'You could sit and speak to him for five hours and get nothing from him. He would never give you a straight answer. He imagined he was a spy and was intrigued by that whole world. He told us everything, but he told us nothing.'

Part of being in control was managing the finances of the business and already in Hillbrow Eric was paranoid about being taken for a ride by his workers. At one stage he accused Keith of stealing from him. The accusation blew up into a dramatic argument that saw Keith storm off and resign. He later agreed to come back.

More than ten years later, when Cranks was operating in Rosebank and Keith and Wayne had left, it seemed little had changed. Only this time, a private detective firm was brought in to investigate.

10.

After offering a chilling explanation of how Betty Ketani was murdered, the hidden letter loops back to the abductions:

4. NDABA BHEBE who is related to THEMBA somehow was picked up from his home (1906 Aintree Place, cnr Tudhope & O'Reilly Streets, Berea) and taken by Mark to Randburg Police Station where we slapped him around for a while with Carel & Monique in attendance. Thereafter we took him to a section of bush near to where Poul used to live in Fourways. Mark, Monique and I did this.

5. Anyway another victim was MALEMLELI MPOFU who lives in 901 Britton Manor, Cnr Kaptein & Klein Streets, Hillbrow. He was "arrested" by Monique and I posing as policemen. I was D/Sgt Richard Wessels (see fake ID) and she was D/Sge Louise Brenner. We took him to the Sandton Hotel Formule One and kept him there for the night, thereafter we took him to the Sandton Park Hotel, where we were staying (room 002), under the name Mac Intosh or Mac Donald. Included in the tin is an 8mm video tape of his questioning. He was kept by us for 3 days and eventually released. Involved were me, Monique, Mark & Douglas. Dirk guarded him once for about 3 hours at Sandton Park. MALAMLELI [sic] was one of the people who deposited one of Monique's stolen cheques in his account.

By now the narrative is repetitive, peppered with new names and new places but recounting similar modus operandi. The latest victim was held for three days and moved from hotel room to hotel room as his captors continued their game, checking in under blatantly fake names like 'Mac Intosh' or 'Mac Donald'.

Whoever these people are, they had access to fake police badges and used the Randburg station as a private interrogation office.

The letter mentions various pieces of evidence contained in a tin, but this has either been lost, hidden elsewhere or never existed to begin with. There is nothing but the letter.

> 6. Included in the tin are some photos of Monique and I, a letter she wrote me, a video of us screwing and other interesting bits and pieces. All of these should be copied and copies given to her father (Eric) who is on (011) 880-3442, as well as a copy of this letter. Use your discression to censor this letter to protect those who need protecting, a black marker pen should do the trick. The large professionally taken photo could also be used by THEMBA to identify me as one of his abductors, as well as to tie me in with Monique. As you know there are more such photos on my desk as well as several cards from her and the A4 "I Love You" certificate on the notice board, which may or may not still be there. Our sexual relationship began 4 weeks after meeting (29 April 1999) each other and started in the Protea Gardens Hotel in Hillbrow. From there we went to the Chamberry Hotel (room 8) in Randburg (Main Road) where we booked in under the names of Louise Crawford, and from there to Sandton Park Hotel.

> 7. Included is a 1.44 MB stiffy with wav files of telephone conversations as well as copies of all letters that I wrote Monique (in Word 97) plus all invoices, etc (including this letter).

> 8. In the box is also a black hood, which Insp. Van Rooyen would be most interested to see, as he has about 4 already from various abductions.

> 9. During the investigation Monique told her father all sorts of stories about a woman called RUTH MNCUBE, whom he believes is dead. RUTH is very much alive and well and all photos to prove this are in an envelope marked 'Ruth'. Also at no stage whatsoever did we ever manage to capture or detain RUTH, only once did I grab her in town, but she escaped as a large crowd helped her. I think Eric should know the truth as to how dishonest and deceitful his daughter really is! She lied to him every step of the way regarding every stage of the investigation.

10. In my cupboard are some of Monique's clothes that she left here, which also may or may not be there, as well as cosmetics and toiletries.

11. At her house in the cottage is a wooden single door cupboard in which all letters, gifts, etc that I gave her are kept. Tell her father this too.

The plot thickens. A near-escape for another would-be victim and a bizarre web of lies between a daughter and father. And what kind of man asks for a sex tape of himself to be sent to his former lover's father? What kind of falling-out must they have had?

At this point, the letter changes tone and becomes a will, with the author passing off a stack of belongings he no longer needs: cars, guns, a business and a safe full of cash.

12. In my gun safe (copy of key included) is an ABSA bank bag belonging to Monique in it is some personal paperwork as well as money in white envelopes, happy birthday Sandor the money is yours, use it to help me. Please note that Monique has a copy of the safe key so I will insert a lock block, the key should also be included. Last count about US$ 3000 and R 10000. There may also be some Australian Dollar trevellers cheques which she stole from her father.

13. Monique opened a Nedbank account at the Hyde Park Branch, using Commercial Services as a front for employment, etc. Let dad know this too.

14. Her full names are Monique Naiyana Neeteson-Lemkes, ID number (770326 0788 080).

15. Inside the box is the Cranks investigation file, which contains lots of information, which you should find useful.

16. Also included is a strange photo of lots of little photos, this can prove a connection between everyone involved. It was taken at a group dinner. [A few handwritten words, afterthoughts perhaps, are crossed out after this sentence and are illegible.]

17. Sandor please do everything you can to avenge me.

18. Speak to Candice, she will also be able to help (if she wants to) and speak to Dirk, he definitely can help.

19. Luigi (Tanfoglio 9mm), the shotgun, 22 pistol, and AMT 9mm short are yours as well as my Astina. Enjoy! Also if you want it C&C Commercial Services cc is yours too.

20. Lastly – fuck them all!!!!!

Regards, best wishes and see you sometime. Alex & I are waiting patiently.
30 September 1999

The letter is signed above the date, with a short, handwritten sentence to end it off:

Also in the voice files are 3 conversation with a det/sgt Erwin Hyde (Randburg) – 2 of them are between him & Monique! Hyde did not do anything but knew about the case.

The Marshalls are still in the kitchen, digesting the information one incredible fact after the next, when Werner, ever impulsive, decides he must do something.

The handwritten letter on the small Howson & Straker notepaper is confusing and may be some kind of a hoax. But this letter is so strikingly detailed. So matter-of-fact in its confessions.

Werner picks up the phone and dials the number given for Eric. First the Johannesburg code 011 and then 880 3442. The letter says Eric should know the truth. It implicates his daughter Monique in every abduction, as well as in Betty Ketani's murder.

'Where am I?' Werner demands when the call connects.

The person who answers tells him he's reached Cranks, in Rosebank. At that moment it all clicks into place. Werner used to work for a company that owned the Black Steer located directly above Cranks. He had seen Eric and was familiar with his mad restaurant and crazy bakkie.

The person on the line claims Eric is not available. Werner tries again a few minutes later but after several attempts realises he's not going to get to speak to Eric, so he leaves a message with whoever answers his final call.

'Tell him his daughter is going to jail for a very long time,' he declares before hanging up. He doesn't give his name and says nothing about the letter. If Eric's past is anything to go by, Werner may well have spoken to him without even realising it.

. . .

It doesn't take long for the family to reach a decision. They agree they must hand the letters over to the authorities as soon as possible, especially the typed confession. They discuss going to the local police station, but play out the scenario and decide against it.

Werner doesn't trust the police. All he can think about are the traffic cops who have tried to squeeze bribes out of him. He and his family also fear the police simply won't believe their story or won't do enough to protect them during the investigation. If the letter is real, then the people mentioned in it are to be feared.

Werner agrees to make any statements that may be required and to shield his family should someone need to testify in court. He will be the spokesman.

Werner also comes up with an alternative to walking into a police station. Instead, he suggests handing the letters over to his manager at the supermarket, Andreas Stephanou. He knows Andreas is close to some pretty colourful characters from a company called VIP Support Systems, who run investigations and protection and have close links to the police. He's confident the letters will find their way into the right hands. Like setting a paper boat sailing down a rain-soaked street, knowing it will eventually tumble into a storm drain. Everyone is okay with the plan.

The next morning, a Sunday, Werner calls Andreas and fills him in about the late-night renovations, the letters, the abductions, the murder and the grave. The manager doesn't know what to make of it all or how to respond, but politely agrees to drop by to take a look.

. . .

Later, standing at the spot where the grave might be, Shama prays to the woman she imagines lying beneath the concrete.

'We were not responsible,' she tells her. 'You have been here for 13 years. You haven't troubled us, please do not trouble us now.'

Shama believes in karma, the philosophy of cause and effect, the idea that what you do to others will come back to you. This is why she has come outside to speak to the woman mentioned in the letter.

The grave – if it exists – is now covered by a slab of cement, which is the floor of a new garage that wasn't there in 1999. Back then, the parking area was narrow and gave way to the garden in the alley alongside the house.

The confession was specific, stating that the body was buried 'in Conway's garden, behind the garage'. Shama remembers the spot and the garden that sprung up there. She remembers the vegetables that were brought to them as gifts, at about the same time as Conway began withdrawing from the world. The vegetables were delicious, but completely out of character, even for One Way Conway.

Shama's prayer ends with a request on behalf of the unknown woman: 'Let your family find out where you are, let them get some closure.'

11.

On Monday, Andreas Stephanou is tied up in the planning of a sting operation with Doc and JB, who are both former agents of the South African Narcotics Bureau (Sanab). He knows they are all going to be far too busy for him to raise the issue of Werner's strange letters, which were found that weekend.

Intelligence has been received that a massive shipment of abalone – also known as perlemoen – is due to arrive in Cyrildene's Chinatown on Tuesday morning. The police are planning to intercept the shipment. Doc and JB are helping out, sweeping the streets for information and assisting with logistics. Andreas is coming along for the ride.

Monday slips by in a blur of phone calls and meetings to make sure everyone involved in the operation is properly briefed. Officers from different stations and units need to be assigned their tasks. The trap must be laid perfectly.

Doc also served as a deep-cover agent at the Directorate of Special Operations (DSO), drawing a small salary and riding a state car. The Scorpions – an elite crime-fighting unit that teamed up investigators with prosecutors to tackle the top layers of the country's organised crime – flew too close to the political sun and was sent hurtling back to earth amidst a storm of controversy and court challenges. It was dismantled and replaced by a new unit, the Hawks, but not before taking down for corruption South Africa's police chief and Interpol president Jackie Selebi.

Doc has been out of the Scorpions for several years. One of his most prized possessions is a 2009 Certificate of Recognition signed by Andrew Leask, the investigator who carried the Selebi docket. 'We acknowledge you for staying the course and demonstrating resilience and patriotism,' it states. 'Best wishes for the future.'

Part of Doc's future turned out to be VIP Support Systems, a small company run by a close friend and fellow member of the Crusaders Motorcycle Club, or MC.

As free agents, both from Sanab and the DSO, Doc and JB now pick and choose their cases. These range from chasing hijackers in Mozambique to helping throw the net over notorious bank robbers like Bongani Moyo. Some missions end in glory, newspaper clippings and photographs for the website, others see them flushing days down the drain without a cent in compensation. Each time a job goes wrong they vow to stop and sell biker gear instead. Each time a new adventure crops up, they make just one more exception.

Once plans for the perlemoen bust are in place, Doc and JB catch a few hours' sleep. The following morning, before sunrise, they meet Andreas to take up their positions in Kensington, on the eastern side of Johannesburg. Their part is to hang back and wait for confirmation of the shipment. They are civilians and have to leave the arrests to the police.

The arranged delivery time comes and goes. With every passing minute, the window of opportunity shrinks and soon it's clear the truck isn't coming. Finally, the mission is called off. No one knows whether the syndicate cancelled its plans or caught wind of the police operation. Or perhaps the informer simply got it wrong. It's one of those things and there's nothing to be done about it.

The policemen involved pack up and head to their stations to stand morning parade. Doc, JB and Andreas decide to hang around. Anticipating an avalanche of paperwork, they have set aside the entire day for the project.

It's very early in the morning, but there is a coffee shop on Queen Street that is about to open. It brews strong coffee and fills up with the smell of freshly baked bread from next door. The trio needs to work down the adrenalin and figure out what to do with the rest of the day. Doc needs to balance out his blood-sugar levels.

Once they're done at the coffee shop, the three friends drive to Doc and JB's cottage in Observatory. They sit around and talk, drinking cheap instant coffee and filling up ashtrays. The cottage belongs to another of Doc's 'brothers' from the bike club, who lives in the house at the top of the garden. It's not much, but it gives them space to set up a couple of work stations and spread out some charts on the walls. On an average day, there's a steady stream of cops flowing through the door. Some simply come to blow off steam, others to fish out some information from the underworld. On sunny days, they sit on the wooden bar bench beneath the weeping willow and smoke cigarettes as Zulu, the giant bullmastiff, cavorts around the garden.

The bizarre letters resurface in Andreas's mind. Two days have passed since they were discovered and he wants to honour the promise he made to Werner. He decides to mention it to the others.

'We're sitting in the office and we have nothing to do. We have planned our whole day and we are sitting here talking shit,' Doc explains. 'So Greek Boy [Andreas] says let's ride through to Werner, the chef in Kenilworth, and let's go and have a look at these letters.'

As Andreas passes on Werner's explanations, Doc begins to voice his opposition. He's chased around enough dud cases and is not ready for another runaround that leaves him and JB poorer than when they started. Cases cost money, starting with the petrol it will take to drive to Kenilworth. Doc suggests that the author of the letters was probably high on drugs or a mental case. Given the facts, nobody can disagree. But even so, they have a whole day ahead of them and nothing better to do. Plus, this is someone Andreas knows personally and can't just blow off.

Had the perlemoen bust gone down as planned, they would probably be filling out police statements by now. As so often happens, they may be chasing down fresh leads or making unplanned arrests, running against the clock before word gets out and suspects scatter. The operation could have had them occupied for days and the letters would have been all but forgotten.

• • •

Werner Nortjé brings out the bundle of letters and allows his guests time to read them before answering some questions from JB.

'Looking at the letters, we can see they're old, but we say, "No man, these people are on drugs,"' Doc recalls. 'It could have been somebody that was on acid going through a bad thing that just wanted to fuck somebody around so they wrote a letter and left it under a mat.'

They have no way of knowing for sure how old the letters are. One is dated 1999, but there's no way to prove the date is legitimate.

ALEX ELISEEV

'The more we read into it, okay, the more we are saying, "Fuck, the *oke* [guy] has got a fantastic imagination." I mean they kill a person, they don't do a good job and then they go and ... I mean it doesn't make any sense. If I am going to kill somebody, I am going to kill somebody, do you understand? I'm definitely not going to go and book them out of a hospital. So at this stage we're looking at this letter and we are saying, "Fuck, this could be a lot of bullshit."'

Werner tells JB about a man named Conway Brown, a good friend of his fiancé's late husband and a previous tenant of the house where they found the letters. Shama is summoned to tell the full story, including details surrounding the supposed grave in the garden.

Ironically, despite the last-minute rush to prepare the house, the tenants who were due to move in never arrived. So Doc, JB and Andreas can explore the room where the letters were found as well as the slab of concrete that's been laid down in the garage. Shama tells them about the vegetable patch and Conway's sudden change of personality. The letter says they are standing directly above a grave, which could be the key that unlocks a 13-year-old murder mystery.

JB is not convinced, but he is definitely curious. Instinctively he already knows the only way to know for sure is to dig up the garage. But they aren't there yet. What's annoying him is why the author of the letter is protecting some of the people mentioned.

'When we first read the letter I thought, is this story out of a book? There were certain things in the letter ... for obvious reasons leave this one out and for obvious reasons leave that one out. So I thought, fuck man, why for "obvious reasons" leave this out? I thought, no man, let's just check how true is this letter.'

JB is no strategist. No Garry Kasparov of criminal investigation. He's the energy, the passion, the sledgehammer. Doc is the older, calmer one, whose life as an agent is starting to catch up with him, forcing him to slow down and consider the angles. They are both street-level operators, men who occupy the shadows between the layers of society, who exist in the grey world between cops and criminals. In their own way, they balance each other out. JB's foot is glued to the accelerator while Doc keeps his on the brake.

Andreas, meanwhile, has his own doubts about the letters.

'When you hear it, you start thinking "movie", like a movie story,' he says. 'But when you read the letter, then you say, "No, there's too much, there's way too much detail."'

In Doc and JB's world, adventure trumps scepticism. Along with Andreas, they have many questions. But each man has just enough curiosity – the faint heartbeat of another quest – to give it a try. What's the harm in running a few basic checks to see whether any truth lies hidden in these pages? And just imagine if it turns out to be true, they figure. Wouldn't that make one hell of a story?

12.

Back at the cottage, Doc and Andreas are on the computer, feeding the names in the letters into online search engines and social network sites. They can't think of a simpler place to start: punch in a few names and see what washes back. They're trying to determine whether the names mentioned in the letters exist in the real world.

JB is on his own mission. His focus is on 'Inspector Van Rooyen', who is mentioned in the typed confession. If he can track Van Rooyen down, and hear from a policeman whether any of this is real, then he can really throw some effort at it. This inspector works – or worked – at the Hillbrow police station and should be easy to trace. If anyone can be trusted, it'll be this cop.

JB calls a senior commander at the Yeoville station. Captain Alan Fagan was once stationed at Hillbrow and may even know Inspector Van Rooyen. It turns out he does, and he offers JB a first name: 'James'. Van Rooyen also has a nickname: 'Skivvies'. Fagan explains that James van Rooyen left the police and now investigates claims at some insurance company. He thinks it's Auto & General. After a little digging around, Fagan passes along a contact number.

JB doesn't skip a beat and dials. He explains the situation and asks to meet Van Rooyen urgently. Somehow, he manages to convince him to drop what he's doing and speak to them about this strange 13-year-old cold case. At Van Rooyen's request, they agree to meet at the Hillbrow police station. No one's getting excited, but if this policeman exists, what else could be out there?

Doc is also moving quickly, and has started building a basic spidergram up on the wall of the cottage. A photocopy of the typed letter has been made and all three pages are stapled to the top of a white noticeboard. The main names and dates are highlighted and pierced with yellow pins. From these, red strings shoot out to connect them to photographs and scraps of paper. It's surprisingly easy to find people on the Internet. The web begins to grow: 'Carrington', 'Conway', 'Mark Lister', 'Warren Williams', 'Candice', 'David Ranger', 'Carel Ranger', 'Sandor', 'Themba Tshabalala' ... and, in the top left-hand corner, 'Betty Ketani'.

As the online searches continue, short profiles are attached to names, and faces – not all of them the right ones yet – begin to observe the investigation from the wall. The letter under the carpet begins to unfold like a delicate origami creation.

. . .

JB has convinced Van Rooyen to meet them right away. The friends leave the office wondering whether Skivvies will be able to remember anything about an investigation that dates back to 1999. It wasn't uncommon for detectives back then – and even today – to carry dozens of dockets at a time. To remember one of them, 13 years later, will require a remarkable memory or a unique case.

At some point along the way, JB calls Van Rooyen again and asks to rather meet at the BP petrol station on Empire Road in Parktown, adjacent to the provincial police headquarters. He's thinking about lunch and doesn't realise that Van Rooyen has asked to meet at his former police station because he doesn't trust JB. Not yet. Having worked so many cases, and especially in internal investigations, he has learned to be careful.

'Over the years you have stepped on a few toes. I mean, you don't know if anybody has got a grudge against you,' Van Rooyen explains.

He agrees to meet at the BP and asks what car JB is driving. Van Rooyen intentionally says nothing about his own vehicle, planning to arrive there, park and assess the situation.

Doc, JB and Andreas pull into the garage and disappear inside the convenience store to buy hot pies and cold drinks. Van Rooyen arrives and parks his car but hangs back, quietly taking in the scene and making up his mind.

Doc rides for an outlaw motorbike club and looks exactly how you would expect a 52-year-old biker to look. His arms are covered in tattoos:

skulls, guns, grim reapers, gravestones, dragons, and choppers with long, ape-hanger handlebars. Inked on his skin are club names and symbols, army badges and slogans such as 'Live fast, die young, have a good-looking corpse' or 'F.T.W', which stands for 'Fuck the world, fuck the war, fuck the women'. On his left wrist, Freddy Krueger is ready to pounce with his blood-soaked claws. 'You fuck with me, I'll be your worst nightmare.'

Most days, Doc wears his leather cut and silver rings that resemble knuckle-dusters. A gun is tucked in the back of his belt and a cigarette dangles from his mouth. On this day he's clean-shaven, but he has been known to grow a mean handlebar moustache. He's the perfect undercover agent, but an intimidating sight to those who don't know him.

JB looks like a street fighter whose powerful frame – a solid block of flesh – has swallowed up much of his neck. It's easy to size him up as a cop or a nightclub bouncer. He always wears a cap, casting a shadow over his narrow-set eyes.

Looking at them as they emerge from the convenience store, Van Rooyen wonders whether he should simply turn around and leave. There's nothing forcing him to honour this meeting. He can barely remember the case anyway.

Just then, a policeman appears in the courtyard and changes Van Rooyen's mind. Lieutenant Colonel André Neethling has a ritual of buying a cup of coffee from the same BP station whenever he comes to report at the provincial headquarters. As he makes his way inside, he recognises Doc and JB and, with Andreas looking on, the three begin an animated discussion about the mysterious letters. Neethling, who is with the Hawks and leads his own unit, has used Doc and JB as agents in the past.

Coincidentally, André Neethling was also once Van Rooyen's mentor at the Parkview police station, not long after Skivvies graduated from police college and before he was sent to Hillbrow. The two of them spent years working together.

Van Rooyen reasons that if Neethling knows JB and his crew, then it's okay to at least have a conversation with them. It feels safe now that there's a witness he can trust. He climbs out the car and makes his way across the courtyard to introduce himself.

13.

Finding Inspector Van Rooyen turns out to be a dead end. Initially, he can't remember anything specific about the case they've come to speak to him about. There are vague recollections, but nothing they can use. Skivvies has worked so many dockets, dealt with so many complainants, that most of them are a blur now. Having left the police, he's tried to forget Hillbrow and all its mayhem. It is only later that he starts remembering and piecing his thoughts together.

But the trip has not been a waste. Far from it. André Neethling is hooked. He's intrigued by the story and offers to help run deeper searches on the names in the letters. He smells an interesting case.

His first suspicion is that this is the work of some kid on drugs. He's seen enough of them while working in the Child Protection unit: 'druggies' on LSD trips who get lost in their strange fantasies. But Doc and JB show him the letters and something about them sucks him in. He leads the others to a nearby coffee shop to get started.

Neethling has short-shaved hair, kind brown eyes, and the tiny white paintbrush strokes in his neat goatee are the only signs that he is approaching 50. What he lacks in physical height, he makes up in his reputation as a fine policeman.

Neethling comes across as a man with purpose, always on the move, always in control. Around his neck dangles a home-made silver pendant of an African river god, NyamiNyami, its crimson eye sparkling above the creature's sharp fangs, its tail corkscrewing into a spear-like tip. Legend has it that NyamiNyami unleashed killer floods in the mighty Zambezi River to punish those who interfered with the balance of nature.

Neethling is a police commander, managing a team of about 30 officers who hunt down the province's most dangerous criminals: ATM bombers, cash-in-transit heist gangs and violent house robbers. Over the years, he has faced many monsters. Along with his team, he chased and caught

Mozambican serial robber and rapist Ananias Mathe, dubbed the 'ultimate criminal' for being the only known man to have escaped from C-Max prison in Pretoria: South Africa's Alcatraz.

Neethling has peered into the squint eyes and tar-black soul of Fanwell Khumalo, who was at the time the country's worst-ever child rapist. There was also Sipho Dube, who strangled and raped young boys and girls.

And yet, for 30 years – aside from the Mathe case – Neethling has managed to stay mostly out of the limelight and away from the headlines. He's not a celebrity cop but a man who likes to operate behind the scenes. With his new unit, he has become an efficient and silent tracker.

Doc and JB call him 'Gadgets' or 'Inspector Gadget', even though he's a lieutenant colonel. He has an entire office in his car and can explore the darkest corners of the police database, which is a galaxy of case numbers, names, dates and addresses. Navigating the data successfully takes an experienced hand with the right access.

Neethling's speciality is tracing cellphones and he gets down to it right away, an investigation into the numbers listed in the mysterious letters. He quickly confirms a few links. The cellphone numbers are, or were, indeed registered to the people mentioned in the letters. One of the numbers is still in use. He checks the number given for 'Dirk' and finds that it's been recycled to a new user. He scribbles 're-issued' next to the digits.

These small confirmations are important. Doc, JB and the others are still trying to convince themselves that this case is real. They want to believe in it, but they need proof.

Neethling runs a company check on C&C Commercial Services, which appears in the letter, and finds that it was registered by Carrington and Candice Laughton in 1998. The company has been closed down but the records reveal identity numbers, addresses and important connections between people.

'Initially I was very wary of it,' Neethling says, referring to the case. 'But, you know, that's the thing; you investigate something, which is what I have been doing the last 30 years, and you test it and in this case the test was definitely positive.'

They leave the coffee shop and head to Neethling's office, where they spend much of the afternoon building up more detailed profiles. After they part ways, they continue to fish out as much as they can from the Internet, filling up the white board with new scraps of information. Doc and JB decide it's time to formally bring in the police. The paper boat Werner and his family set off down the street is about to hit its target.

· · ·

The man Doc and JB call is Gerhard Pretorius, a Yeoville-based detective and a good friend. Pretorius is already familiar with the case. The first time JB spoke to him about it was to ask whether he knew the Ranger brothers Carel and David, who appear to be policemen. Pretorius had never heard of them.

Pretorius was born in Vereeniging and got to know Johannesburg only after joining the police. Now, he's a hardened homicide detective with two decades spent in one of the most demanding jurisdictions in the city. He's the kind of cop who says things like 'Inquests and murders, that's what I know'.

The warrant officer is one of Yeoville's senior detectives and is often handed high-profile cases. He has a particular method of investigating his dockets. He claims that once, many years ago, he slammed the phone down on Nelson Mandela's ex-wife, Winnie Madikizela-Mandela, because she was trying to tell him how to do his job.

When he started in Yeoville, the suburb was predominantly a Jewish neighbourhood, peaceful and quiet. Pretorius was working shifts, focusing on business crimes. Because of the Sabbath, Saturdays saw the small satellite station hibernate. No cases were opened. No statements were written or signed. The policemen in the area would patrol casually, cruising past Rockafellas, the Lizard Lounge and Mama's Pizza, watching families walk to and from the synagogues.

Pretorius spent about three years in uniform and his transfer to the detectives came through as South Africa marked its landmark 1994 election. Over the years that followed, Yeoville deteriorated, suffering the same fate as nearby Hillbrow. Buildings were hijacked, turf split up, and Rockey Street, the suburb's main artery, became synonymous with drugs, booze and violence. If Hillbrow was the Bronx, Yeoville became the grimy part of Brooklyn. Pretorius and his colleagues became very busy.

Pretorius spent years working with Doc and JB. They met while investigating an assault case at one of the Buddy's Cafés in the area. Now they had a long list of shared cases and Doc and JB were Pretorius's registered informers. The detective trusted them completely. He always said that if he was going into a gunfight, they were the guys he wanted standing next to him.

• • •

Gerhard Pretorius meets Doc and JB at their office and is brought up to speed. His reaction is, by this stage, predictable: this is either a cracker case or a gigantic waste of time. Or, in his words, 'There is going to be either nothing from this letter or there's going to be a *moerse* big story.'

Later the same day, Pretorius calls up another detective from Yeoville and brings him into the fold. Lufuno Brian Sono is younger and less experienced than the others, and his background lies in the hijacking unit, but he's under Pretorius's wing and has proved himself to be a dedicated cop. Pretorius likes that Sono investigates with his heart and is always prepared to jump into a car and go.

Sono grew up in Kensington, sharing a single room with his mother, Bertha, a domestic worker who raised five children. She spent 25 years working for the family of Clive Scott, a well-known South African actor who appeared in everything from the TV series *Isidingo* to international films such as *Stander*.

When he was younger, Sono wanted to be an engineer, but with his brothers becoming policemen, and no money to study, he took a chance by applying to join the police service. At the time, he was working at the drive-through counter at a McDonald's.

He's been at Yeoville for around six years but is still a constable, the lowest rank in the police service, with a salary to match. Sono, now in his early thirties, is frustrated at not having been promoted or at least recognised. As soon as he hears about this investigation, he begins to wonder whether it's the kind of case that might just attract a bit of attention.

And so, with Sono on board, the team is assembled and decides to begin where every investigation must begin, with the victim. As things stand, all they have is a name: Betty Ketani. To prove that a crime has taken place, to be able to register a case, they need to find out whether Betty existed and, if possible, exactly what happened to her. What they really need is a body.

If Betty disappeared as the letter says she did, there should be a case registered. A murder docket or at the very least a missing persons report. They know nothing about the case that Betty's brother Ronnie opened all those years ago.

Pretorius starts by searching the police database. Ketani is an unusual enough name and he could get lucky. There are many ways to run searches, but using an identity number is by far the fastest and most reliable. Having a case number and the police station where a case was registered makes things easier. In this instance, however, they have only a name and a surname, and nothing is showing up on the system. No cases. No reports. No Betty Ketani. Careless spelling mistakes made in 1999 are sending the searches astray.

Pretorius tries the same with 'Themba Tshabalala', the first victim named in the hidden confession. Hundreds of results rush back at him. Tshabalala is one of the most common surnames in South Africa, and the number of cases opened either by or against someone with that surname will keep him busy for weeks.

Doc tries another avenue. He calls up a contact and asks him to run a credit check on the name Betty Ketani. If she existed, she probably applied for credit somewhere and may have even been blacklisted. It's a long shot, but they are casting as many lines as possible, hoping for a bite.

JB is growing impatient. To him the case has become real and if the letter says there's a body buried at 21A Leo Street, Kenilworth, then there must be a grave there. The names check out. The cellphone numbers are real. JB has all the proof he needs to do what he does best: follow a scent.

'If we find any human remains there,' he tells the others, 'then we know this letter is true.'

JB phones up a small company and hires a couple of workers to start digging the following morning. He tells them to bring a jackhammer.

14.

Once he was done with the army, Conway Brown moved in with a new girlfriend into a small apartment in Kempton Park. During the day he worked as a salesman at Edgars, the clothing chain store, and nights were spent behind a bar at a local restaurant.

The relationship ended and he was left living alone. At some point he met two Greek shop-owners and started working at their corner café. During this period of his life, the jobs came and went; Conway stayed with one of his two sisters for a while, and eventually decided he had had enough of drifting aimlessly. What he needed was to sort out his head and find direction. What he needed was a change of scene.

Together with a friend named Mike he hatched a plan: he would sell everything he owned, buy a backpack and make his way down to the coast. Mike travelled only halfway with him but Conway went all the way, and soon found himself in Durban, at a run-down hotel a block away from the ocean.

> The cockroaches were almost the size of a packet of cigarettes. The table had this plastic cover over it. In the mornings, you put your plate of food down and your plate would move. It was a real classy joint … but it was a block from the beach and right where all the pubs were.

It wasn't long before Conway was working in one of those pubs. There are gaps in his memory of this time of his life – like there are with many other periods – but he does remember the morning he woke up to find a fresh tattoo on his right arm.

His memories are probably romanticised, but he remembers it as one of those classic moments in which he woke up, looked to one side and found a strange woman in his bed, then looked the other way and found a fresh tattoo. Conway's head was pounding from the 'meanest hangover anyone could possibly have'. Slowly, he walked to take a shower and remembered going to one of the tattoo parlours and picking out a bird design from the reference books. The bird was perched on a branch and had musical notes floating away from its beak, just like Jeffrey Marshall remembered.

> *The reason it was a bird was that you had a sense of freedom because you're away from everything. I'd just sold everything, I'd left the concrete jungle. You've now got the sea in front of you. I could say it was a freedom thing and it was the nicest bird there. They had all the other sailor birds … remember this is right on the docks. And the shape of it is identical to the shape of my dad's tattoo, which he had in the same place. His was a rifle with a helmet on it, with the little mountain behind it. It was an army tattoo that they had done back in those days for the fallen men.*

This wasn't Conway's first tattoo. In fact, he was building up a collection. He would go on to have dragons, Hungarian slogans, tribal designs and a flaming heart with a dagger piercing it vertically. One of these tattoos he did himself, despite knowing nothing about tattooing. He says he went over the same lines again and again and once the ink was driven in, he could barely walk for a week because of the pain.

Conway's Durban adventure was short-lived. He had no car and no money, so he hitchhiked up to stay with his godparents in Dundee. It was there that he met Blanche again, whom he had known since he was a boy.

Blanche had been dating one of Conway's cousins. This cousin was like an older brother to Conway but also a 'loose cannon'. He had made Blanche pregnant and then he split, leaving her with a son.

During their time in Dundee, Conway and Blanche 'clicked'. They returned to Johannesburg and moved in together at an aunt's place. Somewhere along the line they became 'boyfriend and girlfriend'. Further along the line, in March 1993, they were married.

Conway tried to reach out to his cousin, asking him to at least visit Blanche's son Sheldon, but it was no use. Conway decided to legally adopt Sheldon.

Years later, Conway would return to Durban for another three or four months, this time to start a butchery-equipment repair company. The project failed and he and Blanche made their way back to Joburg, where Conway found a job selling toys at Reggie's.

Another job at which he tried his hand was that of a glass medic, someone who fixes cracks in car windscreens. Conway thought it was a neat way to earn money so he bought his own kit and began driving around town fixing windows. In around 1996, he was offered a permanent position at a PG Auto Glass dealership. For him, it was a perfect deal; it meant he wouldn't have to drive around as much and the customers would come to him. But, before long, he managed to get himself tangled up in an undercover police investigation at his new office.

Conway's version is that he landed up working with a corrupt manager who set up a scheme to steal a car. Conway was asked to handle the keys and drive the car around, but he had been approached by the police and was working with them. The operation – which was meant to catch the thieves red-handed – was botched, and Conway ended up being a suspect in a car-theft case. The matter was eventually cleared up, but not without an entry against his name in the police database.

Police records still reflect the incident, but there is no reference to Conway being arrested or charged. Whether he was involved in the original scheme remains uncertain. He says all he can remember is spending a lot of time with the police, showing them sites and writing things down for them.

> *I got involved in something once again … dumb-ass me, much bigger and broader than my IQ. You go in with all good intentions. I don't know if people are gullible or what it is, but you end up on the wrong side.*

Five years earlier, Conway received a minor criminal record without even knowing it. He was working as a manager at a Bimbo's fast-food joint near his house in Rosettenville when the business was sold to a new owner. Bimbo's used to sell soft liquor such as beers and ciders, but on the sale of the business, the liquor licence lapsed.

A couple of undercover policemen walked into his Bimbo's, sat down and ordered burgers. Conway says he served them and didn't think twice before fetching them the beers they wanted. The next thing he knew he was under arrest and on his way to a police station.

They took me to jail. Threw me in a cell there. I went ballistic. I picked up the bed, I threw the bed at the door. There was a little bench. I picked up the bench, I smacked the security gate with the bench. I went crazy. Eventually they came, they unlocked my cell. It was a metal cage. They came, they unlocked the cage and they left it open, and then I calmed down and sort of settled down.

On 5 February 1991, a magistrate tried to explain to a 21-year-old Conway the technicality of the liquor licence lapse, but it wasn't sinking in. The owner of the Bimbo's arrived with lawyers and bail money. Two months later, Conway was ordered to pay a R1 500 fine or spend eight months behind bars. He claims he didn't even realise he had landed a criminal record – 'selling liquor without a licence' – until much later.

Conway and Blanche lived in Rosettenville for a while. Blanche worked at a Stax electronics store and the couple were doing whatever they could to pay the bills. Then, one day Blanche was caught up in an armed robbery at the 7-Eleven below their flat. The Browns decided to find a better, safer place to live.

The couple were battling financially, with Conway bouncing between jobs. He had spent time installing carports and awnings, his car had been written off and, with the arrival of their daughter Toni, they had two kids to feed. Carrington Laughton claims things got so bad for Conway that he would steal coins from public telephone booths. Conway denies this. In any event, when one of Blanche's co-workers offered a cheap accommodation solution, they jumped at the opportunity. Conway and Blanche were introduced to their new landlords, Geoffrey and Shama Marshall. The place they were renting out was a step up from the apartment and, with a little extra effort, was within their price range.

No one remembers exactly when the Browns moved in, but it would have been during 1993 or 1994. Conway recalls meeting Geoffrey for the first time, finding him sitting in his chair, surrounded by books, looking very much like the RAF pilot he had once been. He saw a proud Englishman, a perfect gentleman with a neatly trimmed moustache. He also remembers how much he liked Shama, even though, coming from a sheltered childhood, he was a little taken aback by the mixed marriage.

Conway also has a particularly happy memory of 21A Leo Street: his daughter Toni, still very young, lying in a bathtub at the house, her hair floating on the water. To him, she looked like Medusa. In Greek mythology, Medusa is a monster who has venomous snakes instead of hair and who turns those who look at her into stone. But in Conway's world, which is so abstract and imaginative, the sight is one of the last happy memories from that period in his life. After that, he says, the nightmare began.

15.

Early on Thursday morning, 5 April 2012, the day before Good Friday, JB comes bounding into the office. He's in a rush to drive out to Kenilworth and is checking in before he does. Doc has a breakfast appointment and asks JB to wait for him before starting the excavation at the chef's house.

'Fuck it, man, I'm not waiting for you or for anybody else,' JB replies. 'I'm getting the *okes* and we're going to go and dig.' In JB's world there is no better time to do something than right now, no such a thing as 'later'. There's never a Plan B. Doc knows nothing will change his friend's mind and promises to catch up with him later.

Four days have passed since the letters were found under the carpet and the investigation is moving quickly. Late yesterday, Doc's contact came through for them with the results of the credit check. There were several hits for 'Betty Ketani', but once Doc heard the word 'Cranks' – given as a place of employment – he knew they hit the jackpot.

'Hey, that's the one! That's our Betty Ketani,' he shouted down the phone.

Doc asked his contact to print out everything he had and to meet him in Rosebank. It turned out Betty held a number of accounts at different retail stores and stopped paying all of them simultaneously. A trace alert was put out on her and she was blacklisted. The timing coincided with her disappearance.

The credit listings proved that the Betty mentioned in the letter did exist. More importantly, they gave Doc and the others Betty's identity number. Thirteen digits that unlock all the information contained in the police database, as well as any records held by Home Affairs.

Pretorius ran the ID number and this time the missing persons case popped up on his screen: Hillbrow case number 12/05/1999, the one opened by her brother Ronnie. Betty's names were misspelt on the system: 'Khethane' or 'Khetani' instead of 'Ketani'. There were also variations of her first name. The only one that seemed to have been spelt correctly was her English name: 'Betty'.

Later that same day, the team drove through to the Hillbrow police station, but failed to find the physical missing persons docket. Too much time had passed. It didn't matter; having the statements inside the docket would have been great, but the computer system was enough. It contained names, telephone numbers and addresses associated with the case.

Sono had been sent to the Eastgate shopping mall to check out one of the stores where Betty had run up some bills. The plan was to try to pull her file and, through that, find her family. While he negotiated with the store managers and waited for them to call head office, the others headed to Home Affairs in Alexandra to run Betty's ID number. What came back was a slim profile, but one with a photograph. Seeing that image proved to be a big moment. It was an introduction of sorts, connecting Betty Ketani to the motley crew of men trying to avenge her, 13 years after her disappearance. Being able to see her face, look into her eyes, was confirmation that Betty lived. This was no bullshit case, but a real murder investigation.

• • •

With the missing persons docket and the blacklisting information, there is no more doubt that the grave has to be dug up. For a fresh murder docket to be opened, they will need confirmation that Betty not only lived but is, in fact, dead.

JB leaves for Kenilworth that Thursday morning under strict instructions to stop digging the moment he finds anything. If a body or bones are discovered, he is to call Colonel André Neethling, who can take charge of the scene.

Doc and JB are paying for the excavation themselves. The man they've hired, Chris, arrives dressed in a big safari hat and a loud waistcoat. With him are two workers hired to do the digging.

Werner is told about the plan and agrees, just as long as the hole is covered up afterwards and he is not left paying to fix it. Shama gives JB the mark: a rough location of where the grave must be, given the information in the confession. She knows where the garage used to end and where Conway's garden was.

'We had made up our minds,' Doc says. 'If it meant digging up a swimming pool, that is what we were going to do because the body must be there. Everything has fallen into place.'

The digging begins at around 9am. The soil beneath the concrete is a messy mix of rocks, plastic bags and other rubbish. There are torn pieces of what appears to be woollen clothing. JB drags on his cigarette as he watches the excavation. Soon the hole is deep and wide enough for him to stand in to inspect the progress. Werner's dogs are locked in the back of the property and watch the activity through the fence.

Doc is still at his meeting when his phone rings. It's JB, his voice loud and urgent.

'We found bones.'

'What?'

'We fucking found bones and we've stopped digging.'

'I'm on my way,' Doc says and hangs up.

It's not yet midday and the next call goes out to André Neethling. He arrives at 21A Leo Street and familiarises himself with the scene. Yeoville detectives Gerhard Pretorius and Lufuno Sono are also there now.

Seven small white pieces of what appears to be bone fragments lie on the concrete next to the hole. They are all different shapes and most have been stained a dirty brown by the soil. Some have intricate twists in them, like old seashells. If they are bones, they look like flat shards from a skull or a pelvis.

Neethling calls a forensic pathologist, Dr Shakeera Holland, as well as a police search-and-rescue specialist, Mohammed Waldman. Waldman is a dog handler from the Vaal Rand K9 unit who works with a dog named Buti, which is trained to locate missing people, dead or alive. Other police officers are summoned and the excitement grows with each new arrival.

Doc gets to Leo Street at about noon and immediately begins to photograph the scene, documenting the discovery. He snaps photos of Chris the contractor pointing down at the hole and then of him posing with his two workers. He photographs Neethling, Pretorius and Werner. He hands his camera to JB for a bit, and appears in one or two of the photographs, wearing his black leather biker cut. He photographs what they believe to be bones and the hole that was dug. Doc focuses on the scraps of fabric, which everyone believes to be Betty's clothes. In a video, JB triumphantly declares that the bones must be human. Doc is heard saying that it's time to let the police and forensic experts take over.

Dr Shakeera Holland arrives at a nearby police station with her entourage. She has driven from the Hillbrow mortuary and is escorted to Conway's old house. Along the way she is told about the case. As background, Neethling shows Shakeera one of the letters that was found. It's the small, handwritten one about the robbery.

'I said to André, "Don't you think this guy is psychotic?"' Shakeera remembers. 'This letter looks so strange. Often what happens in psychosis is that you have flight of ideas and pressure of thought, so that as things come into your head you're writing them down, everything is going really fast and you're trying to get it together quickly.'

But Neethling tells her about the typed letter and the policemen who appear to be involved. He says everything else has checked out and assures her that this is a serious case.

Shakeera is shown what JB and the others have unearthed. Her team spends a few minutes dusting off the remains, making sure they are clean and ready for inspection. Shakeera is one of the senior specialists in her department and knows exactly what they are the second she lays eyes on them.

'It's like the smell of blood. Blood has this particular smell that's unlike anything else. Bone has a look to it, whether it is old or new, animal or human; it has a specific look. It's easy to identify bone. You can't mistake it.'

And that is why she's absolutely sure, without a hint of doubt, that what she's holding in her hands are *not* bones.

Shakeera guesses they are small pieces of limestone or some kind of shell. But definitely not human bones. Not even close.

To try to soften the blow, she offers to return should anything else be pulled out of the grave. But the news she has just delivered bursts a bubble, deflating the moment of all excitement.

• • •

The other police officers on the scene find this twist amusing. They look through the confession letter and make smug remarks about the case.

'They look at it and the one guy says, "This paper is not 13 years old,"' Doc recalls. 'I look at the *oke* and say, "Hey, fuck you, can you not see it's a photostat? D'you think we are using the original?" They all have a good laugh at us and they duck. They fuck off. Their whole attitude is telling us: "You people are fucked. You are stupid."'

JB's enthusiasm turns to anger and frustration. He can't understand what has just happened. 'We were *naar* [nauseous]! I *scheme*, "All this digging for nothing." I start fighting with the letter. The names are all right, but there is no body.'

Tempers begin to rise and squabbles break out. Chris wants to know how much longer they are going to dig. Werner is anxious about how much bigger the hole is going to get. JB is just about ready to break the house down to find the body. They decide to push on with the excavation.

Neethling makes a fresh attempt at analysing the contents of the confession. Constable Waldman is in the hole with Buti, trying to pick up a scent. He's convinced the hole is now too deep. Those digging a shallow grave, he tells the others, don't go this far down. Neethling and the dog handler are the only two officers who stay behind. The rest clear off.

As the sun begins to set, the team decides to stop. It's been almost ten hours and they have nothing to show except a heap of humiliation and a couple of pieces of what will later be identified by Conway as a broken tortoise shell. If there was a skeleton here, they would have found it by now. There's no explanation for why there is no body below the concrete. Everything else in the letter checks out. They wonder whether it could be fake after all.

Tomorrow marks the start of the long Easter weekend, and if they are to keep digging further it will have to wait until the following week. They are not ready to give up and agree to regroup then.

'We went there, but we couldn't find anything,' says Sono. 'If we were dogs, our tails would be between our legs.'

16.

Themba Tshabalala is shopping at Makro, buying stock for his wife's restaurant, when his phone rings. It's an unknown number but he answers anyway.

The caller introduces himself as Detective Pretorius. Themba is startled and immediately asks what the call is about. The policeman tells him not to worry and begins asking questions.

In 1999, did he live in flat 1906 at Aintree apartments in Hillbrow? He did. Did he open an assault and kidnapping case with a policeman named Van Rooyen? Correct. Did he know a woman named Betty Ketani? Yes, he knew her.

'Oh, Jesus, at last, I've got you!' Pretorius announces, unable to hide his relief.

The detective tells Themba he wants to meet. He needs more information. Pretorius wants to know whether they can speak in person, as soon as possible.

Themba is frozen by fear. For years he has been terrified of policemen, especially white ones. He remembers the horrors of 1999. Memories of the fake police raids, the abductions and the trips to the 'killing place' have never left him. This phone call sends them all flooding back.

To buy some time, to compose himself, Themba asks Detective Pretorius to SMS him his number and promises to call him back as soon as he has finished his shopping. He asks for an hour and is relieved when the call ends.

As soon as he's done at Makro, Themba drives straight to the restaurant, located a stone's throw away from the Hillbrow police station. His wife, Mighty, used to work with Betty at Cranks. She was a waitress there, on and off, between 1996 and 2008. Like her husband, Mighty has a head full of bad memories from that time and, like most of the staff, had fought with Eric. Although she was never abducted or violently interrogated during the time of the Cranks investigation, she was around during some of the late-night visits to her husband and has never forgotten them.

Mighty still dreams about the past, about Eric and about Betty. She never got over her disappearance. In one of her latest dreams, Betty was standing in a doorway, dressed in her Cranks uniform, with her apron on. Her face was dark, cloaked in shadow. She was crying. And then Mighty woke up.

Hearing about the call from Pretorius, Mighty feels terror wash over her. She tells her husband not to meet him.

'These guys could kill you,' she warns.

But Themba has had some time to think about the request. He has calmed down and tells Mighty that Pretorius sounds like a real policeman. He feels a nervous spark of hope that after all these years, justice may finally be served.

Mighty is unable to convince Themba not to go but she asks him to at least meet Pretorius at the police station, where it's safe. Themba makes the arrangements.

It's taken Pretorius several days to track down the right Themba Tshabalala. The police database contains countless cases linked to that name. Pretorius filtered them down by discarding the ones where the name belonged to a suspect. He was interested in those where Themba Tshabalala was the complainant. Patiently, while the others worked the Betty Ketani angle, he began dialling numbers.

Eventually, Pretorius stumbled across an assault case opened by a Themba Tshabalala somewhere out on the East Rand. It had nothing to do with the 1999 abductions but there was an ID number and contact details. Pretorius typed in the identity number and found what he had been looking for: Hillbrow case 809/05/1999 – the case Themba opened after his abductions.

The charges were of assault, kidnapping and theft. On the computer system, unlike on the physical docket, the complainant's name had been misspelt as 'Themba Tshabalaka', rendering it invisible to earlier searches.

The meeting at the Hillbrow police station goes smoothly. Themba asks the officers in the charge office to watch over him, but after a conversation with Pretorius and JB out in the parking lot he feels confident enough to climb into their car and direct them to Mighty's restaurant. Pretorius can't help himself and, as soon as all the car doors are locked, turns around, puts on a bad-cop voice and tells Themba: 'Now you're going to see who are the real *boere*' (an apartheid-era reference to policemen). Themba panics, but is quickly let in on the joke and relaxes. Within minutes they are at the restaurant, settling down at one of the tables. Themba and Mighty begin to tell their stories, going into great detail. Mighty doesn't feature in the confession but, incredibly, the summary of what happened to Themba is virtually identical to what he is telling them now.

Once Themba is finished, the investigators ask Mighty to look for old photographs of Betty and to put them in touch with other victims or former Cranks employees. Mighty is still in contact with Ruth Mncube and several other ex-colleagues. She can also link them up with Ndaba Bhebe, who turns out to be a relative. Neither Mighty nor Themba know who Malemleli Mpofu is or what happened to him.

Pretorius and JB now have proof that all but one of the victims named in the letter are real. All these people, except Betty, are still alive and are potential witnesses, able to corroborate the confession found by the Marshalls. They leave, promising to send Detective Sono around later to take statements. He will be the official investigating officer of the new docket, once it's opened.

'They said, okay, we are going to come here several times. You guys don't be scared, you are going to be protected,' Themba recalls.

Finding Themba and Mighty, and through them Ndaba and Ruth, is a leap forward in the investigation. It is confirmation of five paragraphs, or almost half, of the three-page confession. But there may still be no case if Betty's body can't be found.

• • •

On a roll now, the team makes another breakthrough over the Easter weekend. Through the missing persons case they trace Betty's brother Ronnie, who is still in town. He is able to fill in some of the blanks about his sister's past, tells them about her three children, Thulani, Bulelwa and Lusanda, and puts them in contact with the family in Queenstown. This is an important piece of the puzzle but one that will have to wait, given the distance between Gauteng and the Eastern Cape.

The following Tuesday, 10 April, the excavation of the grave site resumes. After the disappointment of the last attempt, the team is now desperate. The confession is so clear and Shama has shown them the exact spot.

'Everything in this letter is making sense,' Doc remembers thinking. 'The body must be here. How the fuck are we missing this body?'

The men growl at each other in frustration. JB is arguing with Werner over the location of the grave. JB wants to dig closer to the swimming pool but Werner is refusing, telling them they're not to go anywhere near it. Already, the hole is exposing sewerage pipes running away from the house. JB digs in all directions, wondering if, by some miscalculation, they are a metre or two off target. He's refusing to admit defeat.

'I just thank God that we didn't have a jackhammer on Tuesday because then he would have fucking broken Werner's concrete going back all the way to the gate,' Doc recalls. 'That's the only reason why it wasn't done, because we didn't have a jackhammer. If we did, Werner would have no concrete left.'

Like surgeons operating through an incision in the skin, the team hollow out the soil beneath the cement, working with the opening made the previous week.

'The *okes* were motivating each other and then, every hour on the hour, somebody was selected to go and get us cold drinks, water and chips. There was a lot of bitching going on,' Doc explains. 'But I've always said, JB is the most stubborn fucking *oke* I know and if he gets something into his head, he is like a pit bull. He won't let it go. If the letter says the body is there, it must be there.'

But the more they dig, the more rubbish they find. There is nothing resembling a skeleton or even loose bones.

Finally, at the end of the second day, JB surrenders. He and the team fill up the hole, first tossing back all the stones and rocks and then topping it up with soil. Once they're done, the hole looks like a fresh grave. Werner insists they come back and lay down new cement. Doc and JB promise they will, as soon as they get some money to buy materials.

There's no explanation for the missing body, but it's a major setback.

There have been cases in South Africa where murderers have been convicted without their victim's body being discovered, but resurrecting a 13-year-old cold case without a body seems too far of a stretch. Already they've been laughed at by senior policemen. Even Doc's mother – who has discussed the case with her friends at art class – believes they are tilting at windmills. Doc is tired and pissed off, and decides to go home. JB, Pretorius and Sono have a little fire left and agree to drive to Cranks restaurant in Rosebank to see if they can find this man named Eric.

17.

A few months after Betty Ketani vanished in mid-1999, her boss, Eric Neeteson-Lemkes, appeared on a cooking show broadcast on SABC. Eric was introduced as 'Malon Sangchloury' and was asked to pronounce the unusual name. It was one of several he used in public, creating a riddle around his identity.

Eric appears on the kitchen set of *Spuds: Creative Cooking with Potatoes* in an open-collar white silk shirt with loud orange polka dots and a bright red cap, its square shop tag still dangling off the side. He is jokingly asked whether he wrote the recipe for the day on the tag, to which the stony-faced chef replies that he makes up most of his recipes and keeps them all in his head. Wearing an overall, Eric cooks his restaurant's signature dish 'Kay Bee Too': a fusion of wok-fried baby potatoes with a chilli jam, cashew nuts, celery, bean sprouts and coriander. He either misses or ignores most of the jokes.

The cameras capture the intensity in his pale face. He thinks deeply about questions relating to Cranks and answers them with rehearsed lines. He says Cranks in Rosebank is his twelfth restaurant and that most had lifespans of about a year and a half. He explains that he opened Cranks in Hillbrow in the 1980s, reinvented it as Koula Blue in Melville, then brought Cranks back in Illovo and finally moved it into Rosebank.

Eric explains that Cranks attracts 'exciting' and 'alternative' people who come for the atmosphere and the attitude.

'For us, running Cranks is an addiction. A disease,' Eric proclaims. 'We get a lot of fun out of it. It's not a yes-sir-no-sir kind of place.'

Betty's family members remember watching the show and say she herself appeared as a guest on some other programme, representing Cranks. But there is no trace of this in the SABC archives.

Three years later, Eric granted an interview to journalist Jonathan Ancer, who wrote a profile on him and the restaurant for *Citylife* magazine. This is how Ancer described his first impressions:

> *In front of me is a pineapple, scooped out and filled with a sumptu-*
> *ous mix of chicken, cashew nuts and tamarind. I'm sitting at Cranks*
> *in Rosebank, Johannesburg. The décor calls to mind a psychedelic Thai*
> *knock shop. Above me, suspended from the ceiling, is an array of Barbie*
> *and Ken dolls. Barbie doing Ken; Ken doing Ken; Ken and Ken doing*
> *Barbie; Barbie doing Barbie. And wandering around the restaurant, stop-*
> *ping at each table to chat, is Eric, the owner. He's a big, bulky guy in a*
> *long saffron silk shirt. The patrons either laugh, look confused, or look*
> *confused and then laugh nervously. Finally he arrives at my table, bear-*
> *ing my second course: green papaya salad with tomatoes, peanuts and a*
> *sweet chilli sauce.*
>
> *He gives me a long stare. His eyes are startling, enormous, and a trans-*
> *lucent blue. I shift nervously in my chair.*
>
> *'Beware of the mad dog,' he says. His Dutch accent is as thick as satay*
> *sauce. I laugh nervously.*

The 2002 magazine article states that the restaurant has also attracted well-known South Africans, such as controversial Afrikaans musician Steve Hofmeyr, former Reserve Bank governor Tito Mboweni and politician-turned-activist Jay Naidoo, who 'have been known to kick back with the odd pineapple schnapps and stir-fry'. For the interview, Eric uses the name 'Eric Sangchloury' (perhaps a blend of Malon Sangchloury and Eric Neeteson-Lemkes). He tells Ancer that his parents were born in Indonesia and that his mother was the 'best Indonesian cook in the world'.

Eric continues by explaining that he cooked French cuisine in Holland and then worked in Bangkok, where he fell in love with Thai food.

'I wanted to beat the Thai at their own game. Thai food is an art.'

Eric mentions nothing about his first marriage to Dang Maleerat Sriwattana, which ended in the 1980s, nor about his two daughters, Monique and Naydine, who were both born in Australia and spent a year and a half in Johannesburg between mid-1998 and early 2000. Instead, he talks about his new wife, Jitra, and their young daughter. He claims he picked Jitra out of a photograph album and had met her only once before flying to Thailand to marry her in a Buddhist ceremony. One of her eight sisters was visiting Johannesburg and had set up the entire thing.

'I thought, how can I get married to a stranger? Am I mad dog? Yes, I thought.'

. . .

Pretorius, JB and Sono have never heard of the 'mad dog'. The confession doesn't implicate Eric in anything. In fact, it makes him out to be a victim, whose daughter has been deceiving him.

'I think Eric should know the truth …', the author writes at the bottom of page 2.

The investigators figure that perhaps Eric can help further authenticate the letter. Unlock some more of its secrets. Maybe somehow break the case wide open. Pretorius has called to announce their arrival and they've agreed to meet at the restaurant at 4pm.

Jitra is there to greet them and asks them to wait a few minutes. They are left to process the unusual décor.

'We check this place out and we check it's weird,' JB recalls. 'It's *poppies* and fucking dragonflies. I think these people are on drugs here.'

Eric walks up to them. He's 62 now and has aged since his television appearance.

'Here this *oke* comes. He's got no eyebrows and all his hair is shaved off. He looks like a *malletjie* [crazy one],' JB says. 'He tunes us, "What do you want?"'

Sono is struck by the immediate hostility, watching as Pretorius and JB explain the visit. If they knew the history, they would probably understand …

They manage to confirm a few facts. Eric admits that Monique is his daughter but is living somewhere in Australia, as is his ex-wife. He talks to them about a robbery at his house and about his domestic worker Debbie. But the interview quickly begins to spiral out of control as Eric's anger grows.

All three men remember asking Eric whether he knows or knew Betty Ketani. He tells them he knows no one by that name. This is either a blatant lie – given the years she gave to his restaurants – or a complete misunderstanding, but the team doesn't know enough of the history yet to challenge him.

'I personally asked him, "Do you know Betty?"' Sono recalls. 'He said to me: "Who is that? I don't know Betty, I know Debbie."'

The team is trying to establish the link, if there is one, between the Cranks investigation, Betty's murder and the house robbery described in the second letter and which Eric now seems to be confirming. Did Betty perhaps work for Eric at his house? Did he suspect she was somehow involved in the robbery? Did the robbers try to get rid of her because she saw what happened? No such link will ever be found, but at this moment Eric is shutting down, growing more and more aggressive, rambling on about some 'security guy' whom the police failed to investigate.

In an attempt to rescue the situation, Pretorius shows Eric a copy of the confession. He reads it and makes himself a copy. Absorbing the contents makes Eric all the more furious and he begins to shout at his visitors, saying, 'Fuck the police and fuck you people.' He's ranting about how long it took for the police to investigate his robbery and how useless that investigation was. He keeps repeating 'seven years'.

JB's own temper begins to boil and he's yelling back at Eric, telling him to stop insulting them. Sono leads JB outside while Pretorius tries to defuse the tension. Pretorius has one last try at diplomacy, to get more answers out of Eric, but it's not working. The Cranks visit has blown up. Between the Barbie doll kama sutra and the mad owner with nothing but venom for the police, they feel like they've been knocked out of orbit. So much of the letter has proven to be true, but there's no body in the grave and now the owner of the restaurant where Betty worked denies knowing her.

The team retreats. Back at the police station, Pretorius makes a phone call and jots down a number. They weren't planning to approach any key suspects until the very last moment, until they were ready to make arrests, but they are clean out of options and Eric has the letter now, which means news of their investigation may leak. They have no idea who is connected to whom. One wrong step and the element of surprise is blown. Making the call that Pretorius plans to make is a dangerous gamble that can easily backfire, like the visit to Cranks. It's a hunt and breaking cover can send a herd of suspects darting in opposite directions to hide, destroy evidence or hire lawyers. Sono is anxious about the decision, arguing that they need more time to investigate. If they are forced to make arrests, it could set off a chain of unpredictable events. But Sono is overruled.

The call is an act of frustration and desperation. But there's one man who must know where Betty's body is buried. One man who can explain the confession. Pretorius dials the number and waits for Conway Brown to answer.

18.

Themba Tshabalala hears the pounding on the door and immediately knows he's in trouble. It's after midnight and the knocking is loud and aggressive. A man is shouting from the other side: 'Open! Open! Open!'

The visitors run out of patience and – having already broken the security gate – bash through the door of apartment 1906, spilling inside the small bachelor flat. They confront Themba, announce the raid and begin searching his cupboards.

It's 11 May 1999 and this is the second night in a row the policemen have come. Last night they wanted information about his wife, Mighty. When he told them she was on holiday in KwaZulu-Natal, they hammered him with questions about his past, his job, whether he was living in South Africa legally, and even accused him of selling dagga. There were about six or seven officers, mostly in uniform, including a woman who had her hair tied up under a police cap. Some wore bulletproof vests. They didn't stay long, and left without explanations. Themba knew better then to ask police officers in Hillbrow too many questions.

Themba has been living in the Aintree apartment block for about five years. He's a thin man with small, delicate hands. His face is pockmarked and he carries a nervous but warm smile.

Aintree is perched on the outskirts of Hillbrow, shoulder to shoulder with one of the most recognisable buildings in the Johannesburg skyline: Ponte. Aintree is not as tall, or grand, but is still an impressive building that would have once been prime real estate. Themba's flat is on the nineteenth floor.

After 20 years of working at Mike's Kitchen, Themba has just landed a new job as a chef at the Carnivore restaurant in Muldersdrift. It's a step up and with the extra cash Themba is buying his very first car, an old Mazda 323. He's been saving to put down a deposit and the cash is hidden in his flat.

Themba and Mighty have been married a year. They are sharing their apartment with Ndaba Bhebe and Ruth Mncube, one of Mighty's colleagues from Cranks. Ruth is often away for days at a time and Themba never knows whether she will be spending the night or not.

According to Themba, when the officers return to his flat the second night, they appear to be in a rush. The woman is no longer there. They demand he tell them the truth about where Mighty is. He assures them she's with her family in KwaZulu-Natal.

The officers grill him about Ruth, revealing that she's been accused of stealing from the restaurant. Themba tells them he doesn't know where Ruth is or when she will return. He asks whether Mighty is being accused of anything and is told that Ruth is the one they are looking for. He lies, promising to get Mighty to help them find her colleague as soon as she's back in town.

For a moment it looks like the officers are satisfied and will leave him alone as they did the previous night. But instead they continue searching his house and finally tell him that they need to interview him back at the station. Themba tries to resist, asking why he is being taken away and whether he is being charged with any crime. The men assure him they will bring him home soon. They allow him to fetch a jacket before handcuffing him.

They ride the elevator down to the ground floor and walk past the security guard at the front entrance. Themba says as soon as they are out of sight, they slip a blindfold over his eyes and then pull some sort of a mask over his head. Themba is bundled into a car, which speeds off.

After a brief stop at a police station, Themba is driven for what feels like half an hour. He sits in complete darkness. Those in the car with him speak Afrikaans, which he struggles to keep up with. At some point he hears and feels the car leaving the road, to continue along a dirt track. His heart begins to race. The car stops for a moment and he hears the door of another car opening and then closing. He can also hear a gate. When they drive on, he feels the gradient of the ground change as the car climbs a bumpy hill.

Themba is taken out of the vehicle and forced to walk, someone's hand wrapped around his arm. He manages a peek and sees some kind of a house and a hut, with trees dotted around the property. He's being led through tall grass, over farm fences, towards a small cottage or some other outside structure.

Once there, Themba is forced to sit and the questions start raining down on him. His abductors want to know about Mighty. About Ruth. About Betty. They demand to know whether he's heard anything about the trouble at Cranks. He tells them that he doesn't take any interest in what Mighty and her friends talk about. That's 'ladies' business', he pleads.

The voices soften and someone explains that if he assists them in the investigation he will receive a handsome payout. Themba promises to get Mighty to help the moment she is back. He keeps saying he doesn't want any trouble.

Themba's mask is still in place. The policemen keep changing their story, first telling him they are special investigators, then that he is being kept at a place where special forces and military intelligence detain criminals who are plotting against the state. One moment he is told he is not being intimidated, the next he receives a painful kick for not telling the truth. He's also beaten with some kind of a stick or a sjambok; he feels the blows below his rib cage, on his back and shoulders. The interrogators pull him by his hair. For long periods during the night Themba is left alone while those around him busy themselves with other matters.

By the time he's loaded back into the car and driven back to town the sun is ready to rise. He's dropped off south of the city centre and handed R10 for taxi fare. The officers ask him whether he knows where he is and how to get home. Eager to escape, he pretends he does. When he does eventually return to his flat, he discovers the money he was saving for the car has been stolen. He's exhausted and in pain, and collapses to rest. The following day, he goes to the Hillbrow police station to open a case.

• • •

Listening to Themba relive his abduction, Detective Sono is amazed by how neatly the descriptions align with the summary contained in the confession.

Sono has driven to Hillbrow to take Themba's statement. They are sitting at Mighty's restaurant with Ndaba Bhebe, Rachel Dube and Ruth Mncube.

Hearing the details years later robs Themba's story of its intensity. The memories may still be haunting Themba, but he shares them almost matter-of-factly, wrestling with them on the inside. There is no way he can make someone else feel the terror of being whisked away by these men, handcuffed and helpless, driven through the night blindfolded to be beaten and interrogated for hours.

Themba continues, explaining that he was on duty late in the evening when two men in army uniform arrived at the Carnivore restaurant. Just like the confession says. It was 14 May 1999, three days after his first abduction.

From the kitchen, Themba sees the men speaking to the restaurant's manager. Soon, he is asked to join them and is told the soldiers, from a special unit, have a few questions for him and need him to accompany them to Pretoria. The officers assure his boss that he is not a suspect and is needed only to clarify some aspects of an investigation. They ask Themba whether police officers visited him a few nights ago, which he confirms. He can't figure out whether these are the same men who raided his flat. There were too many of them and their faces are a blur. These two are wearing different uniforms, of that he is sure.

The manager pulls Themba aside and asks him whether he's comfortable going with the officers. Themba is confused and tells him about the earlier abduction, asking him to call the police before he goes anywhere. The officers seem to have no problem with this and policemen from Muldersdrift arrive to note the names of the soldiers and record that they are taking Themba with them.

'The policemen came to me and said, "Okay, Themba, you need to go with these guys; we have done all the work and nothing is going to happen to you." I said fine and went to the office and changed out of my chef's clothes and put on my normal clothes and then they put me in a car.'

The soldiers drive along what is now Beyers Naudé Drive and head in the direction of Northcliff, towards the interchange with the N1 highway to Pretoria. When they get to the interchange, instead of turning north to Pretoria the driver steers south. Themba catches on just as another mask is slipped over his head. The soldiers, who have sat in stony silence until now, tell Themba that today they need 'the whole truth'.

Themba can't be certain, but he believes he is taken to the same location as before. The 'killing place', as he calls it. He is beaten, kicked and shocked with some kind of a Taser. He can't see what it is but he remembers the *tzzzz* sound and the pain and dizziness that follow. It felt like his skin was burning.

His captors are still pushing him for answers, and he keeps telling them he knows nothing. The torture comes in bursts, ten minutes or so at a time. In between, Themba is left to recuperate and think about the demands. Several other men have joined the pair who've brought him here, but he can't see who they are. The beating continues for what feels like the entire night.

In the early morning, Themba's kidnappers tell him that they are fed up with his lies. They force him to kneel and order him to pray. They tell him this will be his last prayer.

'I had to kneel down for a few seconds or a minute and pray. They asked me if I was done and I said yes. Then I heard them whisper to each other, and this other guy said, "Do it, just do it." They were whispering to each other saying, "Do it, do it." But I heard someone say, "No, wait … ".'

Themba thinks about screaming or fighting but knows there's no point. There's no one to hear him and he's hopelessly outnumbered. He pleads with his captors, telling them that if they kill him, they will be killing an innocent man.

Then he feels a cold object touch his neck. He doesn't know what it is but it sends a fresh wave of terror through him. He feels alone and helpless. He waits for whatever comes next. He waits to hear something. Anything.

'It came to my mind that they can kill me at any moment now. That it is my time to die.'

All around him there are whispers. His fate is being decided and he can't do a thing to change it. He's told to stand up, and he rises to his feet.

'I told myself that I'm already dead.'

The interrogators have another run at him.

'Where are these people?' they demand. 'Where is Betty? Have you heard anything?'

Themba has nothing to offer and rattles off the same excuses. After a few more punches and kicks, he's escorted back to the car, driven into town and dropped off in the street. He navigates his way home and, after a couple of hours, calls his manager to tell him what happened. He is given the day off to go back to the police.

. . .

For a week things go quiet. On 22 May 1999, the officers question Themba at his flat once again, but this time they don't take him anywhere. His wife Mighty returns home to hear what has been happening. The next night they come for Ndaba. Themba is alerted by the security guard downstairs and rushes out onto the balcony. He asks the guard to write down the number plates, which he does. As Ndaba is led away, Themba can do nothing but watch.

19.

The mask went over Ndaba's eyes back in Randburg, somewhere outside the taxi rank. He lost all sense of direction after that and can't even judge how long it took them to reach this place. Through the weave of the balaclava, Ndaba Bhebe tries to make out where he is. The place has bright lights and large windows, but that's all he can see. The floor makes a dull 'gong, gong, gong' sound as his captors circle around him. He wonders if he's at a police station. He can hear two-way radios crackling, but it's far too quiet to be a station. There are new voices all around.

Ndaba is 22 years old and unemployed. He's been staying with Mighty, in her and Themba's flat, while searching for work. When the policemen came for him a few hours ago, he immediately recognised one of them. He had been at the flat during some of the earlier visits. They weren't wearing uniforms this time, but he knew who they were. It was around ten at night.

The 'cops' led him downstairs, tied his hands with a white plastic cable tie and shoved him in the back seat of the same car that had whisked Themba away. He remembers seeing a Mazda Astina parked nearby. He saw the same Astina at the Rosebank police station, which was their first stop. He was told he was being taken to another police station, but he doesn't know if that's where he's landed up.

The officers start to question him about Ruth, Betty and Mighty. Like Themba, he tells them he knows nothing. And so the beating begins. Punches. Kicks. Some kind of a hard object smashing across his body. Trapped in darkness, he can't see any of it coming.

'I don't know what it was. I couldn't see,' Ndaba explains. 'A man then spoke and said, "Touch this." I refused to touch anything as I couldn't see. He took my hand and again said, "Touch this!" and placed my hand on the object. I felt that it was a gun. He forced me to hold the firearm and then said that they are going to commit a murder and that my fingerprints are now on the firearm and the police will think I did it. After that, he took the gun away.'

The questions and punches continue. Ndaba is asked whether he can take the officers to see the women they are looking for. He says he can't and is accused of lying. Bursts of electric shock pulse through his body. One man is leading the interrogation, speaking to him in intervals. Trying new angles. The man keeps telling Ndaba that he can save him. If he doesn't talk, the others will kill him.

'They beat me very hard. My mouth was bleeding. I was full of blood all over my face. They said, "This guy is stubborn, let's take him somewhere so that when he screams nobody will hear him." They said, "You don't want to tell us, hey, you don't want to tell us, open your mouth!" And they put a gun in my mouth.'

Ndaba is taken back to the car and driven north. The kidnappers pick a desolate stretch of veld outside Fourways to continue the interrogation. He says their cars were parked in a semicircle, all facing inwards, their lights burning through the cold morning air. Ndaba is placed in the middle. He can't be sure but he thinks they've now armed themselves with a sjambok or some kind of a whip. The blows begin to land. The cable tie around his hands breaks or shakes loose and Ndaba's arms are stuck to his sides with masking tape. His legs are also bound.

Questions about Ruth and Betty are interspersed with zaps from a Taser. The pain is unbearable.

'I wanted to run away but I kept telling myself they've caught me, there's nothing I can do. I was really scared but there were too many of them.'

After a while, Ndaba's mask is lifted and a straw is pushed between his lips. At first he fights it, thinking it's some kind of poison. But when he drinks it, he tastes Lemon Twist or Fresca, some kind of sweet cold drink. He gulps it down.

After hours of beating, whipping and shocking him, his captors finally cut the masking tape and search his pockets. They take his ID book and replace it with two boxes of matches, telling him that it gets cold in the bush this time of the year. They say he can start a fire once they leave. Ndaba is ordered not to take off his mask until they are gone. If he does, he's told, he'll be shot.

He waits for the voices to disappear. Once he can no longer hear the car engines, he rips off the mask and takes in his surroundings. He's next to some road, surrounded by tall grass. In a world of pain, exhausted and cold, he waits until morning. He has no idea where he is and it takes a passing jogger – who is at first frightened by the sight of beaten and bloody Ndaba – to explain that he is outside Fourways, in northern Johannesburg. Ndaba is given directions to the nearest shopping mall, where he begs a taxi driver to take him into Hillbrow for free. Four days later, he gives a formal statement to Inspector Van Rooyen, who is already investigating the abductions.

. . .

Tracking down Themba and docket 809/05/1999 has unlocked a wealth of information. The stories Themba and Ndaba tell Detective Sono are almost identical to what's contained in their statements handwritten by Van Rooyen 13 years earlier. There are discrepancies – Themba struggles with exact dates, for example – but, overall, both have the potential to be witnesses if this case gets to court.

Van Rooyen's old docket contains two statements from Themba, the second given after the second abduction, and one from Ndaba. Sono is told the abductions had a severe impact on their lives.

Themba began having nightmares. He would lie awake at night and worry that the men would come back to kill Mighty. He suffered anxiety attacks.

Ndaba says his beating was so severe that it caused some mild brain damage. He began getting headaches and feeling dizzy. Worse, he battled to remember things and couldn't pay attention for long periods of time. He was fired from his job as a security guard because he couldn't remember his orders. He lost a few more jobs for the same reason and was forced to turn to Mighty for support. All these years later, he still suffers from crippling headaches and sometimes, he says, goes blank in the middle of conversations, forgetting what he was talking about.

. . .

Van Rooyen's 1999 docket also contains a statement from Ruth Mncube, who was, it seems, the real target of the night raids. Ruth heard about what happened to Themba and Ndaba and went to ground, staying with different friends around Hillbrow and Berea, moving from place to place in order to stay safe. She had a boyfriend who lived in Alexandra, a township on the other side of town, and she spent some of her time there, in constant fear of her door being broken down.

The night after Ndaba was taken, Ruth came out of hiding and Themba set up a meeting for her with Inspector Van Rooyen. Ruth signed an affidavit to say she believed Cranks owner Eric and his daughter Monique were trying to have her murdered. To justify this, she gave some background.

Ruth said she was hired to work as a waitress at Cranks and was there only a few months, maybe a year, when the trouble started. She remembers Eric's family arriving from Thailand in 1998 and Monique questioning her about why she wore such nice clothes to work. Ruth explained that she was working two jobs, and was coming to Cranks straight from another restaurant. Monique didn't ask any further questions, but it was clear that she didn't trust her and suspected her of living beyond her means.

Ruth knew Betty, she says, but they were not friends outside of work. She was friendlier with the other waitresses: Mighty, Winnie and Esther.

On 23 March 1999, after a long shift, Ruth says she was told to stay behind when the rest of the staff knocked off for the night. She found herself in an office with Monique, her younger sister Naydine and Eric, who had been away for a while and had recently returned to the restaurant. She was asked to give her home address and the addresses of her closest family. Then, without much emotion, her bosses accused her of stealing from them, showing her a cheque Monique claimed to have found in her work trousers. Eric told Ruth not to bother coming back to work. Nobody was interested in her denials.

The next day, four police officers from Rosebank arrived at her home to escort her to the station. Monique was already there making a statement and Ruth was asked to give her version of events. After a few hours she was released, the police finding that there wasn't enough evidence to charge her. It was a he-said-she-said case and no prosecutor would touch it. Ruth remembers seeing the scrunched-up cheque in Monique's hand.

A week went by and Ruth decided to report the case to the CCMA. None of the dozen or so staff at Cranks had work contracts. Many were illegal immigrants. Ruth says she was working for R700 a month and no tips. But she was livid about being accused of stealing and not being paid her wages. She was convinced Monique had set her up and that Eric had no right to fire her. Betty, who was working legally, was helping the others fight their battles.

Ruth says the CCMA gave her a document that Eric had to sign, but he refused and a hearing was set down for 26 May 1999. By this stage, Betty had also apparently launched a case against the restaurant with the CCMA.

'Early in April 1999 one of the girls I used to work with came to me and said I must move from my flat in Hillbrow,' Ruth said in her police statement, which was dictated to Van Rooyen on the evening of 24 May 1999, two months after the cheque confrontation. 'I asked her why and she informed me that Eric and Monique are getting people to come and kill me. I then moved out of the flat and presently I don't have a place of residence. I sleep at my friends' at different places. I don't know why these policemen are looking for me, unless they work for Eric and Monique.'

Ruth had spent most of May of that year in Zimbabwe, with stories of the abductions reaching her via Mighty. She returned the day Ndaba was taken.

• • •

A week after going to the police station, Ruth calls Inspector Van Rooyen in a panic from a post office in downtown Johannesburg. They found her and almost kidnapped her, she tells him frantically. James van Rooyen rushes over to pick her up.

Ruth's next police statement, signed on 9 June 1999, explains what happened. Many years later, a court will hear the same evidence.

On the first day of June, Ruth is walking along Smit Street in Joubert Park at around 2pm and is passing the post office when a white car pulls up in front of her. She is waiting at a traffic light. A white man in jeans and a T-shirt climbs out of the vehicle. Ruth can see he has a gun tucked into his belt. The man is taller than her and looks strong, with light hair and a moustache or a goatee. Suddenly, he's upon her, his fingers clutching her right arm.

'You are Ruth Mncube?' he demands.

Ruth denies it, but she's not convincing enough and the man begins to pull her towards his car.

'You're under arrest,' he tells her.

As she struggles against him, Ruth asks why she is being taken. She's heard about what happened to Themba and Ndaba, she's been warned by a colleague about a plot to kill her and now she's being kidnapped in broad daylight in the middle of a city street. Ruth knows she has to fight for her life.

The man opens the back door of his car and tries to bundle Ruth inside. She's resisting, screaming out for help, shouting 'No!' over and over again. On the back seat she spots a black ski mask or balaclava. Themba's story rushes to mind and she begins to yell even louder.

'I screamed for my life, so loud that someone far away could hear me.'

Her abductor realises he's not going to get the woman inside the car on his own and asks a nearby security guard for help. But a crowd has gathered, attracted by the commotion. Ruth pleads for help, saying she is being kidnapped, pointing at the mask on the back seat and saying she is going to be killed. People in the crowd start to ask questions, demanding that the man prove that he is a policeman. He refuses and the situation grows tense. Eventually, he releases his grip.

'There were a lot of people around us and this man got scared. He then left me, climbed into his car and raced off. I managed to get the registration number … I'm sure this man is one of the people who tortured Themba and Ndaba,' Ruth says in her statement.

The confession under Conway's carpet sums up this drama in one sentence:

Also at no stage whatsoever did we manage to capture or detain RUTH, only once did I grab her in town, but she escaped as a large crowd helped her.

The car registration number Ruth provides, along with the ones written down by the security guard at Aintree Flats, offers Inspector Van Rooyen some leads. He's been working in Internal Affairs for five years and has grown a thick skin when it comes to accusations against fellow officers. Sometimes criminals make up assault cases against arresting officers in order to frustrate investigations. The same people who claim to have been beaten up don't arrive at identity parades, knowing their story will fall apart. But this case is different. One person can easily tell a lie. But three people telling the same story? Three victims who have signed affidavits. Van Rooyen believes there is something to this case. Something worth investigating. He'll go visit the restaurant, that's the easy part. What he's most interested in, given that his job is to investigate the police, is where the registration plates will lead him.

20.

To describe lapses in his memory, Conway Brown speaks of 'black holes'. Dark, mysterious vacuums that swallow up events, places and people. Conway says his life is full them; periods of existence of which he simply has no recollection.

Carrington Laughton accuses him of using this as an excuse to cover up lies, to avoid accounting for his crimes. Defending himself, Conway says only he knows what happens inside his mind.

Perhaps it *is* a coping mechanism, a way to protect himself against facing up to bad choices, but Conway says the black holes have torn up the timeline of his past and have left him trying to arrange the scraps that remain.

Under pressure, he isn't able to remember the date of his wedding anniversary. He takes a guess, but is two months off. Yet he remembers so vividly posing for a photograph on a porch when he was four. Or, in his youth, watching a swimming pool being dug up and the workers striking a nest of snakes. He also remembers a place where his family once stayed, which must have been built near a cemetery because after a mighty storm, Conway recalls seeing 'coffins popping up all over the place' like something out of a horror movie.

Conway can remember the name of a schoolteacher or what cigarettes his army commander smoked, but entire episodes of his life, he claims, have disappeared. He battles to arrange events – even the simplest ones, like his jobs – into chronological order.

Conway doesn't remember exactly when he moved his family to 21A Leo Street, and relies on the age of his daughter to figure it out. The years that followed are crucial, but many of them, he says, have been sucked into the black holes.

Just before the move to Leo Street, Conway met – under unusual circumstances – a man named Sandor.

Sandor if you are reading this then I am dead.

Conway and Blanche were living in the same block of flats as one of her co-workers, Linda. She was dating Sandor Egyed but was complaining about the way he was treating her. She didn't know what to do and wasn't sure if she should call the police. Conway offered to help. He went downstairs to confront Sandor, but instead ended up making a new friend.

Conway remembers Sandor's long, black curly hair and a goatee, which made him look like the famous wrestler The Undertaker. He says Sandor looked tough, but was a 'Chihuahua wearing a Rottweiler collar'. He remembers him as someone who ran away from fights. Sandor and his family were Hungarian and Conway got on well with them. He and his new friend had both lost their fathers, which brought them closer.

Conway didn't have many friends and had tragically lost a close one a few years earlier. While Sandor went to college to study, Conway would help out at his new friend's house. His mother, who ruled the roost, and sister sometimes needed Conway to play handyman, fixing a tap or a gate or even the car. He was glad to be useful and needed.

When he moved to Kenilworth, Conway remained friends with the Egyeds. He was introduced to one of Sandor's close friends, Mark Eardley, whom Sandor had met while at school in Alberton and who lived on a farm in Kliprivier. This farm would become central to the Ketani murder.

Mark Eardley had recently finished his national service and was living in an old railway bus, which had been converted into a room for him by his father. The red-and-white bus had been bought at a scrapyard and towed to the farm.

Conway began hanging out with Sandor and Mark. They went to pubs or clubs, drank beer and played 'stalk the lantern' out in the surrounding bush. The game involved drinking 'far too much' and then trying to sneak up to touch a lantern that was being guarded by the other players.

Sandor introduced Conway and Mark to one of his other friends, Carrington Laughton. Carrington was from the other side of town, having grown up in Parkview, in the wealthier northern suburbs. He had his own circle of friends and, slowly, the two sets of friends began to merge.

In those years, Conway was working for his uncle at Carnival Foods, building and fixing packing machines in the factory. Carrington, mean-while, was involved in the world of private investigations, the stuff detective novels were made of. It was an intriguing and seductive world and, over time, Carrington introduced most of his friends to it. Conway was quickly sucked in.

> *Carrington, Paul, Dirk, Duncan, Richard, they knew a lot of people. They were influential. It was somebody I was going to aspire to be like, you know, because I was battling my arse off to try to keep my house and my little car going. These guys were driving new cars. The clothes they were wearing was like my month's salary. I suppose there was a certain amount of envy. I was always told that if you mix with a certain group of people, then it will eventually rub off on you.*

Of all the friends, Carrington and Paul Toft-Nielsen had known each other the longest. They met in the mid-1980s, during their primary-school years. They were neighbours in Parkview, with Carrington's family home on Westcliff Drive and Paul's on Dundalk Avenue. As kids, they ran around the neighbourhood together.

On Carrington's twenty-first birthday, at a party at Mike's Kitchen, Paul and some other friends spiked his drink with LSD. Pranks like this – not all quite as reckless, and some far more elaborate – would continue for years and would be played on everyone in the group.

Carrington would tell of the time he and his friends snuck into a cemetery to rig up some fake ghosts to scare Sandor. Conway drove Sandor there and played along by picking the perfect moment to walk ahead and run back screaming in fear.

'We frightened him silly,' Carrington would recall, saying he kept the secret until a wedding speech he made many years later.

There were fake snakes in cars, tins of dog food snuck along on camping trips, snowball ambushes and clothes that went missing when their owner was skinny-dipping.

Carrington attended seven different schools and colleges, finishing with the equivalent of a matric certificate. After two years in the army, he studied a little further. He and Sandor met at the Johannesburg Technical

College. They were pursuing different courses but had classes that over-lapped. They also shared several interests, including music. Ultimately, it was Sandor who brought Conway and Carrington together, with all the other friends meeting along the way. Conway says once they were all intro-duced to each other, they began hanging out, drinking and dancing at the Doors nightclub.

While Carrington joined the volunteer commando corps of the defence force and gradually moved into the field of law enforcement, Paul seemed hell-bent on breaking the law. He owned four powerful motorbikes and named one 'The Warlord', the words printed on the side of the bike. He got tangled up in fights and found himself in precarious situations. Paul took acid and smoked weed – which later landed him a minor criminal record – and was sent to psychologists by his parents, who were concerned about his behaviour.

There were periods when Paul and Carrington all but lost contact. Paul fell in love with the outdoors and worked as a safari guide, leading tour groups around the Kruger National Park and other game reserves. He also chased after wildlife poachers. Carrington, in turn, was starting his career as a private investigator and would sometimes withdraw from Paul after meeting a new girlfriend. And yet, somehow they always gravi-tated back towards each other and remained firm friends for decades. They also worked together a number of times and Paul took part in some of Carrington's army operations.

Carrington seemed to be able to throw a job at anyone – whether you were a friend, an acquaintance or someone he simply met in a cigar shop. There were jobs involving undercover agents, witness protection or general surveillance. Later, with closer friends, there were even overseas adven-tures on offer.

Midway through the 1990s, before he started his second company, Carrington got Conway a job at Shield Investigations, luring him away from Carnival Foods. It was a junior position and, like Carrington, Conway briefed and debriefed agents and wrote up reports. The Shield job, though, lasted less than a year. Conway managed to have an office affair, got into a few fights and eventually returned to his uncle to continue designing and building production lines.

But once Carrington and his then wife Candice started their own business, C&C Commercial Services, Conway was brought in to do the odd job. He had the experience from Shield and needed the cash, willing to work long hours. Simultaneously, their friendship was growing stronger and Conway believed he was moving deeper inside Carrington's 'inner circle'.

21.

A chance encounter at a bank in 1998 saw Dirk Reinecke reconnect with Carrington Laughton and his group of friends. Like all the others, Dirk would land up working with the private investigator for years.

Dirk had first met Carrington in school, but they never became close. Like Carrington, Paul and Conway, Dirk had a fractured education, eventually abandoning school for a technical course in motor mechanics. To make up for it, he later completed a bridging course to get into Studywell College (briefly meeting up with Carrington again), where he matriculated before changing directions altogether and enrolling to study hotel and catering management.

Dirk, the eldest of three brothers, was not able to build a career and bounced between managing a Spar supermarket and an outlet of Roman's Pizza, helping out at a photo lab, answering emergency calls and taking hotel reservations.

He had attention deficit disorder, suffered from 'hyperactive episodes', and in his early twenties was diagnosed as bipolar.

Carrington dedicated 20 years to his career as a private investigator but, intentionally or not, he surrounded himself with friends who battled through life. Conway was a school dropout, a dyslexic and a hooligan, whose moral anchor never quite seemed to catch the ocean floor; Paul was a problem child who took drugs, screamed around on motorbikes and was in and out of psychologists' rooms; and Dirk was bipolar, suppressing spells of depression while working mostly menial jobs. All three, at one time or another, worked for or with Carrington. They all considered him the leader of their group. Paul thought Carrington had a 'dominating personality' and could easily manipulate others, while Conway claimed he had 'a hold over' him and positioned people like chess pieces, never telling them the full truth about what they were involved in. Conway believes Carrington's power was money, which he used to control him. He and the others describe Carrington as a 'puppet master'.

Carrington claims they were all equals. Those close to him say he would never manipulate his friends. They describe Carrington as fiercely committed to the people he chose to let into his life, and whose house was always full of family and friends, who were invited to stay over if they had problems. They say he was obsessed with loyalty, especially when it came to his childhood friends.

Carrington maintains that Paul was physically the strongest in the group and was scared of no one, constantly boasting about killing animal poachers in the bush. He argues that Conway was far more capable than he let on and had the power to draw, from memory, an entire technical plan for a production line, down to the wiring circuits. As for Dirk, he admits he was often the victim of pranks, given his 'dramatic reactions'.

When Dirk and Carrington met up again at the bank, Dirk was unemployed, helping out at his father's medical practice. Carrington offered him work at C&C Commercial Services, taking him along to a client consultation to show him the business, which instantly fascinated Dirk.

The following year, it was Dirk who introduced Carrington to Monique Neeteson-Lemkes, making a connection that led to the notorious Cranks investigation. At the time, Monique was barely in her twenties and Carrington was just about to turn 27, having married a woman who suffered from depression and tried to commit suicide several times. Dirk had heard about the thefts at Cranks while drinking at the pub next door.

Carrington's version is that the Cranks investigation lasted no more than two or three weeks and was a simple matter of placing an undercover agent inside the restaurant. Despite what his friends say, and the evidence of people such as Themba Tshabalala, Ndaba Bhebe and Ruth Mncube, Carrington maintains that no staff members or their family were ever questioned and no one was ever kidnapped and tortured. He says his wife Candice handled the Cranks job while he busied himself in Cape Town.

And yet Dirk tells a different story that, if true, sheds light on what must have been Betty Ketani's final days. Dirk has no way to prove it, and his story won't stand up in court, but he is adamant that Betty was interrogated in a hotel room, questioned about the thefts at the restaurant.

Dirk says Betty was picked up from Cranks late one night in May 1999. He can't place a date on it, but remembers that Carrington fetched him that night from his home and drove him to Rosebank, saying that Betty – the 'chief suspect' in the theft case – was being taken in for questioning. Dirk lived less than a kilometre from Cranks, and when they arrived at the restaurant, he was told to wait in the car as Carrington disappeared inside. Five minutes later, he emerged with Betty and Monique, who was helping out with the investigation.

Dirk says he climbed out the car and moved to the back seat, finding himself next to Betty. They were driven to the Sandton Park Hotel, where Carrington had rented a room. Dirk wasn't introduced to Betty and said his role was to 'ensure she does not cause any problems'. Betty was calm and cooperative.

Inside room 002, she was allegedly told to sit on the double bed and was questioned by Carrington and Monique about the thefts at Cranks. Dirk says Monique was convinced that Betty was involved, or at least knew who was.

'Monique then asked Betty why she was taking money from the restaurant when she was employed there for so long. Betty denied any knowledge of any money whatsoever. The more Monique accused Betty of taking the money, the more Betty denied it and the more tense the situation got.'

Dirk says he stood in the doorway to show Betty that there was no way out.

'Betty became extremely distraught with the questions and allegations and demanded to be taken home. Carrington refused and stated that she will remain there until she provides answers.'

Dirk says Betty tried to leave the room but he blocked her path.

No matter what questions came, Betty maintained her innocence. Dirk says Monique threatened her, stating that the 'guilty parties would be found'. He claims he tried to stand up for Betty and insisted that she wasn't involved and should be released. He says he whispered this to Carrington.

Betty was eventually set free and taken back to Cranks. It was almost midnight.

'Approximately a week after we questioned Betty, I again passed Cranks, where I saw her in the restaurant. We, however, did not speak to each other.'

After that, Betty disappeared without a trace.

'The investigation against the other employees continued until Eric apparently caught Monique stealing money,' Dirk says. 'Thereafter the investigation came to a complete halt.'

Carrington dismisses the entire episode, from start to finish, as a lie. He says Betty was never kept in a hotel room against her will, and questions what she would have been doing at the restaurant at night, considering she worked the day shift. Carrington maintains that the Cranks investigation did not entail any confrontations with suspects and that he, personally, played no role in it.

22.

The year is 1999 and Inspector James van Rooyen has a theory about the late-night abductions of Themba and Ndaba and the close call Ruth had outside the post office. He reckons they are tied to the labour disputes at Cranks and the CCMA cases that have been opened. He can't prove it, but he's convinced the raids are an attempt to make those cases 'go away'.

Beyond a few passing mentions of stolen cheques, Van Rooyen knows nothing about the thefts at Eric's restaurant, nor about the investigation Carrington Laughton's company has been hired to conduct. Van Rooyen's case turns on one key piece of evidence: the car registration numbers given to the police by the victims. Without them, all he has are a few dramatic statements, a couple of balaclavas in the safe and no way to find out who the perpetrators are.

Van Rooyen is with Internal Affairs and his focus, regardless of his private theories or suspicions, is to determine whether any policemen were involved. He throws all his efforts into finding out. The motive can be explored later.

To keep his investigation moving, Van Rooyen takes a statement from Themba's wife, Mighty, who says that in April 1999 Monique asked her more than once how she could find Ruth. Mighty kept insisting she didn't know.

She shares with the policeman a story of how Ruth once came to her in a panic, claiming that Monique had hired two security guards – 'Matthew' and 'Oscar' – to kill her. Ruth says she heard this from a colleague at Cranks who was friendly with Eric's daughter. Although they were rumours, Ruth wasn't about to take a chance, so she went into hiding.

Later, Mighty tells Van Rooyen about an incident when she was walking through Hillbrow and noticed a suspicious white car. Inside, she says, was a white man and a woman, whom she immediately recognised as Monique.

'When Monique saw me, she bent over in the seat as if to hide away from my sight. I then turned around and I ran away as I was scared after hearing what was done, by the policemen, to my husband. I didn't see whether they followed me or not.'

On 2 July 1999, Mighty's home is raided yet again. She is ill and in bed when the policemen come. She says there are two white men in uniform and a black officer in plain clothes. They quickly establish that she is not the woman they are after, but Mighty demands answers. They tell her they have come from Benoni, and one of the officers even gives her a cellphone number, which she passes along to Van Rooyen. The policemen leave without searching her flat or taking her away for questioning.

According to Mighty's statement, two days later, another Cranks waitress, Winnie, knocks on her door at 11 o'clock at night. She wants to warn Ruth of some kind of imminent danger, but is told that Ruth has fled. A nervous Winnie tells Mighty to lock her door because 'the people hired to kill Ruth might be watching'. Five minutes after Winnie slips away, the Benoni policemen are on Mighty's doorstep again, asking for Ruth. This time Mighty plucks up the courage to ask whether they are investigating the thefts at Cranks, but is told they are on a different case. Once they leave, she walks down the stairs and looks through the building's visitors' register. There is no record of them.

· · ·

A police docket is split into three sections. Section A is where detectives file away statements from victims or witnesses. Section B is where important documents or exhibits are kept, and Section C is a diary, where officers keep a record of their progress and receive instructions from commanders or prosecutors.

Inspector James van Rooyen inherits docket 809/05/1999 soon after it is opened by Themba. Some basic work has already been done on the case and there are a few statements and diary entries. In fact, the case has already been closed and reopened, all within a few days of Themba arriving at the Hillbrow police station.

Inside Section B, Van Rooyen says he discovers Exhibit B1: a computer printout showing the results of a car registration-number check done on 17 May 1999. It was a straightforward search into who owned a Mazda Astina with registration number HLJ 194 GP.

Van Rooyen figures that it was either Themba or Ndaba who provided the police with the number plate and that whoever had had the docket first had run it through the system. There's no record of where the registration number came from, but Van Rooyen wonders whether it wasn't given verbally and disregarded because it didn't lead to an official police vehicle. Given the nature of the case, and the allegations Themba and Ndaba were making, Van Rooyen can see how the docket would have been closed after that. Why it was reopened and handed to him, he simply doesn't know.

Exhibit B1 contains no useful information. The car is registered to a 'CR Laughton', who has had it only a few months. His ID number and address are provided, along with some technical information about the Mazda: its weight, engine number, chassis number and other registration details. The owner's address is in Parkview, an area Van Rooyen knows well, having been stationed there after finishing police college. It's a wealthy area and he doubts whether anyone from there would be involved in the Hillbrow abductions, figuring that the number plate may have been taken down incorrectly. And even if that's not the case, his mandate is to find out whether police officers are implicated. This number plate belongs to a civilian.

The detective has another, more promising, number plate to investigate. He checks it against the database and this time the results lead him to the Randburg police station, where a red Mazda 323, registration number BJK 601B, was booked out on one of the nights in question. Given that all cars are signed for by the crews, it is easy to work backwards and establish who used the Mazda and for what purpose.

His first task is to get the names, the second is to establish whether any permission had been granted for the officers to cross jurisdictions. Policing is a territorial business and stations are known to fight bitterly over cases, especially high-profile ones. Randburg and Hillbrow are about 20 kilometres apart, which is a long way for a patrol vehicle to stray.

The logbooks reveal that policeman Carel Ranger and reservist André Coetzer signed out that particular car on one of the nights that Themba was interrogated. Inspector Van Rooyen brings both Carel and André in for questioning and takes witness statements from them. He's not ready to arrest them, knowing how often policemen get accused of crimes they didn't commit, but he does want to make sure that Themba and Ndaba, and maybe even Ruth, can pick them out of a line-up.

By the time Carel and André arrive at his office on 10 June 1999, they have their story prepared. The statements they give are virtually identical, differing only in personal details.

André says he has worked as a Randburg reservist for only a month and a half, having transferred from another station. On 20 May, he claims, he received a tip-off from an informer about illegal immigrants staying in a flat in Berea or Hillbrow. The informer told him fake documents were being used. What André doesn't explain is why, two days later, he and Carel drove across town into another police station's jurisdiction, in the dead of night, to follow up on this information. Illegal immigrants hiding in Hillbrow should have been that station's problem.

André goes on to say that on 22 May 1999, he and Carel dressed in full police uniform and arrived there at around 4.30am, having used one of the official reservist cars. According to him, they knocked and the door was answered by one of the residents.

'After this we asked everyone for their ID documents and everyone gave their books to us. All the books were in order except for one of the men, Themba Tshabalala.'

André says Themba volunteered to accompany them to his brother's house to prove that he was a legal citizen. This was done and, satisfied, they dropped Themba back at his home before heading back to Randburg.

Themba reported that he was kidnapped from his flat on 11 May and then again from the restaurant three days later. He was questioned once more on 22 May, the day before Ndaba was snatched from the same apartment. He says he recognised one of the two officers who came to see him on 22 May from the previous abductions.

But André claims the one and only time they visited the Aintree flats was on 22 May. He swears, under oath, that he doesn't know Monique Neeteson-Lemkes. His story contains no violence and has Themba willingly accompanying them to his brother's house. Themba's statements confirm that on that occasion he was not assaulted.

André says nothing about the fact that he knows Carrington and had started a private investigations company – called LHC (Laughton Heath and Coetzer) – with him a few years earlier. His claim of not knowing Monique is a lie and the two, according to him, even had a short romantic relationship. André will later confess that he and Carel used a police car to conduct an illegal search in another jurisdiction, without permission and at Carrington's request. Worse, he will admit that he was involved in two Cranks-related searches and broke down Themba's door during the second visit. But these revelations are years away, and in June 1999, André provides a short and carefully worded statement, giving only a fraction of the story.

Carel Ranger gives precisely the same version, stating that Themba's ID book looked fake and had to be checked out. His explanation for the early morning operation is that he was helping André outside of his regular shift.

Carel, whose brother David is also a policeman, says Themba spoke to him about other officers visiting the house earlier. Themba suspected they were fake policemen and Carel claims he advised him to open a case. He too maintains that 22 May was the first time he visited apartment 1906 and that he never returned.

Interestingly, he says he was on leave for a week over the period when Themba's abductions took place. Inspector Van Rooyen has investigated several cases where policemen used their leave to do some moonlighting and wonders whether this could have been the case here. Again, though, he can't prove his suspicions.

• • •

By the time James van Rooyen visits Cranks restaurant, Betty is already missing. Nobody tells him about this and her disappearance never features in his investigation. Instead, he has arrived to speak to the owner, Eric, about the Hillbrow abductions. Eric is away and Van Rooyen settles for an interview with his daughter Monique.

Something about Monique immediately makes Van Rooyen uneasy. Most detectives boast about having an instinct – a gut feel – about the people they investigate, whether they are victims or suspects. He can't put his finger on it, but something makes him question her story.

'Her statement, in essence, was taken with a little bit of salt,' Van Rooyen explains many years later.

At that stage, however, there's no link between her or her father and the policemen. Monique is willing to give Van Rooyen a statement. She denies any involvement in the abductions and sheds some light on the stolen cheques. Monique claims the cheques were taken between January and March of 1999. She talks about the allegations against Ruth and how she was fired. She also names Mighty as a suspect.

The young woman also confirms that Ruth opened a case of unfair dismissal against her father's restaurant after she was fired, but says the case was settled and Ruth was paid R1 000. This is contradicted by Ruth, who says she never got a chance to see the CCMA case through because she was intimidated.

But for Van Rooyen that's irrelevant detail. He's searching for a connection between Cranks and the policemen. Monique denies there is one.

'I never hired anyone to threaten any of them,' she says. 'I don't know any policemen except the policemen at Rosebank who dealt with my cases. The policemen mentioned in this case, Ranger and Coetzer, are unknown to me.'

Monique says nothing about hiring Carrington's company to conduct a private investigation and doesn't mention Betty Ketani, who was a prime suspect and who has now vanished. Years later, evidence will emerge that compels André to come clean. It will become clear that Inspector Van Rooyen was misled from the very beginning.

• • •

Midway through October 1999, James van Rooyen arranges an identity parade that includes both Carel and André. His investigation has gone as far as it can and this is the final step. Van Rooyen has collected all the statements, linked the number plates (which tie Carel and André to the scene) and has even taken Themba and Ndaba to a district surgeon, to have their injuries assessed. It was far too late – a couple of weeks after the assaults – but the J88 medical forms are in the docket anyway. If either Carel or André are pointed out in the line-up, the file will go to a prosecutor for a decision on whether to arrest and charge the suspects.

The first date for the identity parade falls through and a second one is set for 22 October 1999. Van Rooyen is counting on Themba to round up all the victims and bring them to the police station. After five months of investigations, he is so close to putting this docket to bed. All he needs is for the line-up to go well.

Van Rooyen books the room and brings in his colleagues to help. Carel and André are informed about the date. But when the day arrives, Themba, Ndaba and Ruth fail to pitch up. Efforts are made to contact them, but they are nowhere to be found. Themba and Mighty have packed up and left apartment 1906, not prepared to go through any further trauma. They were in such a rush they abandoned their deposit. Ruth is in hiding, with no address or telephone number where she can be reached. Ndaba is impossible to find.

Van Rooyen searches 'high and low' for his witnesses. He visits their flat, calls the few numbers he has and leaves a multitude of messages. He asks a black colleague to help, hoping he may be able to find Themba and Ndaba and calm their fears. Speak to them without the language barrier. Van Rooyen wants to offer them protection. Explain that without them the entire case will crumble. He tries his best, but he is carrying many dockets and there is only so much time he can devote to this case.

In late November, a month after the failed identity parade, the abductions case sinks, taking with it all the statements (ten of them by this stage) and evidence gathered by the detective. With no complainants, the docket drowns.

Themba, Mighty and Ndaba try to move on with their lives. Ruth flees to Zimbabwe and returns only seven years later, in 2006, when she feels safe again. She keeps hearing rumours that hitmen have been hired to kill her.

Monique leaves for Thailand. Carel and André never hear about the case again and put it behind them. They are never linked to Cranks, nor to Monique. Carrington remains off the radar.

James van Rooyen continues with his other investigations and leaves the Internal Affairs unit the following year. Soon he forgets about docket 809/05/1999 and what Themba, Ndaba and Ruth went through. He gets a promotion and becomes a commissioned officer, leaving the police as a captain.

Thirteen years later, sitting at a pub in Melville, he takes a drag of a cigarette, mulling over the case and awakening old memories. He's a 45-year-old insurance investigator with a grey beard and a receding hairline. His eyes are sparkling blue, leaping off a face weathered by two decades of police work.

He thinks he can still see Themba's face in his mind, but isn't sure any more.

'Had they come and identified these guys, I think the investigation might have gone a totally different way,' he says. 'It might even have led to everything being solved back then. It might have come out then that Betty was killed.'

23.

With each new assignment, Conway says, he is sucked further into Carrington's world. After a short stint at Shield and a failed business venture in Durban, he returns to Carnival Foods to fix machines on the factory floor. At nights and on weekends, though, he is still playing detective. When he's lucky, he gets to tinker with or set up surveillance equipment like cameras or audio recorders.

> It's exciting. It's like stuff you see in the movies … not everybody gets to do that. But it's not as glamorous. I spent many, many, many hours in a car. You sit there for six, seven hours, your butt is sore, you can't move, you can't get out. You know, it's … it's not as easy as it looks.
>
> The money I was making I needed because times were tough. Getting a decent job was a problem. I didn't have the world's best education. So if I got a couple of hundred rand for doing a job, lekker. If I got a thousand rand for doing a job, lekker. You know, it just added to everything I was doing.

Conway is also beginning to feel like he is earning Carrington's trust and friendship. He sees Carrington as someone he can call on if there's trouble, like when his nephew vanished and his family was in a state of panic. Conway made the call and Carrington arrived with an army of friends, most of whom Conway had never seen before. A search party was formed and the boy was found alive. Carrington had his back, Conway felt.

The detective assignments distract Conway from his real life. The eternal shortage of money. Piles of bills. The rent. The factory job. His inability to stay loyal to Blanche in a world where so many women fill him with temptation – and then the guilt that inevitably follows. Carrington's jobs often keep him busy until the early hours of the morning, providing him with an escape.

His father locked himself away in his workshop until the early hours of the morning, shutting out the outside world. After Vincent died, Conway's mother met a man just two years older than her son. A man barely out of his teens. Conway and the new boyfriend clashed immediately.

His mother spent much of her life working as a personal assistant or secretary at a company selling tractor parts. He says she began to drink heavily and he was forced to come to her rescue when things spiralled out of control. Slowly, their relationship broke down.

With his father gone, Conway also felt a sense of duty to help his sisters. Both have had a string of unsuccessful relationships and have been left to raise their children on their own. He and Blanche even tried to adopt one of the kids. Conway's family dramas never seemed to stop.

Then there's Carrington, whose father is a respected chartered accountant, a former partner at one of the country's top auditing firms. Carrington is his own boss who appears to have a brilliant grasp of law and always seems to be taking calls from people seeking his advice. He drives nice cars and has the latest gadgets. In any situation, it seems to Conway, Carrington is calling the shots.

He wouldn't have a Bic pen, he would have a Montblanc. A status thing. If you smoke a cigar, I'd be like: 'Jeez, this cigar costs more than 20 bucks, what a rip off', and he's like: 'Ja, no, this is 800 rand.'

Carrington's nickname among his close friends was 'Batman', a reference to the lone crusader, stalking the streets in search of justice. Carrington was praised for being thorough with his reports and for his good service to major clients: well-known companies, restaurants and supermarkets. Conway was under the impression that his friend had a wide web of contacts.

We were doing a surveillance job somewhere and he said, look, he's got to go to the police station. We went to the police station. He literally walked in, greeted everybody, like, 'Howzit, Bob; Howzit, Fred', you know, that kind of thing. Greeted everybody, walked behind the counter, picked up a couple of papers, came back this side, wrote a couple of things and handed them back. He was always on the phone speaking to some colonel or captain. He had a lot of police friends and acquaintances.

• • •

The steps leading Conway inside Carrington's world are small. Often, Conway says, he didn't even realise he was taking them. And when he finally stopped to look around, he had come too far to turn back.

Conway tried to hold onto his life on Leo Street, volunteering as a scout master for his son Sheldon and his landlord's son Jeffrey. He worked around the house, getting stuck into little projects, digging a trench or building a cottage behind the house. He went to church, family braais, and for coffee next door with Marshall Senior, whose health was fading. But Carrington's world kept pulling him away.

One weekend Conway was asked to help with a body-painting project Carrington organised on behalf of the South African Naturist Federation (Sanfed). ('I am the leader of the naked people,' Carrington liked to joke.) It was a fund-raising event for a charity. Conway drove to Rosebank and spent the day applying paint to the naked body of a beautiful woman.

On another occasion, he found himself inside a nudist camp near Pretoria, taking a breakfast meeting with Carrington. He claims he had no idea where he was going – Carrington's sense of humour at work – and only began catching on while driving up the farm road, when he saw an old man strolling along the road in a bush hat, a pair of flip-flops and nothing else. He went through to the reception area, where he found a woman sitting behind the desk and wearing nothing but a smile. Conway was led to Carrington's table. He remembers their conversation.

'Come over!' Carrington called out.
'And now?' Conway asked.
'Sit down.'
'But everyone's watching me.'
'Yes, it's because you have your clothes on,' his amused friend replied.

So Conway undressed and sat down to an English breakfast.

In the years that followed, Carrington invited Conway to house-warming parties, birthday bashes and weddings. Some of the parties ended with everyone undressing, Conway included. Holding a drink or a cigarette, climbing up on a bar counter, he happily posed for photographs, grinning from ear to ear.

But, aside from the naked bodies and the detective work, there was a sense of belonging. Invitations to play paintball, a request to show Carrington how to service his Land Rover, a night out at a pub or a camping trip at a private game farm. For someone who had few friends growing up, Conway was drawn to Carrington and his adventures. Not to mention the unusual cast of characters that surrounded him.

. . .

Until Conway met Carrington, he had never ventured beyond the borders of South Africa. That too began to change.

He got invited to a boot camp in KwaZulu-Natal. It was Carrington's way of preparing for a 2004 trip to Germany; a test to see how the group of friends he had selected would get along. The expedition was full of childish pranks, which Conway thoroughly enjoyed.

The Europe trip that followed was like nothing Conway had ever experienced before. To him, it was a covert mission for one of Carrington's clients. In reality, Carrington had been hired by victims of a multimillion-rand investment scam to try track down those responsible. He invited Paul, Conway and a new friend named Barry.

Conway says the trip involved theatre make-up classes so that disguises could be perfected; strict rules about identity (no logos on T-shirts, no branding on pens, no South African currency or identity documents in their wallets) and a surveillance system being put in place at their flat in Hamburg. To him, it felt like they were secret government spies.

There was also the lighter side: seeing snow for the first time, drinking in famous beer halls, seeing Rammstein perform live and being paid for something that felt very much like a holiday.

It's denied by Carrington, but Conway claims he also sent him to Thailand in 2000, exposing him to yet another exotic location. There was another international trip that Carrington had organised in 2002, taking some friends with him, but Conway had not been invited on that occasion.

• • •

Detective Gerhard Pretorius introduces himself politely. He's heard good things about Conway from the Marshalls and has decided to use a soft approach. He's called from a landline at his office to disguise his number. Taking a run at one of the suspects this early in the investigation is a massive risk and Pretorius treads carefully, knowing he can't say anything about the letter.

He confirms he is speaking to the right person and quickly gets to the point. 'We need to speak to you about a murder,' he tells Conway.

Deliberately, he says nothing more.

On the other side of the line, Conway panics. His mind starts to race. He's trying to catch up to the moment, to understand what is happening. He needs time to think. To process. Conway starts to throw back nervous questions at the detective, trying to sound as innocent as possible. What murder? Are you sure you have the right person?

Conway repeats this last question three or four times. He gives his full name and even rattles off his identity number. He asks whether this has anything to do with a car accident. He is told that it doesn't but continues to play dumb.

'I know nothing about nothing,' he claims.

Conway is disorientated. The detective on the line keeps talking about 'a murder'. Nothing more. But on some level, deep inside, Conway knows what this is. He says later that he had been waiting for the call for over ten years. He tried hard to build a wall around those memories, to feed them to the black holes. Now they are stirring. And all he can do is make absolutely sure of what he is up against.

You shit in your pants. I kept saying, 'What the hell are you talking about?' You want to make sure you are not going to get zapped for something that's not yours. So if they phoned me and said, 'Were you at King Williams Town at half past four on Sunday the whatever date?' I'd be like, 'No, thank God, that's not me.' You don't want to take responsibility for something you had nothing to do with.

Whenever Conway speaks to anyone in a position of power – a police officer, for example – he goes out of his way to be polite, calling the person 'sir' or 'ma'am'. He clasps his hands and even bows sheepishly, stepping out the way if need be. He tries to hide any aggression and to appear submissive. He does the same with this phone call, still hoping it might be a misunderstanding – but knowing it isn't.

You don't think about your family at that point; you don't think about your friends, or your work, or any of that. It's just gone. All you're thinking about is the situation and how to sort it out.

Detective Pretorius knows he has the right man. He says he'd like to speak to Conway in person. There is no escape.

'How long will it take me to get from Alberton to Yeoville?' Conway asks.

'About half an hour,' Pretorius replies.

'I'll see you there now.'

The conversation ends. For Pretorius, it couldn't have gone better and he quickly tells the others. They are back on track. About to meet a man who must have the answers they seek.

Conway doesn't think about calling a lawyer or hatching a plan. He wants to try to fix this. Now. To find out how much the police know and how much trouble he is in. He asks his son Sheldon to come along for the drive. Then he climbs into his car and sets out for the unknown.

24.

Conway arrives at the Yeoville police station, walks into the small, busy courtyard and asks where he can find Detective Gerhard Pretorius.

The man he's looking for is standing across the street with his partner, Lufuno Sono, and JB. A small feast of *vetkoek*, Russian sausages, *slap* chips and a couple of cold drinks is laid out on the canvas cover of a double-cab bakkie.

Conway makes an awkward approach but is told to wait for them to finish eating.

'Stand there,' Pretorius orders, pointing a finger.

He wants to knock Conway onto his back foot. To show him who is in control and, secretly, assess what kind of person they are dealing with. Conway submits without question and waits obediently.

Pretorius, JB and Sono put on a show, eating and laughing while Conway and his son look on. JB can't believe the man actually showed up.

Conway Brown turns out to be a fairly tall man with a strong build and a worker's hands. His eyes are an unusual colour. In certain light, they seem almost honey-coloured. He has dark bags under his eyes and a neat soul patch below his lower lip.

Eventually, Pretorius calls Conway over, makes the introductions and starts to question him. He begins slowly, enquiring about his history, his job and his family. Sono is playing the bad cop, watching the scene with fake indignation. He's short and stocky, and likes to wear suits to work.

Finally the murder comes up and Conway denies knowing anything about it. Pretorius and JB have a few gos before changing direction. They've agreed not to let on at this point that they have the confession found at Conway's former home, but begin to drop the names it contains. Conway is asked whether he knows Monique. He denies it. Carrington? No. The Ranger brothers? No. Eric? No. This continues for a while.

They're not breaking through and Pretorius's patience is running out. JB asks him a question and, in Afrikaans, Pretorius replies: '*Hy is nog nie in die selle nie.*' (He is not in the cells yet.)

Conway takes the bait and switches to Afrikaans.

'*Wat het jy nou gesê?*' (What did you say?)

Pretorius repeats his comment.

'But you can't make jokes like that!' Conway pleads nervously.

Suddenly, Pretorius drops the pretence. His eyes are angry now and his voice changes to that of a policeman barking orders.

'I'm not playing with you, I'm being serious. You are going to the cells for murder. I'm going to lock you up!'

Conway realises he has to stop lying. Quickly. He doesn't see through the bluff and surrenders.

'Okay, can we talk?'

He can't understand where all the information is coming from, but with all the names that are being mentioned, he figures someone must be talking. How else would the police know so much?

He asks that they don't speak any further at the police station – it's not safe – and asks the officers to let his son go home, which they have no problem with.

After escorting Conway's son to an off-ramp with which he's familiar, they find the closest McDonald's, which turns out to be the one near Ellis Park stadium (not far from where Themba used to live). They order coffees and settle down to listen.

Conway battles to tell his story. He doesn't know where to begin. All his memories are jumbled. He asks whether his family will be protected, explaining to the officers that the murder has destroyed his life. The emotion starts to well up as he describes how he hasn't been able to sleep; how he buried himself in work …

He bursts into tears, which to everyone at the table appear to be genuine. It doesn't look like an act. Sitting across from them they see a broken man haunted by his secrets. A man who tried to lie to them, but didn't have what it takes to even get that right.

Conway describes the night he was allegedly called out by Carrington. He leaves out his own involvement – holding Betty as she was stabbed in the head – but explains how she was dumped on the side of the dirt road.

How she was left for dead. He doesn't know how much he can say and what the consequences will be. Whether he can even trust these policemen.

Conway can't pinpoint dates or exact places and says he didn't know it was Betty. He talks about how he was called out to bury the body and that it was initially meant to have been at Mark Eardley's farm, but that he, Conway, insisted that the body be taken back to his house in Leo Street. He tells them he wanted to protect Mark, whose parents were murdered on the farm.

Pretorius, JB and Sono can barely believe that everything they've read in the confession is now being confirmed by one of the men who committed the crime. Conway is rolling over.

His story is messy, but it exists. In front of them, with tears in his eyes, is the man who buried Betty Ketani in a shallow grave. The man who was there when an attempt was made to murder her.

They keep throwing each other discreet looks. They struggle to contain their excitement – the urge to burst into laughter, to release the pressure of the past few days – but they must keep up the act in front of Conway. The best thing they can do now is keep quiet and listen. Let him confess. Give him enough rope to hang himself.

It all makes sense now. They have even identified the alleged author of the letter: Carrington. Conway claims he received it from a mutual friend.

Not long ago they were standing over an empty hole in the ground and were being screamed at by a furious Eric Neeteson-Lemkes. Now they have a real-life confession, the break they've been hoping for. They have the man who hid the letters under the carpet.

They seize the moment and ask Conway about the grave and why there is nothing inside it. They want to know where Betty's body is.

'We moved it,' Conway replies.

. . .

Conway explains that a few years after Betty was buried behind his garage, he and a few other people got together to dig up the body. He's vague on why this happened but claims the orders came from Carrington.

Conway tells the policemen that he remembers the strong smell of Jeyes Fluid, an outdoor cleaning liquid, which was mixed with petrol and used to mask the smell of the grave. He recalls seeing bones as they emerged from beneath the concrete. He tells the investigators that almost the entire grave was broken down and loaded into industrial plastic bags and driven to a nearby municipal dump, to be scattered across mountains of rubbish.

JB feels vindicated. His instinct to dig up the grave was spot on. It was the right place but the wrong time. They had no idea the body had been moved.

'Now we can see it,' JB recalls. 'Sono turns around and he says: "JB, Betty is gone. She's on the rubbish dump." I look at him and I *scheme, jislaaik*, this whole fucking letter is true. Pretorius says to Conway, "Are you sure?" and he says, "Yes."'

Pretorius and Sono know they have enough for a formal confession, but can't take it themselves. They aren't high enough in rank; this needs to be captured by a commissioned officer: a captain or higher.

They are hesitant to let Conway go, but decide they have no choice.

Pretorius instructs him to go home and write down everything he remembers. Realising he's not being locked up, Conway eagerly agrees. They arrange to phone him the next day to organise to meet again. Until then, Conway is told to keep the meeting a secret, even from his wife. No one can know what has happened. After so many years of lying to his family, Conway must keep the secret a while longer.

> It's out in the open now and everyone is going to know what happened. I wanted to get it done. And then they took me and said, 'You can't tell anybody.' Once again you go home, and get asked, 'What happened?' 'No, no, no, it was just some other stuff I was involved with, the cops wanted to know some information.' Again, I lied to my wife. Do whatever I need to do or say to make sure she doesn't know what's going on.

After dropping Conway off, Pretorius and the others wonder whether they will ever see him again. They know where he lives and have all of his contact numbers. They're certain he won't be able to run from them, but given the way he was crying and talking about how scared he is of Carrington, about how worried he is for his family, they all share an uncomfortable fear that he may try to commit suicide.

They need him to stay alive and to give a full confession. If that happens, they have enough evidence to apply for arrest warrants for Carrington and the others. They need to keep managing Conway's emotions. To nail down his statement as quickly as possible. Before something goes wrong.

The following morning they call and ask him to come in. Conway tells Pretorius that he didn't sleep and is exhausted. He asks for a day to pull himself together … to get his mind right. Reluctantly, Pretorius agrees. Taking another gamble, he hopes Conway doesn't do anything stupid. That he doesn't change his mind or try to run. Or go out and hire a lawyer.

25.

The hidden camera flickers awake inside Doc and JB's small garden cottage, which is filled with soft autumn sunlight and cigarette smoke. Its gaze falls on Pretorius, dressed in a two-tone farmer's shirt and a black leather jacket, sitting in front of a desk, flipping slowly through the pages of a police docket. The roller blinds behind him are drawn, obscuring the shapes of the trees outside. A breeze is blowing in through an open door, catching the white sail of a cigarette burning lazily in a glass ashtray.

Voices begin to fill the air. Doc stands up and walks past the camera, mumbling something about Carrington. He's wearing a black bomber jacket, camouflage army pants and a loose-fitting checked shirt. JB is out of sight but his voice is booming in the background.

'He knows they *moered* [beat] her dead, he mustn't come talk shit to us,' he bellows. 'He's gonna dig his own grave. He mustn't come play with us. He's a *poes* [cunt].'

Standing at the small kitchen counter, Doc switches on a television and fishes around for a PlayStation remote. He settles down to play a gory first-person shooter set in some science-fiction world. Blood begins to splatter on the screen above Pretorius's neatly shaved head.

Waiting for Conway's phone call, the three banter about the case.

Pretorius lights up another cigarette. Between drags, he watches it burn, hypnotised by the glowing ash, deep in thought. He pushes up his shirt and wrestles a Z88 9mm service pistol from its leather holster. He ejects the magazine, flinging it onto the desk so that it lands with a thump, and pulls back the slide to check that the chamber is empty. He reaches for a glass Coke bottle on the table, wedges the gun's barrel under the ridges of its metal top and, on the second attempt, pops open the cold drink. Looking pleased with himself, he jokes: 'We're not allowed to use it to shoot people any more, so we may as well use it as a bottle opener.'

JB's voice continues to thunder from some invisible part of the room.

'You're gonna see now how I play with this guy's head,' he informs the others. 'We're gonna play mind games. He's gonna *scheme*, fuck it, he must save his arse here. He must *kak* [be scared]. He's got away with a lot of shit. They must all *kak*.'

The conversation keeps circling back to Carrington Laughton, the man at the centre of the investigation. But to get to him and the others, Conway needs to sign a confession.

Fifteen minutes pass with talk about Carrington's background and his previous run-ins with the law. JB finally steps into the camera's line of vision. He's dressed in a grey hoodie and a baseball cap. He begins to fiddle with the camera, making sure it's lined up to film Conway once he arrives. If he arrives. The camera equipment is nothing fancy, just a regular webcam perched on top of a computer screen, which has been switched off to create the illusion that the PC is off.

The camera is an insurance policy. Proof – should it be needed – that Conway's confession was not forced or beaten out of him. It's a smart move considering how often lawyers try to have confessions chucked out of court, collapsing entire trials.

Pretorius's cellphone finally rings.

'Where are you?' he asks, walking out into the garden.

Conway is half an hour early.

Their hunch was right: not only did he not flee after being confronted two days ago, he's ready to be collected – ahead of schedule. Everyone breathes a sigh of relief.

While Pretorius sips his Coke, JB begins to fuss over the open docket. He wants to leave it lying on one of the desks to make sure Conway sees it as soon as he comes in. It's all part of the mind games.

Not wanting to keep Conway waiting, JB and Pretorius leave the cottage and head out to the car. Doc is the last to exit, switching off the TV on his way out. Moments later, the gate at the top of the long, steep driveway rattles closed.

· · ·

Conway walks into the cottage and drops his keys, cellphone and wallet on the kitchen counter. He's dressed in a smart blue open-collar shirt and jeans. His sleeves are rolled up and a cigarette is wedged between his lips.

The secret camera is still rolling.

Before he can sit, JB shows him a photograph and asks him to identify Carrington Laughton. Conway nods to confirm.

As he settles down in the centre of the room, he's offered coffee. He asks for it black, two sugars, but only half a cup of water.

'How's your work carrying on?' JB asks to break the ice. 'You must suffer now since we knocked on your door.' He's trying to get into Conway's head. Assess what he's up against.

Conway shakes his head, trying, but failing, to find words.

'We're gonna take it all right now. We'll look after you, okay?' JB continues.

'You want me to start at the beginning?' Conway asks moments later.

'You need to be straight. No bullshit,' Doc warns him.

The guest raises his open hands. A sign of surrender.

'No bullshit.'

From certain angles, Conway looks like Hollywood actor Robert Downey Junior, with flashes of the same tragic, awkward expression in his eyes. He searches for a way to start his story but is dizzy with emotion. His head is swarming with names and places.

'I'm screwed. I can't remember dates,' he pleads.

He's encouraged to go on, and fill in the dates later.

As he tries to talk, Conway's sentences keep failing him, breaking after only a few words. His head shakes slightly and subconsciously as he tries to answer questions. His breathing seems heavy.

'I'm still trying to come to terms with what I saw and … based on that stuff … you know … every time I was told … it's a complete …'

Conway says something about the black holes in his memory.

'When I saw him standing over there … and … I can't explain it to you, man … the person just dropped …'

He shifts uncomfortably in his chair and slumps over the table to his right. He cracks his neck or rolls his head from side to side, pulls up his socks or fiddles with his wedding ring. He clasps his hands together and slips them between his thighs, folds them over his chest or sits on them.

'I'm gonna fucking cry like a little baby now,' he blurts out, turning to stare out into the garden. His Adam's apple bounces in his throat.

'No, you do … get it off you, you understand,' JB replies.

'That's what I've been keeping inside me all this time,' comes the cracked voice in reply.

As the conversation begins to gain traction, Conway leaps up to illustrate the height of a wall or the depth of a hole and draws imaginary maps on the desk using his finger. He empties ashtrays and politely asks to go to the toilet.

Over and over again he buries his face in his palms, trying to release the pressure. Sometimes he falls into long silences, his gaze suggesting that – for that moment – he's somewhere far away. He often looks directly into the camera, almost as if he knows it's watching.

This is not the formal confession yet. That will come later. For now, Pretorius, Doc and JB are trying to get as much information from him as possible. They need more details to continue their investigation. The discussion at McDonald's was a good start, but it wasn't enough. There are too many parts that don't make sense, too many puzzle pieces in the wrong places. For now, this is off the record.

They've done their homework on Conway. Everyone they've spoken to has had nothing but kind things to say about him. They called him a 'nice guy'; a family man who didn't hesitate to run out of his house to chase robbers in a neighbour's yard; a handyman who could fix anything; a talented artist who could produce the most beautiful sketch of a bird well after it had flown away.

Perhaps it's because of these descriptions that they've decided to do the confession here, at Doc and JB's office, and not at the police station. They chose to approach him first because he seemed less dangerous than the other characters on their list.

They know he is as guilty as the rest and has held onto the same secret. But they don't take him for a tough guy who needs to be dragged between a holding cell and the interrogation room. To them, he's a weak link. A man in agony. He may have tried to lie to them back at the police station, but he's also confirmed many crucial aspects of the case. He appears to be so distraught that they take extra care with their guns.

'Everybody made sure their guns were fastened very, very tight and we kept an eye on him,' says Doc.

Conway claims that many times he thought about turning himself in but was too worried about his family's safety. He says the silence ate away at him from the inside. Tormented him. Changed the way he related to people and forced him to work day and night.

'He said he had been waiting for this knock on the door,' Doc adds. 'Now he wants to come clean. To face judgment day.'

The docket JB prepared earlier is waved around from time to time. The old 1999 Hillbrow file – the one about the abductions – has everything to do with the investigation but absolutely nothing to do with Conway. At least not for now. Its only purpose is to fool him into believing they know everything. It's a theatre prop, just like the bones they showed him earlier, which had been packed into a see-through zip-lock bag for effect. They wanted to unsettle him. And so they used some random bones that had been found and showed them to him, suggesting that they were Betty Ketani's. They even took them out of the bag and laid them out on one of the desks.

The bones weren't particularly effective. Conway didn't believe they were Betty's. But the docket was more convincing.

. . .

The truth is, the investigating team doesn't know nearly enough yet. No new docket has been registered and they are still chasing hunches across all kinds of police jurisdictions. The rules are more lenient for detectives, but the investigation is still very much below the radar. If Conway shuts down now, they'll have to decide whether to abandon the case. This is a make-or-break moment.

Conway has never been in this kind of trouble before. There were those few run-ins with the law, but this time he's at the centre of a murder investigation. Potentially, life behind bars. He tells the investigators that he's worried about what will happen to his house if he's in jail and can't work.

Three months previously, Conway updated his Facebook timeline, saying: '2012 is gona be an amazing year.' Now his life is in a wild tailspin, about to crash inside this small room, surrounded by strangers who have the power to toss him into another cage.

While Pretorius takes notes, Doc and JB continue to nudge Conway towards signing a formal confession. They've done it subtly but they've nevertheless boxed him in, leaving him surrounded. They walk in and out of the room, take phone calls and fire questions from different angles. They keep him busy, trying to deny him a chance to change his mind.

JB is doing most of the talking. For a man whose voice usually sets the walls of an interrogation room rattling, he's being as gentle as possible.

'You must just relax. If you wanna smoke, smoke. If you wanna cry, cry. Just do your thing, Conway. We're your friends now.'

Conway has already surrendered a lot of the background and has explained how various individuals implicated in the crimes know each other. But he still has to explain all the links. He needs to arrange events in their proper order. JB pushes a pressure point.

'This woman had a family,' he says.

Pretorius cuts in: 'That's why he can't fucking sleep … the thing chowed him up for 13 years.'

'Every day,' Conway confirms with a pained expression.

'Imagine if your wife doesn't know where you are and some *poes* has buried you. How sad is that, my brother?' JB continues, slowing down and rolling over some of the words for effect. Elegant turn of phrase is not his strong point. 'Your wife is saying: "Where's Conway?" and we're saying: "We don't know where the fuck Conway is."'

Pretorius tries to add something but JB's arms are flailing about.

'That's why this thing is working on you. This thing will always work on you. I want you to get it off your chest. I want you to be a better person. This thing is over now, it's *klaar* [finished]. Fuck all can come back to you. This is *klaar*. *Ons sal jou help* [we will help you]. And that's it …'

26.

Lieutenant Colonel André Neethling pulls up to the driveway on Eckstein Street and phones Doc to announce his arrival. The white metal gate slides open and swallows up the unmarked police car. The house where Conway is being questioned is perched on a ridge in eastern Johannesburg, in the quiet suburb of Observatory. It's an old, established area, where wide, empty streets rise and fall in the mottled shade of elm trees.

The cottage at the bottom of the garden is completely hidden by a sharp kink in the driveway and the branches of a tree. It's the perfect place for a discreet encounter. A place that must make Conway feel completely cut off from the outside world.

Neethling is eager to meet Conway. He's known about this case from the very beginning ... since that chance encounter at the BP station. Today, he was at a meeting at the police offices in Diagonal Street, in central Johannesburg, when he got the call to come and take a confession. His rank means that the statements he takes can be used as evidence in court.

The timing is perfect. Had Neethling been at his offices on the western side of the city, he probably would not have come. It's too far to drive and he has too much other work to deal with. But the Diagonal Street offices are much closer to Observatory and he can afford to make the detour.

Neethling slows down as he descends the uneven driveway towards the cottage and brings his Mazda bakkie to a stop. He reaches for his diary – full of names, case numbers and neatly filed slips – before opening the door. Doc is there to greet him.

'He's singing like a mossie,' Doc announces.

The words please Neethling, but in the back of his mind he knows how powerful a force self-preservation is. How every man with a dark secret – no matter how dark the secret or how desperate he is to set it free – can still have a change of heart, especially at the moment he has to sign the confession. He also knows how useless a suspect's words are unless each and every step of taking the confession is followed precisely.

For days now, Neethling has felt the pull of this case. He loves a good, old-fashioned whodunnit. He loves to watch the life an investigation takes on as it unfolds. Not the administrative paper-pushing detectives are forced into while juggling dockets, but a *real* investigation.

It's taken everything he has not to get more involved in this case. At one point he was even asked to lead it, but declined.

'My hands are full,' he kept saying. 'I've got too much of my own shit to sort out.'

And yet the case has intrigued him and he's enjoyed the updates he receives from JB. He knows it's the kind of case detectives live for: a chance to bring a stone-cold case back to life and catch those who thought they had long gotten away with it. The sort of case that awakens something primal inside a policeman: a duty to avenge the dead.

Neethling knows that him being summoned here signals a big break in the case. But experience has taught him that no two confrontations with a criminal are ever the same, so he has used the drive to carefully plan his approach. He's determined to make sure that this confession is bulletproof.

He knows the trial ahead will be long and the lawyers sharp. His plan is to be professional and courteous, and to get in and out before anything can go wrong. It's a method he's used throughout his career, an almost businesslike approach. Like his pursuit of the notorious robber and rapist and former Mozambican soldier Ananias Mathe.

'The first time I questioned Mathe, I sat down and introduced myself and I said to him, "You are a soldier and I am a soldier, let's speak now as soldier to soldier,"' he explains. 'He enjoyed that kind of an approach and felt that somebody is dealing with him on his level.'

Neethling adds: 'You concentrate more on the person in terms of what you can get from him rather than all the horrible things he has done. That has always helped me. I manage to get a lot of information that way.'

So when Neethling walks into the cottage, he introduces himself to Conway and shakes his hand. The others spring to attention, greeting him as 'Colonel'. They say it phonetically, as it would be pronounced in Afrikaans: 'Co-lo-nel'.

Conway has been here for over an hour now and looks drained. He knows this cottage as the 'safe house' but he's a nervous wreck.

You've got strangers with guns, you don't know what their motives are …
you don't know who you can actually trust or not, so you're shit scared.
And the guys are asking questions and I was just trying to get through the
questions as best I could.

Neethling disappears for about ten minutes and returns to take up a seat opposite the suspect. He produces a notepad of lined paper and writes 'Conway Brown' at the top.

'You know who I am?' he asks Conway, showing him his appointment card. 'I work with the Hawks.'

'He's Colonel Gadget,' JB jokes to ease the tension, exploding into laughter. Pretorius joins in.

Neethling quickly gets into it and asks Conway what his expectations are.

'I don't want anything to happen to my family.'

Neethling tells Conway the Hawks will be able to handle any threat. He asks what his expectations are for himself.

'I have no expectations,' Conway answers, his voice ringing with resignation.

Neethling takes care to explain the charges and that they involve a murder. He calls it a 'serious situation', taking care to avoid emotive words.

'I can see from your body language that this has been bugging you for a very long time,' he observes.

Neethling makes it clear that Conway does not have to speak to him and that he can offer him no guarantees of immunity from prosecution or deals with the state in return. He says he will only know what can be done once he understands his involvement.

Conway looks up at JB and says: 'It's about honesty, that's what it's about.'

JB's earlier words seem to have sunk in.

Neethling continues: 'We'd like to resolve this matter. I'm from organised crime and this looks like organised crime. We need to put this to rest. And be righteous about it. We can't let people get away with this kind of thing.'

ALEX ELISEEV

The conversation moves quickly to Conway's legal rights.

'The other thing I have to inform you about is that you have the right to speak to a lawyer before you speak to me,' Neethling explains.

He treats the question as a formality but, in truth, it's the final hurdle. Conway has the power to stop the interview right now and leave. To back away. To try to avoid jail, disgrace, exposure ...

But Conway is hopelessly out of his depth. He looks around the small room, and at Pretorius, before giving his answer: 'I'm probably going to kick myself for this, but you look like honest guys. I don't think it's necessary for a lawyer ...'

He has one last flash of doubt and asks Neethling whether he should get legal help. Neethling reminds him that the choice is entirely his, but that everything he's already told JB and Doc – who are civilians – is admissible in court. It's a subtle way of suggesting that he has come too far to turn back. That he must now take the leap.

Neethling deals with more of the formalities. He asks a few more routine questions. Conway's state of mind is important for the record.

The others have already been told to leave the room, to allow Conway to speak freely. Neethling takes down the suspect's identity number, address and contact numbers before recording his own police service number. Paragraph by paragraph he writes down everything that's happened so far and gets Conway to sign his name at the bottom of each one. He notes the time, '12:02', '12:03', '12:04', next to each paragraph.

Neethling also records the discussion they had about lawyers. His notes reflect the following: 'He tells me that the one man involved in this investigation "Carrington" is very rich and will obtain expensive legal representation. I explained that this is usually the case.'

Neethling takes care to document the most important aspects: 'Have you been influenced to make a statement?', 'Have you been assaulted or tortured in any way?', 'Has anyone promised you anything?'

Then, finally: 'Do you want to continue to make this statement?'

Conway has made so many wrong choices in his life. So many bad decisions. This time, he is being asked to be 'righteous'. JB may not have phrased it delicately, but there is a family out there searching for closure. Right now, he is the only one who can offer it.

Without his confession, this case is probably dead. It will likely suffer the same quiet death as the one James van Rooyen investigated 13 years earlier. Conway claims to be the only witness to the actual murder. He admits to hiding the letter under the carpet (making him a crucial link in the chain of evidence). He helped bury Betty's body and dug it up later, shedding light on where it was finally disposed of. Without him, the murder of Betty Ketani will almost certainly remain unsolved.

Conway considers Neethling's question – *does he want to continue?* – and gives his answer: 'Yes.'

. . .

The veteran policeman is meticulous in preparing the confession. At times, up to three minutes pass in absolute silence as he fills in the paperwork. Conway sits still, hunched over in his chair, brooding. During those quiet moments, laughter can be heard from the garden bench outside, where Doc, JB and a few other friends who have since arrived are sitting. There's the occasional shriek of a hadeda flying somewhere above the cottage. The camera is still rolling.

Neethling explains that this is Conway's last chance to report any torture or abuse. Conway is ready.

'Where do we start this?' Neethling asks after another short silence.

Conway takes Neethling inside the Uno, on that dark highway, speeding towards the Blockhouse.

27.

With his confession secured, Conway is given permission to leave South Africa. He is still working at Carnival Foods and his boss is sending him to Italy for a few weeks. Conway is worried that cancelling the trip will jeopardise his job. From the moment he met the detectives, his greatest fear has been his family's safety and finances. He pleads to be allowed to go.

Pretorius and the team weigh up the risks and decide that Conway doesn't have the means to flee the country. He has neither the money nor the connections. Plus, they can always keep an eye on his family here. Pretorius tells him to get in touch the moment he lands back at Johannesburg's OR Tambo International Airport. While he's away, the team will chase up all the new information he's provided. They are not yet ready to make their next move.

They don't know it yet, but Conway has not told the whole truth. He's lied to them again about a crucial part of his story. He's mixed up some of the names and events, falsely implicating people, and has given a watered-down version of how the murder played out. He's described seeing a scuffle as Betty was taken out of Carrington's car but has said nothing about holding her as she was stabbed. These lies will come back to haunt him.

• • •

The investigating team decides to go back to the beginning. They drive to the spot where Betty Ketani was stabbed. Conway has given them a lot to work with, so they head out to the dirt road parallel to the R59 highway, the one behind the tall bluegums.

By day, the area is tranquil and there is nothing menacing about the network of dusty streets that service the local farms and smallholdings. The grass has been trimmed and the T-junction where Conway claims

Carrington made a U-turn before stopping his car and pulling Betty out of the back seat is a lot wider than they imagined. There's even a rusty street pole displaying some road names. The intersection is remote, with the occasional car or bakkie rumbling past, leaving a trail of billowing dust.

The day they visit the crime scene is cool, forcing them to wear jackets. Puffy clouds float across a clear blue sky. Everything around them – the soil with its tyre marks, the trees, the grass – is dry, thirsty for the drenching summer rains that have passed and won't be back for months.

The team is searching for any clues. A witness who saw something and remembers it all these years later. A local paramedic or policeman. Perhaps a farmer who took Betty in before calling an ambulance, or maybe a farm worker with a good memory. Nobody knows how Betty got to Kopanong Hospital in Vereeniging, but she could not have walked there; more than likely she had been discovered and driven there. The answer could lie somewhere out here. All they need is a bit of luck.

With the same energy that drove him to excavate the grave at Conway's old place, JB leads the others in knocking on doors. Many of the properties are far apart, making it difficult to walk the neighbourhood. Getting attention at the gates proves to be a nightmare. JB finds a local resident at a poultry farm who seems to know everything that goes on in the area, but not even he remembers any such incident. The team visits the local police station, but there are no records of the attempted murder or of anyone named Betty Ketani. The chances of a breakthrough here are virtually zero, but JB and the others continue their quest, marching from farm to farm, holding out for a good Samaritan who never stopped wondering what happened to the wounded woman who had been left to die on the side of the dirt road.

When they grow tired of ringing doorbells and hooting at gates, they drive to see Mark Eardley's farm, which is just a few kilometres away. The old red-and-white railway bus is still there, parked perpendicular to the driveway, behind the perimeter fence and a small rotting wooden boat. According to the confession, it is inside this now hollow bus, with its grubby linoleum floor, that Betty spent her final hours. Snatched from the hospital by fake medical transporters, she was locked inside this structure. That night, the letter says, she died. What caused her death will never be known. The confession says it may have been shock. But it could have also been suffocation if she was gagged, or a complication of her earlier injury, which would have been severe. Betty may have suffered a heart attack or a stroke. There's no way to know.

A short drive down the dirt road past Eardley's farm, the team finds a crumbling brick house – an abandoned carcass of a building – perched up on a hill. They stop the car and walk a few hundred metres to inspect it, stepping through thorny, patchy veld littered with rocks. Is this the house Themba spoke about? The 'killing place' he described?

Doc and JB continue the foot patrols, visiting nearby farms, asking about Mark Eardley and his family, trying to fish out an interesting snippet about a local crime mystery that could somehow tie in to this case. Pretorius and Sono break away and head to Kopanong, which is 25 kilometres away, driving south down the R59. When they get there, they ask to speak to the hospital manager and make their enquiry. They are told that they are eight years too late. All patient records from 1999 were destroyed in 2004, after five years in storage. The detectives hear about the act that governs this, but are less interested in the explanation than in the fact that there is now no way to prove that Betty Ketani had ever been admitted to the hospital.

The hospital records – if they were not taken by the men posing as transfer staff – would have revealed what kind of injuries Betty suffered, under what circumstances she was transferred out of the hospital, and, crucially, by whom. This would all be powerful evidence in a trial, especially in a complex case of circumstantial evidence. Instead, there is no hard evidence to show that Betty had ever been treated here, never mind whether she was pushed out in a wheelchair by a brazen group of criminals.

· · ·

Over the following three weeks, during the time Conway is abroad, the investigation slows down. The team continues to work in the field trying to clarify the holes in the case. There are so many unanswered questions: Why was Betty (a cook at a restaurant) killed in such a brutal way? What kind of motive could there possibly have been? How did she manage to get to Kopanong Hospital after being stabbed? Why was her body buried in Conway's garden, in a busy suburban neighbourhood, instead of out near Mark Eardley's farm, which is surrounded by veld for miles in every direction? Why risk driving with it through the city? Why were the bones dug up years later? If Carrington did write the confession, why did he do so? Why did Conway hide it? Why did he not destroy it or at least take it with him when he left his house on Leo Street?

During these weeks, the investigators also open a line of communication with Betty's family in the Eastern Cape. Slowly, they feed them details about the case, breaking the news that Betty is dead and explaining, delicately, how she was murdered and what happened to her body. Betty's youngest daughter, Lusanda, is 13 years old and is only now discovering the truth about her biological mother.

Attempts are made to find out more about the other individuals who feature in the confession. Sandor Egyed – who was the best man at Carrington's latest wedding – now lives in New Zealand and has remained in touch with some of his South African friends. His mother and sister are still here, running a little pre-primary school in Rosettenville.

Monique Neeteson-Lemkes is a Jetstar air hostess with a public profile in Australia, climbing the trade union ladder. The whistle-blower testimony she gave at a Senate inquiry is on YouTube. The footage shows a confident woman in a black dress and rimmed glasses, delivering a brave presentation on working conditions at the airline.

Mark Lister, it will turn out, is also in Australia. He's a senior constable in the Queensland Police's mounted unit. Part of his duties involves protecting senior politicians.

There is no trace of Warren Williams. André Coetzer is still around but there is nothing linking him to the Ketani murder.

Candice, Carrington's ex-wife and business partner, left South Africa years ago. Her movements through immigration are confusing and it's difficult to tell where she is. They visit the address given for Candice in the confession, but the trail runs cold.

The team also tries to chase up a few loose ends, like the wheelchair that was allegedly hired to transport Betty, and the hotels and cars that are mentioned in the confession. They spend time compiling detailed profiles on their suspects.

Conway returns to South Africa and, per his orders, sends Pretorius an SMS as soon as his phone finds signal. He answers some new questions and helps point the investigators in the right direction as much as he can.

As April draws to an end, it is decided that a new case, based on Conway's confession, must be opened. On 24 April 2012, less than a month since the letters were discovered under the carpet, a murder docket is finally registered. Pretorius lists himself as the complainant and Sono is assigned the file, becoming the investigating officer of case 442/04/2012.

In a month's time, a full 13 years would have passed since Betty Ketani's disappearance. Thirteen years for a formal murder investigation to be opened. And, as her family suspected all those years ago, the restaurant where she worked is at the heart of the case.

Pretorius's and Sono's commander, Captain Alan Fagan, receives regular updates on the case. News, particularly good news, flows quickly up the command chain, and before long pressure begins to build. The top brass want arrests. It's time to start delivering them, starting with the man who will prove the hardest to catch: Carrington Roger Laughton.

28.

Herman Broodryk has no meetings lined up for the morning and is surprised when his secretary announces that two policemen have arrived to see him and are waiting in the lobby. He asks for their names but doesn't recognise them, which is unusual because he knows most of the senior officers in his jurisdiction. He's a deputy director of public prosecutions, one of only three Senior Counsel in his division, with an office on the sixth floor of the Innes Court building on Pritchard Street in downtown Johannesburg. He's not the kind of man to receive unannounced visits from low-ranking detectives.

The two policemen introduce themselves as Constable Lufuno Sono and Warrant Officer Gerhard Pretorius, two street-level investigators from Yeoville. They insist they have a murder case to discuss with him. A little bemused, Broodryk offers them the chairs across from his desk and sinks into his own.

Broodryk is large man, an imposing figure. He is a staunch Afrikaner and an old-school prosecutor, who likes to refer to himself as an 'old dog with a long tail'. Those who work with him say Broodryk has a deep knowledge of the law and a thrill for the unpredictable nature of court battles, particularly cross-examinations. He is a prosecutor who guards his reputation and hates his name being dragged into any kind of scandal. A private man who buys cars that best blend into traffic.

But weighing more than a Springbok prop and being one of the most senior prosecutors in town doesn't easily lend itself to a quiet, invisible life. Those who have been on the receiving end of his anger remember it for a lifetime. Broodryk has been around too long to suffer fools, and chases witnesses out of his office if he feels they are wasting his time. Afterwards, his colleagues crack jokes about half expecting those witnesses to have been flung out of a window.

By the time Sono and Pretorius show up at his door, Broodryk has all but stopped taking on his own cases. At his level of management, he can't afford to be in court for weeks on end. Instead, his days are passed signing off plea-bargain agreements or indictments and supervising advocates. More and more he lives in the past now, the kind of man who tends to repeat stories and recycle his proudest court clashes, dropping names of famous opponents or reliving clever legal manoeuvres.

With three decades of prosecutions, Broodryk has no shortage of material. Working with one of South Africa's best-known detectives, Piet Byleveld, he sent the 'Bruma Lake serial killers', Simon Majola and Themba Nkosi, to spend the rest of their lives in jail. The same happened to cop-killer Paul Thabang Khumalo, who murdered a station commissioner in Soweto and became known as one of 'the country's most wanted villains' after escaping from custody on four different occasions. Broodryk also secured the conviction of former Scorpions prosecutor Portia Kgantsi, disgraced after being busted accepting a R40 000 cash bribe inside a police cell from two men accused of fraud.

There were trials built upon massive undercover police operations and others born out of a spontaneous moment, like the case in which a group of drunk friends shot dead a night watchman. Some of his cases forced him to tolerate bodyguards, which he despised. And then there was a rape case he was involved in back in 2006, which led to him retreating even further away from all the journalists and all the headlines.

He wasn't the lead prosecutor on that case, but the weight the trial brought down on him was unbearable. It didn't help that he and his team inherited a flawed case that disintegrated as the complainant, a family friend of the accused, was cross-examined. Three years after the acquittal, the man who had sat in the dock was sworn in as South Africa's president.

The Jacob Zuma trial was the most public case Broodryk had been involved in. The political pressure was crushing. The public attention was piercing. Bodyguards were employed to guard him and his family as they visited close friends or shopped at the local Spar. It was everything he hated, and more.

The defeat was also difficult to bounce back from, as it was his first serious acquittal in 20 years. There had been a few cases where not all of the accused were convicted, but none where he had taken on such a big case and lost.

It didn't help that Broodryk is a competitive man. Catch him on an adrenalin high after a day in court and you'll see him do a fist pump or mumble, 'It's like taking candy from a baby', just loud enough for his opponents to hear.

He's the kind of prosecutor who thinks about his cases late at night in the shower and, if an idea strikes, phones his junior or the police investigating officer and puts them to work. The kind of prosecutor who uses the tranquility of a family holiday at the Kruger National Park to go over evidence in his head. Driving home from court, he listens to radio reports, checking if he's missed something important.

All the years and all the cases have allowed Broodryk to be selective about the litigation work he takes on. Detectives Sono and Pretorius know this, but are hoping that at the very least Broodryk will be able to assign the Ketani case to a capable prosecutor who will give it the kind of attention it needs.

They tell Broodryk all about the written confession and how it was found and about their investigation, building up to Conway's confession. It's a lot to take in. They leap back and forth across time and rattle off all the names. They keep coming back to the odds of this cold case being brought back to life and how all the evidence is now coming together.

Doc convinced them that Broodryk is the best prosecutor to turn to. Doc had played a part in the trap laid for Portia Kgantsi and took the stand as a witness in that case. Doc's role was to wear a wire and act drunk inside the police holding cell where the bribe went down. According to Broodryk, Doc overplayed the part a little, his own 'drunken' ramblings drowning out some of the crucial recording, but ultimately it worked and the trial ended in a conviction.

What the Yeoville detectives have brought Broodryk is certainly an intriguing case, but also an impossibly difficult one. For starters, there is no body to prove a murder. Broodryk can't think of more than a small handful of such cases which resulted in successful prosecutions. Then there's the prospect of trying to secure convictions for a 13-year-old crime. Evidence gets lost, memories fade and witnesses who would otherwise be stars are betrayed by the passage of time. Putting it all back together now, after all these years, is going to be a nightmare. Not to mention trying to preserve any kind of chain of evidence. There is no motive. No weapon. And a long list of suspects.

But the case is a challenge. For someone who has seen it all, Broodryk has never encountered a murder mystery quite like this. Its complexity – the very fact that there is no guarantee that it can ever be proved – is what is so magnetic. So seductive.

'The moment I saw it,' Broodryk says, 'I knew it was a once-in-a-lifetime case.'

. . .

Before studying law, Broodryk spent a year in the police force. His father worked for the notorious Security Branch during the apartheid years and felt his son was better off doing his national service with the police rather than with the army.

During that year Broodryk was taught all the basics: taking statements, protecting crime scenes and handling important evidence. Later in life, he understood investigations right from the A1 statement all the way to when an accused rose in court for judgment. He enjoyed the compulsory camps and riding police horses. The goal was always a career in law, but at some points he did wonder what it would be like to follow in his father's footsteps.

With the sales pitch from Sono and Pretorius over, Broodryk asks them to take him through the evidence. The first thing they do is pull out the original confession, which is being carried around in a plastic sleeve.

'I almost had a stroke,' says Broodryk.

He was expecting to hear that the fragile pages had been sealed inside an exhibit bag and sent to a forensic laboratory for analysis. That somewhere someone was trying to lift fingerprints off the paper or trying to date it. He thought maybe it had already been dispatched to a handwriting special-ist. He wanted to see the letters, but was sure he would be handed some photocopies.

Happier times: A photograph of Betty Ketani that her family has treasured and not shared previously. (Ketani family)

The landmark Blockhouse monument along the R59 highway. Conway Brown says this is near where he and Carrington Laughton met on the night Betty Ketani was stabbed. (© Alon Skuy)

After Betty Ketani was abducted from hospital, she was left to die in an old municipal bus that had been converted into an 'outside room' on Mark Eardley's farm. Eardley was not implicated in the kidnapping and murder. (© Alon Skuy)

A rare look inside the bus where Betty Ketani spent her last hours. She was left there while still recovering after being stabbed in the head. (© Alon Skuy)

Jeffrey Marshall found the confession letter while helping his family lift up some old carpet tiles. (© Alex Eliseev)

PHOTO: 4

Conway Brown's old bedroom, where the confession letter was found by the Marshall family long after Conway and his family had moved out. (Court exhibit)

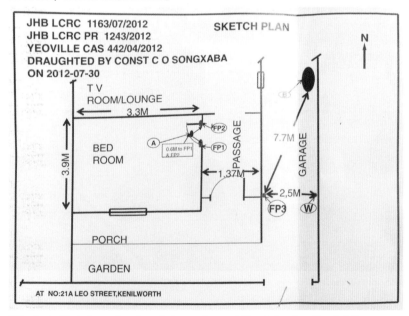

JHB LCRC 1163/07/2012
JHB LCRC PR 1243/2012
YEOVILLE CAS 442/04/2012
DRAUGHTED BY CONST C O SONGXABA
ON 2012-07-30

SKETCH PLAN

N

T V ROOM/LOUNGE

3.3M

FP2

(A) 0.6M to FP1 & FP2

FP1

PASSAGE

(B)

7.7M

GARAGE

BED ROOM

3.9M

1.37M

2,5M

FP3 (W)

PORCH

GARDEN

AT NO:21A LEO STREET,KENILWORTH

Police sketch of the bedroom where the confession was discovered (A) and where Betty Ketani's shallow grave was located (B). (Court exhibit)

Keith Green (Doc) and Jabez Loubser (JB), the private investigators involved in the early stages of the investigation. (© Alon Skuy)

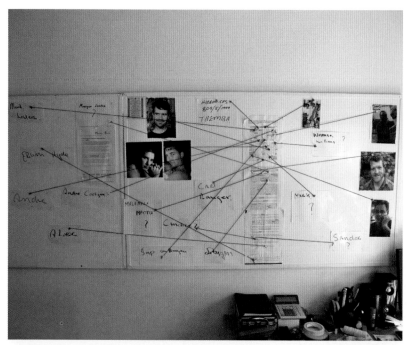

A spidergram on the wall of Doc and JB's office. This was pieced together shortly after the investigation began as an attempt to make sense of all the characters and suspects in the case.

A screen grab of a secret video recorded during Conway Brown's confession when he was being interviewed at a safe house. Conway's confession broke the case wide open.

The shallow grave is excavated a second time. Here a police officer washes the sides of the hole, hoping to find patterns or clues. Nothing of significance was found on this day. (© Alex Eliseev)

ABOVE: Memories: Kitchen staff at Cranks pose for a photograph. Betty Ketani is second from the right, with a blue apron and red hair-curlers.

RIGHT: Monique Neeteson-Lemkes, a suspect in Betty Ketani's murder, poses with waitresses at her father's restaurant. This photograph was likely taken in 1999, the year Ketani vanished.

ABOVE AND LEFT: There are conflicting explanations for why these two doctored photographs (and others like them) were created, but they became an important piece of evidence in the Ketani case.
(Court exhibit)

Carrington Laughton, Paul Toft-Nielsen and Conway Brown on a camping trip.
From Carrington's personal albums. (Court exhibit)

Conway Brown, Carrington Laughton and Dirk Reinecke pose together at Dirk's wedding. (Court exhibit)

An old photograph that compelled André Coetzer (front row, second from left) to turn state witness. It shows a connection between Carrington Laughton (extreme left), Monique Neeteson-Lemkes (centre) and policemen brothers Carel and David Ranger (to Monique's left). (Court exhibit)

A young Carrington Laughton.

It would probably have done no good to try find usable fingerprints on the documents, given how many hands they had passed through, from Werner and the Marshall family to all those involved in the investigation. But holding the pages, Broodryk can't help wonder how much longer they will last. He studies all the folds, tears, marks and moisture stains.

Next, the prosecutor wants to hear more about Conway's confession and whether he has been arrested. Instead, he is told about the Italy trip. He can't believe a suspect was allowed to leave the country. But it gets worse. Sono and Pretorius reveal that the grave was dug up on two separate days with no proper records being kept. And there's the messy visit to Cranks that saw a suspect make a photocopy of a piece of evidence upon which the entire case hangs.

Broodryk knows a mess when he sees one. This is going to be a repair job. But he also knows this is a case worth trying to get back on track. And to do that, there are going to have to be some big changes.

29.

JB braces himself for a 'Bible punch'. He's sure there's one on the way. The man standing in front of them, a part-time pastor who introduced himself as Kevin Clark, has just asked whether he can pray for them.

Kevin is supposed to know everyone in this neighbourhood, but not even he recognises Carrington in the photograph they show him. Now he wants to ask God to help JB, Pretorius and Sono find their suspect.

The team has spent days on Carrington's trail. They've narrowed the search down to an area, but are still wandering the streets, approaching perfect strangers for help. Conway warned them that Carrington never rents a place for long and will be difficult to track down. They didn't believe him at first but have now been to no fewer than six places, each time being told that he longer lives there or never did.

This afternoon they find themselves in Ferndale. It's 8 May 2012. They are close, but they just can't nail down an address.

What JB and the others are going through is no surprise. Carrington purposely made himself hard to find. In the last 13 years, he has lived in 11 different houses. There is no property registered in his name. His business address is long outdated. He made a habit of using his postal address when filling out routine forms and, at some point, even called his cellphone provider to get them to delete his private information from their database. He knew such information could be bought.

Carrington says his work made this necessary. As a private detective, he crossed paths with dangerous people who had to be kept away from his family. And, as a result, JB and the others have walked or driven around Honeydew, Roodepoort and Randburg, sinking hours into trying to catch up with him.

'We were driving up and down the streets,' explains Pretorius. 'If we saw someone walking in the road, we stopped them and showed them a picture. No one could tell us anything.'

Not knowing where Carrington lived was proving frustrating. They had spied on his life through Facebook, had seen his wedding photographs, knew what dogs his wife owned and what car he was driving. They had even spoken to him on the phone, trying to lure him out.

The first such attempt was JB's brainchild. They found out that Carrington was editing an online motoring magazine called *Naked Motoring*. Paul was featured as a contributor. So was Dirk. Even Anel Laughton, Carrington's third wife, was putting her name to some of the car reviews. To JB it seemed like a golden opportunity to make contact.

Once he found a number, JB called Carrington to offer him a 'test drive'. JB had studied to be a mechanic and knew his cars. He spun a tall tale about a 'Z conversion' of a Nissan bakkie and shot his mouth off, one petrolhead to another. He claimed the conversion was a great way to save on petrol.

Carrington wasn't interested. When he got the call he was with Dirk at a Nissan dealership, shopping for a car for his mother-in-law. JB had given him a fake name and was pushing hard for a meeting at his house. If he had known how much trouble Carrington took to keep his address private, he probably wouldn't have even tried. Carrington was suspicious of the call and explained that he would get one of the journalists to contact him.

Next was Sono's plan. He read somewhere that Carrington was also involved in a plastics business, so he called him to try to do a deal. But the information turned out to be false and Carrington quickly turned down the offer. No matter what they tried, they simply couldn't set up a meeting.

Plan C comes to them on the fly, as they drive along the long streets that cut across Ferndale. It's amazing they hadn't thought of it earlier.

They phone Conway and ask him to arrange a meeting with Carrington that same day. The cover story is that he's in the area and wants to catch up. Conway is worried that Carrington will see through the ploy and warns that it's dangerous. He hasn't seen him in a while and doesn't know where he's staying. But they assure him that Carrington has no idea he's working with them.

So at about 3pm, Conway makes the call, creating a story about going to Montecasino that evening with a cousin, asking if he can pop by. Carrington doesn't suspect a thing and tells Conway where to find him. He lets his friend know that he may have to wait outside for a few minutes while he fetches his son from crèche but, aside from that, his plan is to be at home editing video footage for a new motoring TV show he's trying to launch.

Once Conway hands over the address, it's just a matter of finding the right house. The investigators drive straight to York Street, which turns out to be just around the corner. They know they have the right place when they see Carrington's Land Rover in the driveway. Through the gate, they can also see three little Yorkshire terriers.

'So we check these little poodles in the driveway and it's exactly the same fucking poodles as on Facebook,' JB says. 'So I said, "Sharp, we are in the right spot."'

The trio parks just far enough from the gate not to alarm Carrington and settle in for a stakeout. His car is there, but they have to make sure he's at home. He could be using Anel's car or a test-drive vehicle for the magazine. They figure that even if he's out, he has to come back eventually. So they wait. And argue.

'Pretorius tells me, "Let's hit the house,"' JB says. 'I told him we can't just hit the house; if he's not there, it's gone. We are fucked. We are not going to get this *oke* – he'll climb onto a plane and he'll fuck off.'

The dispute is settled for them. A few minutes after 5pm the Land Rover reverses through the gate, Carrington behind the wheel. Pretorius starts the car and drives after it.

With the information at their disposal, the investigators have conjured up an image of Carrington as some kind of an ultimate villain; a former military intelligence officer who is always armed and dangerous. They've heard about his obsession with James Bond. They've checked the records and know he owns several firearms. And if he is in fact the author of the confession, then he is a man capable of brazen violence.

But the man they confront in Ferndale looks every bit the 40-year-old dad popping out to fetch his son at the crèche. Carrington is neatly shaved, wearing jeans and a T-shirt. He has piercing eyes but soft features and impeccable manners.

In an army uniform, as he appears in some photographs, Carrington looks like a career soldier, his beret tipped to the side. In a dark suit and trench coat, clutching a leather legal briefcase, he resembles a lawyer.

In the many motoring videos he posted online, he is an experienced journalist with a need for speed. He fits almost any character. But today, reversing out of his driveway, he is a regular father with an errand to run.

The silver VW Polo sedan rushes after Carrington's Land Rover as he sets off along York Street, catching up at the next intersection. Carrington sees a man rolling down the passenger window and ordering him to pull over, signalling with his hand. Pretorius and Sono are detectives and don't wear uniforms, so he has no idea who they are or what they want. His car is also a lot higher, making it impossible for him to see who else is in the car. As a result, he decides to play it safe and drives off, turning into Hill Street, which is a busier street.

'I was quite scared,' Carrington remembers. 'I felt I would be a lot safer amongst other motorists.'

The unmarked police car shoots past and cuts him off, forcing him to stop. Sono jumps out and approaches him with his gun drawn, ordering him to get out of the vehicle. For a moment, Carrington thinks he is being hijacked.

After identifying themselves as policemen, the detectives ask Carrington whether he is armed and find a pistol tucked into an ankle holster.

The firearm he is carrying is licensed and there is no problem with it. The officers know he has others and ask him where he keeps them. After a quick backtrack along York Street, they are inside his house, being shown the safes in the master bedroom.

Carrington has a collection of weapons, including a shotgun, which match those listed in the confession. The firearms are licensed but there is a problem with one of the handguns, which Anel inherited from a relative. Despite being repeatedly asked, the detectives have said nothing about their murder investigation and use this discrepancy with the gun as an excuse to escort Carrington back to the police station.

Before they do, he asks for permission to call Anel. He's worried about his son, who is barely a year old and is still at crèche, and he needs to tell his wife to leave the conference she's attending to go and fetch him. While on the phone, he asks her to call his lawyer, Michael Trapido. This is not the first time Carrington is being arrested. He knows the drill and what will happen in the coming hours.

He leaves the house with the policemen, who have confiscated six fire-arms, his cellphone and his passport, which is important because it contains a signature that can later be compared to the confession found under the carpet. While Trapido arranges to meet his client at the station, the detectives call Captain Alan Fagan and ask him to come in, even though he's on leave. They want their commander there when they break the news to Carrington that he is not being held for some minor firearm infringement, but for the 1999 kidnapping and murder of Betty Ketani.

Carrington is driven to the Yeoville Crime Intelligence and Detective branch, which is located a few blocks away from the police station. It's an old house with a dusty parking lot and easy access onto Louis Botha Avenue. He is taken to one of the rooms.

There are different versions of what happens next. Carrington claims Doc and JB are introduced as police officers, even though they are civilians. He describes a lot of screaming, shouting, JB 'exploding', and the waving around of Ketani's ID book in his face. Doc, JB and the detectives have a far less dramatic recollection of how they questioned Carrington and eventually revealed to him the real reason for his arrest.

Of more significance is what happens once Captain Fagan arrives. As the highest-ranking officer, Fagan takes control of the situation and, with Carrington's lawyer now present, sits down to ask him some questions.

There is no dispute that the conversation between Fagan and Carrington took place. It began just after 7pm and lasted for around an hour. According to Carrington, it was an off-the-record discussion during which Fagan took no notes. Carrington also claims he made no incriminating admissions during this hour, and kept saying he knew nothing about the murder.

But Fagan goes on to compile a detailed statement about what Carrington told him. He hands over four pages of handwritten notes to his detectives, which they file away in the docket. Two months later, he types out the notes and submits them again, this time in the form of an affidavit, signed under oath.

According to Fagan, he warned Carrington, in the presence of his lawyer, about his right to remain silent. He also made it clear that anything they discussed could be used against him in court. Fagan's statement reflects that Carrington was warned about his rights three separate times during the interview. It notes every time there was a short break or when Carrington consulted with Trapido.

Fagan's statement is a dynamite piece of evidence. It has Carrington confirming key parts of the hidden confession, covers the violent Hillbrow interrogations and the Cranks investigation. It also sheds light on Betty Ketani's kidnapping and the hospital abduction. Fagan states that Carrington explained to him that the hospital where Betty landed up made contact with her employers at Cranks, which seems to explain how and why a plot may have been hatched to kidnap her a second time. Fagan notes an admission that the policemen involved were paid for their assistance.

Captain Fagan is an experienced policeman with 22 years' service. What he's provided may not be a signed confession by a suspect but, the detectives figure, his notes will carry weight during the trial. They call Herman Broodryk and are told to place Carrington under arrest. He is taken to the holding cells at the Hillbrow police station, where so much history relating to this case is buried.

30.

Carrington's arrest is the fall of the first domino and the rest must tumble. Up until now, Conway has been lucky. He's been allowed to travel and to spend time at home with his family while the investigation continues. But his time has come. Broodryk has made that very clear.

Pretorius calls Conway the same night that Carrington is arrested and tells him that they need to speak to him urgently. By the time they reach his Alberton home, it's past midnight. They let Conway know they're outside and watch as he emerges from the house, walking down the driveway to open the flimsy gate. He's wearing a pair of jeans, a shirt and some shoes, but, thinking he will be home soon, hasn't bothered with socks. Conway locks the security door and throws the keys back into the house.

They had asked him to keep quiet about the investigation and about his confession to André Neethling. Conway's wife and children know nothing about his involvement, nor about the murder case. In fact, he and Blanche have just started to patch things up after the near-divorce and it feels like they are finally reconnecting.

Perhaps Conway hoped he would avoid ever being arrested. Maybe he thought he would be taken in as some kind of state witness and granted immunity or taken into witness protection and given a new identity, like in the movies. But that is not what's on the cards tonight and Conway is informed that he is being locked up. He's far too involved and there's no nice way to arrest a man for murder. He must now explain everything to his family.

• • •

The next day, Carrington and Conway make their first court appearance and are formally charged. It is almost routine for courts in South Africa

160

to give detectives a week to continue their investigation before bail is dealt with, and this case is no exception. Both men are to remain in custody until then.

By the end of the following day, 11 May 2012, policemen brothers Carel and David Ranger are behind bars. David, who is still a warrant officer in the police service, is picked up at his station. It's a simple affair that involves his commander summoning him and handing him over to the detectives. David has 18 years of police work behind him.

Carel is a different story. He's left the police and now works as a security consultant with a tactical team based at a casino. He is often armed with high-calibre weapons. If he decides to resist arrest, things could get messy. Pretorius and Sono call André Neethling to help with the 'high-risk takedown'.

Neethling knows the casino managers from past cases and asks the head of security to create a fake undercover operation which requires that the members involved hand in their firearms. Carel is called into the office and, as soon as he's disarmed, is placed under arrest.

Paul Toft-Nielsen is next. News of the arrests is spreading and he has already reached out to the police to arrange a surrender. Conway has told the detectives about Paul, warning them that he can 'snap a person in half like a twig' – his nickname is apparently 'Satan'. But Paul agrees to hand himself over and is taken to a magistrate on the same day in order to make a confession.

During that confession, Paul claims he has tried to come clean over the years but the police ignored him. The magistrate notes: 'The deponent appears to be relieved that someone is finally doing something about this.'

Dirk Reinecke is the last suspect to be brought in. First contact is made on 17 May 2012, three days after Paul's arrest. Dirk hires a lawyer who keeps in constant contact with the police, trying to figure out whether an arrest warrant has been issued. After two weeks, it is arranged that Dirk will hand himself over during an identity parade that is to be held.

His co-accused have been in and out of court four times already. The bail battle is looming. Six men are to stand trial for murdering Betty Ketani.

At the same time, in another court, a default judgment is handed down against Eric Neeteson-Lemkes. Cranks is drowning in debt and he owes his landlords just over a million rand. The court orders an eviction and that his assets be seized in order to try to recoup some of the debt. 'Mad Dog' Eric has dropped public hints that he plans to pack up and leave for Thailand to start a new venture. But even if the team wanted to keep him in the country, they can't. There is no evidence against him in connection with the murder. The rest of the suspects are either thousands of kilometres away, in Australia and New Zealand, or can't be found.

When the bail hearings begin in the Betty Ketani case, a magistrate compares it to a cracked mosaic, with pieces scattered across the globe.

'The contents of the [confession] letter resemble a movie script because it reflects life usually portrayed in mafia or gang-related movies,' the magistrate muses. 'The contents are indeed like a picture puzzle which shows nothing until it is put together.'

PART TWO

Weaving the threads

'Circumstantial evidence is truly the holy grail of evidence. It goes to the root of everything evidence means. It forces us to realise that we have only very tenuous connections with reality. When you think about it hard enough, all evidence is circumstantial, as is our connection to the world.'

— ADVOCATE JAMES GRANT, PHD IN CRIMINAL LAW

31.

As a girl growing up in New Bright, Queenstown, Tandiwe Ketani ran through the dusty, windy streets with her brother Mankinki, buying small bags of ginger and township *vetkoek*. Of the ten children their mother had given birth to, and despite the five years between them, the two shared a special bond.

Tandiwe and Mankinki were both born in George, a sleepy town where their father had found work. But, from a young age, they were sent to live with a relative in the Eastern Cape, the province of majestic landscapes and home of the amaXhosa.

Betty was an energetic child, fast and agile. Along with Mankinki – whose Christian name is Eric (ironically, the same name as her future boss) – she dashed through the streets, covering entire blocks to fetch water or deliver batches of laundry to communal washing spots. Even going to the toilet required a brief adventure through the township.

When they weren't splitting up household chores, Betty and Mankinki played with the neighbourhood kids. Usually, it was girls against boys. This went for card games like 'Ace' or a local interpretation of dodgeball known as *skhululi*.

In the 1970s, deep in the apartheid era, New Bright was a volatile township and many of the locals were pulled into gangs. Mankinki says he ran with the Busy Bees, which perpetually clashed with their arch-rivals the Ama Bhubesi. Betty was always on the sidelines of the skirmishes, chasing after the young men or boys, often in tears worrying about her brother. Mankinki was lucky; he survived the gang wars and found a job that took him out of the township.

The woman who raised them, Agnes Ketani, was their maternal grandfather's sister. She was born a Bikauri and had married into the Ketani name. Betty adopted this surname and, like her brother, intended to formally revert back to her father's surname, Kula, but never got around to it.

Agnes had three children of her own when she took in Tandiwe and Mankinki. Her two-bedroom house on Mayaba Street was too small to accommodate all of them, along with an adult relative who had found refuge there. The kids slept on the floor of the dining room, waking up early to run errands (fetching milk or pushing a wheelbarrow full of firewood) before school began. Apartheid laws crippled education for black South Africans, and both Betty and Mankinki attended a crèche run from a private house and then spent several years in a preparatory school managed by a local church. Betty went to primary and high school, but how far she got remains unclear.

Betty's parents, Wilson and Eunice, divorced after having five children, and her mother went on to have five more children with her new husband. Unlike in Western culture, there were no stepbrothers or -sisters, just one big family with a mixture of surnames: Kula, Bikauri and Ketani.

Betty's father, Wilson, whose birth name was Pitsane Kula, was a descendant of the Mgiqwa clan. He worked for a big construction company, driving tractors and trucks in George, in the Western Cape, and held deep traditional beliefs, which were passed to his children.

On the streets of Hillbrow or Rosebank not many people noticed that Betty was missing part of a digit on her left hand, her wedding-ring finger. The tip had been sliced off by a traditional doctor when she was a girl. The ritual, *ingqithi,* was performed on all of Wilson's five children. As a boy, Mankinki had had the tip of his left pinkie chopped off. For girls of the clan it was the next finger down.

Ingqithi is done to keep children growing at the right pace. It is an old tradition designed to avoid bed-wetting beyond a normal age or various other developmental problems. Mankinki says the amputated part is wrapped in cow or rat dung and mixed into the walls of traditional huts. As Betty painted her nails in glossy red colours in Johannesburg, the missing digit would have reminded her of the culture that remained so alive in the rolling hills of the Eastern Cape, where babies are formally introduced to ancestors and the traditional piercing of ears is still practised.

When their father died (a year or two before the letters were found under Conway's carpet), the duty of keeping these and other traditions fell to Betty's brother Mankinki. With the eldest son, Thubeni, living in George, Mankinki stepped up to lead the family in Queenstown.

Betty's mother, Eunice, or Nontuta, also died waiting for answers that never came. Like her daughter, she spent years working in Johannesburg, cooking and cleaning kitchens. In the nineties, she received a small house in the Unifound township not far from New Bright. Her eldest daughter, Lilly, continued to live there, raising Betty's three children. Lilly lived to hear what happened to Tandiwe but she died, rather suddenly, on 18 August 2012, before the indictments were served on Carrington and the others. From that point on, Betty's children were on their own. Thulani and Bulelwa were old enough to look after Lusanda, with some help from Mankinki, who drove from Barkly East to check in on them.

Betty was 19 when she gave birth to her first child, Thulani. To support him, she went to work in Queenstown and then in Johannesburg. Some say the family she was working for in the Eastern Cape moved and took her with them. Others believe she made the move all on her own.

Mankinki was also forced to get a job and found one as a gardener. To make extra cash he and some friends darted around a golf course searching for lost golf balls, which they could easily sell.

Then, in the late 1970s, the man whose garden he was tending started his own business and took Mankinki with him. First it was furniture, then cars and eventually a petrol station in Barkly East, a tiny grid of streets northeast of Queenstown. By then, South Africa was a different place and eventually the man helped Mankinki start his own small business running a convenience store from a Caltex garage. Mankinki tried to expand by opening a clothing store next door, but there just weren't enough customers.

Mankinki is a shy and awkward man when navigating outside his comfort zone. Back home he is a family leader who consults elders and speaks to ancestors, while caring for his own children and those of his late sister Betty. He invites locals to watch soccer on a big screen inside his shop (he's a Kaizer Chiefs fan) or takes the kids to big matches. He laughs easily and gives willingly, balancing the needs of the modern world – like making regular trips to nearby towns to purchase stock for his shop – against his family's proud traditions. But in Johannesburg, he throws himself at the mercy of those who know the big city, be it his younger brother Ronnie, police detectives or prosecutors. He has a strange giggle, which bursts free at odd times. His big, strong hands are scarred from years of manual work and his eyes are warm and kind. Mankinki has a deep well of patience for any situation, especially when he is far from home.

After news of the confession uncovered at Conway's house and the unfolding investigation reaches Queenstown, Lilly is the first to travel to Johannesburg to meet with the investigating team.

She returns with pieces of information but no real clarity on what happened to Betty. The family tries to put it all together, but aren't sure how Betty died and why her body wasn't found in the grave at Conway's place. The confusion mirrors the uncertainty back in Gauteng, where the full picture is yet to emerge.

Regardless, Mankinki decides to drive to Queenstown to speak to the ancestors. He puts on a smart jacket as a sign of respect for the spirits, and he's always careful to address them either early in the morning or in the evening, never in between. He decides to speak to them at his mother's grave. Eunice died with an ache in her heart, never finding out what happened to Betty. It feels right that the conversation should take place there.

Like so many times before, Mankinki begins by introducing himself and describing his family's bloodlines. He then tells the ancestors that the search for Tandiwe appears to have ended and that she was killed while working in Johannesburg. He asks the spirit world to help guide the investigation.

Days later, while climbing into a long-distance taxi, he speaks to the ancestors again. He asks them to protect him on his journey to Joburg. As a family leader, he's going to get more answers from the police and to face the men accused of murdering his sister.

32.

Doc says his father was an old-school biker who gave him his first drink at the age of 13 and was the kind of parent who wouldn't try to stop his child from smoking.

'Smoke, but don't cry,' Jimmy would growl.

After he died, Doc's mother, Wendy, had four more children, eventually settling down with a man named Lesley, who was an insurance consultant and whose business allowed her to look after their lovely home in Observatory. Doc says his brothers went into the family trade, while his sister pursued a career as a chartered accountant. He chose a different path. He chose the Jimmy way.

After his national service Doc began riding bikes, building brotherhoods and bouncing at Hillbrow pubs and nightclubs like the Pig 'n Whistle or the Jolly Roger. He joined Sanab – the police's narcotics bureau – because it sounded like a 'fucking exciting adventure' and a way to see strip shows for free. The deeper he delved and the older he grew, the more seriously he began to take his job.

Doc worked as an agent through the bloody feuds that raged between escort agencies and, later, through the bouncer wars of the 1990s. As he gained more experience, he was pulled into specialised units dealing with organised crime or intelligence gathering. At the height of it all, he says, he was handling his own informers and reporting directly to top handlers.

On the streets, his reputation invited all kinds of criminal offers. In 1996, while lounging around a tattoo parlour, Doc says he was asked to assassinate a Chinese businessman and his family. The man who wanted to hire him was young, awkward, and looked like an undercover cop, claiming to have been referred to him by 'Preacher', whom Doc did in fact know. By that stage, Doc had had a falling-out with Sanab and was out on his own. He suspected this was a revenge police trap.

Ignoring warnings from his friends, he named a ludicrous price and told the guy to bring him a deposit. He thought he would never see the man again after he walked out of the tattoo shop. But when the money arrived the next day, followed by a dossier of who needed to be taken out, Doc realised the youngster had genuine syndicate connections. He set up a police operation, which led to several arrests that made the newspapers. A few years later, the work he did on that case helped open a door into the Scorpions. Andrew Leask, the investigator in charge of the Jackie Selebi case, sought him out and recruited him.

Doc got his nickname from his biker brothers back in the eighties. It was originally Mad Doc, but over the years was shortened to Doc. Back then he had a reputation for drinking too much, getting into fights and 'doing some crazy shit'.

During his service as an agent, Doc had several aliases: Peter Williams, Mike Jordan and Keith Greene, a variation of the name that stuck: Keith Louis Green.

Doc says his mother knew nothing about his work until his name emerged publicly in the Barry Trigwell murder, which made news in South Africa and in Britain in 1995. Trigwell, a private detective, was bludgeoned to death at his home in Sutton Coldfield, England, in a case that exposed what journalists called the work of 'sinister death squads'. Trigwell's South African-born wife, Anne, was jailed for life for her role in the murder, while two other men, both from Johannesburg, were extradited and convicted years later. Doc says he received information about the planned assassination and passed it on, but this led to a string of unfortunate events that would see him blow his cover, get suspended and go into hiding. With his name in the press, Doc had to speak to his family.

'That is the first time I said to them, "Hey, I'm a deep-cover agent, this is what I do for a living, don't ask questions because I can't tell you."'

If he could speak more freely, he may have told them any number of stories of daring escapades: about how he almost sliced a man's ear off to protect him from a deadly gang of 'enforcers' working at an illegal casino; or how close he once came to killing two dirty cops who had kidnapped him during an operation set up to expose their links to drug dealers; or about how he infiltrated the syndicate around slain gangster Yuri 'The

Russian'. Vlianitski. But his work required him to keep secrets, even from those closest to him.

Years later, while investigating the Ketani case, Doc speaks using his hands, flicking them out like knife blades. His fading tattoos are diary entries dating back two decades, time spent riding for outlaw biker clubs: the Midnight Riders, Gladiators, Gypsy Jokers, Warlords and finally the Crusaders.

While talking about the syndicates he had infiltrated and the split-second, life-or-death decisions agents make daily, Doc mentions something that grips the imagination.

'I'm not dealing with Little Red Riding Hood,' he says.

It's a throwaway line, but the images are powerful. The flowing red cape. The snow-covered trees. The razor-sharp teeth …

What Doc means is that he chose a life away from the safety and comfort of the village. Away from the huntsmen and their rifles. Away from the warm fires. Instead, he chose to help the hunters by lurking in the shadows of the cold forest. He chose a life of running with the wolves.

. . .

Doc and JB met in Sanab and quickly became partners, with Doc teaching his new friend 'the game' and keeping JB out of trouble.

One of five brothers, Jabez Loubser – JB for short – was a school dropout, like many of the men he would help arrest in the Ketani case. After a stint in the army he qualified as a mechanic and joined Sanab after his youngest brother got caught up in drugs. To him, Doc, or Keith, seemed like a 'sharp agent' who would help him stay on the right side of the law in a murky world of blurred lines.

JB has had a few close calls. He survived being shot twice, on two separate occasions, joking that each time the bullets were getting closer to his head. Once, while searching the Saints Hotel in Hillbrow, a criminal pulled a gun on him in a dark corridor and squeezed the trigger. JB's fingers were wrapped around the barrel but, miraculously, the firearm jammed.

His aggressive style of police work has landed him in trouble with the law. Speak to some lawyers who remember the Sanab days and they will call JB a 'thug'.

'I just do the thing,' JB says. 'But Doc is a very paranoid *oke*. He was the *oke* that always kept me *wakker* [awake]. If it wasn't for him, I'd have been locked up a long time ago and in a lot of *kak*.'

Doc describes the work he and JB did as undercover agents as the 'twilight world of sudden death' – a world where the line between good and evil, between light and dark, is faint and illusive. A world with its own rules.

'Death is as close as the person you are having a conversation with. All it takes is one wrong move,' Doc explains.

Before moving to the cottage in Observatory, Doc and JB worked out of a room on the ground floor of a Yeoville block of flats. It was right in the heart of a suburb they called 'the *kas*', the cupboard.

They knew every street. Every corner. From the Green House drug den on Raymond Street to the abandoned Hell's Angels clubhouse on Hendon. Doc would drive around in his black Honda Accord and observe the delicate dance of drug dealers and police vans along the suburb's main artery: Rockey Street. He knew where anything could be bought in the *kas*, from fake identity documents to guns or hijacked cars.

The two friends chased drug dealers or heroin junkies and got caught up in wild shoot-outs. They could introduce you to a Ghanaian giant named Chief, whose gold chain glistened on his massive bare chest through the rising smoke of his joint, or to paramedics working the area. They knew the local cops and the gangsters who hijacked buildings. They existed somewhere in between. In a world of whispers and secrets, where, no matter how hard anyone tried, there was no such thing as a flawless investigation.

33.

It takes 12 and a half years, but the identity parade that Inspector James van Rooyen envisaged back in October 1999 is finally held at his former police station at the end of May 2012. By this point, Themba Tshabalala, Ndaba Bhebe and Ruth Mncube are no longer just names in a strange confession. They are still scared and apprehensive, but this time they arrive promptly at 11am for the pointing out.

The results surprise the police investigators. Carrington Laughton is not identified by anyone. Neither is David Ranger. David's brother, Carel, is picked out of the line-up by Themba, who also recognises Conway and Paul. Ndaba points out Conway too, along with Dirk. Both Themba and Ndaba make several incorrect choices, and Ruth fails to find the face of the man who ambushed her on the street outside the post office.

'It's a long time, people change,' she explains later.

The accused have all aged and some have lost a lot of weight or changed their hairstyles. If the confession is real, and fake documents and uniforms were being used, it's possible that so were physical disguises.

In their initial confessions, Conway, Paul and Dirk claim they had nothing to do with the Hillbrow abductions. And yet all three are pointed out, Conway by two different victims. The letter to Sandor doesn't mention either Conway or Paul in relation to the kidnappings, but then again, they were all close friends at the time and perhaps the author was trying to protect them. Dirk is mentioned in the abduction of Themba and is picked out by Ndaba. In court, he will confess to being involved in the Hillbrow raids, claiming he was asked to watch the cars outside. What the identity parade suggests is that lies are still being told, even by those cooperating with the investigation.

· · ·

Betty's brother Mankinki arrives in Johannesburg to meet the detectives and to attend court proceedings. Before he reports back to the family in the Eastern Cape, he wants to see the men arrested for the murder.

Mankinki describes his sister as a smart lady who loved to dress up. A woman who enjoyed wearing wigs and loud sunglasses. He also describes the pain the family has carried for all these years, and how it's all come flooding back.

'We had hope that she was still alive,' he says.

Mankinki doesn't know the grim details of how Betty – the girl who chased after him through the township, crying at the thought of him getting hurt in a fight – was stabbed and left for dead, then kidnapped again from hospital. Nor about how she apparently died alone in a cold, empty bus in the middle of nowhere. He hasn't heard yet how her body was dug up, her skull broken into pieces and flung into a river. All the family knows is that part of her body was tossed, like trash, on a municipal dump.

'Why would anybody want to kill her?' he is asked in an interview.

Mankinki takes a deep breath. His face twists from a pain deep inside. He rubs his wet eyes. It's impossible not to feel his grief.

'I wish I could speak to the men and ask them,' he finally replies.

• • •

On the first day of June, with Dirk now in custody, all six accused stand in the dock together for the first time. They are being processed at the Johannesburg Magistrate's Court.

At this stage, bail is the most important issue, along with making sure that all the accused are legally represented. To get a trial date onto the court roll takes months and, with all the inevitable postponements, it's not unusual for a case to take years to be finalised. Sometimes three, four or even five years. Even if their case does move quickly, Carrington and the others are standing at the start of a long road. Having worked in law enforcement, Carrington and the Ranger brothers are particularly aware of this.

Conway decides not to apply for bail. Since his arrest, he has been brought before a magistrate to confirm his confession and has helped the police by pointing out certain locations. He knows he is going to be doing time, and decides to start immediately. His lawyer, Nardus Grové, doesn't know what kind of deal he can get his client, but he's certain there will be one. With everything Conway has already confessed to, he has no choice but to bargain. The time he serves while awaiting trial will ultimately work in his favour.

Paul's and Dirk's bail applications go unopposed and they are released. Paul has made an emotional confession before a magistrate but says his involvement, in terms of digging up the grave, began years after Betty was killed. Dirk has told the police about the hotel kidnapping and there's still some confusion over whether he was also involved in the exhumation. But both men are not considered big players and are potential 'flippers' who could testify for the state. Prosecutors downgrade the schedule of the charges they face and agree to set them free on bail of R20 000 each.

For Carrington and the Ranger brothers the situation is entirely different.

The former private investigator is the prime suspect in the case and the alleged author of the confession at the centre of it. If his co-accused are to be believed, he is an intelligent, powerful man – a natural leader – with a solid understanding of the law and the ability to derail or destroy an investigation. In his bail application, he will have to try to shatter that perception and illustrate that he is not a threat.

Carel and David were both policemen when Betty was murdered and when the Hillbrow raids were carried out. Having taken an oath to protect those they serve, they face tougher sentences if convicted. There are different laws for police officers who cross the line. The confession has them wheeling Betty out of the hospital and driving her to her death. Along with Carrington, they will have to show the court exceptional circumstances if they are to be released.

Herman Broodryk assigns another prosecutor to handle the bail application. He will step onto the battlefield once all pretrial formalities are taken care of. Gertrude Market is chosen to assist him and appears once or twice for the state. But a diary clash forces Gertrude to pass the baton to her friend and colleague Namika Kowlas, who takes over the case and will remain Broodryk's partner for the remainder of the trial.

Kowlas is a Durban-born advocate who shot up the ranks to become a senior state advocate, based at the National Prosecuting Authority's Organised Crime Unit led by Broodryk. Kowlas moved rapidly through the lower courts and up to the High Court division. During the Ketani case, she began studying for her master's degree, eager to keep moving.

Her first impressions of the case are mixed. She's never handled a murder case without a body, where it has to be proved first that a crime has actually taken place. The state has no witnesses yet, no scientific evidence, and no analysis has been done on any documents.

'We needed more,' she recalls. 'A lot more.'

But on the other hand, like Broodryk, she was drawn to the challenge. Kowlas kept thinking about the odds of the letter being found and whether it was real, about Conway's confession and how the police had managed to track down all those named in the abductions described in the letter. It all seemed like one of the Jonathan Kellerman novels she loved to read.

With a mixture of anxiety and excitement, and under huge time pressure, Kowlas gets to work on preparing an affidavit to oppose bail for Carrington and the two brothers. She works with Gerhard Pretorius to set out their reasons. The statement they prepare runs to almost 20 pages, with the confession attached as an annexure. It gives a brief summary of all six accused and lists any prior convictions. Carrington has one for perjury (which will become important later), David for reckless and negligent driving, and Paul for drug possession. The others have clean records.

The charges against them include murder, attempted murder, kidnapping, attempted kidnapping, assault and theft. These are likely to be whittled down before trial, but for now the prosecutors are throwing everything they have at the bail application. Pretorius's affidavit describes Betty Ketani's murder as a 'heinous' crime and singles out the policemen for 'abusing their positions of trust'. Although she now resides abroad, Monique is accused of conspiring with the others.

Broodryk and Kowlas have decided to charge all of the accused under the principle of 'common purpose', which means all could be found guilty as co-perpetrators of the same crimes through their association. Their liability arises from their 'common purpose' to commit the crime. Pretorius's affidavit continues:

The accused operated as a gang, sought out and killed the deceased to silence her ... The arrogance of accused 1, 3 and 4 [Carrington and the Ranger brothers] had no boundaries when they presented themselves as medical staff and kidnapped the deceased for a second time from hospital. The accused rented a wheelchair and a kombi [minibus] to make their presentation to the hospital credible. This is a clear indication of how well organised and focused they were as a group in achieving their goal of eliminating the deceased at all cost.

In his statement, Pretorius argues that by living with their 'closely guarded secret' for so long, the men in the dock have shown no remorse or regret. He talks about their 'moral compass' and says they are blind to the agony they have caused Betty's family. He calls them cruel, and accuses them of terrorising Cranks staff to conceal the murder, of 'demolishing and destroying' anyone who stood in their way.

The detective devotes pages to laying out the state's case: the incriminating confession; Conway and Paul confirming much of what it reveals; the identity parade; and all the details that have been independently confirmed, such as Themba's and Ndaba's abductions, Ruth's ordeal, and Carrington's company, car and firearms, all mentioned in the letter under the carpet.

Carrington, Pretorius claims, has the means to intimidate witnesses and possibly collapse the case. Carrington's problems are compounded when Paul hands over a sworn affidavit to the state claiming that his friend of 30-plus years has threatened him inside jail. For someone who placed so much weight on loyalty, Paul's allegations must have caught Carrington off guard. He may have expected it from the others, but not from his oldest friend. Paul claims he was told to stop helping the police, or live to regret it.

'The threats are very serious and I feel that my life could be in jeopardy if Laughton is released on bail,' Paul says. 'I have seen what he is capable of.'

From that moment on, any doubt about whether friends are going to be turning on each other evaporates. New alliances will have to be forged.

34.

Herman Broodryk and Namika Kowlas will get few lucky breaks in the upcoming trial, but the first legal 'gift' falls right into their laps when they read the contents of Carel's and David's bail applications. They have what they consider to be a solid case against Carrington but a far weaker one against the Ranger brothers. Sure, they are named in the confession, and Carel has been pointed out in a line-up, but that's really all there is. In South African law, the confession of one accused can't be used against another.

Carel has also given his version of why he was at Themba's house – to check on his immigrant status – in April 1999 and to prove otherwise will be difficult. Given that several people were incorrectly pointed out in the line-up, Carel may be able to cast serious doubt on his identification. If the defence succeeds in blocking the confession letter – making it inadmissible in court – the case against the policemen will fall to pieces. The confessions from Conway, Paul and Dirk will be of no help to the prosecution, as there's nothing to suggest that they played any part in the hospital kidnapping the brothers are tied to.

But the Rangers are under pressure. They know courts don't look kindly upon policemen who break the law. Denying the crime is not enough; they need to give a version. Show exceptional circumstances. Attack the strength of the state's case.

And so, Carel and David do something extraordinary: in their signed affidavits, they place themselves at the hospital and admit to fetching a woman and dropping her off inside what they describe as a 'bus-like structure'. David even admits to pushing a wheelchair out of the hospital – exactly as the confession says.

The Rangers deny they knew that the woman was in any kind of danger. Both claim they were simply helping Carrington, and if a crime was taking place, they were oblivious to it. Their version departs from some of the key events described in the confession.

Carel Ranger's affidavit states:

> *During 1999, my brother David Ranger stayed with me. I knew Carrington*
> *and (we) were requested by him to accompany him to Vereeniging as I*
> *know the region.*
>
> *Myself as well as David were picked up in a kombi by him and we*
> *went (to a) Vereeniging hospital. There my brother helped him to pick*
> *up a person he allegedly had to take to her uncle in Kliprivier. She never*
> *complained during our trip and I never suspected any foul play.*
>
> *In Kliprivier she was dropped off at a bus-like structure. We left after*
> *we dropped her off. I did not see her again. I thus deny that I abducted her*
> *as I was under the impression that I was only helping a friend.*

David's version is almost identical. He confirms living with his brother and that Carrington arrived to pick up Carel on an unknown date 'during 1999'. These words, 'during 1999', will become the subject of much dispute further down the line.

David offers the court his explanation:

> *I had nothing better to do and accompanied them. We were informed*
> *that he [Carrington] was fetching a person from hospital to take her to*
> *her uncle's place in Kliprivier. He arrived in a kombi and we travelled to*
> *Vereeniging. At the hospital I got out to help him take out a wheelchair.*
> *Carel remained inside the kombi.*
>
> *At the hospital the nurses showed us to a female person and helped us*
> *to put her into the wheelchair. They spoke in their language and seemed*
> *content to help her out. She was released and I helped to push her to the*
> *kombi.*
>
> *I did not wear any doctor's uniform or pretend to be a medical assistant*
> *or doctor. During the trip to Kliprivier I didn't notice anything strange*
> *that one may say could be interpreted that she was taken without her*
> *consent. I constantly believed I was only helping out.*

David also talks about the bus and that after they had dropped her off, they never heard about the matter again. But he adds new detail, such as who performed what duties at the hospital and that the nurses allegedly helped settle the patient into the wheelchair.

In his bail application, David goes slightly further than his brother – himself a father of five – by attaching letters from his church and an organisation called Wings for Life, a school for children with special needs. The letters claim his 10-year-old son is autistic and his 12-year-old daughter is battling with emotional issues. Keeping him in jail, it's argued, will be deeply traumatic for both.

David is the younger brother and is still a policeman. He raises questions about whether a case of murder can ever be proved by the state given that, according to the confession, Betty died of shock. David picks up on the fact that no body has been found and suggests that the truth about what happened to Betty will never be known.

The information Carel and David provide in their bail applications will be used against them during the trial, and, working behind the scenes, Broodryk makes sure Kowlas sees to it that their affidavits are read into the court record once the brothers have been properly warned of the consequences. He wants Carel and David to be bound to their explanations of what happened at the hospital and to the date they have given.

• • •

Carrington goes on the attack immediately. One of the first things he does in his bail application is deny the authenticity of the confession, which he stands accused of writing.

Like the Ranger brothers, he stays clear of the witness stand and applies for bail through a lengthy affidavit. Testifying this early in the case would open him up to cross-examination, with everything he says becoming evidence in the trial. More than likely, he would be forced to give a detailed version. Instead, he tries to knock the state's case.

Unlike the Ranger brothers, he doesn't try to explain anything mentioned in the letter – at least not yet. His lawyers, Boesman van der Westhuizen and Sog van Eck, are both former policemen and know the system inside out. With their help, Carrington issues a blanket denial.

I have been advised, but certainly cannot confirm that what has been styled a 'confession letter' by the media is being attributed to me. I had sight of this document and place in dispute the authenticity thereof.

Carrington paints a picture of himself as a family man, with no plans to live as a fugitive or to abandon everything he 'holds dear'. He argues that if he hasn't fled in 13 years, why would he do so now? The state has already countered this, pointing out that the discovery of the confession a few weeks previously marked the start of the investigation and that until that moment, the secret was safe.

But Carrington maintains he would 'rather die than leave South Africa', and reminds the court that his passport has been surrendered. He talks about his children, explaining that he has joint custody of his nine-year-old daughter from a failed marriage (his second) and a 14-month-old son with his current wife, Anel. His third child, another son, is due to arrive in about four months' time.

Carrington speaks about his father, Harold, who lives in KwaZulu-Natal, and his sister Belinda, who left the country but has since returned. He doesn't mention his mother, Beulah, who died in 2004. His affidavit also describes his new business, *Naked Motoring*.

Carrington goes as far as giving a breakdown of his monthly expenses, trying to illustrate a typical family life: R10 000 for rent, R5 000 maintenance to his ex-wife, R2 000 in medical aid premiums, R4 000 to cover phone bills and R3 000 a month on 'groceries and general'.

While his closest friends and co-accused have made him out to be a criminal, Carrington presents himself as a responsible father, a businessman and the victim of a false accusation linked to his past. He offers R7 500 for bail and begins an anxious wait to see what the court will make of his application and the case against him.

35.

Before Magistrate Vincent Ratshibvumo can deliver his ruling on the issue of bail, another surprise awaits Carrington Laughton. It is another ghost from the past, ushered in by his ex-wife Jayne, a fine arts graduate he met at a tobacco shop in Sandton City.

Carrington enjoyed an occasional cigar, accompanied by a glass of whisky or wine. He was a regular at JJ Cale, a small family-owned tobacconist above the cinemas selling cigarettes, lighters and other trinkets.

Jayne was working behind the counter and met Carrington in late 2000, not long after the Cranks investigation and his brief romance with the restaurant owner's daughter Monique. It was also not long after his first wife, Candice, had tried to kill herself. The following year, Carrington took Jayne to Thailand and proposed, and a few months later, in March 2002, they were married and she was pregnant. By the end of that year their daughter was born.

Sometime during 2001, at the height of their romance, Carrington handed Jayne a white envelope and asked her to keep it safe. She remembers him telling her that it was his insurance policy against Eric Neeteson-Lemkes, who had hired his company to investigate the thefts at Cranks but was apparently refusing to pay. Jayne wasn't told much about the envelope, except that it contained photographs that could be used against Eric should there ever be a need.

The photographs – there were 32 of them – showed a woman in a white long-sleeved T-shirt and black skirt kneeling against a wall, her knees buried in what appears to be thick grass or straw. Her hands are handcuffed, and by the end of the series of photographs, she is lying face down with a bloodstain across her back. Her clothes resemble the uniforms worn by waitresses at Cranks.

Even to an inexperienced eye, the photographs look fake, doctored. The dark bruise around the woman's left eye is clearly not real, nor the blood and her face contains no trace of the fear or terror that would be associated with such a kidnapping.

What seems to have happened is that the scene was staged and a different face was superimposed onto the body later. Ruth Mncube recognised her face in the photographs but said she had never posed for them. She said Monique had a Polaroid camera and took photographs of many of the staff members.

The envelope that Jayne received bore the words:

> The company who did the work on the original polaroids is called Disk Express & the chaps name is Gunther. They are in Parktown in Eaton Road (?). The client is Commercial Services. The photos in the envelope were not used. The face attached to the pics was taken from the colour photo-copy.

Why these Polaroids matter is because the confession mentions them.

> During the investigation Monique told her father all sorts of stories about a woman called RUTH MNCUBE, whom he believes is dead. RUTH is very much alive and well and all the photos to prove this are in an envelope marked 'Ruth'.

Jayne never looked inside the envelope. She remembers being told that the photographs could be used against Eric if he didn't leave Carrington alone, and she simply took his word for it. She asked her stepfather to lock it away in his safe.

But Jayne and Carrington's marriage ended fairly quickly and by 2005 they were separated. A 'long and acrimonious' divorce began and with it a bitter legal fight over maintenance. In 2007, Jayne turned to the courts to secure a protection order against Carrington, whom she accused of 'harassing, threatening, intimidating and verbally abusing' her.

And yet, despite the protection order and whatever led up to it, Carrington and Jayne shared joint custody of their daughter and, many years later, Jayne describes him as a 'great father'. She also refused to hand over to police any of the letters he had written to his daughter. The detectives wanted them for handwriting analysis – to compare the handwriting to the confession – but Jayne was not prepared to break her daughter's trust. In court, when asked how many letters Carrington had written to Jayne while they were a couple, she estimates it was over a hundred.

• • •

For 11 years the white envelope remained locked away inside the safe. Aside from some of the photographs sticking to each other, they were well preserved.

Jayne hears about Carrington's arrest on 11 June 2012. Her ex-husband has made five court appearances by then and news of the case has broken. The radio report she catches states that the father of her daughter is facing a murder charge, relating to a woman who worked at Cranks restaurant. The first thing she thinks of is the envelope at her stepfather's house. She wonders whether it has anything to do with the case.

That same day, a Monday, she drives to her parents' house and asks them to take the envelope out of the safe. Jayne sits on their bed and opens it, anxious about what it contains. The photographs tumble out. She catches a glimpse of the handcuffed woman in the white top and immediately stuffs them back inside. She doesn't want to see any more.

The following day, Jayne takes the envelope to work and calls lawyer Marius du Toit for advice. She is agonising over whether to surrender them to the police and risk incriminating her ex-husband. Her daughter is too young to understand all this but she loves her father. Giving the photographs to the men trying to put Carrington in jail for life feels like a betrayal of them both. She's also unsure about whether she is now some-how implicated in the crime.

Du Toit looks at the situation through the cold, pragmatic lens of the law and advises Jayne to hand over the envelope. He puts in a call to a well-known prosecutor and former head of the Scorpions in Gauteng, Gerrie Nel. It doesn't take Nel long to establish that Herman Broodryk – an old friend and colleague – is in charge of the case and a handover is arranged via a senior policeman who is not involved in the Ketani investigation.

Two days after the photographs are retrieved from the safe, their existence emerges in court, and the bail proceedings are delayed when Broodryk himself submits a surprise affidavit asking for more time to process new evidence that may prove crucial to the case.

If this confession is fake, as Carrington claims, whoever is behind it would have had to have known about the photographs and the envelope. For the prosecutors, it's another lucky break. Jayne is also able to identify her ex-husband's signature and handwriting.

While all this is happening, the police detectives return to Conway's old house on Leo Street and speak to Werner. The chef is angry that despite all the promises, nobody ever returned to fix the concrete in the driveway. The opening still looks like a grave, with a long, narrow mound of soil marking its location. But the detectives haven't come to apologise, nor to fill in the concrete. They want to come back and open the grave up a second time.

36.

By the time Dirk Booysen and Cornelius van Rensburg arrive in Kenilworth on the afternoon of 25 June 2012, the search for a body has been abandoned and the mystery of the empty grave solved. But Herman Broodryk is still holding out for some kind of proof that Betty Ketani's body was once buried at 21A Leo Street.

Booysen and Van Rensburg are from the police's Crime Scene Investigation (CSI) unit and are in charge of exhuming the grave. Broodryk is prepared to prosecute without a body, but he's trying hard to avoid it.

Junior prosecutors joke among themselves that directors at Broodryk's level help themselves to all the 'slam dunk' cases – the ones with a nice clear fingerprint or an accused's confession in the docket – while leaving the difficult ones for them. But by going after Betty Ketani's killers, Broodryk has taken on what he will call the toughest case of his career.

He will lie awake in bed going over legal strategy, trying to make all the different pieces fit together. He will spend days consulting witnesses and chopping through a jungle of state bureaucracy to secure the best possible experts. Throughout the investigation and trial, Broodryk will feel like he's hanging on by the tips of his fingernails, never certain whether he and Kowlas have enough evidence to secure a guilty verdict.

The trial will consume him like he never imagined. It will see him second-guess himself, lead him deep into conspiracy theories and force him to spend the long trips to and from the court in Palm Ridge turning the case over like a Rubik's cube. The trial will also be part of a difficult period in his life, filled with medical problems and emergencies. On at least one afternoon he will be driven to hospital, his shirt unbuttoned, his face pale and drenched in cold sweat.

But Broodryk will push through, determined to finish what he started. He will be demanding on his team, sending Kowlas to the Eastern Cape and communicating so many instructions through her that she will eventually pick up a new nickname: 'Colonel'.

As a young state advocate, Broodryk entered a legal system that was very different to the one that exists today. The gallows in Pretoria cast a dark shadow across courtrooms. Some of the most basic rights, such as an accused being entitled to a copy of the police docket, simply didn't exist back then. It wasn't unheard of for a trial to last an hour and half.

Some prosecutors and judges were tormented by the idea of condemning an accused to death. For Broodryk, there was no such agony, just a duty to make sure he made no mistakes. He prosecuted 40 death-row cases, half of which ended with the accused being executed. Years later, in a magazine interview, he was asked whether he ever dreamt of those men. He said he didn't. Only the victims of those crimes came to him in his dreams.

The death penalty was declared unconstitutional and abolished in South Africa soon after apartheid fell, but the standards Broodryk set himself during his formative years, along with his experience as a policeman, drive him to get the Ketani investigation back on course. To make sure there are no more mistakes.

Broodryk wants the grave to be exhumed again, and this time he wants it done right. He and the detectives know the scene has been disturbed and that the body was apparently moved, some of the contents of the grave thrown away at a landfill site and the rest into a fast-flowing river. But there is always the outside chance of finding a small bone, even if it's just a fragment. There are about 200 bones in an adult skeleton, some no bigger than a pebble, and it's not inconceivable that one or two broke off and were left behind. The first team may have missed a piece of clothing, a lock of hair or maybe some old blood in the soil. DNA has a habit of lingering.

According to Conway and Paul, the grave was robbed in 2004 by those trying to hide evidence and turned upside down in the process. Eight years later, it was dug up by civilians – hired by JB and Doc – on two separate days. But if they find something new now, and that evidence provides a forensic link, it will greatly bolster a case balancing precariously on circumstantial evidence.

With the help of two workers, Booysen and Van Rensburg open up the grave and begin to dig. They take samples of the soil first at half a metre and then at a full metre down. The next samples are drawn from 1.2 metres, 1.3 metres and eventually at 1.4 metres. They pack these samples – eight in total – into little white paper envelopes, label them and line them up on the concrete near the hole in the ground.

By the time it had been moved, Betty's body would have been at an advanced stage of decomposition. After being lowered into the grave and covered with soil and cement, the breaking-down process – autolysis – would have started almost immediately. Acids and gases would have formed inside the corpse; maggots would have moved in, breaking down soft tissue. Writing about the atrocities committed in the former Yugoslavia in the 1990s and the mass graves that were unearthed there, author Christian Jennings describes what is left behind during this process as a 'brownish-white adhesive gloop' that stinks and is commonly called 'grave wax'. As the body dries up, it leaves behind a 'corpse decomposition island', a dark, fertile stain in the ground.

Both Conway and Paul speak about a soapy substance still being present when Betty's body was dug up and transferred into plastic bags. To mask the smell, they poured a mixture of petrol and household disinfectant into the opening.

Booysen and Van Rensburg aren't aware of this, but by taking soil samples they are hoping to find traces of the decomposition island. Detective Sono looks on as Booysen, dressed in jeans and a camouflage jacket, his hands hidden inside thick gloves, jumps in and out of the hole, taking measurements or spraying down the sides with a hosepipe. Unlike those before them, the pair is trying to document as much of the excavation as possible. A pile of debris is rising next to the grave opening. The scraping of the shovels can be heard from the street.

The dry soil is full of bricks, plastic bags, chunks of concrete and other rubbish. The officers keep digging, hoping to find the tiniest clue, a trace that indicates this is the spot where Betty's body lay. Conway has now been brought to the scene and has confirmed the exact location.

Booysen isolates a pile of curious-looking cement pieces that have caught his eye. One by one, he checks each chunk before either tossing it back inside the hole or placing it near the soil samples. One piece makes it inside an evidence bag.

A braid of hair is bagged, along with a fragment of wool from either a knitted jersey or hat. If any of these items belonged to Betty, they may just contain a crumb of DNA, the policemen hope. At worse, her family may be able to identify something.

Booysen and Van Rensburg take photographs of the soil layers inside the grave, aiming the camera at the walls. The interesting patterns there may reveal something. They are trying everything.

It's already evening when the excavation is complete, with the soil packed back inside the hole. All the samples will be taken and locked away until a decision is made on how to proceed and which samples, if any, should be sent for tests. The detectives have no way of knowing yet whether anything of value has been found.

37.

Magistrate Vincent Ratshibvumo's judgment, handed down in late June, deals with the law surrounding Carrington's, Carel's and David's bail applications, but it also does something remarkable: it meanders deep into the human tragedy of the Betty Ketani murder.

After so many years of being invisible, of being nothing more than a reference number floating about in the police archival system, Betty and her children find themselves at the centre of Ratshibvumo's deliberations.

The facts before him clearly affect the magistrate and lead him to use creative metaphors and words seldom encountered in court judgments, especially at the bail stage. Words like 'shocking', 'astonishing' and 'ruthless'.

From the time she vanished and until the confession emerged from under the carpet, the police failed Betty and her family. Magistrate Ratshibvumo isn't about to.

He summarises the case, describing Betty's abduction and murder and comparing it to a mosaic or a picture puzzle that reveals itself only once all the pieces are in their correct places. To the prosecutors' delight, Ratshibvumo highlights that both the Ranger brothers have placed themselves at a potential crime scene, admitting to helping Carrington escort a woman from a hospital. Carel and David may have denied that they were abducting the patient, claiming it was an innocent errand, but the magistrate has a different opinion:

> The two brothers portray a picture of brainless men who operated like robots in taking out the deceased from the hospital, with no idea of where she was being taken to, no knowledge of the reason thereof and still expect a helpless patient who was admitted to a hospital to refuse to go with them. She was just left at a 'bus-like structure' for reasons none of them know … To imagine that the brothers would behave in such a strange way in circumstances they should be asking applicant no. 1 [Carrington] more

questions and maybe arresting him, but they just behaved like good mes-
sengers to him, though they were taking a patient to her death, is shocking
and unbelievable that such can be done by people paid by the taxpayers
with the sole purpose of protecting people like the deceased.

Carrington, Carel and David all claimed they had made no attempt to
flee over the past 13 years and have no intentions of doing so now. But
Ratshibvumo finds that the men were neither suspects nor accused before
a court.

The period of 13 years that lapsed rather depicts a different picture; that of
ruthless men who care little about human life. They did nothing to search
and find out if the woman they removed from this earth had any kids.
Had they investigated, they would have found that she had three kids.
They did nothing to find out as to who is looking after the said three kids
now that they took the only bread winner they had, who is giving them
shelter, do they have food when Christmas approaches and clothes when
winter comes? How is life when they have no person they can call 'mom'
and they have no grave to look at as the resting place of their mother or
ancestor?

Jayne's fears and those expressed by Paul are not ignored by the court.
Neither is the fact that victims mentioned in the confession have been
found and confirm what happened to them. Ratshibvumo feels the state's
case has been bolstered through the confessions given by two of the
accused. Carrington's decision not to present a version, but merely to dispute whether the letter is real, appears to have worked against him.

The signature on [the confession] appears to have more similarities than
differences with the one on Exhibit A, being an affidavit signed by the
applicant.

With unusual force, the magistrate sweeps aside claims that the state's case
is weak.

*When one looks at the case presented by the state, the court can only won-
der as to why the applicants even thought of applying for bail.*

With these words, Ratshibvumo denies bail to Carrington and the Ranger
brothers, sending them back down to the cells.

Over the months that follow, Carrington will appeal the ruling at a
higher court but will lose. He will then bring a fresh bail application based
on what he considers to be new facts. Court transcripts and judgments will
be obtained, pages upon pages of affidavits drawn up, but Ratshibvumo's
ruling will stand firm. At some point there is talk of the bail battle going all
the way to the Supreme Court of Appeal in Bloemfontein, but this fizzles
out over time.

• • •

For Doc, JB, Sono and Pretorius, the bail judgment is a victory. It is recognition that they were not crazy to have poured so much time and effort
into investigating the strange letters under the carpet. Their own families
thought they were mad, but now a court has vindicated them. Not only
that, but a magistrate has commented on the strength of the case they put
together.

*Just like a fly trapped in a spider's web, which gets more entangled the
harder it kicks, the more information the applicants [Carrington, Carel
and David] give, they make the case for the state even stronger or the
picture puzzle even clearer.*

Ratshibvumo's judgment is a mandate to continue investigating. To go
out and find the remainder of the puzzle pieces. The team has new ideas,
like going back to the bus to search for old bloodstains. They need to find
a handwriting specialist and take more statements. There's the forensic
avenue, with the samples gathered at the latest excavation. With the magistrate's words filling their sails, it feels like the case is just beginning to get
interesting. Like the best part is about to start.

Sono, the most junior member of the team and the investigating officer, is particularly excited. He's sunk so many hours into this case, often staying away from home until late at night. He has helped search farms for witnesses, pounded the streets with Pretorius and JB trying to find Carrington, visited hotels and hospitals, and worked late compiling profiles of suspects. Part of what kept him going was the hope of being noticed, of being recognised by his commanders. He also wanted very much to impress his family. To show them what he is capable of.

But in a case full of twists and turns, one of the most unexpected surprises has been reserved for Sono and his colleagues.

38.

Detectives Sono and Pretorius approached Herman Broodryk because they considered him the best prosecutor for the job. They wanted someone senior. Someone who would take a personal interest in the Ketani mystery. What they miscalculated was just how interested Broodryk would become in their case.

From the moment he came on board, he went straight into damage-control mode. Broodryk was jumping moves and looking ahead to the trial. He wanted to straighten out as much of the evidence as possible before he got there.

In the beginning, the chain of evidence was not an issue, but now it is starting to present a major problem. The more he and Kowlas explore the police work, the more they realise how much has gone wrong.

Broodryk wants some of the statements redone. He's haunted by how the original confession was handled and that is still hasn't seen the inside of a forensic lab. The first excavation of the grave was a disaster; they still don't have a decent sample of Carrington's handwriting; and one of the pieces of paper found under the carpet (the one with 'Do not throw away' written across it) has gone missing. On top of it all, a suspect in the case has not only been shown a crucial piece of evidence, but has been allowed to make himself a copy of the typed confession. Broodryk is anxious that other information about the case could leak through the Yeoville detectives.

He knows what needs to be done and, once the bail applications are completed, he instructs Kowlas to get him a new investigating officer.

'The case was too big for them,' Kowlas explains.

Broodryk wants someone more experienced. A detective he can trust and who can take a decent statement or hold his own on the witness stand. He wants a Piet Byleveld or someone like him.

Kowlas calls Sono's superiors but is met with reluctance from them to reassign the case. It has already bounced between jurisdictions (the crime was not committed in Yeoville so the docket had to be transferred) and Sono's bosses don't want to pull the case away from him. But Broodryk refuses to hear excuses and Kowlas is forced to go higher up the chain of command. After a while, the orders are given and the docket is briefly handed over to a more senior detective in the cluster and then to a Hawks detective stationed at Johannesburg Organised Crime.

This all happens without Sono's knowledge. The original docket is locked away in the office of his commander while he's carrying around a duplicate. So handing it over to a new detective is a simple matter. When Sono is eventually told, he is devastated. He feels angry and betrayed.

> If they came to me and said: 'Sono, there is a lot of work here and you have other dockets at the station, it's going to affect them', maybe I would have understood. Or if they came to me and said: 'We think this case needs a highly experienced officer', I would have understood. But the way it came across was that we were simply not competent enough to deal with it. Why not make us work with [the new investigator] so we can gain experience? Not just shut us out.

In his mind, Sono and his colleagues have done all the hard work. They spent weeks running down leads, preparing the paperwork and eventually arresting the suspects. There were nights when it was almost midnight and, instead of being with his partner, Sono was still at work.

> You spend most of your [free] hours, you are fighting at home, but you tell yourself that she will understand some day … You go all out and do everything and at the end of the day a person comes and takes it away.

This was supposed to be his big break. His moment to shine. Sono wanted it to be known inside the police that there is a crew in Yeoville solving difficult cases. But now, some new hotshot detective from the Hawks will step in and get all the credit.

Sono meets his replacement at the end of June and is forced to drive him out to Eardley's farm, where the CSI team is preparing to tear up the floor of the railway bus and search for old bloodstains. Captain Gerhard van Wyk introduces himself to everyone on site and informs them that he is taking over the case.

39.

After Betty Ketani was buried at his house, Conway began retreating from the world around him. He says he began to shut out the people who cared most about him, building a wall between himself and his wife Blanche and his children, Sheldon and Toni. When his father died, he had done much the same, closing himself off from his mother and her new boyfriend.

Conway began ploughing all of his time into his work, coming home to bath or eat and then disappearing again on some late-night assignment for Carrington. If there was no work from Laughton, he would simply stay at the factory until the early hours of the morning or go get 'shit-faced' at some pub.

He began to drink heavily. He tried to drown the demons with Cane or whatever else he could get his hands on. At the pubs, he 'looked for shit' or chased women, knowing full well how much it would hurt Blanche if she found out. When she did suspect something, he piled on the denials. His marriage was breaking down and at one point he went as far as to ask for Carrington's advice on divorce. He consulted a lawyer and moved out for a while. He even got himself a 'promise' tattoo for another woman, but in the end he returned to his wife to patch things up.

Blanche was his 'personal saint' and although she couldn't keep him out of trouble, she seemed to always forgive him. When he was in court, Blanche took time off work to be there. She arrived early in the mornings and sat quietly in the back row. She visited him in jail and brought the entire family for special occasions. She was proud of his art, eagerly showing off his latest creation: a pencil drawing of a cupid with all of their names hidden in the background patterns, or his soap sculptures, some of which he traded for cigarettes and other prison supplies. What Conway was able to do with a bar of soap and a wooden splinter broken off a chair handle was extraordinary. He would transform a slimy green brick into a heart, a teddy bear, a pair of praying hands or some other miniature masterpiece.

He could carve out a lion or a rhino, even the face of someone famous. The detail was unbelievable, every scale of a snake's skin or the tiniest tooth in the mouth of a 3-D skull, all chiselled out as though under a magnifying glass.

But after 'the incident' (Conway can't bring himself to speak of a 'murder') and long before things came to a head, he began spending more and more time away from Blanche. He claims he would backpack through the Drakensburg for days, eating tinned food and climbing dangerous rock faces. He disappeared into the bush or rode his motorbike – a Honda Fireblade named Eve – at kamikaze speeds. He tried extreme sports.

> You find things to do that push you to the edge because you are trying to fill something that is gone. And it doesn't matter what you throw in it, I can tell you, it doesn't matter what you throw in it, it's useless. It's a bottomless pit.

When Shama Marshall asked him whether everything was okay, he lied and told her it was just work. He told his family even less. He didn't want them to pry. He thought that by staying away, he was protecting them.

Conway never wrestled with thoughts of suicide, but admits he got to a point where he was prepared not to wake up the following morning. He wanted to take out good insurance policies on his life, to provide for his family, but didn't have the money.

He also thought about telling someone his secret, but couldn't find the strength. Telling Blanche was never an option. She had forgiven so much but he was sure that this was something she would never understand or accept.

As for the police, Conway claims he had no idea who to approach. Almost every day, he says, brought news of another corrupt police officer, some new spy scandal at crime intelligence or policemen arrested for being on the payroll of underworld figures. He believed Carrington was far too well connected and would find out. He didn't know how deep it all went and who was involved.

Conway says he thought about it hundreds of times; about going to a police station, a court, a priest, someone. But he could never settle the question of *who* he should turn to. He didn't know how to do it without incriminating himself in the murder. He keeps referring to his 'rough' and 'messed-up' childhood, but in reality he was probably too scared to take responsibility given the consequences.

In Dostoevsky's words, Conway was prepared to stand alone up on a cliff top, on a square foot of rock, with the wind howling around him for eternity, rather than jump into the swirling abyss below. He convinced himself that he was protecting his family and would take his secret to the grave.

Paul claimed the same thing: that no matter what he tried, no matter how many policemen he spoke to, nothing was ever done. He described trying to set up a meeting with a detective at a McDonald's but claims that he was double-crossed. He says on the day of the meeting, he called the detective but gave him a description of another car parked outside. Moments later, policemen surrounded that car and Paul decided to flee. He also claimed that during other encounters with police he was threatened and warned to keep quiet.

And yet, while both spoke about distancing themselves from Carrington after Betty was killed, of no longer trusting Laughton, Conway and Paul remained friends with him until they were all arrested. Photographs show them at nudist parties, birthday bashes and weddings where they all celebrated together. In May 2012, the month of the arrests, Carrington, Paul and Dirk were still working together on *Naked Motoring*.

Carrington's version is that they never feared him because he was never the criminal mastermind they made him out to be. He called them liars who conspired against him. Conway explained it differently:

You keep your friends close, but your enemies even closer.

. . .

In the 13 years since Betty's murder, Conway may have struggled to face his family but he claims he tried to make up for it in other ways. He began overcompensating at work by getting to know the workers and trying to assist them. He would help them secure extra shifts if they needed cash.

He got to know some of the workers by name and learned a little about their lives and history. In his mind, he connected Betty to the staff at his factory. The link was more than likely based on crass comparisons of race and class, but it made sense to him. He says he carried thoughts of her with him every day.

> I'd push my family one side and say, 'You know what, I'm going to go and help this person', thinking that if I keep doing right by everybody, then maybe God will forgive me.

Conway says that even after Betty's body was exhumed and disposed of, he felt a connection to the woman who had lay buried in his garden for so long. When he looked out the window and prayed, the woman was, in a strange way, the only other being or spirit that shared his secret. No one else around him knew. He was in a house surrounded by his family, but completely alone with his secret. He says he thought about her family and her children:

> I can't even begin to imagine how hard it is for kids to grow up without parents. I mean, I lost my dad when I was young and that still messes me up, even now. The hurt doesn't go away. It doesn't become easier. I wish I could have stopped ... I wish I could have stopped it. I couldn't stop it at the time. I don't think I was strong enough.
>
> What would I say to them now? The only thing I could do is literally get on my hands and knees and beg them for forgiveness and understanding. I would ask them for forgiveness. I can't say anything else. Anything else doesn't really matter.

Conway's relationship with his own children suffered too. He says he missed out on most of their childhood. He has fragmented memories, but most of it has been lost. Torn. Swallowed up by those black holes.

> It kills you. My life came to an end. My life went to shit that night that this incident took place. The love and the laughter and everything you get afterwards, it's fake, it's not real, it's pretend.

I used to spend as much time as humanly possible away from my family because I disappointed them.

• • •

In early 2004, the year the Marshalls went on that Durban holiday and Shama started noticing a change in Conway, a decision was taken to exhume Betty Ketani's grave and hide the evidence. There are three conflicting versions of how this came to pass.

Conway says it was Carrington who ordered him to dig up the grave, asking Paul to help him. Paul recalls Conway asking him to do some 'gardening' while they were talking at a hotel near Heathrow airport, on their way back from Germany. They had had a fight in Hamburg, he claims, and were making up, so Paul agreed to help. He has no memory of there being any mention of opening a grave. Later, Paul says, Carrington asked him whether Conway had spoken to him, confirming for him where the instruction originated.

Carrington denies all of it, saying he issued no such orders and had nothing to do with the crime or the exhumation.

What Conway and Paul agree on is that on the day after they arrived back in South Africa, which would have been 19 February 2004, they met to 'move the begonias'.

40.

Conway's and Paul's words in court paint the scenes of how Betty Ketani's body was dug up, carried off in thick plastic bags and disposed of at two different locations. The descriptions are vivid and haunting, transporting those listening to them to the side of the grave as delicate neck bones crumble in Paul's hands and to the bank of a river where Betty's skull is broken with a hammer and hurled into the fast-flowing water.

Both Paul and Conway pull Carrington, and other people, into the narrative, implicating them in trying to conceal the murder. Those overseas are yet to break their silence but Carrington says that his friends are lying.

Paul begins the story, saying that on the day after they got back from their Germany trip, he arrived at Conway's house to find his friend nervous and shaky. Conway looked like he was about to burst into tears.

'I'm in big trouble,' Paul remembers Conway saying as he leads him through the house, past the bedroom where the confession is lying hidden under the carpet and towards the garden behind the garage. The moment they get there, Paul understands.

Conway has already started digging and his shovel has exposed part of a human skull, with some hair clearly visible. Having expected to spend the day digging up a flower bed, Paul is horrified by what he sees and lashes out at Conway, demanding to know how he landed up in this mess. Through his anger, though, he also feels sorry for Conway.

Paul begins to simmer down. He is offered some coffee and told about what, according to Conway, happened at Eardley's farm shortly after Betty was taken from the hospital.

Conway tells him he received a call from Carrington and was asked to go and deal with the situation at the farm. When Conway arrived, he says he saw a man – later alleged to be Mark Lister – pacing up and down, testing the ground with a shovel, trying to decide where to dig. Nearby, a white minibus was parked. On the floor, in between its seats, lay a body wrapped in a sheet.

According to Conway, Monique was also there and the two of them got into a fight over where the grave should be dug. Conway lost his temper, shouting that Mark Eardley's parents were murdered on the farm and he would not allow them to bury a body there. Under pressure to provide an alternative, he escorts the minibus back to his house in Kenilworth.

The vehicle is reversed into the driveway and, with Blanche at work and the children at school, Conway began to dig a hole behind the garage. He remembers digging most of the grave himself and claims it was Monique's idea to fill it with cement. She and Mark then drove away in the minibus, leaving Conway to finish the job. By the time he was done, the ground was level, his tools were washed and everything was back to normal. Nobody would suspect a thing, he thought.

Conway can't remember who lowered the body into the grave and suspects it was done while he was out buying cement. He also says he never saw the person's face – only the sheet she was wrapped in and some of her hair. Based on her height and build, he assumed it was the same person he left to die near the R59 highway.

With the grave covered over, Conway went inside the house to wait for his family to return. He says he lay down on the floor and cried.

. . .

When they meet to move the body, Paul and Conway realise that breaking open the cement cannot be done with any of the tools they have at their disposal. Conway runs out to buy an industrial-sized hammer, but that doesn't work either. They drive off to hire a jackhammer, which proves more effective.

Conway says he was freaked out by the idea of exhuming the grave. The prospect brings back childhood memories of horror movies, with half-decomposing zombies rising from the earth. But the memories that really torment him are those of how he held the woman as she was stabbed and how, in a moment of madness, he offered to bury her body in his own garden. For over four years he has lived with the consequences of that decision. Looking out at his little garden … at Betty's tomb. He's emotional and it's decided that Paul will handle the remains inside the grave.

Conway and Paul claim that at some point Carrington arrived to help, bringing a trailer, thick refuse bags and gloves. Paul remembers Conway admitting that he had panicked and filled the grave with too much concrete. Now they're paying the price and it's taking a lot of effort to break open the sarcophagus.

The hole is growing. Eventually it will be so deep that Paul – who stands 1.8 metres tall – will be able to climb inside it. One of the first body parts to be removed is the skull. It's close to the surface and Conway isn't prepared to touch it. When Paul picks up the skull, it comes away easily from the rest of the skeleton. There is no flesh on the face, only the hair he saw when he first encountered Conway and the grave. Paul gives a chilling account of the moment.

> When I lifted the skull up, the neck bones just sort of crumbled. They fell away. They were broken, the neck bones. I had to scrape them up with the gloves and put them in the packet.

The grave is being pulverised by the jackhammer. As they work their way down, layer by layer, Paul realises that the body was left in a kind of upright, foetal position. He can make out the ribs and the arms, later the pelvis and the legs. He also notices the remains of what appears to be a diaper. Conway also mentions the diaper.

Much of the body was encased in quick-drying cement. Through decomposition, what's been left behind is some kind of a 'grease', which helps separate the bones from the concrete, leaving behind hollow cavities. Conway compares it to sticking a finger into a bar of soft soap and then removing it.

At some point, Paul says, the skeleton breaks in half. Not all of the tissue is gone and some of it clings onto the bones. Paul scoops what he can into the rubbish bags.

The stench is unbearable. To fight it, they mix the disinfectant Jeyes Fluid with petrol and pour it into the grave.

. . .

Hot summer days in Johannesburg are often extinguished by cool evening showers accompanied by the cannon fire of thunder rolling across the sky. Late in the afternoon on the day the 'begonias' are being moved, it starts to rain. The sun has set and the grave has been hollowed out, its putrescent contents sitting inside garbage bags, some of which have already been placed on top of the trailer parked inside Conway's garage. But time has run out and the rest will have to wait until morning. They can't dispose of the bags in the dark, especially now that it's raining.

Conway has lost all sense of time. Running on adrenalin, in full survival mode, he can't say whether they've been digging for an hour or all day. Everything around him faded into the background and all he has been thinking about was getting the job done without getting caught. Without his wife and children finding out.

Conway covers up the hole as well as the bags with tarpaulins. He packs everything away and locks both the garage and the back door of the house, making sure that nobody will venture there. His cover story is that he had to tear up some concrete to get to a blocked pipe. It's an old house and the lie is convenient. When he delivers it, he warns Blanche that there is Jeyes Fluid and petrol all over the place and asks her not to let the children out. His nose and throat are 'on fire' because of all the chemicals they used to mask the smell.

The grim project is on hold and Paul departs. He feels sick thinking about what they have done. He can still feel the skull in his hands and the sludge he had to scoop up with his fingers. He vomits inside his car.

> *I left it and went inside. Left the car, sick and all, closed up and went and got drunk. It helped.*

· · ·

The next morning, Paul says he has second thoughts. He gets cold feet and simply can't face the idea of going back to Conway's house to finish the job. Plus, there's puke inside his car that has been there all night. He and Conway speak on the phone and he is finally convinced to keep going. Conway picks him up and drives him back to Kenilworth.

Together they start loading the heavy bags onto the trailer. They say Carrington joins them as they work. The bags are separated, half containing mostly broken concrete and soil, the other full of human remains mixed with debris.

The atmosphere is tense and they argue about where to dispose of the bags. Aside from figuring out logistics, they aren't speaking much. Paul says that Carrington seems aggressive, not in a mood to discuss anything, eager to get on with it.

In the end, they cart the bags off to a nearby municipal dump a few kilometres from Conway's house, find a discreet spot up on a hillside and scatter some of the contents among the rubbish. Even if someone found out about the murder and knew exactly where to look for the remains of the body, it would be impossible to find any trace of it here. As the bags are emptied, whatever is inside them is lost in an ocean of waste.

Carrington and Paul drop Conway at home so that he can finish filling the grave while they tackle the remainder of the bags. The bags they have held back are those containing most of the bones and the decomposed body. Paul claims he and Carrington decide that these need to be thrown away somewhere safer. Paul's version is that Carrington came up with a place and they drove through to the bank of the Kliprivier. (Paul tried to return to the place later to give a more specific location, but there had been so much development in the area that he was never able to find it again.)

Paul remembers the river being swollen from the overnight rain, flowing quickly past them. He says they carry the bags to the water's edge, tip them upside down and begin emptying them into the river. Paul notices a problem.

> Carrington had put one of the bags in and the arm stayed floating on the water. It was like a waxy substance with some bones. It had fingers. It looked human. If someone downstream saw it they would know it was an arm.
>
> I said: 'We can't have that', and I took the skull and put it on the ground and smacked it with a small hammer.

Paul smashes the skull to make it less recognisable. When questioned about why he would have a hammer with him, especially if they were in Carrington's car, Paul claims that during those years he always carried a small toolkit with him because of an old car that constantly gave him trouble. Carrington uses this detail to try to expose Paul's story as a fabrication. He maintains he was not there on either of the days.

After the skull fragments are thrown into the water, Paul says he and Carrington take care of the rest of the evidence.

> All the other bags were unloaded. We could see them being taken away by the water. It was flowing very strongly.

What is left of Betty's body vanishes out of sight. The cement and soil had preserved her bones remarkably well for years. Like a fossil, her skeleton lay protected, hidden from extreme heat and moisture, deprived of oxygen, all factors that speed up decomposition and rob forensic scientists of clues. Had her bones been found any time during that period, nothing would have been easier than to extract some DNA from them and to identify her as the victim. Her family could have used the rest of the bones to give Betty a traditional funeral, to bring her spirit home to the Eastern Cape. Instead, whatever evidence of her life existed is gone, erased forever.

Her family and friends were right: Betty did not run off with a new boyfriend and abandon her children. Evidence is fast emerging that she was captured, interrogated, stabbed in the head, kidnapped a second time and, after what must have been a torturous death, was buried in a cube of concrete that would later be torn to pieces by the chisel of a jackhammer. And now, to complete her violent end, her bones have been strewn across a garbage dump and flung into a new watery grave.

· · ·

As soon as he takes over the Ketani case, Gerhard van Wyk, the new investigating officer, moves quickly to retrace some of the steps of the original team. On 10 July 2012, three weeks after the CSI team exhumes the grave, he arrives at the now familiar house on Leo Street in Kenilworth with his own excavation team.

After spending a year with Baltimore homicide unit, American journalist and author David Simon wrote that 'a victim is killed once but a crime scene can be murdered a thousand times'. In the last eight years, Betty's grave has been emptied and filled three times. Whatever evidence it contained has surely been lost. Opening it up again seems pointless. But Van Wyk has a new plan.

41.

Captain Gerhard van Wyk became a policeman not because of some romantic childhood dream, but because of an argument with his father. It was 1983 and he had just finished school with plans of becoming a forensic scientist. Everything appeared to be on track and, as a final step before carrying on with his studies, young Gerhard had an aptitude test lined up in Modderfontein.

He asked his father to drive him there from their home in Vereeniging. It was a long way to go, further than the distance between Johannesburg and Pretoria. Instead, his dad handed him the car keys and told him to find his own way there. This blew up into a fight that somehow ended with Gerhard threatening to abandon forensics and join the police force instead.

The threat backfired. His father was a police reservist and rather liked the idea. He picked up the phone and called the station commander in Vereeniging to arrange an interview for his son. Some 30 years later, the Ketani docket is handed to a balding, bespectacled detective who, quite by accident, landed up devoting his entire life to chasing criminals.

In those three decades, Van Wyk worked house robberies, firearms, hijackings and murders. He was one of the detectives who investigated a brutal spree of police killings in the late 1980s, when around a dozen officers were murdered in and around Johannesburg. He spent time at the now infamous Brixton Murder and Robbery Squad and led a provincial task team dealing with crimes relating to precious metals and endangered species. He worked with undercover units and side by side with intelligence operatives, and had been deeply involved with projects to stem the tide of illegal cars into South Africa.

Van Wyk knew Broodryk well and, as a provincial coordinator for undercover operations and traps, had spent years visiting his office to get authorisation forms signed off.

In his younger years, Van Wyk was athletic. He cycled and ran the Comrades Marathon. But by 2012, time has sculpted him into a middle-aged man who looks a little frazzled. He has a droll sense of humour and the aura of a detective who has seen just about as many murders as he can cope with.

Divorced, he lives in a small, neat townhouse on the West Rand that has the feel of a three-star hotel room. When he gets caught up in a case, he spends his nights and weekends working: consulting witnesses, delivering documents or using a friend's computer to send emails.

Van Wyk never had children of his own. His mother died when he was still in high school and his father, who didn't have much luck as a farmer and took a government job, died in 1997. Having lost touch with his sister, he channels much of his free time into police work.

He is meticulous and dedicated. His eyes light up with childish excitement when he makes what he considers to be a particularly smart move in an investigation. Speak to a lawyer, even one whose client is in jail because of Van Wyk, and he or she will describe him as a 'bulldog' who never stops running around gathering evidence.

'If my family fell victim to a crime, I'd feel good if Van Wyk showed up at my doorstep,' a lawyer who knows him and the Ketani case explains. 'He sits in court and listens and if something important is said, he's out the door …'

Van Wyk gets sucked into his cases. To him they are more than dockets on a desk. If a court witness has been brought in from another province but is left stranded due to a postponement, he spends hours of his free time trying to arrange accommodation. On occasion, he has had to settle hotel bills himself.

Broodryk and Kowlas are pleased to have Van Wyk on the case. In him they see an old-school detective who puts in the time and believes in doing legwork. The prosecutors like that Van Wyk is pedantic about details; in their eyes he is a perfectionist. Aside from taking new statements and following through on the new CSI tests on the bus, Van Wyk starts planning a new identity parade for early August. He's determined to cover all bases.

Early on in his investigation, Van Wyk is forced to speak to the old investigating team. Broodryk will later take a decision to cut them out of the trial, but at this stage Van Wyk is still trying to take statements from Sono and the others, find certain bits of evidence and get his head around how the first leg of the investigation unfolded.

For Sono, the betrayal is still raw and he is bitter at having lost what American detectives call a 'red ball' case. Doc's and JB's allegiances lie with Sono and his partner. Doc gives the new Hawks detective a rough time and many heated arguments erupt. Threats of arrest and subpoenas are flung about. The tension dilutes as time wears on, but will never fully wash away.

At about the same time, Gerhard Pretorius leaves Yeoville. He applies for and is granted a transfer to the sleepy streets of Meyerton, which is far closer to home and cuts out hours of travel each day. If Pretorius is holding a grudge about the Ketani case, he doesn't show it and gets on with patrolling the quiet neighbourhood. While he waits for a detective position to open, he gets back into a uniform and drives around dealing with complaints.

They may be embroiled in a cold war, but all the policemen know the truth that author David Simon found on the streets of Baltimore, that three things solve murders: evidence, witnesses and confessions. The holy trinity.

Van Wyk has confessions and some potential state witnesses but what he doesn't have nearly enough of is forensic evidence. And that's why he returns to Conway's old house to dig again. The crime scene has been lost, but he isn't about to wrap police tape around Werner's garage and place a night watchman on duty. What he is looking at now is an archaeological site.

42.

Gerhard van Wyk and the new team arrive early in the morning, park along the pavement on Leo Street and find what remains of the grave. Curious neighbours peer out of windows in the small block of flats across the road.

Captain Teunis Briers and Lieutenant Melanie Pienaar, both from the police's Victim Identification Centre (VIC), are accompanying Van Wyk and will be responsible for the dig. Briers takes charge and begins to set up.

The first time the grave was disturbed it was by those trying to conceal evidence. The second by JB and his hired workers. The third by the provincial CSI team. Now it's time for a special unit from the national office to have a go.

The VIC is led by a smart and ambitious commander, Brigadier Helena Ras. It was established in August 2011 to deal with an ever-increasing number of unidentified and missing people across South Africa, particularly victims of car and bus crashes, burnt or crushed beyond recognition. After its formation, the VIC began building its own database, gathering as much forensic evidence as it could from both the victims and the families of those reported missing. This included DNA samples, dental records, fingerprints and all other scraps of useful information. It didn't take long for the unit to become the custodian of thousands of samples, many relating to unsolved murders.

Helena Ras – or Leonie, as she is known – has almost 10 000 investigations behind her. She has studied in America, taking courses in everything from how the FBI analyses human hair to establishing contingency plans for attacks involving weapons of mass destruction. She's trained in bloodstain pattern analysis, crime scene reconstruction and disaster management, her work taking her across Africa – to Kenya, Zambia, the Democratic Republic of Congo – and to the far-flung tropical islands of the Maldives. All the travel has not only opened her eyes to what the rest of the world is doing in the realm of forensics but has sharpened her diplomatic and bureaucratic skills, which she puts to good use.

A petite woman who wears bright jewellery and has manicured nails, Leonie Ras describes the work her unit carries out in one sentence: 'We are the voice of the dead.'

To lead the exhumation of the grave in Kenilworth on 10 July 2012, Ras assigns one of her top members. Teunis Briers specialises in facial reconstruction, mostly from skulls, and has been involved in some high-profile serial-killer investigations. He also assisted the work of the Truth and Reconciliation Commission.

Melanie Pienaar doesn't have the same depth of experience in the police, but is a trained entomologist whose skills include determining time of death in murder cases or inquests. She has also been involved in fingerprint and post-mortem analysis at the VIC. One of Pienaar's duties on this day will be to keep notes.

On a printed-out form, Pienaar writes down the time of their arrival – 8am – fills in a few standard details and indicates the last time Betty Ketani was seen alive: '1999/05/20'. Thirteen years and counting. Pienaar then draws a rough sketch of the site, showing the rectangular shape of the garage. She plots the coffin-sized grave at 11 metres from the gate leading into the street and shows how close it is to the opposite corner: just 30 centimetres from the boundary wall. Back in 1999, the grave would have fallen behind the garage. The rest of the form will be filled in as they work.

Briers spends most days in his office, so being out in the field is a pleasant change of scenery. Digging up the grave is hard labour, but he's enjoying it, happy not to be at a computer or a laboratory desk. It feels good to let his muscles work. The soil has been compressed into the hole, but the shovel is cutting through it readily enough.

Briers knows the odds are against them. They can't even say they are searching for the proverbial needle in a haystack because they don't know whether the needle is actually in the haystack. All they have is the 'hay': a lot of soil in a hole deep enough for a man to disappear in.

Bones tend to absorb colouring from the soil around them and even from clothes, which means they will be difficult to spot and may look like tiny, dirty twigs. Briers is prepared to look carefully and to dig slowly.

The fact that he is not the first person to try to find a trace of Betty Ketani's body is what makes this particular job interesting. Exciting even. He's been looking forward to it for days. Briers likes the idea of being called in to try to rescue a case. He also likes the fact that the person they are searching for has a name. That it's not a John or Jane Doe, some missing person marked down as 'unknown'. While he was at university, one of his favourite professors would always make a point of referring by name to the people whose bones were being examined. It made the experience more personal. Like they were dealing with human beings, not merely hard formations of proteins and minerals.

'There was a real person attached to it,' Briers says. 'She had a life and a history. There was a family connected to it. With those thoughts in mind, I said to myself: "I'm going to find Betty."'

• • •

By now the grave is essentially a rubbish dump. A mix of chunks of concrete, rocks, bricks, plastic and other waste that has been tossed like a salad. All of these are discarded and moved out of the way. What Teunis Briers is looking for is far smaller.

He and Pienaar have set up a tripod in the centre of the garage, with a large plastic sieve dangling from where the three bars meet. It's a large contraption that takes up the entire width of the garage and stands taller than Captain Van Wyk, who is helping sift through the soil, dressed casually in jeans and takkies. Two wooden sieves, with finer nets, are used to examine the contents of the same soil more closely. Three scoops of the shovel are processed at a time. The soil that has been examined is piled up on the side.

Tired of the intrusions, Werner Nortjé had put up a fight against this excavation but Captain Van Wyk changed his mind with a court-sanctioned search warrant. Regardless, Shama Marshall plays the perfect hostess and prepares lunch for the police officers, anticipating a long day of hard labour. The soil flows through the sieves. The work is repetitive and requires a great deal of concentration. The first hour is uneventful, the nets catching nothing even remotely interesting. The second hour is much the same. But then, early into the third hour, Briers spots something that grabs his attention.

Van Wyk steps away to make a phone call. He dials the number for Claudia Bisso, a forensic anthropologist and archaeologist from Argentina, currently working in South Africa. He's briefed her about the case and tells her about Briers's discovery. He says they think it might be bones. He asks if she would be willing to drive out – just like Dr Holland did when the fragments of tortoise shell were discovered – to give them her opinion. Bisso takes down the address and, in her thick, playful accent, tells Van Wyk to hang on.

Bisso's career over the past 20 years can be summed up in the same words Leonie Ras uses to describe her unit. Bisso truly is the voice of the dead. Since 2005, she has been working with the National Prosecuting Authority, exhuming the remains of anti-apartheid fighters murdered during the struggle. Working with Madeleine Fullard and others at the NPA's Missing Persons' Task Team, she has brought closure to dozens of families by opening up graves identified by security police assassins like Eugene de Kock during and after the TRC hearings. As with so many other countries around the globe that have experienced atrocities, finding the bodies of apartheid victims and allowing their families to bury their loved ones is a crucial part of healing. In some countries, along with bringing those responsible to justice, it can be the difference between peace and further bloodshed.

Bisso would know. She has worked in some of the darkest corners of the globe, where the wounds of war or genocide continue to fester. Places like Chad, Sierra Leone, the Sudan, Bosnia and Kosovo.

Bosnia – which will play an unexpected but integral role in the Betty Ketani case – was one of six republics of the former Yugoslavia, which broke apart in the last decade of the twentieth century. Along with Croatia and Kosovo, Bosnia suffered through the horrors of ethnic cleansing, as the conflict between the Serbs, Croats and the Muslims burned for three years, claiming the lives of an estimated 100 000 men, women and children.

There were mass civilian casualties and suffering on all sides, but the largest massacre of the Bosnian War happened outside the industrial town of Srebrenica in July 1995. At the hands of the Bosnian Serb forces, around 8 000 Muslim (Bosniak) men and boys were captured, separated into groups and, in the sweltering heat, executed with Kalashnikov machine guns. Their bodies were dumped in five primary mass graves near the execution sites, but were later dug up with construction vehicles and hidden in dozens of smaller, secondary mass graves scattered around a 30-kilometre radius. By the time the shadow of war began to pass, forensic investigators were finding the body parts of a single victim in three or four different graves, kilometres apart.

Author Christian Jennings writes that by some calculations, to identify the dead, scientists in Bosnia had to sort through more than a million bones concealed across 500 square kilometres of countryside. This quest, accomplished through DNA fingerprinting, became known as 'the world's greatest forensic puzzle'.

Claudia Bisso had heard about the Betty Ketani case and was more than familiar with the concept of robbed or disturbed graves. She had worked in the Balkans, examining sites where hundreds of people had been slaughtered. She had encountered situations where bodies were buried among bags of rubbish. In such cases, the position of the bones became meaningless and recording their exact location inside the graves was pointless. What counted was the forensic work that followed.

When Bisso arrives at Conway's old house, she is pleasantly surprised by what is unfolding there. She has witnessed how badly some crime scenes are handled but this archaeological dig, in her mind, is the 'perfect approach' to a difficult situation.

One of Bisso's key forensic skills is osteology, which, simply put, makes her a bones specialist. If anyone can determine whether the three small objects Briers has discovered – tiny yellowish sticks, no longer than five or six centimetres each – are in fact bones, it's Bisso. She finds them lying in one of the smaller wooden sieves and picks them up to take a look.

43.

Experience has taught Claudia Bisso that when corpses are hurriedly relocated from grave to grave, the hands and feet often break off and are left behind. Both are collections of short, narrow bones – phalanges, metatarsals, metacarpals – and tight clutches of even smaller, nugget-shaped bones in the wrists and ankles. Combined, there are more than a hundred little bones in the hands and feet.

Through decomposition, the muscles, ligaments and tendons that hold the bones together wither away or disappear, leaving little or nothing to prevent them from crumbling apart. Just like Paul Toft-Nielsen describes. Finding these small bones afterwards can be difficult if not impossible. Even trained archaeologists can easily miss them.

Nobody at the excavation site knows exactly where inside the grave the three objects came from. No one can tell on which shovel load they rode up to the surface or where they were hiding. One by one, they simply got caught in the nets and revealed themselves to Captain Teunis Briers.

All three are stained a dirty yellow-brown and caked in dry soil. Two are shaped like miniature clubs, with one end broader than the other. The third looks like it belongs in a ball-and-socket joint, with a round tip and a wide, flat surface on the opposite side. In the palm of a hand, they weigh virtually nothing, a gram or two at most. They are smaller than a cigarette and look delicate, brittle even, despite having probably been dug up and thrown back into the ground several times.

The curious objects give off a strong, unpleasant smell. To an inexperienced eye, they look nothing like bones. The shapes are odd and the colour is all wrong. Even if one of the earlier teams had found them, they likely would have paid no attention to them.

Bones have a fibreglass-like structure and protect DNA long after a body has decomposed. Teeth and strong bones such as the femur (upper leg bone) and the tibia and fibula (lower leg bones) lock away DNA securely.

Softer bones, which aren't designed to bear weight, are more spongy and less dense, making them weaker bodyguards against the elements, which destroy cells and the DNA inside.

A single strand, or molecule, of DNA is said to be one-tenth of one-billionth of a centimetre wide. Inside its now famous double-helix structure lies the biological code, the blueprint, that creates diversity in all living species.

The instructions contained in tightly coiled bundles of DNA, called chromosomes, are passed down the generations from parent to child. Each parent contributes to the genetic make-up – the genome – of his or her offspring and is forever linked through a series of unique sequences.

The study of DNA has reached such an advanced stage that scientists are able to map out these sequences at various locations – markers – along the threads and use them to mathematically compare samples, working with the principles of probabilities. DNA profiling has become an immensely powerful and accurate forensic tool with a myriad of applications, from throwing rapists in jail or freeing wrongly convicted suspects to unravelling ancestry.

. . .

Claudia Bisso needs no more than a few seconds to study the little yellow sticks Teunis Briers has found. She knows exactly what they are. Not only can she say with absolute certainty that they are bones, but she can also identify them. Two are definitely foot bones, probably the fourth and fifth metatarsals, the bones that run across the arch of the foot. The third is a phalange (the actual digit) but could be from either a foot or a hand – it's tough to say without running tests. (Later, it will emerge that all of the bones are in fact from the feet.)

Bisso is intrigued and decides to hang around a little longer. As the afternoon wears on, she watches as three more bones, similar to the first group, emerge from the grave.

'They always forget the hands and feet,' Bisso testifies in court months later.

According to the police officers on site, the six bones are split equally and sealed in two evidence bags. There's no one to photograph them, so Briers packs them away.

An official police photographer did come by early in the morning but spent less than 15 minutes at the scene, took just three photographs and ran off to the next call. He claimed to have been covering the jurisdictions of more than 10 police stations and couldn't spare the time, despite being booked in advance.

Dirk Booysen, who excavated the grave before Briers, heard that Bisso was there and dropped by to show her a sample he had collected, which turned out to be of no importance. While there, he photographed the first three bones that had been found and had, by then, been placed on top of two see-through evidence bags. Dirk Booysen left before the other bones surfaced.

It seems insignificant at the time, but a failure to photograph all six bones together at the scene will cause major problems down the line. During the trial, Broodryk will have to defend the chain of evidence, relying on witnesses and photographs taken later. But for now, all that matters is that bones have been found. Even if they don't contain usable DNA, they can always be identified as human by an expert such as Claudia Bisso. For Broodryk that's hugely significant. If the letter says Betty Ketani was buried at a certain location and human bones are found there, the statistical probability of the confession being genuine multiplies tenfold. In his cross-examination of the accused, he will be able to ask them to explain what human bones are doing at that specific location.

In the microscopic world of DNA, the more markers – known as *loci* – scientists can isolate, map out and compare, the more accurate the findings become. The odds of unrelated people sharing the precise codes at up to 15 specific points on a particular chromosome become so unlikely they can be ruled out. The reverse, of course, applies. Simply put, it's like comparing two cars. If the only information one has is that both cars are red, the comparison is weak. But if both red cars have a white leather interior, 17-inch alloy wheels with V-shaped spokes, a broken left tail light, an identical scratch on the front bumper, a sun-warped dashboard and a spider-web-shaped crack in the right-hand rear-view mirror, the match becomes all but impossible to dispute. The more unique identifiers there are, the more astronomical the values become.

Similarly, Broodryk's mission with this case is to find as many pieces of circumstantial evidence as possible – the bones included – line them up and convince a court that the odds of them all leading to a false conviction are virtually zero. The defence will come from a different angle, casting doubt on each piece of evidence and asking whether it can be proved, *beyond a reasonable doubt*, that the accused in the dock are guilty. In a murder case, even an outside chance of a mistake should lead to an acquittal, it will be argued. But all that is years away.

Late in the afternoon, Briers and his team pack up their equipment, close up the grave and head home. Captain Teunis Briers had set out to find Betty Ketani. Driving out of Kenilworth, he's convinced the mission has been accomplished.

. . .

Determined to start the investigation afresh, Gerhard van Wyk puts together a second identity parade a few weeks after the bones are found. It turns out to be a waste of time, but after what happened in Kenilworth, any lead seems worth following.

At about the same time, he asks a colleague to drive down to the Eastern Cape to find Betty's children and to take samples of their DNA. Warrant Officer Hlengani Malele is handed three swab kits per child – which to him resemble 'lollipops' – and heads down to Queenstown. It's a simple errand and as soon as he tracks down Thulani, Bulelwa and Lusanda, he escorts them to a local hospital, where a doctor sweeps up some DNA from inside their cheeks.

Some of these samples, along with three of the bones found inside the grave, are sent to the police's forensic laboratory in Pretoria. Scientists there are asked to pull DNA from the bones believed to be Betty Ketani's and to compare it to the samples taken from her children. In scientific terms: a reversed parental determination.

Leonie Ras knows there are going to be problems. The bones are small, spongy and degraded, having spent over a decade in the ground. Extracting DNA from them is going to be exceptionally difficult. Scientists in Pretoria are going to have to grind the bones down to a powder while searching for DNA molecules. The process will destroy the bones and if the search is unsuccessful, the samples will be lost. There will be no second chances. For that very reason, she and her team decide to split up the six bones.

In early 2005, Ras was part of an Interpol mission dispatched to the coral beaches of the Maldives, an archipelago of postcard-perfect islands out in the warm Indian Ocean. Following a colossal undersea earthquake and the deadly tsunami it triggered, Ras and the team she was working with, which included prominent Johannesburg-based forensic patholo-gist Hendrik Scholtz, exhumed graves on several islands in order to obtain DNA samples. These were fed into a global database that would help iden-tify those who perished.

Incidentally, the Boxing Day tsunami was also the first time the International Commission on Missing Persons (ICMP), a forensic labora-tory situated in Bosnia and Herzegovina, was called to apply its forensic skills to one of the worst natural disasters in history. Until then, the centre's focus was squarely on the Balkans.

The ICMP was born out of a need to stabilise and bring peace to the region. The process included identifying the dead and returning remains to families. What the ICMP was doing was a fusion of science and human rights.

The pioneers of the ICMP developed a cost-effective way to process mass amounts of DNA samples. The new model worked on the same principle as a car-manufacturing plant, where each employee had just one function to perform before the DNA sample moved along to the next station. It was a conveyor belt which relied on an unbreakable chain of custody, which involved piles of forms, countless signatures and even photographs.

In order to depoliticise the ICMP's work, DNA samples were bar-coded and all names discarded right at the start. Those carrying out laboratory tests had no idea whether the sample before them belonged to a Serb, a Croat or a Bosnian Muslim. It was the idea of 'blind justice', which served the ICMP well when it came to criminal cases.

The ICMP honed its skills and perfected its system. Its success was unprecedented and soon the tap of foreign funding opened up. During this time, the ICMP also became a world leader in extracting DNA from degraded bone samples, where victims had been buried in mass graves for years. Where others failed, ICMP employees – working in laboratories as sterile as hospital operating theatres – were able to pluck out DNA molecules from pockets hidden deep inside old, crumbling bones.

Less than a year after the Boxing Day tsunami, Hurricane Katrina smashed into the Bahamas, tearing through New Orleans, claiming almost 2 000 lives. Once again, the ICMP was called in to help. Then came the *Princess of the Stars* ferry disaster in the Philippines in 2008, where more than 700 passengers and crew went missing after the boat capsized. By that stage, the ICMP was already working with Interpol and had opened its doors to the organisation's member states.

In the years that followed, the ICMP assisted with DNA profiling in Libya, Columbia and Chile, where mass graves were being discovered but many victims remained unaccounted for. The centre also dispatched teams to Iraq, where hundreds of thousands of people had disappeared during Saddam Hussein's regime and the subsequent wars.

But one of the most fascinating and least reported on cases the ICMP took on was the identification of a group of soldiers from Norway who died during the Second World War in a Russian pine forest outside what is now St Petersburg but was then Leningrad. The soldiers, from a special battalion, clashed with Russian forces in June 1944 and, despite putting up a fierce fight, were overrun.

In his book on the Balkan wars and the ICMP, Christian Jennings describes this battle, writing that the bodies of the Norwegian soldiers lay where they fell for 60 years. Their remains were discovered by historians only in 2003 and 2005 and were sent to the ICMP for identification. For six decades, the bodies lay under the pine trees and on the edge of a lake. They froze and thawed each year, lying in the open air, and some were partially eaten by foxes and wolves. The acidic soil damaged the abandoned skeletons. And yet, ICMP technicians were able to generate 29 DNA reports and see to it that, despite the difficult politics surrounding Norway's decision to side with Germany in the war, those remains were returned to their families.

The Maldives mission provided the context for Leonie Ras's introduction to the work of the ICMP, and over the years she became familiar with the organisation that had been able to extract DNA from the skeletal remains of Second World War soldiers. She knew that just because Betty Ketani's bones had spent a decade underground didn't mean they had nothing to offer.

Ras decides to send half of the bones to the local laboratories and, if that fails, to send the remainder overseas to an organisation with more advanced technology and refined skills. Ras knows what they are up against and wants to keep her options open.

Sending the bones abroad will be expensive – especially with the exchange rate – and will require comparative quotations and top-level approval. Ras wants to wait and see what will happen in Pretoria before she begins approaching the international laboratories. What she has going for her is that South Africa is under the Interpol umbrella and turning to an organisation such as the ICMP, which too is connected to the global policing body, makes the process logical. But the costs are daunting and nothing like this has been done before by the South African Police Service (SAPS).

Leonie Ras's fears are soon confirmed. The local laboratory has done its best to extract nuclear DNA – the most reliable for identification purposes – but has failed. The bones are too old and contain too little DNA.

In late July 2012, two extractions were attempted on the first bone, which had been sent to the forensic laboratory in Arcadia, Pretoria. Both attempts failed to produce any DNA samples. In August, two more extractions were done by the same laboratory on a second bone. Although this time a tiny trace of DNA was indeed found, it was insufficient for technicians to map out enough markers for comparisons. Those who worked on the extractions say it was like trying to 'get DNA out of a mummy'.

The laboratory was left with a single bone and some crumbs. But with an inflow of three to four thousand samples each month, including cases from Durban, no further time could be devoted to this case and the last bone was filed away.

With two of the six bones destroyed, and zero results, the time comes to approach the world experts.

44.

By the next court date, in August 2012, plans are well under way to send the remaining three bones found in Kenilworth overseas. Prosecutor Namika Kowlas speaks about it in open court. The development buys the state time and the case is rolled over until November, when a trial date is likely to be set.

Carrington Laughton is still trying, without success, to get the bail judgment overturned. During August, Betty's sister Lilly dies in Queenstown, leaving Thulani, Bulelwa and Lusanda to fend for themselves.

At the same time, Gerhard van Wyk's investigation continues. He starts to cast his net wider, looking into Eric Neeteson-Lemkes's money and how it left the country after Cranks closed down. For a man who ran restaurants for a living, he accumulated a great deal of wealth. Van Wyk gathers information about Eric's daughter Monique and about Mark Lister, who is now a policeman in Australia. He tries to contact Sandor Egyed, who has been very quiet and remains well out of reach. He manages to speak to him on the telephone and sends a letter to Interpol to ask that officers in New Zealand take a statement, but never hears back from them. Sandor's family in Johannesburg is not helpful.

The detective takes a statement from Mark Eardley, whose farm is central to the case but who offers nothing of value to the investigation. Van Wyk sorts through existing affidavits and examines cellphone records and old bank statements. He starts pulling together all the exhibits. Despite assurances that the records are gone, he returns to Kopanong Hospital to manually search for them, but doesn't find what he's looking for. For days he is referred from one storeroom to another. The books that cover 1999 are no longer there.

Van Wyk drives from police station to police station in the area where Betty was stabbed. At one of them, in Kliprivier, he discovers a promising entry while flipping through an old 1999 occurrence book. The date is 20 May, the day Betty was last seen alive. The handwritten entry, made by a constable at the charge office, notes that they received a call from a nurse at the Randvaal Clinic at 8.30pm that night. The officer recorded that the nurse asked them to summon an ambulance and called back later to report that the paramedics had taken almost two hours to arrive.

'The lady, Mrs Mphuthi, phoned us again, asking that we must make a report concerning the matter for her,' the entry states. It's signed at 10.40pm.

The fact that Captain Van Wyk is able to find such records 13 years later is in itself a small miracle. Each station has its own filing systems and going through them takes days. The Kliprivier entry leads him to the Randvaal family clinic, where there is a faint glimmer of hope: one of the staff members who worked there during 1999 seems to remember a woman being brought in and that an ambulance was summoned to take her to hospital. This is the kind of break JB and the others had hoped for.

The nurse, whose name turns out to be Monafu Mphuting, tells Van Wyk that she would only have called the police if a patient's injuries suggested some kind of a criminal act: a hit-and-run car accident, an assault, a stabbing or a shooting. During 1999, the Randvaal Clinic operated at nights but did not have an emergency ward and referred all serious cases to nearby hospitals. She says they were used to summoning ambulances and did not call the police each time this was required.

Van Wyk shows Mphuting a photograph of Betty Ketani but the elderly nurse doesn't recognise the face. She has no recollection of the actual incident. Too many years have passed and she hasn't worked at the clinic in over ten years. Her only explanation for why the police entry claims she had asked for an ambulance is that the inexperienced constable must have got some of the facts wrong. Van Wyk traces the officer who made the entry but is not able to interview him. The man who scribbled in the police book was subsequently involved in a serious car accident and has suffered brain damage.

The police entry is an astonishing piece of circumstantial evidence. Van Wyk can't imagine that it's not linked to the Ketani murder, even if there is no way to prove it. The Randvaal Clinic is less than ten kilometres from the Blockhouse and possibly even closer to where Betty was stabbed. On the very night she disappears, 20 May, a nurse there calls the police to report a patient being brought in and requiring an ambulance. The nurse says she would only have called the police if she suspected a crime. In Van Wyk's mind, this is the missing link that explains how Betty got to Kopanong Hospital.

Captain Van Wyk also burrows through inquest dockets and missing-persons reports dating back to mid-1999 and which cover the geographical area. He finds nothing and, like his predecessors, looks into the hiring of the wheelchair mentioned in the confession. Even though it has moved, he finds the company, which confirms it used to hire out wheelchairs, but has kept no records of transactions dating that far back.

The case has so many layers, so many characters and events, so many unexplored avenues and conflicting versions, that following up everything is impossible. Van Wyk is going to have to be selective about which leads he chases.

Any negotiations there are to be had with Conway, Paul and Dirk will be handled by Broodryk and Kowlas, who have made a tactical decision to wait for the lawyers to come to them. It's a wait-and-see approach, a legal game of chicken that Van Wyk has nothing to do with. Broodryk will have to authorise any potential plea bargains. The policeman also has no control over the DNA tests that are being done. As the investigating officer, his role is to make sure the process gets under way and then to receive the results.

What Van Wyk can get stuck into, however, is the handwriting analysis. Carrington has refused to hand over any samples of his signature or handwriting. Carrington has every right not to cooperate with the investigation and there is nothing they can do to, quite literally, force his hand. It's up to Van Wyk to get creative and find a sample without the accused's permission.

He begins by plucking the low-hanging fruit: Carrington's passport is in police custody and bears his signature. The accused also signed a warning statement soon after his arrest, leaving eight signatures across a 16-page form. Then there's his bail application, also signed. Not all of these are immediately available, but Van Wyk knows he can get them.

After Carrington's ex-wife Jayne came forward with the photographs, new samples emerged. There's the white envelope with some writing on the back. Jayne also gave the police a batch of divorce papers from 2007, which are initialled and signed. There's even a signed delivery note relating to a television the two of them bought in 2003.

When Van Wyk asks Jayne for the letters Carrington wrote to his daughter, she refuses. She's trapped between trying to help the police solve a murder and a nine-year-old daughter who adores her father. Jayne has gone as far as she is prepared to.

All these samples are usable, but there is a problem: they are not old enough. The confession was written and signed in September 1999, and the earliest trace of Carrington's signature or handwriting so far is from 2003. So Van Wyk digs deeper, and eventually tracks down the original forms Carrington and his then wife Candice signed while opening up their company, C&C Commercial Services. This was done in 1998 and 1999 with the Companies and Intellectual Property Commission. The time frame is spot on.

All these and other documents (the 'Howson & Straker' letter found under the carpet, a copy of the 'Do not throw away' page, the paper containing names and phone numbers, and a laminated photograph with the word 'Ruth' on it) are gathered and submitted to the police's forensic science laboratory. Conway Brown's handwriting samples – which were given voluntarily – are also handed over for purposes of elimination. The file lands on the desk of Warrant Officer Magendree Govindsamy, from the Questioned Document Unit. She's fairly new to the unit, but the report she produces will be critical. Proving that Carrington wrote the confession is the heart of the state's case.

• • •

Leonie Ras shops around and sources quotations from three different international laboratories. The ICMP turns out to be the cheapest and arrangements are made to fly the bones over. To avoid any further complications with the chain of evidence, there are discussions about sending Gerhard van Wyk to Bosnia to deliver the package personally, but there are already so many costs to cover and a cheaper option is simply to courier the bones across.

What Ras is about to do has never been attempted before. It will be the first time that the ICMP will be asked to analyse samples for a criminal investigation by the South African police. Never before has a South African court, hearing a murder trial, had to consider forensic evidence from the ICMP, which has different systems to local laboratories. More likely than not, someone from the commission will have to fly to South Africa to testify, which will in itself carry further expenses and complications. As soon as two countries start working together, there are diplomatic protocols and all kinds of red tape, with the reputation of both nations at stake. For law-enforcement agencies, working outside the borders of your own country is a bureaucratic affair.

But the challenge is exciting. After investigating thousands of cases, this is a chance for Ras and her unit to try something new. Something ground-breaking. If the ICMP cracks this case, how many others will it be able to help the SAPS solve? How many slumbering dockets – some much older than the Ketani case – will be reopened with fresh DNA evidence? Ras already has two cases in mind, one dating back to 1989.

She thus includes samples from these two unsolved and unrelated cases in the Ketani package destined for Bosnia. In both investigations, which were registered at about the same time as the Ketani case, the local laboratory had tried but failed to extract DNA.

The first case involves a skeleton found buried under a swimming pool at a house in Bedfordview, in eastern Johannesburg. The discovery was made by a group of construction workers hired to remove the pool. What lay beneath was a human skeleton and the remains of clothing and jewellery, which suggest the victim was a woman. Detectives investigating the case determined that the swimming pool was installed in 1989, which meant they had a murder on their hands that was at least 23 years old.

The owners of the house from those years had long since left South Africa and the victim's identity remained a mystery. The case was stone cold.

In the second case, there's even less to go on. The police have been left to investigate the remains of a child's body found in Diepkloof, Soweto, in June 2012.

Given that this case involves a child, this murder can't be as old as the others. If a DNA profile is established, the detectives may well be able to track down the victim's family. Given the likelihood that the murderer was a relative or a friend living in the same area, the Soweto case has every chance of being solved.

Ras writes up short summaries of each of these cases in a letter that will accompany the samples. She describes the Betty Ketani case, taking care to mention the fact that the body had been partially buried in cement 'to prevent any leakage of odours and to avoid any detection'. She describes how the grave was opened and how the concrete was broken up into pieces, along with the body inside. She feels it's important to give the ICMP an idea of the kind of conditions to which the bones were exposed as well as an overview of the case.

Because there is already a criminal case under way, she asks the commission to prioritise their examination of the bones believed to be Betty Ketani's. She requests that nuclear DNA tests be carried out, but states that if this is not possible, then mitochondrial DNA profiling – DNA passed down only via the maternal line and thus less reliable, especially when trying to prove murder in a court of law – will have to suffice.

The three bones set aside by Briers while exhuming Betty's grave are repackaged into a little white paper envelope and transferred from a big evidence bag into a smaller one. This is to prevent the bones from moving around in transit and to avoid any further damage. The DNA samples taken from Betty's children are placed into separate envelopes.

The Bedfordview and Soweto samples contain teeth and fragments of the femur, which are more likely to contain DNA. They too are packed away and sealed. Once the package is ready, it's dispatched on its 8 000-kilometre journey to Sarajevo, the capital of Bosnia and Herzegovina. If the ICMP was able to profile the DNA of dead Second World War soldiers, perhaps its scientists can solve a much smaller puzzle and bring closure to a Queenstown family still waiting patiently for it.

45.

Going into October, Herman Broodryk feels like he and Kowlas have managed to steer the Ketani investigation back on track. Despite all odds, bones have been found in Kenilworth, the handwriting analysis is under way and their new investigating officer is hard at work, unearthing gems like the old occurrence-book entry.

Their hard work has also been met with a good dose of luck. The Ranger brothers surprised them with those bail statements, Carrington's ex-wife came forward with the Polaroids and Paul's claims of intimidation helped keep his oldest friend behind bars and away from the investigation.

Broodryk likes to compare his cases to the tides of an ocean. He imagines evidence flowing in and out as the investigation unfolds, sometimes changing the entire landscape of the case. In his mind this is an inevitable, rhythmic cycle that forces prosecutors to adjust their strategy. This case is turning out to be a perfect example.

But sometimes, the sea that Broodryk describes in court is stirred up by a sudden change of wind.

On 6 October 2012, Captain Alan Fagan commits suicide.

The man who interviewed Carrington in those golden hours before his arrest slips away without warning or explanation. For Sono, Pretorius, JB and Doc, this is a personal tragedy. For Broodryk, Kowlas and Van Wyk, it is a serious setback.

Two months ago, Fagan signed an affidavit detailing his conversation with Carrington Laughton. Knowing how important this was to the case, Van Wyk oversaw the process personally, signing as the commissioner of oaths. The team was relying on Fagan to come to court to defend his notes. They wanted him to explain all the admissions he says Carrington made to him during their discussion. Without Fagan on the witness stand, his statement will remain locked inside the docket, supressed by laws governing hearsay evidence.

The statement contains startling confessions about the Cranks investigation and Betty Ketani's kidnapping. It also offers a possible explanation for how those who took her from hospital found out where she was. In Fagan's statement, he said that he was told that hospital staff called Monique Neeteson-Lemkes – Ketani's boss – after she was brought in. There is so much more detail … from allegations that the Ranger brothers were paid for their involvement to explanations for why people like Themba Tshabalala were tortured.

But now, Fagan's statement will remain sealed, to be discussed only in passing during the trial. Broodryk will push the boundaries as far as he can to flag that the version Carrington gave to Fagan and what he testifies to in court are completely different.

Carrington will retaliate by claiming that Fagan was part of the wider plot to set him up. He will present no proof of this, nor will he be able to explain why Fagan would potentially jeopardise a 22-year career by lying about their interview, but he will maintain that he never said the things reflected in the notes and the affidavit.

Carrington will further claim that Fagan was not writing down anything while they spoke and that he denied knowing anything about any of the events he was being questioned about. With Fagan not there to answer for himself, this will prove to be another puzzle piece that will never fall into place.

46.

One of the last cars Carrington Laughton got to test-drive before his arrest was a R2-million Aston Martin V8 Vantage S. For a man who saw supercars as 'spoils of success' and 'objects of desire', and who wrote for his online magazine, *Naked Motoring*, about how people looked in 'awe and envy' when he was behind the wheel of these 'masterpieces', the experience must have been a thrill. And of course Aston Martin is also the signature car of James Bond, with whom Carrington had a lifelong fascination.

Naked Motoring was an amateur product, compiled by Carrington and his friends. It was laid out in PDF format, available for download on the website. The articles contained spelling mistakes and most played on predictable stereotypes and clichés. Sandor Egyed, one of Carrington's closest friends, appeared in the letters section. 'I'm your biggest fan,' he is quoted as saying, adding that he had bought his wife a car based on one of the reviews.

The videos were shaky, crammed with the same adjectives used to describe different cars. Whether it was a 'ballistically fast' Audi or a 'grand' Bentley, most of the luxury cars were 'exquisite', full of 'beauty, grace and poise'. The low-quality camerawork was accompanied by dramatic music, from Mozart's *Requiem* to Patrick Cassidy and Hans Zimmer's 'Vide Cor Meum', a piece composed for the film *Hannibal*.

Naked Motoring, which started in 2011, also had a venomous edge to it, with Carrington and his crew dismissing cars as 'horrible' and 'hateful' or calling a potential owner of a hybrid 'Mr Stupid'. When Mercedes-Benz refused to give them vehicles to test-drive, Carrington used his editor's slot to hurl abuse at the company and its representatives, saying that they must 'live and die by their stupid, childish and idiotic decisions'. He called on readers who drove Mercs to submit their private cars for test drives and then, in his April 2012 edition, had one of his writers throw together an April Fool's story about the company launching a line of raunchy lingerie.

Paul claims it had all been done in jest.

'For me, it was always a kind of fun thing to do. I never received payment. It was humour, which is what I think people enjoyed about it,' he explained.

One of the more unusual reviews that Carrington got to do was of a 12-ton armoured Paramount Marauder. Strapped into the driver's seat of this war machine and speaking directly into the camera, he declared with excitement that it could 'take a landmine and suck it up like a peppermint'. In another video, this time of a supercar, Carrington counts along with the speedometer: '190 ... 200 ... 210 ... 220 ... hard on the brakes ...'

Paul may have considered writing for *Naked Motoring* a hobby, but for Laughton, the magazine was a serious venture. When reviewing the blue Aston Martin Vantage S, Carrington revealed a fascination with the imaginary spy world in which James Bond existed. Those close to him say it was an obsession that consumed the private detective. He wrote:

> *Ever since I was old enough to watch movies I was intrigued by the antics and adventures of the immortal James Bond, MI-6 agent 007, licensed to kill and all that other good stuff. Maybe he is responsible for me pursuing a career in the intelligence sector fighting crime and/or evil for 20 years before venturing into motoring journalism ... makes you wonder! I loved the toys and gadgets that Bond used. He always had the coolest stuff ... Many of you will remember his DB5 fitted with rockets, machine guns, oil slick sprays, retractable armour plating and the legendary ejector seat. Now that was a really nice car ...*

Paul would also reveal that shortly before their arrest, he and Carrington crashed an Aston Martin. It's not clear whether it was the same one Carrington wrote about, but Paul said he stopped writing reviews for the magazine after the accident.

Paul was behind the wheel as they attempted a 'high-speed pass' in front of a camera. He claims they were arguing but Carrington says Paul was looking at the speedometer and wasn't paying attention to the road. Laughton says he decided to take responsibility for the crash, by claiming he was behind the wheel, because Paul should not have been driving in the first place and neither of them wanted to pay for the damages. In court,

Carrington tried to explain why he did not consider this fraud, while Broodryk kept insisting that it was.

If Paul was reckless enough to crash an Aston Martin and Dirk nervously stumbled through his reviews (hopelessly out of his league in the cabin of a BMW 5-series), Carrington appeared to be in control of whatever car he was passing judgment on. Unlike his friends, he had grown into a confident man who could quote South Africa's Constitution in his reviews and speak comfortably about the history of the models he was driving.

Not long before he was arrested, Carrington spoke on Radio 702 about the naturist federation he was leading. He quoted international statistics and ventured into whether naturism could help grow South Africa's tourism, and by how much. He spoke about being comfortable in his own skin and how he had introduced his family, including his young son, to the lifestyle, which he called a 'family sport'. By that stage he had been into naturism for around eight years and answered criticism about racial dynamics and whether there was anything sexual about the lifestyle. He came across as a knowledgeable advocate for his hobby. His other hobbies included scuba-diving.

Carrington had a talent for appearing to be in control of any situation. He came across as organised and precise, at ease with any topic of conversation, from how car windows are tinted to laws governing the formation of companies. Every day during his trial he brought with him his black leather briefcase and lever-arch files full of notes and documents. He wrote down everything – creating a complete transcript of the trial in his own handwriting – and would reach into his space case for highlighters to mark important sections in the documents spread out in front of him. Unlike the Ranger brothers, who often arrived for court in knitted jerseys or tired-looking jackets, Carrington always wore a suit and tie, his crisp shirt cuffs fastened with cufflinks. (When his father, Harold, attended court, he too was dressed up, in an outdated but smart three-piece suit.)

Everything around him in the dock had a place, from the pack of baby wet wipes to a cushion with the words 'hope', 'joy' and 'love' embroidered in shiny sequins. No state witness would be released from cross-examination unless Carrington was confident that his defence team had done what he expected. He wrote countless notes, which he passed to his lawyers. When a court orderly wanted to lock the accused in the holding cells during a tea or lunch break, he would loudly declare that it was an opportune moment for a cigarette break – as if the decision had been his to begin with.

Inside prison, he wrote formal letters to managers of various prison sections requesting family visits or everyday items such as an MP3 player, a television or an extension cord. Each handwritten letter was neatly laid out with his name and prison number in the top right-hand corner, the date, the full name of the intended recipient, a subject line and a 'Dear Sir'. Each letter ended with the words 'Yours Faithfully, Carrington Laughton'.

But behind what Broodryk will call the 'veneer' of Carrington's public life lay a very different reality. Carrington had a criminal record and had been arrested and released at least four times; his second wife had taken out a restraining order against him; a fight he had with a landlord in Sharonlea over rent ended in legal action, during which allegations were made that he forged a document; his name had appeared on the front page of a major newspaper over allegations that he was a con man; his father was helping him financially; and the kind of cars he drove in real life were certainly not the kind that filled the pages of his online magazine.

Carrington's life never stood still for long, his roots always shallow enough to be pulled up and planted elsewhere. He attended seven schools; lived in 11 different houses; was married three times; and was capable of building and breaking down businesses, which ranged from private investigations to manufacturing car parts.

Conway aspired to be like Carrington. He was mesmerised by the cars, cigars and gadgets, the overseas trips and his friend's spy world. But on Carrington's cellphone, which was analysed by the police, sat messages about overdue medical bills, an outstanding TV licence fee and an SMS from his father confirming that he would be paid back R500.

Laughton's criminal record for perjury surfaced in court. He confirmed he pleaded guilty and received a one-year suspended sentence and a fine of R3 000. The case was heard in the Randburg Magistrate's Court but there is no trace of a case file by the time of his arrest in 2012. What the investigators are able to find out quickly, though, is that the case involved a fast, German car and its suspicious disappearance.

• • •

In late January 2001, Carrington hired a black, convertible Audi TT Roadster from the luxury division of Avis. It was a 2000 model with a touch over 5 000 kilometres on the clock. He needed the car for an investigation he was conducting.

The Audi was due back about two weeks later, on 8 February, but on that day Carrington contacted Avis and told them he had been hijacked in Midrand and the car was gone. When he came in to speak to the company's internal investigators, he elaborated on what happened to him, explaining that he was ambushed while he pulled over on the side of the road to close the convertible roof. Carrington said five armed men had driven up to him in an Isuzu bakkie, forced him out of the vehicle and sped off.

For some or other reason, the Avis investigators listening to all this didn't believe the story. They weren't impressed when Carrington shared with them tales about his work as a private investigator and all his undercover operations. Something about him annoyed them and they were left with an impression of a man 'lost in a dream world'.

The investigators couldn't figure out why the hijackers wouldn't have taken his gun, which he was still wearing in an ankle holster. Or why he didn't use it to fight them off. They grew even more suspicious when it emerged that the tracking device on the car appeared to have been disconnected two days before the hijacking.

Carrington opened a police case but Avis decided to do its own investigation. Those responsible for it visited Carrington's complex in Jukskei Park, near Fourways, and asked the security guards there to let them know if they spotted a black Audi TT.

Nine months later, Avis received a call from a security guard at Riverglades. A car fitting that description had entered the complex. By that afternoon, following a short stakeout, Carrington was in custody. It turned out he had not only kept the Audi, but had fitted it with fake diplomatic number plates.

The case against Carrington began as one of fraud, but in March 2003 he landed up pleading guilty to a lesser charge of perjury.

. . .

When profiling their suspects, the Yeoville detectives pulled all the information that existed on Carrington on the police system. The records, which Gerhard van Wyk took over, reflect all the cases he opened as a complainant or those that were opened against him. His job as a private detective exposed him to greater risk, but even so, his file ran to 36 printed pages.

Carrington's record reflected that the first time he was arrested he was just 20 years old. It was a shooting that saw him kill a man he says was a robber.

> Towards the end of 1992, I was on my way home and I witnessed a fight of sorts, so I stopped to render assistance. The victim of the fight as such reported or informed me that he had been robbed by armed robbers. He then pointed to where they were. I approached these men with the view of apprehending them and there was a bit of a scuffle. Most of them got away and I ended up shooting and killing one of them.

The case of murder was opened but withdrawn and an inquest into the shooting was held instead. Carrington says that was the end of it.

Five years later, he was arrested again, this time for extortion. He claims it was a 'misunderstanding' involving a client who was owed money by an interior design company. That case was also withdrawn.

When the detectives had tried to follow up on some of these and other dockets, which could have potentially offered context to the murder case they were investigating, they found that just about all of the files were missing. There were records of the cases on the computer system, but many of the actual dockets were gone. There was a letter from a senior officer at provincial level requesting the transfer of several of the dockets, but it was impossible to determine where the files went. What the investigators were particularly interested in were two robbery cases, dating back to 2001, which led to Carrington being arrested again and saw him spend two months in jail before all charges were dropped. These dockets were among the missing ones and it was difficult to piece together what they were about. What did emerge, however, was that the dockets shared a common denominator: Cranks owner Eric Neeteson-Lemkes.

47.

Within a month of the arrests in the Betty Ketani murder case, Cranks closed its doors. After 30 years of running one of the most iconic restaurants in the city, Eric Neeteson-Lemkes began preparing to leave South Africa. He left quietly, owing his landlord a million rand and forcing the sheriff of the court to dismantle the psychedelic Asian fantasy he had created in Rosebank.

Without Eric there, the place was broken down neatly into an inventory of 48 dining tables, 129 plastic and steel chairs, refrigerators, gas stoves, fryers, freezers, pots and pans, buckets, cutlery and crockery, a cash register, a silver statue and a cheap radio. There was also a washing machine, a broken umbrella and a wooden photo frame. With the restaurant's doors firmly closed, the space stood empty until it was eventually demolished as part of a major revamp at the mall, destined to become another Woolworths.

Eric had spoken about leaving to set up a new venture in Thailand. He either ran out of time or simply had no inclination to sell his car and motorbike, and abandoned them both. In his apartment he left only his empty safes.

But Eric would not leave before driving what he saw as one last dagger into Carrington Laughton.

After Eric was approached at the restaurant by the police, his lawyers immediately made contact with Herman Broodryk. Initially Broodryk resisted, but eventually he agreed to a meeting. He was prepared to speak to the lawyers, but Eric arrived too and was told to wait outside. He was now a 62-year-old man who looked like a regular pensioner, without the dazzle of his colourful bandanas and sarongs. There was no evidence against Eric, but he remained a suspect and policy dictated that prosecutors don't talk to suspects.

Soon after the meeting, Neeteson-Lemkes signed an affidavit that illuminated certain aspects of the case. It was a bulky document that was never formalised into an affidavit but which covered numerous key events, the most important of which were backed up by police reports and statements. It's not known how he came into possession of these.

Eric's affidavit, which will become a court exhibit later on, revealed that he still carried a deep resentment for Carrington, 13 years after first meeting him. In fact, Eric was prepared to put his signature to a declaration that he would not rest until Laughton was brought to justice. So desperate was Eric to see Carrington in jail that he confessed to bribing police officers as well as a prosecutor. Eric's declaration also made it known that he had hired an array of private investigators to spy on Carrington and dig up dirt on him.

Eric Neeteson-Lemkes had met Carrington through his daughter Monique, who had been introduced to the private investigator by Dirk Reinecke. The length and scope of the Cranks investigation, along with who actually carried it out, is disputed, but it was at about the same time that Eric says he began growing increasingly suspicious that money was being stolen not just from his restaurant, but from his personal stash at home. He suspected that his daughter and Carrington were behind it.

Eric, it appears, grew paranoid and angry, and eventually confronted Monique. There's no way to know what happened between them, but in late January 2000 Monique flew out of South Africa, leaving the scandal behind. She spent some time in Thailand before returning to Australia, where she and her sister were born. She had lived in South Africa, on and off, for a year and a half.

Carrington tells a different story of how he and Eric became arch-enemies, but in his statement Neeteson-Lemkes describes two key events he says set him on the warpath.

The first was a late-night robbery at his Parkwood home in June 2000. While Eric was at his restaurant, a gang wearing balaclavas broke in, held up his domestic worker and two-year-old daughter, and cleaned out his safes. Eric says whoever stole from him made off with R300 000 and that no matter how much information he gave them, the police were not able to solve the case.

He was sure it was an inside job because there was no forced entry and whoever was behind it knew that one of the keys to the larger safe was kept in the smaller one. Eric pointed the finger at his daughter, even though she had already left the country, and at Carrington, with whom she had been romantically involved. He suspected that Monique had already stolen close to R150 000 from him.

If JB and detectives Pretorius and Sono knew some of this history when they went to visit Eric many years later, they would have understood his anger and his disdain for police officers. They would also have known that the house robbery was just the start of the ordeal.

• • •

Two and a half months after the home invasion, on 30 August 2000, there was another robbery, this time at the discreet workshop of an Orange Grove jeweller. Eric knew nothing about this robbery until much later, but it would become intertwined in his life as well as his quest to put Carrington behind bars.

The owner of the business had his suspicions of who was behind the heist. Carrington was one of his clients. He had designed a diamond engagement ring for him, which was then given to his first wife Candice. Shortly before the robbery, the jeweller claims, Carrington returned to discuss another order. But he had no evidence to pursue his suspicions and even though he reported the crime to the police, no progress was made in catching those responsible.

• • •

Eric refused to let his case go. Realising that the police were making no progress, he hired private detectives to try to shake something loose – more specifically, to find evidence that could be used to arrest Monique and Carrington in connection with the robbery.

He turned to an outfit called Associated Intelligence Network (AIN), which carried out private investigations and later featured on the periphery of the Brett Kebble murder investigation. According to the invoices that have survived, Eric spent well over R100 000 settling AIN's bills and then went on to hire another company, Incom Investigations, to keep digging. In court, it was claimed he had parted with a quarter of a million rand or more on private investigators – almost as much as was stolen from him.

Eric's investigators chased every lead: they dug into Carrington's life, ran checks on his company, monitored his international travel, obtained what appear to be illegal copies of his itemised telephone bills (where certain numbers were painstakingly highlighted and linked to names) and even took covert photographs of him at restaurants. Carrington and his friends were also followed around town.

There was nothing Eric was not willing to do. He even had his domestic worker questioned (or as AIN put it, 'interrogated') and subjected her and his new wife, Jitra, to a polygraph test. The test cleared them both but Debbie, despite her long service, eventually took Eric to the CCMA at the end of 2000 and was awarded a small settlement. Eric also suspected that his ex-wife was somehow involved.

In the meantime, Eric's army of investigators ran international crime checks and carried out 'electronic surveillance'. They typed up reports that alleged that Carrington had financial problems and was relying on his father for support. The reports went into great detail about those close to Carrington, even chronicling affairs and new relationships.

But none of the investigators was able to give him the proof he so desperately desired.

As the year drew to a close, Eric reported another case to the police. This time he claimed he had been ambushed as he arrived home with Jitra on 14 November 2000. It was late at night, almost 11pm, when four 'armed assailants' attacked him moments after he and Jitra climbed off his motorbike and walked into the house. Eric says he heard someone scream, 'Put your hands up, otherwise I'll shoot', at which point he drew his own gun and a shoot-out ensued. Eric fired five rounds and claims the intruders returned three more while fleeing. By this time, Eric had moved his family from Parkwood to Rosebank.

Then, on 23 November 2000, Eric opened yet another case at Rosebank police station, relating to the R140 000 that had allegedly been stolen from him between 1998 and 2000. He asked the police to investigate his daughter Monique.

Three months later, Eric says he flew out to Thailand to speak to Monique. She denies having ever been arrested for any crime, but Eric, in his affidavit, claims the purpose of his trip was to help her while she was detained for fraud or theft in February 2001. It is during that visit to Thailand, with what appears to be powerful leverage against his daughter, that Eric finally makes the connection between the robbery at his house and the jewellery store.

• • •

The link between the two robberies, in Eric's eyes, is a cryptic letter that he claims was faxed to Monique by Carrington. It's a 'Fax Transmission', allegedly sent to the Bansabai Hotel in Bangkok, where she rented a room. The cover page has her name, room number, the name and fax number of the hotel, and Carrington's own name and return fax number.

The actual message is contained on the second page, and begins with two underlined words in the centre of the page: *'The Actors'*. A list of six names follows, in neat bullet points. Some of the names are followed by telephone numbers and addresses or even explanations of who the individuals are ('My friend of about 15 years' or 'Ziggy's friend of many years').

The list takes up roughly half the page and is followed by the second headline, once again in the middle of the page: *'The Helper (remember the name)'*. Here the author gives the name of a lawyer.

The last headline is *'The Performance (more or less)'*, followed by a detailed explanation:

> *Act 1 Scene 1: To visit a man. Those visiting will be Ziggy, Reginald, Michelle & Jacques. Alex & I will be driving. Travis will be the third vehicle as a Telkom man & may or may not be on the premises when the scene is acted. Ziggy & Michelle will be husband and wife. Reginald will be a bodyguard. When they leave the set in Alex's car they will drive and switch cars, and off they go. Names and car numbers will be changed to protect the innocent, naturally! Oddly enough so will faces.*
>
> *Hope the script sounds OK so far. The performance will take place around 10h00 tomorrow (give or take an hour or two either way).*

Eric says he returns from Thailand with this letter and some of the jewellery that he reckons was stolen from the jeweller. He claims to have bought it at a pawnshop in Bangkok. Also in his possession are statements made by his daughter implicating herself and Carrington in both the house robbery and the jewellery heist.

These statements – which Eric hoped to use against Carrington – were not commissioned and thus proved of little value in South Africa. Monique also subsequently performed a dramatic U-turn, and it's not possible to know whether they were real to begin with.

By this point in the saga, so many statements and counter-statements have been made that the truth begins to fade into a dense fog of allegations, which cannot be proved either way.

Carrington's version is that he was set up and was never involved in any of the robberies. He says Eric held a grudge against him because he helped Monique and her family members leave South Africa, which Eric saw as taking sides or 'crossing him'. He claims Eric has asked him to kill a Cranks employee, Ruth, which led to the Polaroids being doctored. It was because of this grudge, Carrington alleges, that Eric fabricated all the evidence against him, including the faxed letter.

Interviewed in 2013, Monique claimed that her family always came first and denied that there were any conflicts. She also denied having anything to do with either of the robberies. But to the bitter end, Eric believed he knew who had stolen from him, even if he eventually softened towards his daughter.

What rises above the fog, however, is that at some point in their lives, Eric and his daughter were involved in an ugly battle over stolen money.

Eric's house robbery and the heist at the jewellery workshop are well documented in police records and are substantiated by a number of interviews and documents. It's also clear that Eric took it upon himself to find proof that Carrington, whose company investigated the Cranks thefts, was involved. There's no dispute that Eric and Carrington were enemies.

The authenticity of the faxed letter was never determined, but Eric used it as ammunition against Carrington, while Laughton used it to try to show that Eric was trying to set him up for murder.

. . .

In his parting 2012 statement, Eric says that a month after his return from Thailand, he was introduced to a woman who bragged about having good contacts at Norwood police station. After hearing his story of failed justice, she arrived at Cranks with two Norwood detectives. Eric briefed the officers about the 'evidence' he had gathered – the statements, the fax, the jewellery – and how desperate he was to see Carrington arrested. The two policemen offered to help, but for a price.

Eric says he agreed to pay. He was furious at the police for failing to solve his cases, and he had poured a vast amount of money into private investigations, which too had gone nowhere. He felt betrayed by his own family and by the man whose company he hired to investigate the thefts at his restaurant. His house had been broken into, his daughter was held up and his wife was lucky to have escaped the crossfire in the latest attack. Bitter, angry, he was now willing to break the law himself and pay the officers to, in Eric's words, 'juice the system'. They wanted R10 000 to have his house robbery case transferred to their police station and another R20 000 to pay off the right people in order to secure arrest warrants. It was agreed that further payments would follow. The corruption went beyond the officers themselves and, Eric claims, extended to a state prosecutor who was paid R50 000 to keep Carrington locked up by opposing bail. Eric parted with the money.

In his affidavit, Eric names the woman who had introduced him to the police officers, the detectives themselves and the prosecutor. But none of the individuals has been arrested, charged or prosecuted and cannot be named here. They may also be the subjects of future investigations.

With the system 'juiced', Carrington was arrested a month later, on 12 May 2001. The charges against him related to the robbery at Eric's house. He was detained at Norwood police station and later moved to the Johannesburg Correctional Services prison, known as 'Sun City'– an ironic reference to the luxury holiday resort by the same name.

Carrington fought for bail and launched several applications. Eventually, a month later, he succeeded, but enjoyed only a few hours of freedom before being rearrested, this time for the jewellery-store heist.

While he was in jail, the policemen who had been bribed by Eric secured arrest warrants for all six people named in the cryptic fax, as well as

Monique. An official letter was even sent to Interpol requesting the extradition of Monique, her sister Naydine and her mother Dang – although this appeared to have been premature and was more than likely never followed up.

During Carrington's battle for bail, the prosecution argued it had enough evidence to prosecute Carrington, but his legal team maintained the state's case was flimsy. Eric hired lawyers to sit in on the court proceedings and take notes.

Finally, by the middle of July 2001, Carrington succeeded in illustrating how weak the state's case against him was. After her falling-out with Eric, the police were having trouble finding Debbie, the victim of the house robbery; Monique was overseas and there was little chance of her coming back to testify against him; and the forensic evidence simply could not tie Carrington to any crime. Two months after being arrested, Carrington was released on bail. He waited another month before all charges against him were withdrawn and he was finally able to put the episode behind him.

'There is no hope in hell that we can ever prove this case,' the prosecutor wrote at the time in the police docket. 'It rather appears that Lemkes has a personal vendetta against the accused. No prospect of successful prosecution.'

. . .

The allegations didn't stop there. Eric believed that the same prosecutor he bribed had received payment from the other side, leading to the collapse of both cases. Carrington categorically denied it.

Either way, Eric was outraged. Nothing he did, legally or illegally, could give him what he wanted. So in September 2001, he decided to take a wild gamble. What he did was closer to Russian roulette, but Eric decided to spin the gun's cylinder anyway. He approached the Scorpions.

He went directly to one of South Africa's top prosecutors, Gerrie Nel (known as the Bull Terrier for the way in which he prosecuted Jackie Selebi and later Oscar Pistorius) and Scorpions investigator Andrew Leask. Eric told them his story, but the part he thought they would be most interested in were the bribes he had paid.

A case was duly registered and an investigator named Byron Decker was assigned to follow up Eric's claims. The Cranks owner produced what he claimed were copies of the cheques he had written in favour of the police officers: at least three cheques for R20 000 each, signed in May and June that year. In return for the information he provided, Eric wanted immunity from prosecution. He wanted to be what is known as a section 204 witness, admitting his role in the corruption but handing the authorities a couple of dirty cops and a prosecutor in return. Paul Toft-Nielsen called these policemen Eric's 'pet detectives'.

It seems that Eric was so desperate for revenge that he was prepared to approach the country's most elite unit – boasting a near 100 per cent success rate with its cases – and admit to bribing police officers and a prosecutor. If he wasn't able to secure immunity, he was opening himself up to the possibility of criminal charges and prosecution.

But at least this way, he figured, the Scorpions would investigate everything and make progress where others had failed.

The move didn't backfire on him, but neither did it lead anywhere. It's not clear why, but the Scorpions never pursued the case far enough to execute any arrests. Perhaps Eric was not a reliable witness or their suspects gave Decker an explanation for the payments that could not be disproved.

In the statement Eric signed before he left South Africa more than ten years later, he remained baffled by why the policemen were never prosecuted.

Eric's version is an extraordinary tale of how he paid a fortune to private detectives, flew to Thailand to gather evidence, navigated an ugly family feud that involved his ex-wife and daughters, fought off intruders in a shoot-out, committed crimes by bribing policemen and, when all else failed, threw himself at the mercy of the Scorpions. And still, his robbery remained unsolved, Carrington was a free man and Monique had a new life in Australia.

Eric Neeteson-Lemkes never came to terms with what happened during that period. Carrington claimed it made him 'bitter and twisted'. Detective Gerhard van Wyk received an alert when Eric passed through passport control at the airport and rushed over to try to speak to him one last time – but was too late.

Before he slipped quietly out of the country, Eric left prosecutors with his statement, which spoke of his 'hopeless' and 'desperate' quest for justice. His final words, just above his signature, were: 'Notwithstanding the severe toll that my relentless pursuit of justice against Carrington and Monique has already cost me and my family (not only from a financial perspective but also an emotional one), I will not rest until justice has been dealt to Carrington and his co-perpetrators.'

48.

Carrington says Eric's obsession with him was nothing short of a 'campaign of terror'. He describes Eric as a stubborn and arrogant man.

Laughton says he met Eric Neeteson-Lemkes in 1999 while chasing up an invoice for the Cranks investigation. He says Eric was initially hostile and rude, accusing Carrington and his wife of ripping him off because the agent planted at the restaurant failed to find out who was behind the thefts. Eric, however, warmed up to him – so much so, Laughton says, that during a meeting at his house Eric allegedly asked whether Carrington could help him kill one of his staff members.

Carrington's version is that he manufactured the fake Ruth photographs to 'satisfy Eric's bloodlust'. He says he agreed because he didn't know how else to escape the situation, and lied by telling Eric that a friend of his owed him a favour and could do the job, for free.

But, according to Carrington, what led to the real enmity – all the bribes and the dodgy arrests – was his willingness to help Monique and her relatives as they left South Africa in early 2000. This included booking and paying for a hotel room for them to stay in after they were kicked out of their house and arranging their flights. In the process he became their 'personal ATM' and says Eric saw this as a betrayal.

> Eric started threatening me, saying that I had stolen his family. That I had stolen his control. He swore blind that there would be vengeance and that I would be punished for crossing him.

In October 2001, after he had been arrested and released, Carrington reported an armed robbery at his Northriding home. He told police that he was fast asleep when his cellphone rang, showing that the call was coming from his then-girlfriend Jayne. What was strange was that Jayne was sleeping next to him and her phone was lying on the kitchen counter.

FOTO: 69

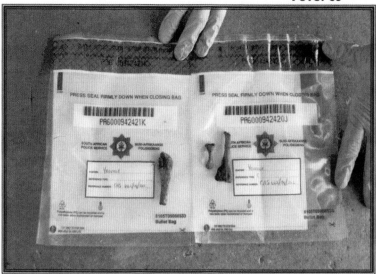

FOTO: 70

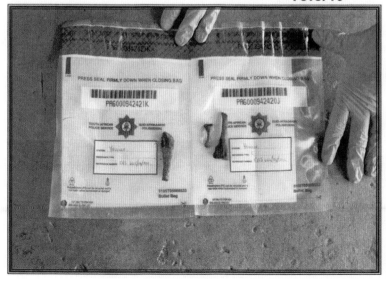

Photographs from a police album showing three of the six feet bones that were eventually unearthed from Betty Ketani's grave. Half of these bones were sent abroad for DNA testing. (Court exhibit)

Investigating officer Captain Gerhard van Wyk (standing, far left) helps sift through soil during the third and final exhumation of Betty Ketani's grave. This was the day that six bones were discovered. (Court exhibit)

The last known photograph of former Cranks owner Eric Neeteson-Lemkes, or 'Mad Dog', as he called himself. Shortly after giving the prosecutors a lengthy statement, he left South Africa.

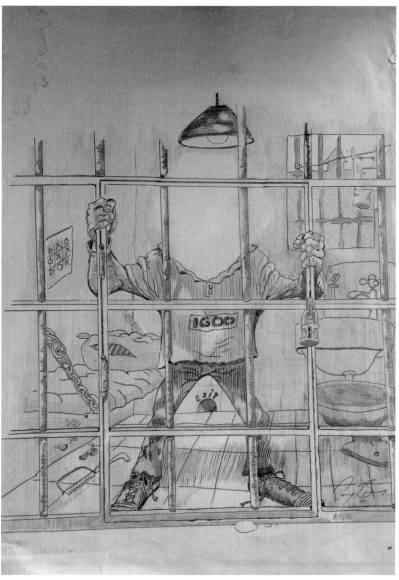

Premonition: A 1997 pencil drawing by Conway Brown. He is unable to explain why he did not draw a face but, 18 years later, he will spend time in jail in connection with the murder of Betty Ketani. (Conway Brown)

Carrington Laughton prepares to testify in his own defence. He will spend 13 days on the witness stand.
(© Alon Skuy)

Prosecutors Namika Kowlas (centre) and Herman Broodryk (back) in conversation with lead detective Captain Gerhard van Wyk (right). In the foreground is Carrington Laughton's lawyer, Laurance Hodes. (© Alon Skuy)

The six accused on the day half of them pleaded guilty and turned state witness. From left: Carrington Laughton, Conway Brown, David Ranger, Carel Ranger, Paul Toft-Nielsen and Dirk Reinecke. (© EWN)

Carel and David Ranger photographed during a break in court proceedings. (© Alon Skuy)

The three accused who went on to face trial: Carrington Laughton (back), David Ranger (centre) and his brother Carel Ranger (front). (© Alon Skuy)

Judgment day: Betty Ketani's brother Mankinki Kula and Betty's eldest daughter, Bulelwa, in court to hear the verdict. (© Alon Skuy)

Prosecutors Namika Kowlas and Herman Broodryk share a lighter moment in court. (© Alon Skuy)

A dedicated sleuth: Captain Gerhard van Wyk spent over a week testifying for the state.
The pressure of the case eventually saw him hospitalised. (© Alon Skuy)

A tense moment in court for Carrington Laughton. (© Alon Skuy)

Monique Neeteson-Lemkes is a suspect in the Ketani murder case. Like Mark Lister, she left South Africa in 2000 and now lives in Australia. She too faces possible extradition. This is a screen grab of *Hostie or Hitman?*, a documentary for Australia Channel Seven's *Sunday Night*.

Betty Ketani's family and the team that set out to send her killers to jail. From left: Prosecutor Namika Kowlas, Bulelwa Ketani, Mankinki Kula, Captain Gerhard van Wyk and prosecutor Herman Broodryk. (© Alex Eliseev)

Mark Lister, a former policeman currently residing in Australia, is mentioned in the written confession and now faces possible extradition. He is seen here in a screen grab of *Hostie or Hitman?*, a documentary for Australia Channel Seven's *Sunday Night*.

Betty Ketani's daughter Bulelwa travelled up from the Eastern Cape to be in court on judgment day. Here she processes her emotions. (© Alon Skuy)

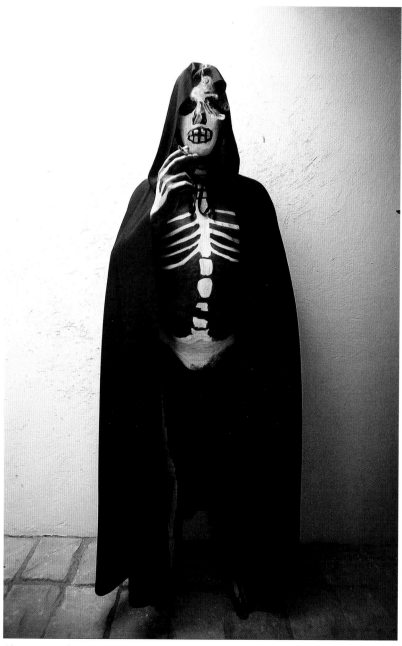

A haunting coincidence: Carrington Laughton at a Halloween party several years before the truth about Betty Ketani's abductions and murder emerged. (© Alon Skuy)

The final journey: Betty Ketani's children and relatives travel to Johannesburg to summon her spirit and escort it home to the Eastern Cape. (© Alon Skuy)

Tears for a mother: The Ketani family visits the bus where she died and the location of her shallow grave (pictured here). For the youngest daughter, Lusanda, confronting these sites is a painful experience.(© Alon Skuy)

It was just after 4am and Carrington went to investigate. He walked down the passage and found an open kitchen door and a man crouching in his TV room. As soon as the intruder saw him, he fired several shots in Carrington's direction, the bullets striking the walls and the ceiling. Carrington retreated and shouted to Jayne to call the police, after which the intruder fled, taking Jayne's cellphone and a set of house keys.

Carrington suspected that Eric was behind the break-in but had no proof. He could think of no other reason why the robber would have called his cellphone.

Later, Carrington claims, Eric also tried to extort money from him by demanding he pay R1 million to be left alone. This, he says, was done through a private investigator. In court, Carrington said he had recorded this conversation but couldn't explain why he did not turn to the police.

It was only in 2015, while standing trial for Betty Ketani's murder, that Carrington had his lawyers open a case against Eric and the policemen and prosecutor he allegedly bribed. He used Eric's statement as the basis for the complaint.

Eric believed Carrington was behind most, if not all, of his misfortune. Carrington called Eric the 'puppet master' who played havoc with his life. Like Eric, Carrington was angry at the country's criminal justice system. In 2009, he wrote an article titled 'Crime and Punishment in South Africa'.

'The system lets us down …', he wrote. 'This allows criminals to continue their criminal activities with impunity and little fear of arrest.'

The history these two men shared – all the suspicious robberies, bribery, extortion, planned hits and spying – seems as surreal as the rest of the circumstances around the Ketani case. But as difficult as it is to know where the truth lies, the events are important because they are to form the very foundation of the defence Carrington is waiting patiently to present in court.

49.

By late November 2012, the bones Teunis Briers unearthed from the grave in Kenilworth are at the ICMP laboratory in Bosnia. It's going to take months for the final analysis to be issued and sent back to South Africa. The ICMP is meticulous and if any DNA is found in the bones, whatever conclusions are reached will be checked and double-checked, subjected to a statistical review and will eventually be signed off by a senior official. In the meantime, Captain Gerhard van Wyk, Herman Broodryk and Namika Kowlas have a more urgent problem to deal with.

The handwriting report has arrived and it's not at all what they had hoped for. Warrant Officer Magendree Govindsamy has issued a standard seven-page document explaining her findings. Like most other Section 212 affidavits (which can be introduced in court without the author testifying), the report begins with her qualifications, runs through the exhibits and the methodology, and ends with her conclusions.

Govindsamy has carried out a routine examination, breaking the signature and handwriting on the hidden confession into various elements, exploring style and execution, rhythm and form, a unique loop or the pressure of a pen stroke. These elements are compared between samples and an expert opinion is provided.

The examination of handwriting is an indefinite science that by its very nature is more subjective and therefore less reliable. Although it has proved useful in courtrooms, handwriting reports are more open to interpretation and thus vulnerable to attack.

Govindsamy had been given as many samples of Carrington's signature and handwriting as the investigating officer could find, along with samples from Conway, who supplied them willingly. Her task was to compare the signature and handwriting on the confession to these samples in order to determine whether Carrington was the author. She was also asked to offer an opinion on whether Conway could have signed the confession.

As part of the investigation, Govindsamy accompanied Van Wyk to the Department of Trade and Industry in Pretoria, where the 1998 and 1999 company documents are stored. They were not allowed to remove the originals but were permitted to study the paperwork on site.

Govindsamy is fairly new to the Questioned Document Unit, having spent about two and a half years learning how to analyse documents or spot fake banknotes. Examining signatures was part of her training.

At first, the report is encouraging. Govindsamy finds 'sufficient evidence' that Carrington could have signed the confession and that there are 'correspondences' in respect of the handwriting. But Govindsamy then starts to qualify her findings with the kinds of statements that no detective or prosecutor wants to present at a trial.

'A definite conclusion could not be reached at this stage of the examination,' she writes. 'The current specimens are qualitatively and quantitatively insufficient (i.e. the current specimen handwriting submitted for comparison does not adequately address all of the features within the handwriting in question).'

In other words, while Govindsamy has found evidence to link the signatures, she's not prepared to commit to a finding on the handwriting. Her problem is clear: she needs more specimens to work with.

The handwriting analysis is one of the main pillars of the state's case. It is a link between Carrington and the hidden confession.

Govindsamy is also not prepared to make a finding on the photograph (with a single word on the back) and the white envelope (with several lines of writing), stating that they 'consist of very limited writing with limited characteristics to examine'. As far as these exhibits are concerned, she believes that not even additional specimens to compare them with would take the investigation any further.

Herman Broodryk is not pleased. The report is far too inconclusive. The words and phrases Govindsamy has chosen – 'correspondences', 'qualitatively and quantitatively insufficient' – are sure to be picked apart by the defence and she would have to survive days in the witness box defending her conclusions. Broodryk also discovers that Govindsamy has never testified in court about handwriting analysis. This would be her first case.

He is not prepared to carry the risk of putting an inexperienced witness on the stand. He feels this case is far too important and complex for someone who only has two years of actual, practical experience.

A couple of weeks previously, during the most recent court appearance, he and Kowlas served their indictments on the six accused and a trial date has been set for 22 July 2013, which is fewer than eight months away. They don't have a lot of time but a new expert will have to be found and a new report issued. As was the case with Yeoville detective Lufuno Sono, Broodryk wants a substitute – the best handwriting analyst the police has to offer. Someone senior enough to stand up to the best defence advocate.

The man Broodryk is looking for is hundreds of kilometres away, sitting in a police office in Amanzimtoti, KwaZulu-Natal. Colonel Marco van der Hammen has more than 20 years with the Questioned Document Unit, has been involved in thousands of cases and has testified in court more than 200 times. At one point he was Govindsamy's mentor, teaching her the techniques she would apply in the Betty Ketani case. Marco van der Hammen literally helped write the manuals and textbooks police forensic analysts around South Africa use daily. Two of his recent high-profile cases were the Baby Jordan trial, in which a woman named Dina Rodrigues was accused of plotting the murder of her lover's baby, and the trial of Thandi Maqubela, found guilty of the murder of her husband, Acting Judge Patrick Maqubela.

Colonel Van der Hammen is a polite, friendly man with a generous smile and a deep love for his work. He's an impressive witness who arrives armed with presentations and doesn't try to hide the fact that handwriting analysis, although a scientific discipline, relies on human interpretation. In the witness box he shuffles around, gesturing almost theatrically and smiling ever so slightly when facing predictable questions from lawyers. Even when an advocate accuses him of being a 'hired gun', Van der Hammen can come back with something measured like: 'My Lord, I've been called many names before … I've been called a hired gun before as well … I'm here not as an advocate, I'm here as a professional in a certain field.' That's exactly why Broodryk wants him.

The problem he and Kowlas face is getting Van der Hammen on board. This case has no link to KwaZulu-Natal, and Van der Hammen – should he be interested and available – will not only have to take on additional work outside his jurisdiction, but will have to spend time preparing for court and then travelling to Johannesburg to testify. Not to mention all the consultations. In court, getting through his evidence will likely take days. Transferring the case to Van der Hammen may also be difficult and could be accompanied by the same bureaucracy and emotion that followed when Gerhard van Wyk took over from detective Sono. But Broodryk knows the value of the evidence and is convinced that securing Van der Hammen will pay off during the trial. Again, he won't take no for an answer.

At the same time, Broodryk instructs Van Wyk to go out and find more samples of Carrington's handwriting. Govindsamy's report has made it clear that what they have is not enough. Carrington is not cooperating but Van Wyk has an idea. Later, he will call it one of the smartest moves he made during the entire investigation.

50.

After several burglaries and attempted break-ins at his Kenilworth house, Conway began hiding things in places he was sure nobody would look.

He stitched a secret sleeve into the hem of the bedroom curtain and used it to store his most treasured possession: his family sword. The thinking was that no thief would ever open the curtains because the window looks out onto the street.

Conway hid money and other items inside and beneath his mattress, leaving his safe empty to serve as a decoy. He removed the outside handle from the back door, making it impossible for anyone to enter the house through the kitchen, and built a high wall to protect the back of the property. Conway also figured out that some of the carpet squares in his house made perfect secret compartments, and stored important papers under them.

Like his father, Conway considered his garage his sanctuary. He did not have nearly the kind of workshop that Vincent kept and his options for places to hide things were limited. Because of this, he resorted to using his car to keep letters or notes he didn't want Blanche to read. He cut a secret pocket into the roof lining near the rear-view mirror.

When the confession about Betty's murder came into his possession, Conway says he briefly kept it in the garage and then took it inside the house. He first read it while sitting in the lounge but was disturbed and forced to hide it. When the coast was clear, he took the letter to his bedroom, found a good spot and slipped it under the carpet.

The question of why Conway hid the confession under the carpet is often asked. But to Conway, it seemed natural to hide it there because it was just one of many hiding places he had around the house. He didn't want his wife to find it so he chose what he considered a safe option. The question of why he didn't destroy it, however, is far more difficult for him to answer.

While giving his confession to André Neethling, Conway said he thought the letter had been handed to him by Sandor. Later he changed this, saying it was Dirk who gave it to him. Dirk confirmed this, saying he received it from Carrington. The timing, says Dirk, would have coincided with Carrington's arrests in 2001 and the height of his war with Eric Neeteson-Lemkes.

Sometime during that year, Dirk says, he was handed a brown duffel bag by Carrington and asked to deliver it to Conway. Carrington denies he did any such thing, and while Conway doesn't remember a duffel bag, he does speak of a box, made of silver galvanised metal, with a latch in the middle. To complicate matters, the confession refers to a 'tin'. Much will be made of this in court, with questions around whether the metal box could have fitted inside an army-style duffel bag and why Conway's and Dirk's recollections of this handover are different. Conway says the box was in the boot of Dirk's black Opel Corsa when they met at a McDonald's near the Turffontein Racecourse in southern Johannesburg. After a brief discussion, he took it over.

Dirk claims his instructions from Carrington were to give the bag to Conway for safe keeping, but Conway remembers being told to 'get rid of it'. Whatever the intention, Conway says he began discarding some of the contents as he drove home. He says he was warned that some of the items were of a personal nature, including a sex tape.

Conway says when he first opened the box, several folded letters or documents sprung up. He remembers the confession was right at the top. Underneath the papers, Conway saw all kinds of items, from handcuffs to bullets, from videotapes to name badges and from police epaulettes to a black hood. He says he threw a handful of these into a municipal rubbish bin along his route home, and also tossed some items out the window, figuring they would be picked up in minutes. Conway destroyed the rest of the items, with the exception of a wallet, which he liked and kept a bit longer.

When he arrived home after seeing Dirk, Conway says he hid the box in his garage, returning to it a little later. This time, he read the letter.

Sandor if you are reading this then I am dead.

His name appeared in the third paragraph.

> *We drove her about 10 minutes further down the highway and 'killed'*
> *her ...*

The word 'we' jumped out at him, filling him with both fear and anger. Fear gave way to fury, as he realised that right there, in black and white, was evidence to implicate him in a murder. He was 'beyond furious'.

After Conway read the letter, he took an on-the-spot decision that would lead to his arrest more than ten years later. It was a decision that would ripple across time and result in many unintended consequences, from the resignation of a policeman in Australia to the truth emerging about an Aston Martin crash.

Conway decided to keep the confession.

• • •

If his story is true, had Conway torn up the letter, thrown it away or burnt it, none of the events that unfolded would have come to pass. Betty Ketani's murder would have remained a secret. Her children would never know what happened to her. Six men, including two policemen, would never have been arrested. Eric may not have left South Africa. Interpol may never have issued arrest warrants for Monique Neeteson-Lemkes and Mark Lister. David Ranger would have continued working at the police station, his brother Carel at the casino. Dirk would have carried on selling trinkets to travellers at the airport. And Carrington may have launched that television programme he was busy preparing the day he drove out of his house not noticing the silver VW Polo in his rear-view mirror.

Instead, Conway decided to hide the letter. His explanation is that he could no longer trust Carrington and couldn't be sure of what other evidence was out there. He was angry and confused. He was scared. He wanted something he could use as leverage against Carrington should the need ever arise. Something that incriminated him, but also incriminated his friend. He wanted an 'insurance policy'.

Conway says he felt like the people he was up against were smarter than him and a lot more powerful. His back was against the wall and holding onto the confession seemed like a good idea. The many years that have passed haven't helped him make sense of his decision:

> *You can pull out my teeth without anaesthetic and I'll still say to you: 'Can't help you, bud.' It's just something ... in hindsight, yes, it was stupid. I should have burnt those papers or thrown them away or done whatever I was told to do with them because then this wouldn't have come out. But then I would still be living like I was living and not having any rest. After so many years, when they said they found the letter, it was like you can breathe again.*

Once he discovered the confession, Conway says he began keeping notes about snippets of information he either overheard or was told by his friends. He claims he wanted to piece together as much of the murder as possible. His memory was poor, so he wrote things down in order to trigger the memories later.

The list detailing the names and telephone numbers, Conway says, was created using the information in the actual confession. He didn't want to damage the original. He says the coffee stain was his, as was the sheet of paper inscribed with 'Do not throw away', which served as an envelope in case Blanche ever found the package. It was also a reminder to himself that the papers inside were important.

Despite having written the 'Howson & Straker' letter to Blanche, Conway denies he took part in the June 2000 robbery at Eric's house. The robbery described by Eric's domestic worker, who lived through it, is nothing like the events described in Conway's note.

The letter to Blanche claims the intruders hooted outside the house and allowed the 'maid' to open the door. Deborah Mashigoana reported being ambushed by men who stormed in through the back door. The note claims the domestic worker was pepper-sprayed, had her mouth taped shut and was bundled into a car boot in order to be driven far away from the house to disorientate her. Nothing like that happened.

But some of the information does appear to correspond with the real-life events, such as the existence of the two safes and the reference to Eric's restaurant and Monique's whereabouts (in Thailand). The rest of the information he had noted down appears to be hearsay. This is how he explains its existence:

> God forbid something should happen to me, at least you have this information because I'm not strong enough to hand it in, I don't know who to hand it to, I don't know what to say …

These thoughts are similar to those Conway says flashed through his mind while giving his confession to André Neethling at the safe house in Observatory. Neethling had shown him his appointment card and told him he was with the Hawks. Conway thought of Neethling as one of the 'untouchable' policemen and there was thus some sense of relief in getting his story down on paper, so that it could not be undone.

> You finally felt comfortable. You felt safe that you're telling them something, that they're writing it on paper. And if something happened to me that day on the way from their home, fuck it, it didn't matter because they … Mr Neethling had that paper. I don't know if there's such a thing as a dead man's confession, but that was the kind of thing that came to my mind. Even if I'm dead it's all there. These assholes can't take it away …

Conway seems to have had an aversion to throwing things away, especially items with sentimental value. He hung on to his paintings, poems and notes for years, singling out ones that were particularly important to him. Some of his drawings, which he has kept at his house, go back 20 or more years. There are paintings in a suitcase, stacked up against walls and hanging up on display.

Conway's art collection opens another window to a man blessed with an active imagination and an undeniable talent, but who battled to find his own identity. There is no real thread or style running through the body of his work, with the drawings careening from dolphins and unicorns to gods and goddesses from Aztec mythology.

There are pencil and pen sketches, but also colourful abstract paintings of women with names like Misty, Cindy, Miss M and The Dancer. Conway's comic strips depict witches, trolls, dragons, pixies and self-created super-heroes such as Roach Man, who looks remarkably like Spider-Man and is seen smashing, head-on, into the side of a brick building. There are nudes with a touch of the erotic but also hideous, saggy creatures. There are ter-rifying monsters, robots and cyborgs, but also happy bugs with captions such as 'doof', 'thud' and 'flump'. Conway drew Japanese warriors and aliens with dark glassy eyes, but also Madiba with his trademark smile. He copied Picasso paintings and even had a go at Edvard Munch's *The Scream*.

In 1997, Conway drew a pencil sketch of a muscular man, his face never drawn, standing inside a prison cell, his arms spread out to grip the bars, his legs wide apart. Behind him, a bunk bed hangs on chains from a wall, a piece of paper above the bed with a completed game of noughts and crosses and a small hacksaw on the floor. There's a mouse hole in the wall with the word 'Exit' above it. It is a haunting image, which draws the eye to the gaping, empty white space where the man's face should have been.

Conway speaks about his paintings, admitting that although several were on display at a restaurant in Alberton, selling for between R400 and R800, none had actually been sold.

Conway's writing was similarly bizarre. There's a four-page story about a house fly that ends up splattered under a human foot. There are also col-lections of short poems, with the usual countless spelling errors.

'What is life if not a dream ... The light has gone yet I know it will return to me ... My boddy unchained, my mind not yet, why have we got this desire, to be free ...'

While in jail, Conway continued with his art. He sketched his cell or mystical religious symbols. He helped wardens with their children's art projects and some of his creations were even pinned up in their offices. He carved beautiful and detailed sculptures out of soap that could fit into the palm of a hand. He didn't know it, but Carrington Laughton and his defence team were preparing to use his artistic ability against him in court. The question they would ask is: if he could draw and sculpt, what else was he capable of creating or, more specifically, forging?

51.

In February 2013, almost a year after the discovery of the confession under the carpet, Doc and JB are escorting a client out of Dragon City, a Chinese shopping mall situated near Ellis Park stadium.

Investigations like the Betty Ketani one are exciting, but they don't always pay the bills. So Doc and JB pick up extra work where they can. They've been driving this client to and from her husband's clothing store since December. It's an easy way for each of them to score R100 a day.

As usual, JB meets the woman at the store at 3.30pm and walks out with her. Doc connects with them in the street. Their cars are parked where many of the local minibus taxis wait for customers: JB's white Nissan Almera is in front and Doc's Opel Astra is parked behind it. JB climbs into the driver's seat, while Doc opens the back door of his car for the client. Once she's in, he opens his door and is about to get behind the wheel when two cars screech to a halt next to them. Seconds later, a minibus appears behind them. Armed men spill out of all three vehicles and open fire.

'The *okes* let crack with the AK-47s ...'

Doc and JB are trapped and can't get into defensive positions. They barely have time to draw their weapons.

The storm of bullets blows in from all directions. JB is hit first. He is shot five times and slumps over in the driver's seat. Doc is next, collapsing onto the pavement. The bullets tear into his back, near the right shoulder, ripping apart muscles and nerves. A stray bullet slams into the ground nearby, bounces up like a menacing jack-in-the-box and burrows into his head.

Amazingly, their client escapes unharmed. The gang snatch her handbag and flee. Some of the local taxi drivers fire off a few rounds as the three cars speed off. JB manages to make a call on his cellphone before losing consciousness.

Doc and JB are rushed to the emergency ward at Milpark Hospital, one of the best hospitals in town. Doctors there do what they can to try to save them.

Combing the scene for clues later, police find dozens of casings where the gunmen stood. Doc's car bears the scars of almost 30 bullets.

It seems the gang was acting on rotten underworld intelligence, believing that a large amount of cash – as much as half a million rand – was being transported. Doc and JB are the collateral damage.

The twilight world of sudden death ...

•   •   •

A few days later in hospital, JB is on the mend. The damage done by the bullets is limited and he is in a fine mood, his loud voice filling an entire section of the ICU ward, the nurses rolling their eyes. JB is still joking that every time he's been shot, the bullets have crept closer and closer to his head. He's in pain, but glad to be alive. It doesn't take long for JB to recover fully and he's on his feet within days. He will go back to being the 'bouncing ball' Neethling knows him to be.

Doc, though, remains critical. The bullets that struck him – seven AK-47 rounds – have damaged his nervous system. Doctors fear he could remain a quadriplegic. A tube has been inserted into his throat and when he's awake – drifting in and out of consciousness – he can barely communicate.

In June 1999, while in Richards Bay, Doc was in a terrible car crash. The vehicle he was in drove through a barrier and plunged off a cliff. He injured his spine and spent three months in intensive care, after which he had steel pins inserted to secure his vertebrae. He sold everything he could – including his Harley-Davidson – to pay the hospital bills.

Nobody knows whether Doc's body can recover from another massive trauma. He's in his fifties now, trying to keep his diabetes at bay. He proved his doctors wrong in 1999 by walking again, but can he pull through this time?

52.

When the bone samples arrive at the International Commission on Missing Persons in Bosnia, they are unwrapped, photographed, weighed, measured, placed into test tubes and assigned individual bar codes.

The ICMP – its chain-of-custody protocols designed to satisfy international war crimes tribunals at The Hague – was one of the first laboratories in the world to focus mainly on nuclear DNA, finding its own method to extract it, amplify it, locate molecular markers and study the patterns they reveal.

If the ICMP laboratories are like a car-manufacturing plant, then the first stop of the assembly line is the decontamination station. That's where the bones from South Africa begin their journey.

DNA can be found almost everywhere, and foreign traces of it must be removed from the surface of all samples. The laboratories where this and all other tests are done are absolutely sterile. Instruments are radiated and protective clothing – white suits, masks and gloves – are worn by employees. The challenge is not to introduce new DNA to any of the samples.

The bones are washed and scoured with a hand-held sanding tool to remove any dirt, soil or foreign DNA, and to create a clean surface. Scientists then do something counter-intuitive: they place the fragile samples into a strong solution of bleach, which is a proficient DNA killer.

It seems odd to subject the bones to such an erosive chemical, especially if there isn't a lot of DNA to spare and considering how much trouble it took to get the samples to the laboratory. But the exposure is brief and the bleach helps to decontaminate the bones. The molecules that matter are deep inside, safe from the chemical.

Staff then rinse off the bones, grind them down and soak them overnight in a new solution of extraction buffer. The liquid eats away the bone, setting free the DNA molecules inside. By the time the minerals and proteins are gone, what's left behind is a solution containing all available DNA.

An intricate scientific process follows to pluck out DNA molecules, which are then split and copied to reveal sequences and patterns. The results are displayed on electropherograms, which resemble graphs used to record a heartbeat, known in the medical world as electrocardiograms or ECGs.

The sharp peaks, and the sequences they represent, allow ICMP staff to apply Bayesian calculations to arrive at possible matches. This is the realm of statistical probabilities, a way to attach a percentage of certainty to a hypothesis.

The question that needs to be answered is whether any DNA sequences retrieved from the three bones found at Conway's old house in Kenilworth will match those in the DNA collected from Betty's children.

But this is where the complexities creep in. Betty Ketani's children are all from different fathers, with no DNA samples available from any of the men. Thulani, Bulelwa and Lusanda are half-siblings, having inherited half of their nuclear DNA from their mother and half from their fathers. This will play havoc with the algorithms generated by the DNA identification process executed by the ICMP. To make matters worse, if any of Betty's DNA is found, it will likely have been damaged, which will result in what is known as partial matches.

Given all these scenarios and countless other factors that impact on the DNA analysis, the ICMP is thus forced to take a conservative approach. This translates into a percentage of probability – and the ICMP doesn't settle for anything less than 99.95 per cent.

Feet bones are not the worst vessels of DNA but they are by no means the best.

The first bone refuses to surrender enough DNA and is discarded. The second meets the same fate. Between Pretoria and Bosnia, four of the six bones have failed to offer so much as a hint of proof that Betty Ketani was ever buried at 21A Leo Street. The fifth, still in South Africa, has been filed away and won't be tested.

Only one more bone has the potential to offer a forensic link.

When it arrived in Bosnia, the bone – with its new bar code 4101016 – was 5.9 centimetres long and weighed just 0.84 grams. It had a unique shape with a splinter that looked like the thumb of a cupped hand, probably the result of a small piece breaking off at some point. Like the others, the remaining bone is reduced to its molecular level and scientists begin their search. They must determine whether there's enough DNA to amplify and sequence.

53.

The first time prosecutor Namika Kowlas accepted a plea-bargain deal with a criminal, she cried all the way home from the office. It was an agonising decision to have to make. She knew the man had done terrible things, that he was a 'horrible human being', and letting him off with a lighter sentence seemed to go against everything she stood for as a state advocate. It played on her conscience and made her want to do what she always did in times of emotional turmoil or confusion: drive down to Durban and spend a few days with her mother.

Kowlas grew up in what she describes as a typical family. An only child, she accompanied her father to watch all the sport he enjoyed: cricket, tennis, rugby ... He made a staunch Manchester United fan out of his daughter. Later she found her own hobbies in hiking, reading, visiting art galleries and travelling. Like Broodryk, she became competitive in her career.

Kowlas didn't really have a choice in taking that first Section 105A plea bargain. Based on the available evidence, there was no other option. The case demanded it.

> *It was about compromise. And I don't like compromise.*

When it came to the Betty Ketani investigation, Kowlas knew from the start that deals would have to be made. She had come a long way since that first experience, but that didn't make negotiating with criminals and their lawyers any easier.

Early on, she began carrying the Ketani case around with her, thinking about it when she was at home or having coffee somewhere. It was always on her mind everywhere she went. It became her 'baby'. She thought about Betty Ketani and how her family fell apart without her. She thought about the men who took a mother away from her children, and how those children suffered in the years that followed.

265

> *She looked like she had a good life. Like she was a fun-loving, outgoing person. And then, suddenly, it was all gone and they didn't know where she was. It was an unfinished life.*

Kowlas travelled to the Eastern Cape with Captain Gerhard van Wyk. She met Betty's children and got to know them. When the two daughters came up to Johannesburg for the trial, Kowlas says she took the youngest, Lusanda, to her first movie at a cinema.

Kowlas and Broodryk are confident that Paul Toft-Nielsen and Dirk Reinecke will flip for the state. Paul has given a full confession and Dirk has admitted to his role in kidnapping Ketani and holding her captive in a hotel room. They both face serious charges but, with the right lawyers, can avoid jail time.

Conway Brown's situation is different. His lawyer is angling for the best deal to keep his client from serving any more time than he already has. Conway never applied for bail and has been in jail for over a year. But unlike Paul and Dirk, the crimes he has confessed to are far more serious.

Conway admits to being present when Betty was stabbed, to burying her body and then digging up her skeleton to help get rid of it. So there's no way that Broodryk can sign off a deal – nor does he have any desire to – that would see Conway escape a murder sentence. Both sides are refusing to blink, waiting as the clock counts down to the start of the trial.

Negotiations with Paul's and Dirk's lawyers go smoothly. Both clients are out on bail and agree to bargain. Paul will plead guilty to being an accessory after the fact to murder and will receive a five-year suspended sentence. He won't have to serve any time in jail but will have to testify against Carrington and the others.

Paul has reached a point of no return. He's already accused his childhood friend of threatening him inside jail and has signed an affidavit that contributed to Carrington being denied bail. His confession was taken by a magistrate and is on record and in Carrington's possession. His options are either to take a deal or be convicted by a court, which may not be as lenient on the sentencing. In exchange for staying clear of jail, Paul will have to come clean on his role in digging up Betty Ketani's grave and discarding her bones. Having known Carrington for 30 years, Paul could be an extremely useful man to have on the state's side, even if he is volatile and unpredictable.

Dirk, in turn, will have to accept a kidnapping conviction but he too will not see the inside of a prison cell. He'll tell the court about how Betty was interrogated at the hotel and fill in the blanks about how the confession made its way to Conway. Dirk is an important link and will receive the same sentence as Paul, plus three years' correctional supervision.

Broodryk and Kowlas will have the option of calling them both to testify and will receive statements from each detailing their crimes. They know they are probably going to be torn apart by the defence and their credibility will be tested, but Broodryk has dealt with worse witnesses in the past and understands the value of corroborative evidence. He calls putting such witnesses on the stand 'grin-and-bear-it time'. No one is going to try to convince a court that they are angels. But in this case, Broodryk says he doesn't need angels, he needs criminals. It's the old 'use a crook to catch a crook' approach.

The court will, of course, have to give its stamp of approval, but the plan is for Paul and Dirk to become Section 105A witnesses. On the first day of trial they will plead guilty and will be sentenced immediately. A separation of trial will follow, with the remaining accused receiving new indictments and being offered more time to prepare, given the new evidence against them. All this will play out on Monday, 22 July 2013, when the Betty Ketani trial is scheduled to get under way.

On the Friday before, 19 July 2013, negotiations continue with Conway's lawyer. The deadlock remains in place and Nardus Grové is not budging. He's an experienced lawyer and is not ready to play his hand.

Dirk signed the first plea-and-sentence agreement two days earlier. Paul came to the party the following day. But by Friday afternoon there is still no agreement and no word from the only man who can take the court to the scene of the stabbing and who can explain how, and by whom, Betty's body was buried.

More than a year has passed since Conway was arrested and now there are just two days – a weekend – before the trial commences. Conway is yet to commit to giving a supplementary affidavit and his lawyer is still pushing for a better deal, one that entails no jail time. Broodryk, however, knows

Conway has no chance in court and has dug in his heels. He and Kowlas leave the office that afternoon not knowing whether, come Monday, they are going to be prosecuting Conway or calling him as a witness.

• • •

Back in Milpark Hospital, Doc pulls through. His recovery will be a long one but he has survived the shooting and is regaining some movement. Gradually, he is moved out of the intensive care unit and into a general ward, followed by a rehabilitation centre. Eventually, he will be allowed to go home to his mother's house in Observatory. He is weak and pale, trapped in a wheelchair. He has lost a lot of weight and is being fed by family members or a nurse, who has been hired to assist him. Everyone who encounters Doc says it's as though the life has drained out of him, all but a few precious drops.

It is this recovery period that exposes the contrasts of Doc's life. On the one hand is his undercover work with Sanab and the Scorpions, his brothers at the bike clubs and the tales of mayhem tattooed along his arms and back. It's the bullet wounds in his shoulder and the flattened 9mm round that bounced up from the tarmac, which he will turn into a pendant and wear around his neck. It's JB bringing him the latest news from the *kas*.

On the other hand is the warm tea his mother makes for him. It's her home in leafy Observatory, with its sparkling pool and intricate mezuzahs on the door frames. And it's the yellowing letters from the Guild Cottage children's home, where Doc did volunteer work, such as escorting a girl to a matric dance or cooking Christmas meals for the kids.

It takes months for Doc to start walking short distances. He misses out on a lot of the court case, but follows it in the news or on Twitter, monitoring the twists and turns and coming up with new theories. He waits anxiously to hear about the handwriting and DNA results.

54.

Broodryk and Kowlas may not have their most crucial witness nailed down and are still stuck with a weak handwriting report, but they know that whatever happens on the first trial date, they'll be given more time to prepare.

Even if the deal with Conway falls through, Dirk and Paul will still have to be formally separated from the other accused once their plea bargains are read into the record. The next trial date will be weeks or even months away.

Plus, there is news from Bosnia.

Scientists there have failed to extract DNA from two of the three bones submitted to the ICMP. But the third and final bone turned out to contain just enough DNA for a match. An invisible speck of molecules floating in a solution of buffer has offered the first forensic proof that Betty Ketani was buried in Conway's garden.

A year ago, Captain Teunis Briers set out to find Betty Ketani, and the ICMP is now confirming that he succeeded. The DNA results are below the ICMP's threshold for issuing a match report and Ana Bilić, who signs off the final review on 20 May 2013, cautions that the evidence is not strong enough to stand independently. That's because the bone was badly degraded and contained only a small amount of DNA. The fact that Betty's three children all have different fathers also messed with the comparison.

And yet, the DNA Statistical Comparison Report suggests that the bone that was tested belonged to Betty Ketani. Or, as the ICMP phrases it:

> The DNA results obtained from the bone sample are 4 740 times more likely if they originated from Khetane [sic] Thandiwe Betty than if they originated from another unrelated individual in the general population. The factor by which the DNA evidence supports the hypothesis that the bone is from Khethane [sic] Thandiwe Betty rather than an unrelated person is 4 740.

From the DNA profile that emerges from the third bone, the absence of a Y chromosome means that scientists were easily able to tell that the bone belonged to a female. For Broodryk, that alone is significant. He was prepared to go to trial without any DNA results at all, and would have relied on the testimony of Teunis Briers, who found the bones, and Claudia Bisso, who would identify them as human. To back them up, he could always call his investigating officer and Melanie Pienaar.

But now he is able to prove scientifically that the bones are human, female and contain DNA that partially matches that of Betty's children. Broodryk may still not have a body, but this is as close as he is going to get. And it's a whole lot more than what he was expecting.

The DNA report is a game changer. Broodryk wonders whether the defence will dispute the link and how the accused could ever hope to explain the existence of a bone containing a DNA profile that matches – however faintly – those of Thulani, Bulelwa and Lusanda Ketani. What's more, how could they explain this bone, and others, being found at the exact location where Conway and Paul say they dug up Betty's body?

Unlike a murder weapon that can be planted or a witness who can lie, this is a sequence of genetic codes locked deep inside a human bone, accessible only to the best DNA scientists in the world.

The test ICMP staff ran to map out the DNA targeted eight *loci* or markers. Of these, three offered a clean and complete profile, while two gave partial results. For the purposes of court cases and databases around the world, nine, 13 or more *loci* per sample are generally compared and reported on. The results in this case fall short of that, but, as the ICMP's Thomas Parsons will argue in due course, nothing precludes a court from accepting a partial profile as a match. This evidence is also not being used to directly implicate an accused but rather to prove the identity of a deceased person.

Parsons leads a team of 85 scientists at the ICMP and has a PhD in molecular science, specialising in ancient DNA and population genetics. He has testified at The Hague, in a war crimes tribunal relating to the former Yugoslavia, and will fly to Johannesburg, along with quality controller Ana Bilić, to testify in the Ketani trial. It will be the first time ever that ICMP officials give evidence in a criminal case in South Africa. Parsons will go on to describe the country's legal system as fair and mature. For a man who is not prone to hyperbole, he will call it an 'edifying experience' on par with proceedings at The Hague.

From the moment it arrives, the DNA report from Bosnia becomes one of the strongest aspects of the state's case. To the scientists at the ICMP, where the bone was found, who handled it and how is irrelevant. The information that provided the link was inside the bone, matched later to the DNA samples taken from Betty's children.

If any errors occur during the extraction process, Parsons explains, the results are faulty and are not reported. Asked about false incrimination and convictions through DNA matching, Parsons smiles and says: 'Boy, I don't know many instances where that's happened.'

55.

On the morning of Monday, 22 July 2013, Johannesburg is in the grip of a cold winter snap. Carrington Laughton enters the dock from the holding cells wearing a black trench coat over his suit. Carel and David Ranger are ushered in with him. Paul and Dirk, out on bail, are anxiously milling around in the corridors outside, both neatly shaved and smartly dressed for the first day of trial.

Conway Brown is brought in separately, wearing a pinstripe suit and glasses, a rosary wrapped around his wrist. His lawyer has been in court for a while, putting the finishing touches to his client's plea-and-sentence agreement. Nardus Grové has set up a small mobile printer next to his MacBook Pro. He has waited for the fifty-ninth second of the eleventh hour, holding out for the right deal. But time is up and Conway must sign the documents or go on trial.

As the other lawyers leave the courtroom – the noisy conversations floating away behind them – Conway settles down to read through the agreement. Nardus has been sending his juniors to consult with Conway in prison and the two of them have not had a lot of time together. The deal on the table now is quite possibly the best Conway can hope for.

He has to plead guilty to a charge of attempted murder and being an accessory after the fact to murder. Each charge comes with a five-year jail sentence, one of which will be suspended. Of the remaining five years, Conway will only have to serve about a fifth before being placed under correctional supervision, as long as he completes all the right programmes in prison, passes his assessments and is not blocked by an objection from the victim's family. It's a good deal, but to earn it he will have to spend days in the witness box testifying against Carrington and the Ranger brothers. Page by page, Conway reads the document, initials each page and eventually signs it.

The prosecutors have their third and most important witness.

Now and again Conway looks over his shoulder at Blanche, who is sitting at the back of the courtroom. Like the time he signed his first confession, which was caught on a hidden camera, he spends minutes lost in his thoughts, clutching his rosary beads and shutting his eyes. Before proceedings begin, he finds a moment to give Blanche a kiss.

Carrington's wife Anel is also here, her hair covering a discreet tattoo on the back of her neck made up of three letters: 'CRL', Carrington Roger Laughton. His father, Harold, is sitting beside her, dressed in a smart blue jacket and tie. Just a few weeks previously, Carrington's lawyers, Boesman van der Westhuizen and Sog van Eck, were still trying to get their client out on bail, and they know full well what to expect today. Carrington will, however, soon part ways with them, arguing over strategy and legal fees, and will appoint Howard Woolf and Laurence Hodes SC to take over his defence. To secure Hodes's services he will have to spend a few extra months awaiting trial in jail.

Betty Ketani's brother Mankinki has caught an overnight taxi from the Eastern Cape and will report back to the family once proceedings are over. He is alone, wearing a warm leather jacket, and seated in the middle of the public gallery.

Lieutenant Colonel André Neethling pops in to see what's happening. He has three other cases on the go in the same building at the Palm Ridge court but he can't help his curiosity. The confession he took from Conway more than a year ago has led to all the arrests and everything else that unfolded. Neethling is on the list of state witnesses but won't need to testify now that Conway is pleading guilty. Conway lied to Neethling about his role on the night Betty Ketani was stabbed near the R59 highway, neglecting to mention anything about holding her as the silver shaft was plunged into her head. But the statement Conway has just signed contains this and other confessions.

The public benches fill up and the lawyers are back, huddled in a circle, talking and laughing loudly among themselves. Broodryk is at the prosecutor's podium, assuring reporters setting up sound equipment that he has been accused of many things, but whispering is not one of them. Namika Kowlas and Gerhard van Wyk are by his side. Gerhard Pretorius, who has taken a transfer from Yeoville to Meyerton, is also in court in what must be a bittersweet moment for him. He had never had a case like this and didn't think he ever would again. His former partner, Lufuno Sono, is absent, as are JB and Doc.

Shortly before 11am the court is convened and all six accused file into the dock. Conway sits shoulder to shoulder with Carrington. The Ranger brothers are to his left, followed by Paul and Dirk. Three other accused from a separate case are also brought in, forcing everyone to squash up. The men no longer have any room to move their arms and sit with their hands clasped in their laps, avoiding as much eye contact with each other as possible. Old friendships are dead, new alliances have been formed and those moments waiting for the judge and his assessors to enter are passed in uncomfortable silence.

Eventually, Broodryk addresses the court, dealing with a few minor logistical issues. These include the fact that although the case is being heard in Palm Ridge, it is a South Gauteng High Court matter. He announces that three of the accused have entered into plea bargains.

Conway is up first. His agreement is read out in court by his lawyer. At the end, Brown confirms the arrangement with a polite but incorrect 'I agree, Your Worship', which is the way magistrates are addressed, as compared to 'Your Lordship' for judges in the High Court.

It takes an hour for Conway's, Paul's and Dirk's plea agreements to be placed on record. Each gives an explanation of the charges and a summary of the confession, and ends with mitigating and aggravating factors. The proceedings are standard.

Right at the end, Mankinki Kula is called to the stand to confirm that he was consulted about the deals. With the assistance of an interpreter, he agrees to them. Although he gets to look into the eyes of the men accused of murdering his sister, he is still a long way off from getting the answers he wants.

Conway, Paul and Dirk are then asked to stand. The judge declares that he is satisfied with the agreements and convicts and sentences the three. It all happens quickly, but it is a big moment: three men have finally been convicted in connection with Betty Ketani's murder, 14 years after she disappeared. And all because of three pieces of paper that lay under a carpet.

The trial is postponed for two days for the state to serve new indictments on the remaining accused: Carrington and the Ranger brothers. But that will just be a formality. The actual trial will now resume in November. As soon as the judge has left the courtroom, Conway Brown shares his feelings:

> I don't want to say relieved. It's been a year and a half awaiting trial. It's nice to know there is direction now and everything will come out. I would like other people to come forward with the information that they should come forward with. Then it will be fair.

Before heading back to Queenstown, Mankinki says he is happy that three of the accused have turned state witness. He says he feels comfortable going home to tell Thulani, Bulelwa and Lusanda about what happened and is sure they will be happy too. Mankinki admits that listening to the plea bargains was painful and brought back memories of his sister.

Asked about the lengthy postponement, he replies: 'We've been waiting for 14 years. We can wait for November.'

56.

With the trial more than three months away, the Section 105A witnesses lined up and the DNA results in, the focus falls back on the handwriting analysis.

Herman Broodryk wants more samples of Carrington's handwriting so that Colonel Marco van der Hammen doesn't run into the same problem as his Pretoria colleague who compiled the first report. He wants definitive answers. If Broodryk is going to fly DNA experts out from Bosnia and the United States, he wants the same level and quality of evidence when it comes to the handwriting. He likes 99.98 per cent probabilities.

Captain Gerhard van Wyk has been in and out of prison, following up on whether Carrington has been illegally using a cellphone from inside his cell. Carrington didn't take kindly to this and laid a charge of intimidation against the policeman. The case didn't go anywhere but the prison visits did give Van Wyk an idea.

The detective has heard that Carrington has sent a number of letters to the managers of the prison requesting various items or complaining about his family not being able to visit him on certain days. Van Wyk wonders whether he can intercept those letters and seize them as evidence.

He is prepared to apply for another court warrant but is told he doesn't need one. The police and prisons are organs of the same state and can share resources, especially in a criminal investigation. The process turns out to be fairly painless and within weeks he has seven handwritten letters in his possession. Carrington had refused to write as much as a single word to assist the police investigation. Now Van Wyk is holding 11 pages of his handwriting.

Carrington's prison letters were written between May and August 2013. They are neat and old-fashioned. On each one, he has written his name, prison number and the section where he is being held, the receiver's details, the date and the subject of the correspondence.

The first thing that catches the captain's attention is that Carrington is now using a completely different signature. Van Wyk has unearthed samples of Carrington's signature from 1998 through to 2012. Over a period of 14 years – from a television receipt to his passport – the signature had remained the same. The one that appears above his name now is a brand-new design.

Van Wyk has a theory about why Carrington would suddenly create a new signature that looks nothing like the one on the confession – a point of dispute during the trial – but he has enough samples of Carrington's signature from the crucial year of 1999, so what matters more is the actual handwriting. And for that, these prison letters are perfect. They range from a request to meet another inmate to discuss a case in the Constitutional Court to a request for permission to receive a 4gb Apple iPod that had been sent for repairs, was brought back by Anel and was now stuck in some official's office. In another letter, Carrington asks to receive a television, a short extension cord and an electric steam iron.

In some of the letters Carrington tries to convince prison authorities to grant him special visits. First, he asks for his sister and daughter (from his marriage to Jayne) to be allowed to visit him on a weekend instead of a Friday. He says that because of work and school, they can't make it any other time. A rejection note is written on this letter in red pen, explaining that weekend visits are for sentenced inmates.

Carrington then approaches a social worker to ask for a meeting to discuss 'matters of a personal nature'. What he is after is a special visit from his two sons:

> I debated the point with her [social worker] that 'visiting' my children, especially the two-year-old and the baby through a glass window is not a good idea and would not in any way at all serve the best interests of my children.
>
> For your information I saw the baby last when he was about three weeks old and the two-year-old some 15 months ago before my arrest. In fact I dropped him off at crèche the day of my arrest.
>
> … Trying to connect with small children, in these circumstances, through glass and bars would do more harm than good.

I respectfully request your intervention in this matter to help facilitate making these arrangements at your soonest convenience.

Thanking you in advance for your kind consideration and assistance.

Yours faithfully, Carrington Laughton.

Like Conway's art and poetry, the letters offer insight into their author. Carrington wanted the prison authorities to make an exception for him and let his sister visit him on days reserved for other prisoners. He called this a 'special visit', explaining that she was not available during the week.

While Conway struggled to get a pair of sneakers in which to exercise or spent a month getting a tin of coffee from the prison tuck shop, Carrington requested a steam iron for his clothes. Where Conway couldn't string together a few words without making a mistake, Carrington's letters are formal and eloquent. In one of them, he wanted to authorise the unit manager of his prison section to hand over all his belongings to Carel and David Ranger should his bail application be successful.

Where Conway cowered and bowed to prison warders, Carrington wanted to be taken seriously, demanding his rights and 'debating' his points of view. During his legal fight with his landlords in Sharonlea, Carrington used Latin phrases in his emails while his digital signature contained a family crest. To create the impression that his company, C&C Commercial Services, was bigger than it was, and more established, he listed some of his friends as 'associates' on the letterheads. Carrington cared deeply about his image, even as he communicated from inside his prison cell.

Van Wyk takes great pleasure in telling the story of how he managed to get Carrington's handwriting samples without him knowing.

'Not bad for a dumb cop,' he jokes.

There is little time to gloat and Van Wyk's next task is to get the new samples to Marco van der Hammen as quickly as possible.

57.

In 1993, when he flew off to marry his second wife, Jitra, in Thailand, Eric Neeteson-Lemkes left Cranks in the hands of Toby Shapshak, who had just finished studying at Rhodes University and was eager to make a little money before going travelling.

Toby went on to become one of South Africa's best-known tech journalists, but back then, in the early nineties, Toby was still on his way to becoming a regular news reporter and was introduced to Eric by a mutual friend.

Like everyone else, Toby remembers Eric as a 'strange character' and calls him 'a bizarre enigma'. He recalls the stories Eric told about serving in the French Foreign Legion (which is difficult to reconcile with the history he sketches in his affidavit) and about fighting off robbers in his restaurant. Eric told him about his father, who was Dutch, and his mother, who was Indonesian.

In all the time he worked for Eric, Toby admired his ability to run a restaurant and saw him as a sound businessman. He couldn't help feel that the 'Mad Dog' or 'Strange Eric' was just an act performed by someone who was in complete control.

What Toby also picked up on is that, despite being a wealthy man, Eric was running Cranks on a shoestring budget. He would make Toby drive all the way downtown to pick up an order of duck because it was cheaper. Or he would cut an A4 sheet of carbon paper into four pieces to fit the cheaper and smaller Oom Dik notepads he used for orders, making sure nothing was wasted.

'He didn't spend on anything. He liked that his restaurant had a cheap and crappy feel to it,' Toby recalls.

Toby wasn't at Cranks long enough to witness the upheaval that began in 1998, but he did work there, on and off, for a few years. He got to know Eric's wife Jitra and he knew Betty Ketani, the woman with a great sense of humour and the colourful headscarves. When Eric left him to run the restaurant, Toby never interfered with what Betty was doing in the kitchen. She was far too good a cook for that and could get the orders out quickly.

'She was the ideal employee. She was headstrong and feisty, but great. She ran the whole kitchen,' Toby remembers. 'She was hard-working and diligent. She took no nonsense.'

Toby remembers Betty's smile. He also noticed that Eric treated her differently to all the other staff.

'He always treated her with respect,' Toby says. 'He was even proud of how good and quick she was. She ruled the kitchen as her own preserve.'

• • •

Betty Ketani's oldest brother, Thubeni, says his sister was usually the life of any party. She laughed easily and overcame a tough childhood to find a job she enjoyed. If she had financial problems, she kept them to herself and certainly didn't mention anything to him when they spoke on the phone. She sent money home and always came bearing gifts.

'She loved her friends and she was well liked,' he remembers. 'She liked dressing well and looking after herself. She took a lot of pride in her appearance. She always seemed happy.'

Thubeni moved to George, in the Western Cape, when he was still a teenager. He went there to find his father, who had recently divorced their mother. When the investigation into his sister's murder began, Thubeni was in his late fifties, working as a driver at the local airport. He followed developments in the case through his brother Mankinki. The more he learned about the crime, the more anger filled his heart. Unlike Mankinki, he had no desire to face the men accused of killing Betty.

'They killed her like a dog. They buried her and poured concrete over her. I couldn't bear to see them. What they did was cruel and inhumane. We'll never get over the pain and we'll never forgive.'

In Queenstown, Eastern Cape, Betty's children use similar words when asked about their mother's death.

'She was buried like she was not a human being. It's painful to hear that they threw her away to the rubbish. That was very painful,' Bulelwa said during a *Carte Blanche* interview. 'In our culture when someone is dead you bury her and then you go and visit her. We don't even know where to visit her and tell her our problems, so she can look after us.'

For Bulelwa and Lusanda one of the most frustrating things is knowing there are people out there, including in other countries, who they believe know things but are staying silent.

Bulelwa comments, 'It hurts because if they were here, maybe the truth would come out.'

58.

Once Conway Brown pleaded guilty, was sentenced and began serving his time, he agreed to a series of candid interviews. These conversations lasted for hours, and were recorded over a period of four months. Conway was responsible for the continued existence of the single most important piece of evidence in this case: the 1999 confession hidden in his bedroom. Without it, the trial that was approaching would not be taking place.

There were so many questions only Conway could answer. Why did he confess so quickly to the police? Why did he follow Carrington deep into his world? Why did he stay silent for so many years? How could he leave Kenilworth without retrieving the papers under the carpet? And, most importantly, given all of his lies, had he finally told the truth?

Journalist and author Jonny Steinberg once wrote: 'I do not pretend to know what goes on in the heads of those about whom I write. But I do try to imagine, as fiercely as I can, how the world seems to them. The best way to do this, I think, is to pay attention to those moments when a person decides.'

Conway made many decisions, which all added up to where he now found himself, serving time for Betty Ketani's murder. He tried to explain some of his decisions but wouldn't even attempt others. He saw the interviews as part of his journey and spoke willingly about his life.

Conway's days in prison were taken up by the simple tasks he set himself. These included meeting a social worker or attending a programme he had to complete in order to qualify for early release. He beamed with pride at having been asked to teach a class in the prison workshop and was especially happy to have found the Buddhist centre, which may not sound like much, but considering prisons are divided into sections, moving between them takes a full-blown expedition. He had also painted a giant Women's Day banner that was hung up to mark the occasion.

Conway would show off his tattoos or his latest soap sculpture, if he hadn't already traded it for cigarettes or sugar. One sculpture he was particularly proud of was a three-dimensional snake with a tiny red tongue made out of a matchstick or a piece of cardboard. He had carved it using a piece of wood broken off the armrest of a chair.

During the interviews, Conway spent a lot of time going over the actual crimes, reconstructing scenes, clarifying details or placing various individuals. He struggled to organise anything into sequential order and his whole life seemed to be a series of strobe-light flashes, or broken memories. His interests had swung from researching Vlad the Impaler to learning magic tricks, his art went from copying Picasso to drawing childlike cartoons, and his spiritual belief system was a weird blend of Christianity, Buddhism, Wicca and some strange cult originating in India. He would talk about going on a retreat where the spiritual leader would make the rain start or stop at will. He dabbled in everything and knew a little about the things that interested him – but all of the parts just didn't seem to fit together into a whole.

The interviews kept circling back to why he hid the confession under the carpet and how he could have forgotten to take it with him when he and Blanche moved homes. He could never offer a proper explanation.

> It wasn't an accident. It can't be an accident. For everything to just line up like it did. I'm going to use the wrong words here, but it's like divine intervention. Somebody just put their hand on this and said: 'This is the right time, this is the only way it can be done.' I couldn't do this any other way. I couldn't get my head around it because everything was so complex, so busy, so many facets of all these other things …

Doc, JB and the Yeoville detectives all felt the same: how could it be possible for everything to just fall into place and for the arrests to be made so quickly? They too felt a guiding hand.

For Shama Marshall, it was karma. For Claudia Bisso, it was science. For Herman Broodryk, it was a once-in-a-lifetime alignment of random events and coincidences, fate conspiring against those involved in the crime.

Conway was pushed on whether he understood the difference between right and wrong and whether he knew he was crossing a line. He said it all happened gradually, one misguided step at a time, and before he knew it, he was in too deep. After the stabbing, he was inextricably tied into all the lies and secrets, and his instinct simply took over.

> To keep this quiet, there is nothing you're not prepared to do. Nothing. If someone came to me tomorrow and said: 'Listen, we need to blow up X, Y and Z, otherwise this is going to come out', it wouldn't even be a question because it's your life you're talking about. At the end of the day, it's about self-preservation. Your morals don't come into it.

Conway claimed that if he had been asked up front to abduct somebody or murder someone he would have refused. He described himself as 'a fixer', someone who was called upon to sort out situations. But, he said, he had watched enough Hollywood movies to know that things don't end well for villains. He claims he didn't really have a choice.

> If you said to me, 'Listen, I need you to go and shoot somebody', I'd be like, 'No, you're barking up the wrong tree here.' So there is clearly stuff I won't do. But maybe having witnessed what I witnessed, that shit goes out the window, because now you need to do whatever you need to do to make sure that this doesn't come out. And you say, 'Well, why don't you go to the cops?' But you're trying to make sure that you're still alive. You've got a family to look after. You don't know who to trust. It's like you're giving me a gun, you're going to put the bullet in and say, 'Pull the trigger.'

To illustrate the point further, Conway used yet another metaphor, stating that keeping the secret was like driving on a highway and pushing back against a car trying to run you into a ditch. It was like self-defence. Conway tried to justify his decisions by referring to his dysfunctional childhood, his family's dire financial situation and the seductive pull Carrington had on those around him. He spoke about his life falling apart and how he wanted to make things right with Betty's family, even though he didn't think he ever could. How he communicated with her spirit or how he cared for the garden above where she was buried. The woman with the great smile and colourful headscarves entombed in ready-mix cement inside a shallow grave outside his window.

Conway said he used to speak to her. Pray to her, with her. She was the only one who knew the secret he was carrying. He thought about going to the police, but didn't trust them. Betty, it seemed, was the only one he could speak to. This woman without a face. Without a name. Buried outside his living-room window. Never more than a few metres away, no matter what part of the house he was in.

Conway claims he wondered about her. He thought about her age, about her children and about what she could have possibly done to deserve such a brutal death.

He wondered how he got tangled up in the crime. He asked why he was the one to be called out that night. How would it have played out if Candice hadn't shot herself and he was never asked to go to Mark Eardley's farm? Would the body still have landed up at his house? He drowned in self-pity, seeing himself as the victim. He called himself a 'sucker', an 'easy target'.

When he prayed, Conway asked for forgiveness. If he knew who the victim was, it might have been easier. In his mind, he could rationalise or justify the murder of a hijacker, a rapist or a violent robber. But the scraps of information he had managed to gather suggested that this was not the case. He tried to 'make it right with God', who, he was convinced, knew exactly what part he had played. Over and over, he would offer different versions of his personal prayer to Betty:

> *Look, I'm helluva sorry you got caught up in this. It was not my making, I'm just trying to do the best I can with the messed-up situation.*

In prison, he spoke about a wound that would never heal:

> *A part of me died the same time and you can say what you want, but you don't get it back. You become dead inside. This wound has killed me.*

Conway kept describing the hole that was torn in his life when his father died and how he had nobody to ask for advice or to help him out when he lost a job. ('I've been on my own since *frikken* day one.') He grew angry with himself for the way he treated Blanche (his 'couldn't-give-a-shit' attitude) or how much of his children's lives he missed out on. He agonised over what his son and daughter think of him – the man who was supposed to teach them right from wrong. ('Whatever Dad taught us is a load of shit because Dad is a criminal.') He kept wondering why he didn't try to stop the stabbing.

But when it came to the web of circumstances around Betty Ketani's death, there were many contradictions and almost every answer Conway gave evolved into another question. Many more questions would be raised by Carrington's defence during the trial.

Why would two separate victims of the Hillbrow abductions (Themba and Ndaba) identify Conway in a line-up when he claims he had nothing to do with them? Why would Carrington call him out to the side of the R59 if all he needed was someone to hold Betty Ketani, who was already restrained and helpless? Why does the confession state that Conway met the author at a house where Betty was being 'slapped around for a few hours' and not on the side of the highway? Did he play a more significant role in the abduction than he has admitted to? Why was Conway's first confession so different to his final one and to his evidence in court? How could he not remember whether he had read the letter, who had given it to him and who his accomplices were at different stages of the crime? How could so many details be lost, such as who lowered Betty's body into the grave? Were the black holes – or these 'brick walls' he built around painful memories – even real?

From the moment he arrived at the Yeoville police station to meet the detectives, everyone with whom he came into contact saw a man riddled with remorse and exhausted from keeping his secret. Conway was Dostoevsky's Rodion, driven mad by the crime he had committed.

But Carrington and his legal team didn't see it that way. They saw a 'sadistic' liar who was trying to save himself. They found letters he had written in prison on behalf of other inmates, suggesting he wasn't dyslexic or as hapless as he pretended to be. They grilled him about why he pleaded guilty to attempted murder if he claimed to have never planned to take part in the stabbing. They described as absurd the suggestion that the stabbing could have happened in absolute silence and was never discussed afterwards. Or that Conway stayed friends with Carrington right up until their arrest.

Conway was called out for lying to André Neethling, of conveniently using the gaps in his memory and implicating Paul and Dirk in crimes, only to take it back later. Carrington claimed Conway was able to draw a blueprint of an entire factory production line from memory, down to the electrical circuits.

Conway was forced to explain why he had left so much detail out of his statements and why his story didn't align perfectly with Paul and Dirk's. The smallest details were amplified: was Betty in the boot or the back seat? If she was in the back seat, how did he not see her when they first met? What shoes was he wearing on the night? Was the victim later wrapped in a blanket or a hospital sheet? What did Mark Lister look like? Who mixed the concrete? Who asked Paul to come and help dig up the grave? Who drove the car? What colour were the rubbish bags? Who brought the gloves? Was he told to keep safe or destroy the contents of the metal box containing the confession? Did he throw them away or burn them? The questions went on and on …

There can be no doubt that Conway was now parting with some of his secrets. That there was truth among the lies. But a judge would have to decide what to make of Conway's story, especially what he claims happened near the Blockhouse. It will be up to that judge to determine whether he has made a 'full and frank' disclosure, or whether he never stopped lying.

• • •

If Conway considered granting interviews cathartic, Carrington was the complete opposite. He guarded his privacy and refused all requests. During a prison visit in October 2012, he agreed to write down some notes, but never did. Later he was sent around 50 detailed questions via his lawyers, but declined to answer them. During the trial, standing in the dock, he said the answer to each one of them was the same: 'None of your business.'

His line never changed: 'You'll get nothing from me. I have nothing to say because I wasn't involved.'

In a final attempt, his lawyer received and signed for a letter asking him to participate in the writing of this book, but again there was no reply.

Carrington was prepared to discuss neither the case nor his private life. Instead, he spoke about how, once the trial was over and he was vindicated, he would apply to Google to erase any search results that linked his name to the case. Standing trial for murder, he was concerned about what people would find when they entered his name into an online search engine.

Chatting to lawyers in the courtroom or his co-accused, Carrington maintained that his only crime was to have made bad friends. In his mind, Conway, Paul, Dirk and all the others had 'wasted' years of his life.

'The wheel turns,' he would say, musing about how everyone who had done him wrong was on his radar.

Carrington went on about the difference between public interest and the interest of the public, arguing that trials should not be reported until they are finalised. He watched the videos that emerged about the Ketani case and gave what he considered to be tips on how to report on camera.

He accused the police of conspiring against him and prosecutors of believing they were 'doing God's work' while lying to get convictions. He never stopped being dismissive of the state's case, taking every opportunity to downplay 'rubbish evidence' or mock witnesses. He created an impression that the trial and his detention were temporary inconveniences. He kept notes of everything, instructed his legal team, and was in control of every aspect of his case. He spoke about fighting for his life, but there were also times when it seemed like it was all just a game.

One day, chatting to a lawyer in the public gallery, Carrington explained his approach, loud enough for everyone to hear.

'Our defence is simple,' he said. 'Prove it!'

59.

Once Carrington's prison letters arrive in Amanzimtoti at the end of August 2013, Colonel Marco van der Hammen is able to isolate 13 'discriminating elements' within the handwriting samples.

Like the scientists at the ICMP who searched for unique molecular markers along threads of DNA, Van der Hammen's task is to compare handwriting elements – quirks – and to pronounce on any matches. Humans are creatures of habit and these habits manifest inside a person's handwriting, sometimes even through attempts to hide them.

Carrington's writing is full of idiosyncrasies. His *g* looks like the number 6, his *q* is a circle sliced in half by a vertical line, the *w* has a tiny flick to the right and his *e* can look like either the Greek sigma or a sharp sideways *w*. Van der Hammen finds these and other examples – like Carrington's *m*, which has a 'peculiar' sag in the middle – and picks up on the way some of the letters connect to each other, a *c* that runs into an *e* or an *n* that links into the top of a *y*.

He scans in all the samples, zooms in on the relevant sections and compiles slides that point out these elements using bright red arrows. Under a microscope, Van der Hammen explores the symmetry of the letters: how in words such as 'face' or 'files' the tops of all the letters fall in a neat horizontal line below the downward hook of the *f* or how a capital *A* tends to slant upwards. He uses all the examples of handwriting at his disposal: the confession, the white envelope that contained the photographs, the television receipt, Carrington's warning statement and, of course, the seven prison letters.

Van der Hammen's findings must show whether the few lines written at the bottom of the September 1999 confession were penned by Carrington Laughton. While he now has a lot of reference samples with which to work – exhibits that Magendree Govindsamy never got to see or examine – the confession itself offers only about 30 words of handwriting, comprising 127 letters, a couple of numbers, a set of brackets and a few punctuation marks. Just like the minuscule amount of DNA that was pulled from the bone, this is a limited sample within which to search for patterns.

Although handwriting analysis is considered to be a pseudoscience, open to human interpretation, the process of arriving at a finding is rather similar to that followed in a DNA laboratory. An examiner such as Marco van der Hammen will study the samples and identify unique elements, after which he will construct hypotheses, test them and present his findings. The hypotheses will look similar to those of the ICMP, with one option suggesting a common author and a second proposing no link between the samples. The method is known as ACE, which stands for analysis, comparison and evaluation.

When analysing handwriting and signatures, Van der Hammen and forensic experts like him explore the style and execution, the rhythm and form. This deals with the design and construction of the letters and words, how they are arranged or how fluent a particular stroke is. He also looks at the speed with which a signature is made, the pressure applied and whether it contains an unusual loop or a unique 'flying finish'. These are all subtle features that reveal themselves to those who seek them out.

But, as Van der Hammen notes in all his reports, humans are not machines and cannot reproduce letters like a computer printer. This introduces what is known as 'natural variations', which can occur for a great number of reasons, from the author being in a rush or running out of writing space to the effects of stress. Once the style and execution are studied and natural variations accounted for, a report is issued.

Aside from Carrington's handwriting, Van der Hammen also studies Conway's and works through the ACE process on these samples too. But the style of handwriting is visibly different and he can find no matches in the letters or the links between them. Again, Van der Hammen lays out the samples on PowerPoint slides, this time using black arrows to show the differences.

Thanks to Gerhard van Wyk, Van der Hammen has examples of Carrington's signature over a period of 14 years. There are gaps, but he has samples from 1998 through to 2012, and they are all similar. The 2013 signatures Carrington started using in prison are new and, having studied them, Van der Hammen calls it a 'deliberate change in form and execution'. Van Wyk suspects Carrington intentionally changed his signature after his arrest because he realised how crucial it would be to the case against him. Carrington has a different explanation, which he will share later.

Setting aside the new design that Carrington came up with in prison, Van der Hammen maps out his real signature. He locates where it begins, where it breaks and where it continues into a series of sharp twists and loops, rising and falling, curling like two ocean waves and eventually circling around the entire creation, disappearing in a long slanted stroke towards what would be the two o'clock mark on a watch face. It is an unusual and complex signature, which the colonel breaks down into 14 points for the purposes of comparison.

Marco van der Hammen finds that the signatures on the 1999 confession were written quickly with a ballpoint pen, evident by the marks inside the lines, which are consistent with the turning of the ink ball. The first two signatures are small and are designed almost as a way to initial each of the pages. The one on the third page is large and formal, made with purpose and similar to signatures that appear on legal contracts.

'All three signatures are mutually consistent in respect of signature design, line sequence and continuity,' Van der Hammen notes. He then compares them to all the other available signature samples.

Before offering his findings, the policeman conducts a general examination of the confession. He identifies the font and the folds that run across all three pages. He lines up the margins and the staple marks, which reveal 'reddish-brown residue marks', probably rust. The corner of one of the pages has been torn, but aside from that, the letter is intact, the top half of the last page stained brown by what must have been damp from the carpet.

Van der Hammen believes that the document is genuine, and says so in his report. He even offers his opinion that it emerged from a laser printer, which is disputed by Carrington's team. What he can't determine is how old the confession is. That would require chemical tests on the paper and ink, which he doesn't have the skills or equipment to do. In court, Van der Hammen will come under fire from the defence for not outsourcing these tests, given that the bones were sent all the way to Bosnia for analysis. But

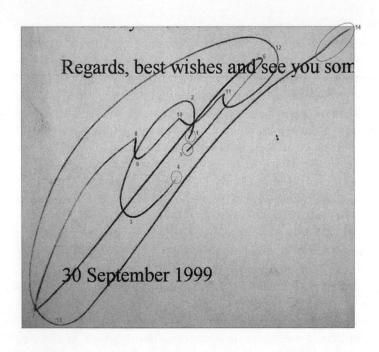

Regards, best wishes and see you som

30 September 1999

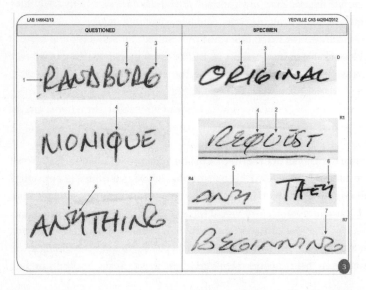

he will maintain that the letter must be old because of the rust marks and the stains.

When the colonel issues his report at the end of November (finalising his presentations later), it is a far cry from the one produced by his colleague Magendree Govindsamy. On both the signatures and the handwriting, Van der Hammen is willing to commit to firm conclusions. With his 16-page report in hand, he will testify that 'in all probability' Carrington Laughton signed the confession and wrote the four lines at the bottom of the third and final page.

On the three-level scale he uses in all his cases, from 'probably written' to 'conclusive', Van der Hammen's verdict falls midway on 'high probability'. In the realm of handwriting analysis, this makes any other alternative 'highly unlikely'. The reason Van der Hammen can't award the top-level finding is due to the limited writing sample on the confession and the quality of some of the signatures.

This is the report Broodryk was hoping to see. He knows that Marco van der Hammen will be able to explain his findings and how he arrived at them, and will be able to defend them on the witness stand. Carrington's lawyers have a copy of the first handwriting report and will question why a second expert, from another province, was brought in. They will accuse Van der Hammen of being called in to 'save the situation' by any means and of excluding evidence that didn't fit his findings. Having been in the witness box hundreds of times, Van der Hammen will smile under his breath and politely counter the accusations, going over his findings.

. . .

While Marco van der Hammen is wrapping up his presentations, the trial is postponed yet again. This time, it rolls over to the following year, and is now due to begin in mid-February 2014. By the time Broodryk and Kowlas will call their first witness, almost two years would have passed since Jeffrey Marshall and his girlfriend abandoned their movie date and drove home to help his family tear up some old carpets. The Ketani family will have to wait yet another three and a half months.

The reason for the most recent delay is that Carrington has fired his legal team and the new one needs time to prepare. Laurence Hodes is in court to confirm that he has taken over the case, but his diary is full and the December holidays are around the corner. His first available date is 17 February 2014.

Like Broodryk, Hodes is a silk and a brilliant lawyer. He and his father are well known in legal circles. Hodes has appointed a junior, Advocate Thabang Mathopo, to help him, while Howard Woolf will be his instructing attorney and the link to Carrington Laughton.

With no objections from the state, it takes just a few minutes to stand the trial down. The final chapter will have to wait.

60.

Before the unravelling can begin, Broodryk, Kowlas and Van Wyk discover a mountain of chain-of-evidence mistakes that need to be rectified.

Carrington's new legal team is refusing to make a single admission and is planning a merciless attack on the process surrounding the investigation. Known unofficially as 'Stalingrad burning', the defence will use every weapon in its arsenal to try to break the state's case before opening its own. The strategy will force prosecutors to call endless witnesses, some of whom performed menial tasks such as sealing an envelope or fetching DNA samples from another province. This will drag out the trial by weeks and cost Carrington a fortune, but it will expose each state witness to cross-examination, during which further mistakes may emerge.

It is a house-by-house, street-by-street battle, an assault on an entire city, where victory is often reached only through relentless attrition. It's a tense chess game of legal moves, where a great deal of thought goes into the order in which witnesses are called, where heads of arguments are drafted months before the applications that warrant their existence are launched, and where lawyers and prosecutors rehearse questions in their heads for weeks before delivering them in court. At this level of legal warfare, cases crumble on technicalities or collapse through Section 174 applications, which come the moment the state has closed its case and challenge whether an accused has a case to answer. The trial of Shrien Dewani is a well-known example of a case falling apart before an accused has to present his evidence.

As the trial draws nearer, Broodryk's job is to head off as many attacks as possible. He and his team ran into some luck with the DNA tests, held out for the Section 105A witnesses and got them, and now have a strong handwriting report. But they've also inherited a nightmare in the amount of mistakes made by almost every police officer involved with the Betty Ketani case.

Dirk Booysen took photographs on three separate occasions but mixed them up while compiling his statement. Having excavated the grave on 25 June 2012, he confused the date of the final and most important excavation, which took place two weeks later. This played havoc with the photograph albums that had been compiled and led to confusion over what date Captain Teunis Briers was in Kenilworth. As a result, the state faced the ridiculous situation of having to prove that Briers was actually present at the exhumation during which he uncovered the bones.

Briers landed up making three statements, while Booysen had to sign a second one to correct all the dates and explain the confusion surrounding the photographs from the June excavation, the 'blue light' tests for old bloodstains carried out inside the old railway bus on Mark Eardley's farm, and those he snapped when he had dropped by to see Claudia Bisso in Kenilworth on the day of the dig.

The mistakes might have gone unnoticed, but Broodryk and Kowlas had been under pressure to serve indictments and to reveal the police docket to the accused. So the defence was already in possession of the initial affidavits containing the errors.

For Teunis Briers it got worse. After the DNA swabs from Betty's children arrived from Queenstown, he opened the evidence bag containing the samples to remove the J88 forms – a record of the outcomes of medical examinations – that had mistakenly been sealed inside. Briers resealed the swabs in a new bag but didn't properly record the transfer from one sealed bag to another. When Hodes and his team got to the swabs, the seal numbers didn't add up and it appeared that the chain of evidence had been broken. The oversight would lead to a fierce legal dispute, which would require the court to make rulings over whether Broodryk would be allowed to re-examine Teunis Briers in order to explain what had happened (which he ultimately was). At one stage, the fate of the state's entire forensic evidence – and everything that had transpired at the ICMP – was under threat because of the way one policeman in Pretoria had opened and closed an evidence bag.

Briers's colleagues, Leonie Ras and Melanie Pienaar, both had to submit new statements to rectify minor mistakes relating to dates and serial numbers of evidence bags, as well as the handling of the bones. In one instance, a '4' had been left out of a serial number, which the defence spotted.

But nothing illustrates what Broodryk and his team were up against better than the work of Constable Cebisa Songxaba, from the police's Local Criminal Records Centre. Songxaba was called out to the exhumation led by Teunis Briers on 10 July 2012, but left after less than 15 minutes at the scene, having taken just three photographs. His justification was that he needed to rush to another crime scene. The search for old bones – which may or may not be found – did not appear to be a priority, but the result was that there was no photographic record showing all six bones before they were separated, bagged and taken away. This opened a line of attack for the defence that questioned every aspect of the discovery.

Later, Constable Songxaba had been asked to take a few more photographs at the house in Leo Street – of Werner Nortjé pointing out where the confession had been found – and, back at the office, to photograph new evidence Captain Gerhard van Wyk had secured. When the time came to compile an album for court, Songxaba mixed up the dates, times and addresses.

Once the mistakes were pointed out, he was forced to go back to his records and reconcile the events with the correct dates and places. A new affidavit had to be written and signed in order to protect the chain. In early 2014, Songxaba proceeded to cut and paste chunks of his July 2012 affidavit, fixed what needed to be fixed and submitted the statement. In court, it emerged that he had also failed to sign a new prescribed oath, retaining the old one that reflected the date 16 July 2012. His explanation was that he didn't believe it was necessary to 'change everything'. Hodes left Songxaba in a pile of smouldering rubble.

The Ketani case thus presented polar opposites of South African police work. On one hand there was the dogged determination to find the bones and, although it had never been done before, to send them overseas for DNA testing. On that same side of the investigation lay the countless hours of overtime devoted to the case and the smart thinking from Captain Gerhard van Wyk, who took over the docket. On the other hand, however, was the reality of overworked and undertrained officers who, daily, risked ruining cases through careless mistakes.

And they weren't the only ones. The Eastern Cape doctor had done a poor job of filling in the J88s, claiming that he had been on duty in the emergency unit on a busy day. In court, the doctor was confronted by Laurence Hodes, who told him in no uncertain terms that being busy was not an excuse for not filling in basic details on crucial forms. There was also an issue with the way in which Carrington's cellphone was seized and handled and claims of irregularities relating to his arrest.

Mopping up these mistakes proved to be a frustrating and time-consuming task. New photograph albums were produced and new statements taken. But if Broodryk was to defend the chain of evidence – which stretched over 13 years – there was no alternative. As in a drunk-driving trial, if the blood tests were not done properly, the accused would be entitled to an acquittal.

At the same time, Van Wyk was still exploring new avenues in the investigation. Through stubborn perseverance, he tracked down Carrington's ex-wife Candice, who was now living in England and had reverted to her maiden name. Candice claimed she knew nothing and had no information that could help the investigation. She insisted she wanted nothing to do with her former life and was not prepared to give a statement or go further than to corroborate a few details.

Van Wyk understood the sensitivity, given what Candice had been through, but pushed her to agree to allow them to use her medical records in court. These confirmed the date of her attempted suicide, mentioned in the confession. The suicide attempt also served as an anchor, fixing the events around Betty's murder to a date.

There was a long legal fight over the admissibility of Candice's medical records, which was eventually won by the state, but not before Van Wyk was forced to find one of the doctors who treated Candice after her suicide attempt in 1999.

Gerhard van Wyk also leaned on Sandor Egyed's family and eventually got to interview him over the phone. But he failed to glean anything substantial from Sandor – certainly nothing worth introducing into the trial – and he had no evidence against Sandor that he could use as leverage to gain further information from him. Plus, the man was on the other side of the planet in New Zealand and was under no pressure to return or even to speak to the police.

Carrington, who remained a close friend to Sandor, claimed he left

South Africa rather quickly, without planning far in advance. Once in New Zealand, Sandor began working in IT. Like Carrington, Sandor refused all requests for interviews. A local reporter from TVNZ, Jehan Casinader, managed to get through to him on the phone but says Sandor wasn't willing to discuss the case or his relationship with Carrington.

'Friendships are private,' he kept saying to Casinader.

. . .

Captain Gerhard van Wyk's investigation spans five countries. The heart of the case is in South Africa, Candice is in the United Kingdom, Sandor in New Zealand, Eric Neeteson-Lemkes is believed to be in Thailand, while his daughter Monique and Mark Lister are in Australia.

Van Wyk is helping Broodryk and Kowlas prepare for trial, fixing all the mistakes and still following up leads. The extradition of Monique and Mark has now also come into the picture, along with all the paperwork it will demand. Sourcing up-to-date photographs of them is in itself a challenge. Later, arrest warrants and Interpol Red Notices – international alerts again the names of suspects wanted for possible extradition or prosecution – are issued for both.

The postponement of the trial to February 2014 allows Broodryk to step back and try to see the bigger picture, to look at the case holistically. He is already lost inside it, constantly trying to figure out strategy, putting himself in the shoes of his witnesses or the remaining accused, exploring motives, running through each step of the chain of evidence and trying to anticipate the defence's moves.

Considering how much is going wrong leading up to the trial, Herman Broodryk often jokes that if there is a conspiracy against Carrington Laughton and the Ranger brothers, as is alleged, whoever is behind it has done a terrible job of it.

61.

By February 2014, word of the trial has spread through the corridors of the National Prosecuting Authority and Captain Gerhard van Wyk begins hearing it being referred to as the 'battle of the lions'.

Herman Broodryk and Laurence Hodes are formidable opponents, two legal heavyweights who will run the kind of trial other prosecutors and lawyers will talk about. Hodes is fast, agile, forever circling his rival, searching for new ways to pounce. Broodryk reserves his energy, knowing the fight will be a long one. When he strikes, his blows are heavy, but a lot of the time he stands back and lets Kowlas charge into the fray.

Both teams have spent months preparing. Broodryk and Kowlas have to consult a witness like Marco van der Hammen several times. He travels all over the country and pinning him down is no easy task.

Kowlas has also been meeting with Conway Brown to prepare him for what lies ahead. He has taken a deal but seems nervous and keeps complaining about his memory. Kowlas thinks he is holding back.

> I kept asking him for the truth but I kept feeling that he wasn't telling us everything.

Eventually, she asks Conway to write things down, which seems to work. Carrington knows Conway and the others intimately and will use their past against them. Conway must be coached to speak clearly in court and not to lose his temper.

Paul is perceived to be aggressive and unpredictable. During one of the occasions he came to Broodryk's office to consult, he stormed out screaming and threatening to place a bomb in the building. He had to come back and apologise to the prosecutors. Dirk is all over the place, unable to concentrate for long, which makes interviewing him incredibly difficult.

Broodryk and Kowlas are forced to meet their 'accomplice' witnesses six, seven or more times each.

There's a prisoner who approaches Broodryk and his team offering them information. He claims to have overheard some conversations and is volunteering to testify against Carrington and the Ranger brothers. In return, he wants his fraud sentence reduced. He is brought to meet Broodryk at Palm Ridge court but is exposed as a charlatan within minutes. Broodryk is furious and shouts for him to be taken away.

Van Wyk is still finding pieces of evidence. The old missing persons docket – the actual paper one – which was opened after Betty Ketani's disappearance is tracked down two days before Broodryk has to open his case. Ketani's original ID book also surfaces at about the same time. There are still no hospital records from 1999, but James van Rooyen's docket into the Hillbrow abductions is eventually found.

Broodryk and Kowlas have witnesses coming in from other provinces and other countries, and sorting out all the logistics eats up their time. They have one chance to bring someone like Professor Thomas Parsons over and once he's in Johannesburg there can be no delay. This means Broodryk has to structure the order of his witnesses carefully.

Carrington and his team have also been getting ready. Lawyer Howard Woolf has been tasked with finding DNA and handwriting experts who can testify on Carrington's behalf. Hodes has placed every piece of evidence in dispute and will cross-examine all of the state's witnesses. This requires a great deal of research and preparation. Hodes is particularly lethal when he's well prepared to meet an expert witness.

At a pretrial conference it was made clear that neither side would be doing the other any favours. There would be no compromises. Hodes and his team were 'putting the state to the sword' – as Carrington liked to put it – to prove each and every link in the chain of evidence. Nothing would be let through without scrutiny. No exhibit would be accepted without proof of where it came from. For the prosecutors, this meant having to call extra witnesses, including doctors or even a retired policeman.

Broodryk retaliated by giving the defence no clues about which witnesses he was calling and in what order. When asked, he would reply:

'Buck Jones.' If asked, 'How long?', as in how long the witness would be led for, Broodryk would answer: 'Six foot four.'

This made preparation difficult and meant that Hodes would often not know who he would be cross-examining until that person walked into the courtroom. Broodryk also refused to shut down the investigation, and new evidence emerged throughout the trial. Hodes complained bitterly, calling it a 'trial by ambush'. Broodryk thought that that was rich given that Carrington was keeping his defence a secret and would not reveal it until the state's case was finalised.

Hodes will launch applications to have the trial declared unfair, while Broodryk will shuffle and reshuffle his witnesses for maximum damage. The simplest of things, such as the handing over of the ICMP's standard operating procedure, deteriorated into legal squabbles. They don't know it yet, but the lions will fight for two full years.

. . .

It was widely thought that Broodryk would begin the trial by trying to get the 1999 confession admitted into evidence, which would then spark a 'trial within a trial'. If not, he would surely start with his Section 105A witnesses. Conway's sentence was already starting to run out and once he was released, there was a risk that he could disappear, so Broodryk and Kowlas would surely want to get him into the witness box while he was still in prison and thus easy to manage. But Broodryk has come up with a different strategy.

On the morning of 17 February 2014, the courtroom at the Palm Ridge court fills up once again with lawyers, family members or relatives and court officials. The recording equipment is switched on and every microphone around the room is tested. The two red bulbs on the metal box containing the court recorder light up to signal the start.

The three accused – Carrington, Carel and David – are brought in to the dock. The 13-year-old murder mystery for which they will stand trial has turned into a 15-year-old murder mystery.

Carrington is wearing a short side parting in his hair and, as always, is dressed immaculately. Surrounded by his files and briefcases, he chats to his wife and hands her a list of things he needs in jail. His father has come up from KwaZulu-Natal and gives him a warm hug, stretching over the wall of the dock.

The Ranger brothers have hired Roelof van Wyk, a former-magistrate-turned-lawyer, to represent them, but will soon run out of money and he will be forced to apply for funding from Legal Aid in order for him to continue acting for them. He's a friendly man who gets on well with everyone in court and is happy to pass the time chatting rugby.

The defence – Laurence Hodes, Howard Woolf and Thabang Mathopo – still has no idea who the state's first witness will be. Conway has been led into court in leg irons and Blanche is fussing over whether he has eaten and whether he will be entitled to lunch. Werner Nortjé, the chef from Kenilworth, is seated on a bench outside with Shama. His hair is tied into a ponytail and he's attempted a suit. There are other people milling around outside, but the state's witness list bears almost 60 names and who will be first is anyone's guess.

Privately, Broodryk has taken a decision to lead the forensic evidence first. He wants to present the evidence he believes to be indisputable: the hard science that proves that Betty Ketani was murdered and that the confession is real. Calculating that there will be a postponement after the first three weeks, Broodryk wants to do the DNA and handwriting before he throws Conway, Paul and Dirk into the den with Hodes. But the ICMP team is only arriving early next week and he wants Marco van der Hammen on the stand once the DNA has been dealt with. To buy himself some time, he'll have to call a few local witnesses.

The plan is to start strong and leave the judge with a favourable impression for the remainder of the trial. He wants Judge Natvarial Ranchod to remember the facts rather than versions from criminals.

Once Judge Ranchod and his two assessors bow and settle down, and all other the formalities are taken care of, Carrington and the Rangers plead to the eight charges against them. They maintain their innocence and enter pleas of 'Not guilty'. For the first time, Carrington gives the court a taste of what his defence will entail: he's being framed, probably by Eric Neeteson-Lemkes. He doesn't explain how or why. His plea explanation is one sentence.

Eric is not around to dispute the claim, although it is more than likely that he is watching from afar. Two separate lawyers are in the public gallery with watching briefs, to document proceedings in court..

Herman Broodryk calls his first witness.

Policeman Johan Reynecke, commander of the police's Missing Persons unit and the man who, in May 1999, recorded Betty Ketani's name in his register, makes his way in through the back door. His role is to explain to the court the police process that is followed once a person is reported missing, from the charge office to the alerts that go out to the country's border posts. Warrant Officer Reynecke – with the change in the police ranking system, all inspectors were now warrant officers – has with him the original notebook from 1999 and is shown the yellowing forms Betty's brother Ronnie was asked to help fill out at the Hillbrow police station.

Broodryk has decided to start at the very beginning.

They may not have the complete mosaic Magistrate Vincent Ratshibvumo spoke about, but Broodryk and his team believe they can see the whole picture now. Except for two people, Warren Williams and Malemleli Mpofu, they have tracked down or identified every key person mentioned in the confession, either victim or perpetrator. They have built a case that stands on the DNA link, handwriting analysis and the witnesses whom they have managed to turn. The motive remains elusive, but there's nothing in South African law that demands it. Broodryk has his 'pot of evidence' and is ready to stir it.

Walking into court, lead detective Captain Van Wyk spots a black-and-white photograph of Betty Ketani on the laptop screen of a reporter sitting in the public gallery, doing some last-minute research. He stops for a moment to look at her.

'Betty can't say we didn't try,' he says and walks off to take his seat.

PART THREE

A broken chain or a strong rope?

'*Everything is already known to everyone, and everything hidden will be made manifest.*'

— FYODOR DOSTOEVSKY, *CRIME AND PUNISHMENT*

62.

It doesn't take long for Herman Broodryk, Namika Kowlas and Gerhard van Wyk to fall into the rhythm of a long-running trial.

Palm Ridge court is a sleek, modern building on the outskirts of Katlehong. It's new and comfortable, but it's an hour's drive out of the city and the usual route would be along the R59 highway – not quite as far as the Blockhouse, but close.

Broodryk likes to get to court early and uses the long drive to think about the case. By 6am or 6.30am, he and his team are generally locked inside their third-floor office, drinking coffee and eating pastries. With a desk and a couple of steel filing cabinets, there's little room to move. Rows of lever-arch files are lined up on the floor.

Court begins daily at 10am and runs until teatime at 11.15am. There's an hour-long lunch at 1pm and prisoners are usually taken down to the holding cells by 4pm. The police officers transporting them try to miss as much of the morning and afternoon traffic as possible. Because of the number of support staff it takes to run the courts, this routine is seldom changed.

Sometimes, after a particularly good day – or a really bad one – Broodryk, Kowlas and Van Wyk meet at the Keg in Hillfox to wind down. Van Wyk also introduces Kowlas to a pub in Rosettenville where cops like to hang out. When there's cause for celebration, Broodryk and Van Wyk drink Johnnie Walker Black while Kowlas toasts with red wine. Difficult days are soothed with beers.

Broodryk and his team use the early-morning sessions to plan the day ahead. The afternoons are a bit more social, but are inevitably spent discussing the case and analysing witnesses, evidence or the opposition. Kowlas describes the trial as a chess game, with moves and countermoves that take days or weeks to execute. She calls it 'lawyering'.

. . .

The first session of the trial runs from 17 February to 4 March 2014. In that time, the teams manage to get through nine court days and 10 witnesses. It's a short but important burst.

Broodryk begins with Betty Ketani's disappearance; how it was reported by her brother Ronnie and handled by the police. He then calls Werner Nortjé to describe the discovery of the letters and to confirm that the three-page confession had not been changed or altered in any way. Werner testifies that it looks exactly the same as it did the day it was discovered. In Broodryk's opinion, that means that the chain of custody is proved and that Doc, JB, their friend Andreas Stephanou, Sono and Pretorius need not be called as witnesses. The defence doesn't see it that way, but in Broodryk's mind it's a neat solution, since Van Wyk had effectively started the investigation afresh. During cross-examination Werner is questioned about inaccuracies in his statement, the excavation at his house and why he had not handed the letters to the police. He keeps reminding the court that he is not a policeman, but a supermarket chef.

Next, Broodryk brings in Carrington's ex-wife Jayne to explain how she found the Polaroids, as well as to identify her ex-husband's signature and handwriting. Jayne's voice is soft, her body language screaming that she does not want to be in court, testifying against a man she describes as a 'good father'.

The ICMP's Thomas Parsons and Ana Bilić are on their way from Bosnia and America, but have an inflexible schedule, so Broodryk fills the days before their arrival with evidence from Claudia Bisso, who identified the bones as human, and Teunis Briers, the policeman who unearthed them.

Bisso is unshakable and confirms that, even though only three were photographed, six bones had indeed been found. Briers's testimony, however, detonates an explosive legal bomb, which leads to a clash over how he handled the evidence bag containing DNA samples from Ketani's three children. Briers had opened the sealed bag to remove medical forms – the J88s – but failed to place the original bag inside the new one. The fight is long and involves legal submissions and a special date for judgment, but ultimately the court hands Broodryk his first victory and allows Briers to submit the old evidence bag.

Once Broodryk's international witnesses touch down, they spend three days testifying. Bilić is there to talk about the scientific process and the ICMP's chain-of-custody protocols. Her evidence is fairly routine. Watching Parsons and Laurence Hodes do battle, however, is as close as cross-examination can get to Shakespearean theatre.

Hodes is impeccably prepared, armed with articles, books and documents compiled by the FBI. Standing at the podium, clenching his fist like a Roman emperor and teasing his fine hair, Hodes challenges Parsons on everything, from how the grave was dug up to whether DNA is reliable enough to be used in criminal trials.

But Parsons has testified in war crimes tribunals at The Hague and is not going to be pushed around. He is a thin man with neat white hair and an American twang, who never rushes an answer, processing every word or fact like a supercomputer. The CV he presents in court is over 20 pages long and he is perfectly at ease with terms such as 'polymerase chain reaction' or 'capillary electropherogram'.

In his unpacking of the ICMP's DNA findings, Parsons – who splits his time between his home in America and his office in Bosnia and Herzegovina – runs spontaneous calculations based on different probabilities of the bone that the ICMP tested belonging to Betty Ketani. The calculations are different if, hypothetically, the bone had been found in a random, unexpected location as opposed to being pulled out of a shallow grave that had been pointed out by Conway, the man who claims to have buried the body there. With a 50/50 chance of being true – which Parsons points out is a conservative calculation given how much information the police had at its disposal – the probability of a match is 99.98 per cent. For the sake of argument, Parsons drops the prior probability (the sense of certainty in the location) to just 10 per cent and arrives at a match of 99.81 per cent.

Parsons is a formidable witness, who brushes aside concerns of contamination, sample switches and broken chains of evidence. He testifies that molecular information cannot be manipulated or forged, and the results his team reached would stand even if the bone had been found on the side of a road, 'brought there by a blackbird'.

At times, the exchanges between scientist and lawyer grow tense, even fraught. At one point Parsons raises his voice: 'I object, sir, to your characterisation that I have attempted to mislead this court in any way and overemphasise the strength of this evidence.'

Hodes does not flinch. 'You may object, sir, but I can assure you I'm not done ...'

Later, Hodes cuts Parsons off: 'I ask the questions here, sir.'

Parsons leaves the court with his assessment that although the DNA comparisons are not as strong as the ICMP would have liked, there is overwhelming evidence that the bone that was tested *is* that of Betty Ketani.

Staying with his plan to try to leave the judge with a good first impression, Broodryk then calls Marco van der Hammen to present the handwriting analysis.

63.

The search for witnesses continues even as the trial gathers momentum. Herman Broodryk and the others have a particular interest in Eric Neeteson-Lemkes's daughter Monique, who is central to the Cranks investigation, and Mark Lister, whose name appears throughout the written confession. But they are not the only ones scratching around for information on Mark and Monique, who are now both living in Australia. Two Australian journalists have also been investigating.

Ean Higgins, a senior writer for the *Australian*, publishes several articles on the case and even manages to pin down Mark Lister. But the Queensland police officer denies any involvement in or knowledge of the Ketani kidnapping and murder.

'I did some surveillance work for Carrington when I was at university,' Mark tells Higgins, 'but we had a bit of a falling-out.'

According to Higgins, Mark claims this happened before Betty Ketani vanished in 1999 and insists that he has nothing to hide; in fact, he is keen to sort everything out with prosecutors in Johannesburg. Mark explains that he had dropped out of university before finishing his zoology degree at Unisa and was encouraged to pursue a career as a policeman in Australia, where his sister had already settled.

When he left South Africa in March 2000, Mark was part of the army reserves as well as a police reservist in Randburg. He rode for the police's mounted unit based in nearby Douglasdale. He had been dating his girlfriend for around six years and, although she accompanied him to Australia, she returned after a couple of months and their relationship ended.

Mark is described by those who knew him as a sweet man who looked like that kid in *Mad* magazine, Alfred E. Neuman, and who had a desire to protect others. Once, his girlfriend – who was still at art school at the time – talked him into pawning his CD collection to help her run away from home. He didn't want to, but he just didn't know how to say no. The young couple returned home after running out of money on the road between Durban and Mozambique.

Ean Higgins tracks Mark down, but he never confronts him in person. Ross Coulthart, a well-known television reporter for Channel Seven's *Sunday Night*, does.

Mark is a senior constable serving in an elite mounted unit at the Queensland Police Service. When Ross confronts him on camera, Mark is on horseback and in formation, dressed in full ceremonial regalia and preparing to escort the Australian governor-general, Quentin Bryce, into an arena prepared for Brisbane's annual agriculture show. Ross presents Mark with the indictment that has been served in South Africa, but Mark, while trying to keep his horse steady, points towards his commander and tells the journalist to address any questions to him.

'I have no comment to make at this time. Thank you,' he repeats as politely as he can, his fellow officers looking on bewildered until his inspector eventually intervenes and blocks any further engagement.

The Queensland police later issues a vague statement about taking the allegations seriously and promises to keep working with the authorities in South Africa. At the end of February 2014, Mark resigns from his job. When emailed for further comment, he replies: 'I believe you have the wrong Mark Lister. I'm sorry I can't help.'

Despite claiming he is prepared to assist South African prosecutors, Mark never engages with Broodryk and Kowlas beyond a couple of emails.

• • •

Unlike Mark Lister, Monique Neeteson-Lemkes opens up to Ross Coulthart and allows him to interview her. They spend hours together, talking on and off camera. Their discussions culminate in a *Sunday Night* exclusive titled 'Hostie or Hitman?', a reference to Monique's former job as an air hostess.

Monique is fast becoming 'a mover and a shaker' in the trade unions and has testified about working conditions in her industry at a special Senate inquiry. She fought against being dismissed by Jetstar after a bizarre incident in August 2011, when she found a fake bomb floating in the toilet on a Sydney-to-Darwin flight. Monique claimed she was being punished for speaking up about how Jetstar handled that bomb scare, while the airline maintained she was not only too traumatised to return to duty, but was battling a pre-existing personality disorder and was not fit to fly.

When she learns about the allegations emerging from South Africa, Monique secures the services of one of Australia's top lawyers, David Galbally QC, who reaches out to the South African prosecutors in early 2013 via a local firm. There are requests for information and email exchanges, and eventually Monique's legal team fly to Johannesburg for an off-the-record meeting. In the end, no deal is reached. The prosecutors have placed her at the centre of the murder and are probably not willing to bargain.

In her conversations with Coulthart, Monique repeatedly denies having anything to do with Betty Ketani's murder and claims she will never receive a fair trial in South Africa, which she describes as a 'terrible', crime-ridden place. Her lawyer, Galbally, interjects and claims that South Africa's political and judicial systems are 'not as pure and clean as our systems' and that those making the allegations against his client are doing so to 'save themselves'.

The Monique who appears on camera in the *Sunday Night* broadcast looks very different to the young woman who worked at her father's restaurant in South Africa in 1999. Gone are the bandanas and tomboy attire. Her face has filled out and is now rounder, with a sharp chin and narrow lips. Her hair is now blonde, her eyebrows perfectly shaped. During short breaks in filming she asks for her make-up and touches up her powder. When asked a direct question, such as 'Did you kill Betty Ketani?', Monique's eyebrow rises and she replies: 'No, Ross, never!'

Monique happily shares the romantic story of how her parents met in Thailand in the seventies. Eric had apparently walked into a restaurant where Dang was working and ordered a chicken dish. When the waitress brought it out he was so disappointed that he complained, but was told that if he felt he could do it better he was welcome to go into the kitchen and try. She says her father did just that, and there he met his future wife.

Eric and Dang subsequently moved to Australia and began running restaurants. Monique says that as an infant she slept in a basket at the back of the restaurants and, by the time she was four, was helping out. In her words, she was the 'adorable, cute little girl' who worked for small tips and saved them in a piggy bank.

Monique speaks of a happy childhood, when she and her sister Naydine played in the neighbourhood park where they were chased by dogs and had family picnics. She remembers meeting the Prince of Thailand on his trip to Australia. She also remembers her parents divorcing, and claims that Eric invited her and Naydine and other members of the family to South Africa so that he could make up for lost time and so that they could 'be a family again'. She says nothing about what happened between her and her father that led to her leaving in early 2000. Eric, in his statement, accuses his daughter of stealing over R100 000 from him.

If the Betty Ketani investigation is a mosaic, then Monique is one of most significant pieces – the link between Cranks, her father and Carrington's company. Her name features in every abduction described in the hidden confession and she has been implicated in the burying of the body. But Monique describes herself as a good person who was 'gutted', 'sad' and 'surprised' to hear the allegations. Monique denies being involved in the robbery at her father's house and insists that she had nothing to do with the jewellery-store heist. She also denies ever being arrested in Thailand. Monique speaks of being a practising Buddhist – praying for her family and for world peace.

In her interview, she keeps circling back to workers' rights and how passionate she is about helping the underdog. She does not deny dating Carrington Laughton or knowing Mark Lister, but uses words such as 'absurd' and 'ridiculous' to sweep aside allegations of abductions, torture and murder. Whenever Monique is asked about the actual case in South Africa, she offers what appears to be a well-rehearsed answer about the legal proceedings being *sub judice* and how she has been advised by her lawyer not to venture there.

Monique is asked if she remembers Betty Ketani and whether – as Dirk claimed in his telling of the hotel kidnapping – she had ever confronted her about the thefts at the restaurant.

'Absolutely not,' Monique replies. 'My heart goes out to her. I would like to bring Betty Ketani's children to Australia, to tell them to their faces that I had nothing to do with it. To take them to a temple and celebrate her life.'

Monique describes Betty as a 'nice lady' and 'the best cook Dad has ever had'.

. . .

Through her lawyers, Monique declines to answer any questions for this book.

'At this point in time, my client will not be making any comment or conducting any interviews,' is the response from David Galbally.

Coulthart, a journalist and author with 25 years of reporting behind him, is willing to share some of his impressions of Monique and the allegations against her. Having travelled to South Africa to conduct research for his *Sunday Night* feature, he knows the case well.

> *Monique is an extremely charismatic and likeable person. I find the allegations against her in South Africa very confronting. I have spoken to union officials and airline executives who speak about her with awe. She fought back and won a convincing victory against one of the biggest corporations in the country. I've also spoken to people she's helped along the way, young flight attendants who have won their jobs back because of her campaigning on their behalf.*
>
> *The most extraordinary thing about this whole story is the contrast between Monique we have got to know in Australia and the Monique who is cast in the court allegations as this appalling femme fatale who brutally orchestrated the murder of a woman and then concealed her body.*

The same contradictions can apply to just about everyone implicated in the Ketani murder. By the time it all unravelled, Mark Lister is a policeman assigned to escort senior politicians in Australia. The Ranger brothers are police officers who took an oath to uphold the law. Conway is so likeable that his landlord treated him like a son. Cranks owner Eric is eccentric but enchanting. Paul Toft-Nielsen is an animal lover and a safari guide who chased down wildlife poachers. And Carrington spent 20 years working as a private investigator who was often described as a 'charming' man with a wicked sense of humour (he had the pianist play a few seconds of a horror movie soundtrack as Jayne entered the church on their wedding day) and who has a deep love for his children. Carrington published articles in which he portrayed himself as a crusader against criminals and testified in some of the cases he investigated.

Perhaps these contrasts play no small part in driving local and international media to continue reporting the Betty Ketani case as it unfolds. Peter Munro is another Australian reporter who conducts interviews in South Africa and writes a feature in the weekend magazine of the *Sydney Morning Herald*, titled 'Betty Ketani Murder: The Body under the Begonias'. He speaks of a 'bizarre murder case that won't stay buried'.

News of the trial travels as far as Canada, where the *Toronto Star* commissions its South African correspondent to write a story. One of South Africa's most respected investigative programmes, *Carte Blanche*, does their own take on the Ketani mystery, as do publications ranging from *The Times* to the *Citizen* and from the *Daily Dispatch* to *You* magazine.

The coverage in Australia helps Broodryk and his team gather information about suspects beyond their reach. They apply for arrest warrants for both Mark and Monique, but decide to leave any formal extradition request until after the trial. The outcome will determine whether they will attempt to bring them over.

The last person Gerhard van Wyk tracks down while the trial is still under way is Warren Williams, mentioned in the confession in relation to Betty's kidnapping. Warren, it turns out, has never left South Africa. When approached, he says he has nothing to offer the police and promptly hires a lawyer. Van Wyk has no evidence against him except the mention in the confession and although he works a few angles, he eventually has to let it go. Another blank square in the mosaic.

When Warren is approached for an interview for this book, his lawyer steps in: 'Our client emphatically denies being involved in the kidnapping and/or murder of the deceased. He takes exception to the fact that the name Warren Williams is being dragged into the matter. He has no interest in the matter and sees no reason as to why he should supply you with a response, save to state that he denies any involvement in the matter.'

The trial will have to continue without Warren, Mark, Monique and 'Mad Dog' Eric.

64.

Conway Brown is slumped forward in the witness box, his head bowed, his eyes shut. Like a boxer beaten down into a corner, then left for a moment, he waits to face a fresh storm of punches. Despite the bulging muscles, Conway is drained, physically defeated. His thoughts are drifting, melting. He's already pleaded for two toilet breaks, shuffling out of the stifling courtroom in leg irons, a prison escort in tow.

He's trying to follow the questions, process words he's never heard before, swallow his anger or at least let only small flashes escape. He has been advised on how to perform on the stand, but advocate Laurence Hodes has been delivering agonising blows for around four hours, accusing him of being a liar, a sadist who took the easy way out by turning state witness.

Conway is battling to concentrate and has started answering Hodes with a rehearsed 'Yes, My Lord' just for the sake of getting through the day. It's after three in the afternoon. The court session is about to end and Conway will then be taken back to jail. But the next court day will come and Hodes will appear in front of him again, draped in his black robe, armed with a hundred more questions. Hodes will pick up exactly where he left off. The pressure of the interrogation will be on again. The advocate will glare at him from his podium. His voice will rise and fall, every word designed to trip Conway up. To catch him out. To expose and discredit him. To break him.

This is Conway's third day on the witness stand and second under cross-examination. He doesn't know it yet, but another three days await. Evidence-in-chief had been tough but straightforward and yesterday got off to a good start, with Conway pushing back against Hodes and even daring a touch of sarcasm. But today the questions have gone beyond the contradictions in his evidence. They cut deeper than the many lies he told during the police investigation. The questions cracked open his private life: from all the times he cheated on his wife, Blanche, to the fights he was involved in. From reminders about how poor he was in the 1990s to the nudist parties he attended. From the abstract paintings he never sold to the petty criminal record he says he should never have had. He'd been grilled about his childhood, his army days, the jobs he couldn't hold down and his limited understanding of the law. Hodes even turned a printout of his Facebook profile into a formal court exhibit. The same is about to happen to a delicate sculpture he carved out of prison soap.

Wooden rosary beads slither through Conway's fingers. His faded aviator jacket is folded up next to him. The men he is testifying against are sitting just a whisper away.

He'll be 44 next month. A grandfather now, with light-grey frost settling on the dark hair around his temples. When the questions resume, Conway denies he took a plea-and-sentence deal from the prosecutors to save himself.

'The truth is the truth,' he testifies, with the little energy he has left. 'It will come out eventually.'

It's been 15 years. Some have died waiting for this truth. Now, in this quiet room with its wood panels, soaring ceiling and humming air-conditioning, before a judge and his two assessors, Conway is once again inside his wife's Fiat Uno, speeding down the R59 highway ...

. . .

It's mid-May 2014 and the second session of the trial is under way. Conway is the state's eleventh witness and the first of Broodryk's 105A 'grin-and-bear-it' trio. He's been called to testify straight after Marco van der Hammen is excused from court.

The handwriting expert had been cross-examined for three days, with lengthy disputes over the reliability of handwriting analysis (sarcastically called a 'wonderful science'), varying interpretations and analysis of the tests Van der Hammen conducted. Hodes had wanted to know why Colonel Van der Hammen had been brought in to do a second report, why he hadn't mentioned the first one and why he didn't attempt to date the paper or ink. There were disagreements about what kind of printer was used and whether the third page may have been created separately from the others. The colonel had been accused of ignoring important discrepancies and eventually of being a 'hired gun'. He didn't take the attacks personally and stood by his evidence, leaving the court to decide on its merits once the defence called its own handwriting expert, which it would no doubt do.

During Van der Hammen's re-examination, Hodes and Kowlas had clashed. Hodes launched a series of dramatic objections, accusing her of being 'underhanded' and 'dishonest', which is about as far as lawyers can take insults inside a courtroom. Hodes had fumed and argued that Kowlas had led the witness, slipping him information to guide his answers. He had told the court he would not sit by and watch such a travesty unfold. Judge Natvarial Ranchod assured him that his concerns had been heard, and Kowlas rephrased or abandoned questions, knowing that her points had been made. Broodryk sat on the edge of his seat and almost intervened on a few occasions, but in the end had decided to let the exchanges play out. Letting Kowlas handle some of the more controversial parts of the trial, and take some of the heavy blows, had always been part of their strategy.

Calling Conway after such strong witnesses as Van der Hammen, Parsons and Bisso is another part of that strategy. Broodryk wants to start strong. Conway has already admitted to lying and Broodryk knows Hodes is going to beat Conway into a corner and leave him bloodied.

Conway spends a total of six days testifying. He is accused of implicating others to get himself the best possible deal with the state. Hodes takes him to task about every discrepancy and tries to force answers as to why Conway remained friends with Carrington.

> In the past 15 years, did you ever ask what went on there [near the Blockhouse]?
>
> No, M'Lord, I never did. I did not want to know, M'Lord.
>
> Through parties, through house-warmings, through travelling overseas, through working together, not once did you ever ask, 'But what happened that night?'
>
> Not once, M'Lord.
>
> Why not?
>
> What would it have mattered, M'Lord?
>
> You would have understood what had happened.

I do not think anybody could have understood.

You just left it. Did you not feel that it was incorrect [of Carrington] to involve you in this manner?

At that point it was too late, M'Lord.

Even after it was too late, did you not say, 'How can you involve me in this type of conduct?'

No, M'Lord.

Why not? Instead you became close mates. You travel around the world, you go to parties together, you visit one another, you introduce family, you confide in one another, you undress in front of one another, but you never ask what happened that day?

M'Lord, you keep your friends close, you keep your enemies closer.

Some exchanges are so charged that the formalities of the courtroom all but slip away.

Why did you not say to him [Carrington], 'How could you do that to me?'

M'Lord, I just witnessed what I thought was a killing of somebody. I am not going to go and antagonise the guy and ask him, 'What the hell were you thinking?' I'm not stupid.

No, sir, you became closer friends after that. There is almost like a sadistical characteristic of yours that now you are in envy of the guy and you become closer friends, you keep him even closer to you.

M'Lord, I do not understand the exact contents of what you just said but the reference to me being sadistic, that is your opinion and I suggest you keep it to yourself.

I am putting it to you, sir, it is not an opinion.

You never put it to me. You told me.

Yes, I am telling it to you.

There is a difference, M'Lord.

You became closer with a person that you have just watched kill and you remain silent.

Of course, M'Lord. If you were put in the same situation you would not say a word.

This goes on for hours. Hodes can't understand Conway's claim that there was complete silence between him and Carrington during the alleged stabbing. He keeps referring to it as a 'silent movie', raising the possibility that Conway's involvement went a lot further than he has confessed to. Hodes keeps pushing the fact that the two remained friends.

> *Did you not feel scared travelling to Germany? Did you do anything to actively disassociate yourself from him?*
>
> *I did, M'Lord. I started working more and more. More hours, until eventually I was working 16, 18 hours a day, seven days a week, until the day I was arrested. I distanced myself from him as well as my family and my loved ones.*
>
> *Where is that in your statement, sir?*
>
> *It is nowhere in my statement, M'Lord, because it is reality.*
>
> *It is the opposite. Your statement says you became very kind to people and overcompensated on account of the guilt you felt. Why did you not say that you worked 16, 18 hours every day thereafter, neglecting your family and friends?*
>
> *Nobody ever bothered to ask me, M'Lord.*
>
> *Nobody has to ask you, sir, you undertook to tell the truth and give a full and frank disclosure. It is not a case of them having to extract answers from you.*
>
> *Sir, I had an ingrown toenail. Do you really want to hear about that?*
>
> *No, it is of no interest, sir. It has nothing to do with the case.*
>
> *Exactly.*
>
> *It is absolutely pathetic what you have just said, sir.*

Conway battles with the legal questions around his plea-and-sentence agreement and although he tries to fight back, he stands no chance against Hodes. Some of his answers are broken, as they had been at Doc and JB's cottage, and carry a degree of sadness.

> *M'Lord, if you were subjected to the pain ... and ... what happened ... that will be burned in your memory forever, M'Lord ... and you don't want to go there ... it's a dark place you don't want to go to ... When you*

do recall those memories, they come back to you.

What pain? The pain that, on your version, you blocked out and kept out of your mind for 14 years? That pain?

Mr Hodes ... you're very good at your job, I give you that. I can't ... I can't ...

If you give me that, will you admit you're lying, sir?

I can't explain to you how I feel inside ... when you say what pain I can't explain it to you ... M'Lord, please can I have a few minutes?

With these words, Conway breaks down and cries. As court is adjourned and the judge and his assessors stand to exit, Carrington turns back to look at his wife, Anel, and smiles ever so slightly. Winning this case requires destroying the credibility of those testifying against him.

. . .

Over a period of six days, Conway is led back and forth over his evidence about the stabbing, about how the body was buried and how it was later dug up, and about how he came into possession of the confession. Hodes all but accuses him of forging Carrington's signature and asks him to comment on his friend's denials about having written or signed the letter.

'I didn't expect him to confirm it,' Conway replies.

His cross-examination ends in yet another stalemate. Hodes repeats Carrington's claim that he is being set up by Eric Neeteson-Lemkes and then asks one final question.

What I want to put to you, sir, is that throughout your 'keeping your enemy closer to you' and 'having your insurance', accused one [Carrington] was always a true and genuine friend to you, do you agree with that?

I don't know how to respond to that, M'Lord. If accused number one was a true and genuine friend, he would talk the truth. He would say what happened. He's being deceitful, which means he's not a true friend, M'Lord.

He says he has been telling the truth and that you're the one being deceitful.

I don't have a comment on that, it's not true.

• • •

After Conway, Broodryk calls Paul Toft-Nielsen to the stand. Given the fiery consultations, he is especially anxious about how Paul will behave. He is sure Paul's friends don't call him 'Satan' for nothing. But as Carrington's oldest friend, and the man who confessed to digging up the body with Conway, he has to testify.

Like Conway, Paul's credibility takes something of a bashing, from allegations that he invented an older brother to his strange claim that, in 1999, he used to carry a hammer (along with a small toolkit) around with him everywhere he went. Paul is accused of being a drug dealer, of telling tales of murder while in the bush, and of lying about how the body was dug up and on whose instructions. Paul tells the court that he had tried to warn others about his childhood friend Carrington.

He is not all he seems to be. There is a dark past.

Hodes asks Paul why he had made no mention in his earlier statements of 'dramatic' details such as the hair sticking out of the ground. He calls him an 'experienced serial killer' and an 'accomplished liar'. At one point, Hodes is forced to apologise for asking Paul whether he is delusional.

Paul speaks about the Betty Ketani secret eating him up. About the rages he would get into and how nervous he had become, leaping off his bed if someone entered the room. He says he embarked on a mission to destroy himself with drugs and booze. Wrapping up his evidence, he appeals to the others to confess, 'so that the Ketanis would know what happened'.

Once again, the court is left to sift through the debris in search of the truth.

To fill the remaining days of the second court session, Broodryk calls a series of policemen to deal with the chain of evidence. He also summons

Ruth Mncube, who narrowly escaped being snatched outside the post office in 1999.

Hodes continues his assault on the state's case by pointing out mistakes in the police work. He goes as far as picking up spelling mistakes and raises questions about why a certain note was made over one line, not three, on an official form.

As the trial is adjourned for a further four months, Broodryk is still deciding whether to call Dirk Reinecke and how to deal with the remaining victims of the 1999 abductions. Some 21 witnesses and almost 30 court days later, Carrington is sticking to his version. And he has a big surprise waiting for Broodryk and his team.

65.

With Conway Brown and Paul Toft-Nielsen's evidence done, Dirk Reinecke is the next obvious witness. But to open the third session of the trial, Broodryk decides to call André Coetzer instead.

Coetzer is the police reservist who, along with Carel Ranger, had denied so emphatically that the 1999 raids in Hillbrow were in any way related to the Cranks investigation. After the discovery of the confession in 2012, Coetzer signed a second statement standing by what he had told Inspector James van Rooyen 13 years earlier. But when Gerhard van Wyk finds and shows him an old photograph in which he appears together with Monique Neeteson-Lemkes, having repeatedly denied knowing her, Coetzer is ready to start talking.

In court he confesses that the statement he had given in 1999 had been 'a pack of lies' and claims that he had gone to Hillbrow because Carrington was searching first for Themba Tshabalala and later for a woman implicated in the thefts at Cranks. He tells the court how he broke down the door of apartment 1906 in the middle of the night and details how the illegal searches were carried out.

Coetzer had been in business with Carrington and had worked as an undercover agent for him. His codename was 'C5' or 'Charlie Five'. Coetzer and Carel Ranger had also been arrested in connection with an armed robbery at a Makro store in August 1999.

Coetzer testifies about the brief romance he had had with Monique and, like others before him, identifies the handwriting and signature on the confession as Carrington's. The fact that he has secured himself immunity from prosecution opens him up to allegations from the defence that he will lie about anything to earn his Section 204 deal, which the court must approve. The fact that he had lied under oath, twice, doesn't help him either.

Carrington and Carel Ranger deny all of Coetzer's revelations, but for

Broodryk, his evidence supports the accuracy of the information contained in the hidden confession, particularly the Hillbrow raids. Whether Coetzer has earned his Section 204 will be decided at the end of the trial.

. . .

Dirk Reinecke's testimony comes like bursts of gunfire. He speaks quickly, making it difficult to take notes. He tells stories by squeezing and releasing a trigger in his mind, firing off facts into the microphone. He assures the court that he is off his medication (to treat his ADD and to manage bipolar episodes) and is able to 'perform in society'. His wife sits in the public gallery, unable to hold her tongue during three days of cross-examination.

The man nicknamed 'Chicken' testifies that he, Carrington and Monique kidnapped Betty Ketani and questioned her in a hotel room for two hours before setting her free. He claims he later asked about what happened to Betty, but was lied to and told she had moved to Zimbabwe.

Dirk confirms that in or around 2001 he received a duffel bag from Carrington – allegedly containing the confession – and explains how he handed it over to Conway at a McDonald's. He also gives evidence about taking part in one of the Hillbrow raids.

Dirk explains how he was introduced to Monique while having a drink at a pub above her father's restaurant and how he arranged for her to meet Carrington. He says he was again lied to about the Audi TT saga, with Carrington telling him that he had purchased the car from a diplomat.

Dirk's testimony meanders into how rejected he felt when the army wouldn't take him, the fights he and Carrington had and all the pranks to which he had fallen victim, including a drunken whipping at a strip club. Dirk describes Carrington as a generous man who gave freely and without expecting anything in return. Once, he said, Carrington had offered him free use of his lawyer.

Carrington, however, denies everything that incriminates him. He also uses Dirk's cross-examination to play one of the cards he has been holding close to his chest. Through his lawyer, Carrington describes a peculiar incident during which, he claims, he received a call from his friend Leon

Rehrl, who wanted to warn him about a letter that had been manufactured, which would 'change his life forever'. The warning – which he did not take seriously – allegedly came in 2004, while Carrington was overseas. Leon's claim was that he heard about the letter from Dirk, who in turn heard about it from Paul. Dirk denies it all, as does Paul, who is recalled at the end of the trial to deal specifically with this new allegation. But Carrington is determined to call Leon to testify about what he feels is further proof of a conspiracy against him.

• • •

Themba Tshabalala doesn't get far in the giving of his evidence before Laurence Hodes again complains that his client is not receiving a fair trial. Hodes charges that they are being ambushed by witnesses who deviate from their original statements once they come to court. He calls it 'trial by ambush', claiming that they – the defence – are thus not able to prepare properly. Broodryk fights back, explaining that it is impossible for witnesses to write down every detail in their statements and that their oral testimony is more important. He argues that it is also impossible for prosecutors to commission a new statement every time a witness remembers something new in consultation. A full court day is lost to these arguments and once more the judgment is in favour of the state.

Hodes's attempt to have the trial declared unfair disrupts Themba's evidence-in-chief and his time on the witness stand is thus set to continue the following Monday, but that weekend he approaches Gerhard van Wyk with what he claims to be an old diary with entries in it relating to the 1999 abductions. Themba says he has found it at his house and wants it to be handed in as evidence. Neither Broodryk nor Kowlas really want to introduce new evidence this late in his testimony – especially after the fight they have just had – but Themba insists, and they worry that if he mentions it in cross-examination, they will be accused of trying to suppress the diary. It's a lose-lose situation. They have no choice and lead Themba through the entries he wants mentioned. He also, for the first time, claims that Monique Neeteson-Lemkes was the woman he saw in his flat, the one wearing a police uniform.

Hodes rips the diary part of Themba's testimony to shreds. The diary's dates don't match up to the 1999 calendar and the entries appear to have been made later. Van Wyk had confirmed some of the details in the book, such as the number of a former manager at the Carnivore restaurant where Themba worked, but the dates speak for themselves.

Themba tries to explain why he had not mentioned Monique back in 1999, claiming that he had been scared, but it remains a glaring omission. He also battles with the detail around exactly where he was held and by whom. Hodes calls Themba a 'shocking witness' who manufactures evidence. Broodryk does what he can to draw the court's attention back to the fact that the circumstances around Themba's abductions match the descriptions in the confession and that, regardless of what happens now, the witness had signed statements back in 1999. But the man who had waited so long for justice has done damage to his credibility and possibly to the state's case.

. . .

Ndaba Bhebe then takes the court through his 1999 abduction and Rachel Dube is called to describe her last encounter with Betty Ketani at Cranks restaurant.

Betty Ketani's brother Mankinki explains to the court the various branches of their family tree, but Broodryk also wants the judge to hear from the children. Thulani isn't well enough to travel, so Betty's daughters Bulelwa and Lusanda make the journey to Johannesburg without him. They are collected by a policeman, driven for eight hours and put up at the Parktonian Hotel near the Civic Theatre. It is Lusanda's first time in the city.

The sisters have mixed feelings about the trip. They want to face the men accused of murdering their mother. They have so many questions they want to ask them. Bulelwa wants to know how they all feel now, all these years later. Regardless of the legal process, in her mind they are guilty. But

Bulelwa and Lusanda are also scared, anxious about what will happen if the accused are ever set free.

Waiting to testify, they laze around their hotel room watching TV. Lusanda is missing school exams but she feels it is her duty to testify. When she gets to court she is overcome with sadness. She looks at the men in the dock and resents the way they stare back at her.

They were looking at me in a strange way. It's like they had seen a ghost.

The court interpreter, a smart, charming man named Charles Moloi, who speaks every one of South Africa's official languages and will shortly qualify to be an advocate, calms Lusanda down and makes her feel a little more at ease in the witness box. She and Bulelwa face questions about their fathers and about the DNA tests to which they had agreed. Hodes, in turn, treads carefully, not wanting to bully two orphans who have made a difficult decision to testify.

Bulelwa is a mother herself now. Her two girls are a little over a year old. She has named them Hlonipha and Msomhle, which mean 'respect' and 'a beautiful tomorrow'. At 16, Lusanda has also given birth. She hid the pregnancy in order to avoid being booted out of school and delivered her son, Amvuyele, on 8 October 2014, less than a month before she testifies. She had fought hard to stay in school but now she is missing her Grade 11 exams and doesn't have the money to register for 2015. She has decided to drop out, promising herself it will be only for a year.

Bulelwa is sure that had their mother been alive, she and her sister would never be in the situation in which they now find themselves.

Having to leave her son – who is just a few weeks old – with family in the Eastern Cape and missing school poisons an already horrible trip for Lusanda. She says she hates Joburg. When asked why, Bulelwa cuts in: 'Because it took my mother.'

66.

The Betty Ketani investigation and trial unfold during an exceptionally difficult time for South Africa's police officers and prosecutors. The Marikana bloodbath, which took place in the same year the confession was found, shook the foundations of the country and led to the suspension of National Police Commissioner Riah Phiyega. The two commissioners before her had either been fired or criminally charged, vacating their posts in disgrace.

The gunning down of miners on the platinum belt in August 2012 damaged even further the relationship South Africans had with the men and women who are meant to protect them. Video footage of officers handcuffing a suspect to the back of a police van and dragging him through the streets, or, later, the execution of an unarmed suspect who lay prostrate on the ground, did little to repair it. The period saw constant scandals inside crime intelligence, the suspensions of top police officers, badly handled protests and bungled cases, including the murder of Bafana Bafana captain Senzo Meyiwa. Crime statistics, which had been a good-news story for the police for years, had swung around and were now spiking where it hurt most: murders, hijackings and house robberies.

In the meantime, the National Prosecuting Authority has a leadership crisis of its own. There are deep political cracks running through management structures and the top post of National Director of Public Prosecutions remains a poisoned chalice. No NDPP has managed to finish a term in office since the fall of apartheid. There are inquiries into fitness to hold office, golden handshakes and endless controversy over a handful of cases, including the corruption charges against the man responsible for appointing NPA bosses, President Jacob Zuma.

At the same time, South Africa finds itself the focus of a global media frenzy over two high-profile trials: the Shrien Dewani honeymoon murder and the case of Oscar Pistorius, which overshadows even the death of Nelson Mandela.

The Dewani trial falls apart before the British millionaire accused of hiring hitmen to kill his wife in a fake hijacking has a chance to testify. It takes four years to extradite Dewani to South Africa, and just days to put him on a plane back home.

In the Pistorius case, the lead detective who handled the crime scene is exposed for having done a shoddy job and is replaced after it emerges that he was facing his own, unrelated criminal charges. The fact that the Blade Runner is found guilty of culpable homicide and not murder at the end of his trial (later overturned by a higher court) puts the NPA under even more pressure.

All of this means that Broodryk, Kowlas and Van Wyk have taken on a difficult, messy case at a time when they can least afford to fail. From Johannesburg to Australia, to Canada and back, there are eyes watching them. The police have spent a lot of money to have DNA tests done at the ICMP, and flying overseas witnesses in to testify also comes at no small cost. They are up against the best defence team money can buy. And, of course, there is a deeper narrative, as reporter Ross Coulthart explains:

> It strikes me that South Africa has a lot of credibility on the line with this case. It should matter to any country that a woman was murdered 13 years ago and that her killers have not all been brought to justice.
>
> The story says so much about modern South Africa because one of the most common complaints I hear from South Africans is the rampant crime that goes unpunished. This case really matters. If the allegations against these men and Monique are true, then it says so much about those early days of post-apartheid South Africa that they felt they could get away with these terrible crimes … That a group of white people, including policemen, felt that they could get away with this.
>
> This is a compelling whodunnit and I am waiting to see what happens in the trial with great anticipation. Justice demands Betty Ketani's family gets answers.

Determined to lead the best possible witnesses, Broodryk calls two experts who had made an appearance in the Pistorius trial. Police Colonel Mike Sales testifies about the analysis of Carrington's cellphone messages, while pathologist Gert Saayman gives his opinion on whether a person can be killed in the way Conway described. Saayman's evidence is hypothetical and deals with the kind of injuries a spike could cause to a human brain, whether a decomposed arm would float on water (as Paul had testified) and the science of what a body goes through if buried in a shallow grave and covered with cement. Because Betty's body has never been found, and no post-mortem was possible, Saayman's testimony is dismissed as 'speculative' by the defence.

Given the weight of his evidence, Saayman spends only a few hours in court. What follows next is another fight between Hodes and Broodryk, this time over the admissibility of medical records. The records had been found by Van Wyk and dealt with Candice Laughton's attempted suicide in 1999. They are important for one main reason: to pin down the date of the failed suicide, which is mentioned in the confession and which Carrington had earlier disputed.

It takes a lot of convincing, but Van Wyk manages to speak to Candice, who is now living abroad. She agrees to her medical records being used but makes it clear, in writing, that she will not travel to South Africa to testify and does not want her contact details shared with anyone, especially Carrington Laughton.

Once again, the fight over the medical records requires legal submissions from both sides and postponements. In the end, the records are admitted and the date of the attempted suicide is conceded. Broodryk narrowly escapes having to call a representative from the hospital to explain how records are kept, but does have to lead the psychiatrist who treated Candice at the time. The evidence touches on the relationship between Carrington and Candice, her suspicions that he was cheating on her and the time he spent working away from Johannesburg.

In mid-November 2014, nine months after the start of the trial, the time arrives for Broodryk and Kowlas to wrap up their case. It has taken them over 50 court days and more than 30 witnesses to get to this point. Their last witness will be Captain Gerhard van Wyk, who will tie everything together and fill in the gaps.

What they don't know is how much stress the case has placed on Van Wyk and that the man who relentlessly ran after every scrap of evidence – and will now have to testify about each step of his investigation – is buckling under the pressure and is on the verge of a nervous breakdown.

67.

By the time he has to testify, Gerhard van Wyk is clearly in distress. He has spent two years investigating this case and another watching what Laurence Hodes puts people through on the witness stand. The detective looks unwell. He is eating badly. He calls himself *mal* (crazy) and makes morbid jokes about suicide. Outside court he speaks about his 32 years with the police and how he can no longer 'take the blood'.

The whole team feels the pressure. Namika Kowlas describes the intensity of the trial as 'massive'. She, Broodryk and Van Wyk are never able to put it out of their minds, to shake it off for a while. They think constantly about the evidence and the men in the dock. It is the kind of case that floats into their thoughts just before they go to bed and as soon as they open their eyes again. Not even the breaks in between court sessions offer respite. There is always a niggling fear they are missing something.

Van Wyk has taken a huge amount of the responsibility upon himself. Most of his stress comes from managing witnesses, whom he has to subpoena and get to court. Some are lost in the system and arrive in Johannesburg with no money and no place to stay. It falls to him to help them. Handling Conway Brown, Dirk Reinecke and Paul Toft-Nielsen is also taking its toll.

He is the custodian of the docket and all the statements that have been taken, and will be cross-examined about each and every decision he and the prosecutors took. Broodryk directed the investigation but Van Wyk will be the one in the witness box explaining it all. Hodes will pick apart the slightest mistake and turn every one of Carrington's accusations into a courtroom spectacle.

Van Wyk also knows Carrington and his legal team will go after his credibility and accuse him of being part of the dark conspiracy orchestrated by Eric Neeteson-Lemkes. He is sure they will try to find dirt on him.

The detective bottles up all of these feelings, allowing the anxiety to incubate inside him like a virus, and by the time he steps into the witness box, he is weak, hurtling towards a breakdown. His answers are sufficient, but they are not as sharp as Broodryk wants – or needs – them to be. Van Wyk knows he isn't fighting back as hard as he knows he can. He always seems to be thirsty and his team have to force him to eat. They share their food with him and wonder whether he has developed diabetes.

Van Wyk makes it through five days, three and a half of those being led by Broodryk, going over the investigation from start to finish. Then the tanks roll into Stalingrad. Hodes grills Van Wyk about Carrington's arrest, the use of private investigators, the excavation, the bones, the handwriting, cellphone records and every single other aspect of the case. He accuses the detective of double standards, of treating Eric Neeteson-Lemkes with kid gloves, and allowing him to leave the country while relentlessly pursuing Carrington. Hodes claims Van Wyk is grabbing only the pieces of the puzzle that suit him. Van Wyk is made to answer for every mistake that was made – including those committed by the Yeoville team.

On the second day of cross-examination the defence team reveals how far back they had dug to try to discredit the investigating officer. Hodes and his team have unearthed a suspension from over 20 years previously. Now they are going to use it to try to undermine Van Wyk's credibility.

It was a murky set of accusations relating to an attempted murder and the possession of an AK-47 and hundreds of rounds of ammunition. Van Wyk was working as a young detective in Vereeniging at the time and was arrested with two other officers and suspended. One of the policemen went on trial, with the second testifying against him. Van Wyk was never charged and never even signed a warning statement. All cases involving police officers received special attention from the office of the Director of Public Prosecutions. He was released and his suspension was lifted immediately.

Hodes reveals that his team tracked down one of the two officers arrested with Van Wyk. The judge and Broodryk question whether any of it is relevant to this case, given that Van Wyk was never charged, never mind prosecuted, but Hodes argues, 'It goes to credibility.'

Being confronted with a scandal that had blown over more than two decades previously must be the final straw for Van Wyk. The stress overpowers him and he can no longer continue. He is not thinking clearly, is muddling his facts and thus risking a case he cares so much about. He complains of crippling headaches, trying to keep them at bay with pills. Eventually, he is struggling to read exhibits.

Van Wyk takes a sick day. Then another. A weekend passes, but by Monday he is still not back. On Tuesday, the court is informed that the detective is in hospital. He is being treated by a psychiatrist and is suffering from an 'acute stress reaction'. The doctor books him off for a month.

With another long postponement now inevitable, Hodes takes the opportunity to tell the court they are going to launch a fresh bail application. This will be Carrington's fourth attempt, excluding aborted plans to approach the Supreme Court of Appeal. The new application will be based on the delay caused by Van Wyk's health and the fact that there is no longer any threat to the state's case, as it is all but done. The court record is secured and legal documents are exchanged deep into the festive season, but the bail application never materialises. It is decided that Van Wyk will finish giving evidence in early January and the defence will prepare to open its case in April, once Judge Natvarial Ranchod is back from extended leave.

68.

Gerhard van Wyk finally recovers and returns to court to finish what he started. Hodes keeps up the intensity, but the policeman is stronger and able to work his way through three more days of cross-examination – eight days in total spent pulling together all the strands of the state's case. There is never going to be agreement between the two sides. The defence focuses on all the problems with the investigation, all the discrepancies, while the prosecutors continue to highlight all the pieces of evidence that corroborate each other.

The state closes its case in April 2015 and fights off an attempt by the defence to have the matter thrown out of court with a Section 174 application, which allows an accused to ask the court to determine whether the state has proved that there is sufficient evidence to prove the offence. If not, the accused is entitled to be discharged at the close of the state's case and is spared further legal costs and, if in custody, further incarceration. Through the Section 174 application, Carrington and the Ranger brothers manage to shave off a few of the charges, but still face the main charges of murder and kidnapping.

For Broodryk this is a good sign. The judge would not have kept Carrington and his co-accused behind bars if they had no case to answer to. Hodes, meanwhile, is pleasantly surprised that some of the charges – such as the one relating to the alleged hotel interrogation described by Dirk – have been dismissed. He takes that to be a positive omen.

At the end of April, Carrington Laughton, dressed as always in a smart black suit, shuffles across the dock, lets a police orderly unlock his leg irons and makes his way over to the witness stand.

Three years have passed since his arrest. Carrington's family is no longer attending the trial. His current wife, Anel, has met another man and, along with their two sons, has moved in with him. Carrington's second wife, Jayne, who had testified against him, is finalising arrangements to leave

South Africa with their daughter. She is not prepared to wait for judgment. His closest friends – Paul, Dirk, Conway and André – have betrayed him, accusing him of murder.

Carrington is alone, but this is the moment for which he has waited so patiently. Up until this point, his lawyers have done all the talking, trying to break the state's case and keep him out of the witness box. But the court has refused the Section 174 application and so, finally, it is his time to speak.

If Carrington is nervous, he doesn't show it. He sits on the wooden bench and dips his head below the microphone, letting only his eyes peek over the edge. For a second, he looks like a soldier in a bunker as he playfully illustrates to the Ranger brothers how low he will be sitting during his testimony.

Hodes begins to lead his most important witness. He starts at the very beginning, allowing Carrington to stitch together a neat narrative of his life, from his birth, through his schooling and into his career as a private investigator. The evidence flows smoothly along a timeline and Carrington speaks clearly and firmly, giving long answers where necessary, without rambling.

He comes across as a strong witness. He is familiar with courtrooms, knows the language and is not afraid to flex his powerful memory. He knows the docket back to front, down to some of the exhibit numbers assigned to various documents. He has written out virtually every line of testimony heard during the trial.

Carrington watches the judge as he writes his notes, trying to speak only once he has finished. He spells names without being prompted, and his stories come complete with dates, locations and names, such as the man he met while exploring business opportunities in England in 1998. He can remember number plates, like the one on a car driven by one of his friends in the nineties, and if he can't, he at least gives the court the first few letters. His Mazda Astina did not just have tinted windows ... they were tinted to precisely 18 per cent.

Whether it is raw skill or a case of meticulous preparation, or both, Carrington has his story ironed out and navigates the witness stand with ease. He does not shy away from addressing the judge directly: 'Would M'Lord prefer Accused 3 or Carel?' He chooses his words carefully, describing a confrontation with a gang of robbers, which ended with him shooting a man dead, as a 'scuffle'.

On his first day, Carrington outlines how he had met all the friends who have testified against him and takes the court through his military history and his relationship with Candice, who, when they met, was a receptionist at an advertising agency in a building in which he worked. The two of them went on to form C&C Commercial Services.

He speaks with confidence about his time in the army, maintaining that he had obtained the rank of full lieutenant by doing a fast-track course before joining the commandos. Carrington testifies about serving in army intelligence and being posted to lead a unit of the 61 Mechanised Battalion in Namibia. He claims they had some 'contact' with enemy forces and listed the medals he had been awarded, including one for helping secure the 1994 elections.

The records Gerhard van Wyk had obtained from the South African National Defence Force (SANDF) state clearly that Carrington had left the army with the lowest possible rank of 'private', but Laughton simply maintains that the SANDF's records are incomplete.

Asked for clarity, the SANDF issues a media statement defending its records: 'The member had the rank of private until the final termination of his duty of service on 20 December 2006.' It details his time with the commandos and the compulsory camps he attended.

Broodryk and his team, in turn, secure expert opinion on photographs in which Carrington poses in his army uniform, and the consensus is that he could not have earned the badges and medals he displayed. Carrington gives detailed explanations and argues that the opinion being offered is wrong. Like many other parts of his life, Carrington's military history remains disputed. Not even the simplest of facts – his rank – can be agreed upon.

· · ·

One of the most important parts of Carrington's evidence was always going to be how he explained the statements made by Carel and David Ranger during their bail applications. In those statements, both confirmed being asked by Carrington to drive to a hospital, fetch a woman and take her to a smallholding in Kliprivier, just as the confession outlines. Both had started their statements with 'During 1999 ...', and David even mentioned a 'bus-like structure'. As they had been charged with the murder of Betty Ketani, it stood to reason that she was the woman to whom they were referring.

Carrington disagrees and offers a detailed explanation.

His story shifts the events back by four years, to September 1995.

Carrington testifies that during that time he was still working for Shield Investigations and had bought a new car, a white Mazda 323. He gives the court the car's engine size and number plate, and adds that it had a manual transmission.

The reason the car is important is because he had kept a log of all the kilometres he travelled in it for work so that he could claim back the money spent on petrol. Carrington can show that the mileage he recorded dropped significantly in the month of September, and rose to normal levels again in October. Later, his attorney Howard Woolf would submit Carrington's old diary to the court to confirm the odometer readings.

The reason the recorded mileage was low in September, Carrington claims, was because he had been given a white minibus – a Mazda or a Mitsubishi – by his employer in anticipation of a music concert, for which Shield had been hired to provide security. Carrington tells the court that American singer Clarence Carter was due in Johannesburg and his task was to secure the various venues. There were almost 30 shows over some two and a half weeks, starting in mid-September 1995 at the city hall in downtown Johannesburg.

Carrington says he was given six security guards to manage. To cut costs, three guards were brought in from the East Rand office. Carrington is asked whether he remembers their names. He does. There was Godfrey, Lawrence, Isaac, Jack, Sibusiso and Lucky. Lawrence had a driver's licence.

Carrington remembers the meetings he held in the build-up to the concert. The first was with a 'chap by the name of Ashby' (Carrington spells out the name: A-S-H-B-Y) who had an office at the Carlton Centre. The meeting took place at 12.30pm on 7 September 1995.

Still following up with this kind of detail, Carrington continues his story, explaining that the concert was cancelled at the last minute and they were asked to stand down. The security guards had been reporting to Carrington each morning and one day Godfrey asked him for a special favour. He needed to fetch a relative from a hospital in Vereeniging. Carrington says the request was vague, but he agreed to help and made all the necessary arrangements.

He and Godfrey took the minibus to pick up Carel and David Ranger from Norwood. Carel knew Vereeniging and would be their 'human GPS', while David had nothing better to do but tag along. In court, Carrington claims, Carel and David had confused the year 1999 with 1995, but they were referring to the same event.

Carrington then describes how they drove to the hospital and double-parked outside the entrance, and how he, Godfrey and David Ranger went in to fetch the woman, while Carel stayed in the vehicle in case it needed to be moved.

> We alighted from the vehicle. David, Godfrey and I went inside. I went inside as I needed to use the bathroom, M'Lord, which I did. When I came out the bathroom, M'Lord, David and Godfrey were nowhere to be seen, but surfaced a few minutes later with a young lady, a young black lady who was seated in a wheelchair, which David was pushing. Godfrey was carrying a large red suitcase, M'Lord.

Carrington says Godfrey took care of the formalities at reception, after which they returned to the minibus.

> We – myself, Godfrey, David and the lady still seated in the wheelchair – went out the front entrance to the vehicle. Godfrey then, and possibly David, helped her into the vehicle. I was at that stage climbing into the driver's position in the vehicle, M'Lord, and the wheelchair was left behind at the hospital. M'Lord, I am not entirely sure what David did with it, but it was left behind …

Carrington is asked to describe the woman.

M'Lord, she was of average height, slender build, fairly young, I would
say probably in her twenties, short hair. She was fairly unremarkable ...

According to Carrington, the woman moved with some difficulty but there
were no visible injuries. Hodes asks one more question before moving on
to the next phase of the story:

Did you ever ascertain her name?
Her name was Mary, M'Lord.

Broodryk, Kowlas and Van Wyk can't believe what they are hearing. Three
years into the case and after a full year of trial, this is the first time they are
being offered this information. At long last, *this* is Carrington's version.
They have called over 30 witnesses and none were confronted with this
detail. It is all coming out now.

Carrington is claiming that he and the Ranger brothers *did* fetch a
woman from a hospital in Vereeniging, albeit in 1995, not 1999. The trip
was at the request of one of Carrington's security guards and the woman
they fetched was not Betty Ketani, but a Mary. They used a minibus but not
a VW, and the woman may have had some kind of an injury or surgery but
she had definitely not been stabbed in the head.

For some reason, what sticks in Broodryk's memory is the big red suitcase. It is such a vivid detail, and one that he will return to many times
during cross-examination. That and the name 'Mary'.

Carrington's story continues with the five of them leaving the hospital and driving towards Mark Eardley's farm. Along the way, he claims,
Godfrey received a call from someone and spoke in a language he couldn't
understand. Carrington says he found it strange that a security guard
would own a cellphone at a time when they were still new to South Africa
and very expensive.

'Perhaps we were paying our guards a bit too much if they could afford
cellphones If I was struggling to pay for mine, M'Lord,' he quips.

Carrington gathered that Godfrey had arranged to meet another relative at the farm and was giving directions to Mark Eardley's farm, which
Carrington had suggested as the meeting place. When they arrived at the

farm, a man – later introduced as Shadrack – was waiting for them in a large white car, possibly a Toyota Cressida or a Mitsubishi Colt Galant.

Carrington says he went to check whether Mark was home. He wasn't, and by the time he returned, everyone was standing around waiting to leave. He excused Godfrey for the day, Mary was helped into the other car and the three of them – Mary, Godfrey and Shadrack – followed the minibus off of the farm and onto the dirt road. After that, they all went their separate ways.

Broodryk has so many questions he doesn't know where to start.

The burning question is why Godfrey and Shadrack didn't simply pick Mary up from the hospital. Shadrack had a car, Godfrey had a phone, so it would have saved them the detour to Mark Eardley's farm, which neither had ever been to and was located along a dirt road and not, in Broodryk's opinion, easy to find. Why would Godfrey go to so much trouble to ask his boss for help when Shadrack drove a car? And even if he did, why not just meet at work or at the Blockhouse or some other established landmark?

Why did Carrington wait until the state had closed its case before giving this version of events? Broodryk is convinced that he had waited until all the state's evidence was led and only then put the final touches to his story, figuring that there would be no time for the state to test it.

Broodryk's take is that Carel and David were invited along to the hospital so they could flash their police appointment cards and thus fob off any questions. He finds the names Mary, Shadrack and Godfrey far too predictable and clichéd. He also wonders whether the red suitcase wasn't used to block the door of the minibus and to keep the woman inside.

In their statements, the Ranger brothers stated that the wheelchair had been taken with them to the plot. Why was Carrington now saying it was abandoned at the hospital? The questions keep popping into his head, but they will have to wait until cross-examination. Carrington isn't even nearly done.

69.

Throughout the trial so far, Carrington has offered no alibi for the night Conway claims Betty Ketani was stabbed in the head and left on the side of a dirt road. On the second day of his evidence-in-chief, Carrington drops the bombshell that will become his alibi.

Once again, Broodryk and his team sit listening to a defence that is being offered 14 months into the trial. Carrington explains how he met Mark Lister and his friend Warren, how their Cape Town franchise operation came into being and how he spent the whole of May 1999 training the two of them in the Cape.

To back up his alibi, Carrington produces the franchise agreement signed in early April 1999. Although he can't prove that he was in Cape Town during those weeks in May, he argues that the state has led no evidence to prove he wasn't.

Broodryk and Kowlas have no access to Mark Lister, who is in Australia, and Warren had not appeared on their radar. In any event, reopening their case will require a special application to the judge. All they can do for now is listen as Carrington rolls out his defence.

Through his testimony, Carrington shifts the state's entire timeline. He does not deny that he had a romantic relationship with Monique Neeteson-Lemkes, but says it was not in 1999 but in 2000, following a trip to Thailand. His timeline contradicts the confession and stands in opposition to the state's contention that it was his affair with Monique that led to Candice's attempted suicide. Candice is overseas and refused to testify, so there is no way to challenge the version.

Carrington admits that his company investigated the thefts at Cranks, but testifies that Candice had handled the case while he was away. Again, Candice is not available to confirm or deny the claim. His version is that food items, not money, were being stolen. This, he says, led to a brief investigation during which an agent was placed inside the restaurant but was removed after Eric pulled the plug on the undercover operation.

None of this information was put to any of the state's witnesses, but Carrington anticipates the questions from Broodryk and tells the court he had held onto all this information on instruction from his legal teams.

Carrington has an explanation for everything.

The confession is a well-crafted forgery, he says. Four of his closest friends turned on him because Eric had got to them and they needed to save their own skins. The DNA results are inconclusive. The handwriting analysis can't exclude forgery. The witnesses from 1999 can't be believed because there are too many holes in their stories. The chain of evidence is broken. Plus, he claims, it can't be proved with absolute certainty that Betty Ketani is actually dead.

Carrington cries foul over his arrest and the involvement of Doc and JB. He explains that his lawyers instructed him not to give a handwriting sample right from the start and that he changed his signature in prison because he was warned that warders have been known to commit identity theft and clean out the bank accounts of inmates. He says this was the 'word around the campfire' inside jail.

As for the Audi TT and the perjury conviction, he now claims that Dirk had played a prank on him by hiding the car, and by the time Dirk did come clean, Carrington had already reported it hijacked. He can't explain why this was never put to Dirk when he had testified or why he had made up an elaborate story about a violent hijacking instead of simply reporting the car stolen.

Carrington admits he doctored photographs of Ruth Mncube, but says he did so not to lie to Eric about having killed her but to protect her from the Cranks owner. Yes, he spoke to Captain Alan Fagan after his arrest, but the notes the senior policeman made and the affidavit he later signed – which made no mention of any of the details Carrington was now offering – are lies.

Carrington testifies that he does have army uniforms at home, but that they are rare collector's items from as far away as Switzerland. He admits to owning a white coat (mentioned in relation to the hospital kidnapping), but says that this is not a doctor's coat but rather protective clothing from a mine where he had run an investigation.

Carrington draws parallels between his 2001 arrests, and the fax that formed part of the case back then, and the confession letter that surfaced in 2012. He also, for the first time, testifies that the 'Howson & Straker' letter that Conway admitted to writing had appeared in the 2001 case. This is meant to prove a link between Conway and Eric Neeteson-Lemkes. There is, however, no way to verify the claim because the dockets of those 2001 cases were never found.

Having at first denied that Candice had shot herself on 12 June 1999, and then being shown the medical records, Carrington now says he had battled to reconstruct the timeline but had eventually been able to do so. He claims it was difficult to prepare for the case because so much time had lapsed and because of the state's conduct. Hodes leads him through every line of the confession and Carrington zooms in on the smallest oddity, such as the township Alexandra being spelt as 'Alexander'. He says he would not have made such a mistake.

It takes Hodes three and a half days to take Carrington through his evidence-in-chief, during which time he goes over the evidence of everyone who had incriminated him and casts doubt on all of it.

Broodryk, meanwhile, has spent months thinking about what his first question to Carrington will be. He considered something dramatic, such as, 'Mr Laughton, can you tell the court what perjury means?' This, he thought, might unsettle Carrington right from the start. But Carrington's evidence over the last three days has thrown up so much new information, including a new alibi, that Broodryk's focus is redirected and he scraps the theatrics, choosing instead to start with a fairly tame question about Carrington's school days. Broodryk recognises that he is up against a very capable witness and that it will take a lot more than a one-liner to get under his skin.

. . .

Broodryk is into his third day of cross-examination when he knocks over his glass of water onto his notes and fumbles around apologising.

'I suddenly don't feel so well,' he says, before asking for the case to stand down.

The moment the adjournment is granted, he shrugs off his robe, slumps into his chair and loosens his collar. When he has gained enough strength, he leaves the courtroom and takes a seat on one of the benches outside, where the air is cooler. He has broken out in a cold sweat and his breathing is shallow. It looks like all the blood has drained from his face. Hodes comes out to express his concern. Arrangements are quickly made for him to be driven straight to his cardiologist at Olivedale Clinic.

It is not a heart attack, but Broodryk is nevertheless admitted for observation. The previous year, his doctors had picked up that his heart had developed an irregular beat and had to be set right. Crudely speaking, it needed a reboot – what the medical fraternity refer to as a cardioversion.

Like his investigating officer, Broodryk worried a great deal about the case, putting himself under enormous pressure, and was nervous about the confrontation with Carrington. Although he had been looking forward to it from the start of the trial, he also knew how much was at stake.

Broodryk rests for four days and comes back the following week to continue. He has let Kowlas lead and cross-examine many of the witnesses, but their arrangement from the beginning was that it would be him doing battle with Carrington. After just one day in court, Broodryk is back at the doctor and is booked off again, this time only for a day. So worried about having another episode in court, he has now suffered an anxiety attack. He hates that his heart is tripping him up at such a crucial moment. He doesn't want to show weakness when jokes about witnesses developing 'Carrington-itis' have begun doing the rounds.

So it is that Broodryk comes back and, although he battles, he keeps Carrington in the box for another seven days. With a brief re-examination, the witness spends 13 days testifying, each one starting with a polite bow and a 'Good morning, M'Lord'. At an average of five hours per day, Carrington is on the stand for over 60 hours. Only once, towards the end, does he say he is tired, but assures the court that he has no problem continuing.

Carrington is an unstumpable witness.

No matter what Broodryk tries, the accused concedes nothing. The prosecutor feels he has won some important victories, but if he was hoping for a grand unravelling and a teary confession, he gets nowhere near it.

Carrington doesn't move an inch from his version, repeating sequences of events as many times as he is asked.

Most of the days are taken up by the details: dates, names, places or conversations. There is so much to cover. Broodryk keeps circling back to key events, such as the hospital visit or the time Carrington claims to have spent in Cape Town.

There are dramatic exchanges between prosecutor and accused as Broodryk tests whether there is any evidence that Eric Neeteson-Lemkes – alleged by Carrington to be the 'puppet master' – is behind the confession under the carpet and everything that followed.

> *What did he [Eric] allegedly do that had anything to do with the charges that you are facing? How was he involved in that, according to you? What evidence is there to that effect?*
>
> *That I do not know.*
>
> *But it is your words, Mr Laughton, that you were surprised that he is not an accused.*
>
> *Well, M'Lord, yes.*
>
> *What did you mean by that?*
>
> *What I mean by that is I am surprised he is not an accused. I mean I have been arrested in this matter and I have no involvement in it, whereas the connection between Betty Ketani and Cranks, that is Eric Lemkes. Instead what happened was a statement was procured somehow, not by the police, and the man was allowed to leave the country, M'Lord. It just surprises me that he was not …*
>
> *But what evidence, according to your knowledge, is there against Mr Lemkes, that he was involved in this case? You have had lots of time, take meticulous notes, you have had copies of everything, you had three years to think about it, what evidence is there linking Mr Lemkes to this case?*
>
> *M'Lord, as I said the fact that Betty Ketani worked for Mr Lemkes, the way in which he absconded, it is not a question of … I am not investigating this case but I believe that he is involved in it in some manner, means or fashion.*
>
> *In some fashion?*
>
> *Yes, M'Lord.*

> *You are an experienced private investigator, Mr Laughton. I ask the*
> *question again, what evidence is there to link Mr Lemkes with the offences*
> *of which you are charged?*
> *M'Lord, I do not know.*
> *You do not know?*
> *I do not know what evidence there is against him.*
> *There is no evidence, not so, Mr Laughton?*
> *If you say so, M'Lord.*

Broodryk keeps pointing out that the war between Carrington and Eric had subsided in 2001 or just after, and the two of them had had no contact for more than a decade. His point is that if Eric had set him up, he had been prepared to wait an awfully long time for his plan to be realised.

At times, Carrington accuses Broodryk of asking unfair or misleading questions. Broodryk, in turn, growls when Carrington steps too far in trying to mirror the terms he and Hodes are using.

> *… It is my submission, M'Lord, that who is to say this is …*
> *Submission? You are not here to make submissions. Just answer the*
> *questions. Continue, Mr Laughton. You are not a lawyer.*

The advantage swings back and forth. Late in the cross-examination, Carrington asks for a document to be handed up to him before he will answer a question. Broodryk tries to resist, but Hodes intervenes and convinces the court that his client is entitled to see the exhibit. This relates to Candice's medical records and the debate is over a single sentence. The request sees the teams scramble to find the right document and a brief adjournment is taken, but when the court is reconstituted, Carrington does something extraordinary and decides to address Judge Natvarial Ranchod directly. The exchange begins with Broodryk passing him the medical records.

> *A copy for you, Mr Laughton.*
> *Thank you, M'Lord. Before I begin on this page, M'Lord, sorry, I seem*
> *to have been the cause of a bit of an issue here. I just firstly would like to*
> *thank Your Lordship for the indulgence …*

That's as far as he gets before a stunned Judge Ranchod cuts him off.

> *Mr Laughton, no need to apologise or anything. This is something between*
> *the counsel and the court.*
> > *I understand that, M'Lord, it is just that …*
> > *You can continue …*

But Carrington isn't finished.

> *This has been a lengthy cross-examination and I am quite tired, M'Lord.*
> *Now I just want to be absolutely certain of what I tell Your Lordship, that*
> *is why I wanted it. It was not for … I was not disputing it or anything, I*
> *just need to be absolutely sure of what I am saying so I do not get confused.*

There are times when Carrington pushes the boundaries too far and the judge is less forgiving, such as when he is trying to convince the court that he holds the rank of an officer in the army.

> *I do not understand why such a considerable amount of time has been*
> *devoted to something in this court which has nothing to do with the mat-*
> *ter at hand. It has never been in dispute that I performed military service,*
> *in fact it is a matter of public record almost. I do not understand why*
> *Captain Van Wyk enjoyed such a personal interest in pursuing this rea-*
> *sonably fruitless line of investigation. But I …*

At this point Judge Ranchod runs out of patience and stops him mid-sentence.

> *Mr Laughton, I think you should just answer the question or deal with*
> *what was put to you. You are giving a lot of your own opinions. That will*
> *be for this court to determine.*
> > *Of course, M'Lord. I apologise.*

Eventually, Broodryk gets to deliver the line with which he had wanted to open his cross-examination, but it comes unexpectedly during one of the most heated clashes. Carrington is talking about the photographs he had doctored for Eric, explaining that he agreed to 'kill' Ruth only to satisfy the restaurant boss and that he had no intention of actually doing it. He maintains he had not charged Eric for the favour he had promised to do for him. But Broodryk is not buying it.

> *You are a private investigator, you work for money.*
> *That is correct, M'Lord, yes, but I have, I had ethics, M'Lord. I have a personal code.*

The word 'ethics' ignites something inside Broodryk, and he charges like a bull towards a matador's crimson cape.

> *You have ethics?*
> *It is not something I could do.*
> *You have got ethics, is that what I heard?*
> *Yes, M'Lord.*
> *What does the word perjury mean, Mr Laughton?*
> *Yes, M'Lord, I …*
> *What does the word perjury mean?*
> *It means to lie under oath.*
> *We know you have been convicted of lying under oath.*
> *I pleaded guilty, yes, M'Lord. That is correct.*

Broodryk hammers on about the fact that Carrington had driven around in the Audi TT for months before being arrested and that he had installed fake diplomatic plates. But even being confronted with that, Carrington refuses to give any more than he absolutely has to.

> *You agree driving around with a vehicle which is not your own with dip-lomatic plates on it, that is fraud.*
> *Well, M'Lord … it certainly is wrong, yes.*
> *I am sorry?*
> *It certainly is wrong, yes. I mean, as I said, I pled guilty to it, M'Lord, I accepted responsibility for what I had done.*

Again the judge interrupts.

> *You say just before the last answer, it was not fraud?*
> *M'Lord, yes, I do not believe it was fraud. I said it was wrong, it was a stupid, wrong thing to do and I acknowledge that.*

Broodryk charges back in.

> *I am sorry, I did not hear that. Why do you say it is not fraud?*
> *Well, M'Lord, I ...*
> *An experienced private investigator like you not knowing that that is fraud.*
> *Well, M'Lord, for fraud there is, one of the requirements is prejudice, M'Lord.*
> *Yes. The car rental company believed that the car was stolen, meanwhile it was not, you were driving around with it.*
> *Yes, M'Lord, that is correct.*
> *So is that not prejudice?*
> *M'Lord, the vehicle was insured and I paid the excess on it. There may well have been prejudice. As I said, as Mr Broodryk said, M'Lord, that the initial charge was fraud.*
> *Ja.*
> *But it was then reduced, I mean I do not know if that is the correct terminology, M'Lord, to perjury. That was actually ... what I had done wrong.*
> *Actually you drove around in it for eight months.*
> *Well, M'Lord, I did not drive around.*
> *Is that correct, Mr Laughton?*
> *M'Lord, I had it for eight months.*

From there, Broodryk brings up the Aston Martin crash, following which Carrington had lied in the accident report and said he was behind the wheel when in fact it had been Paul. He then goes to the legal fight Carrington had over rent with his Sharonlea landlords, where he was accused of forging a signature for the extension of the contract. To finish, he questions Carrington about the snorkel business he had run with Conway that saw him accused of being a con man on the front page of a newspaper. Carrington fights back but eventually backs off.

> *M'Lord, I am not trying to portray myself as being lily white. I am the first to admit that I am no saint. I have made mistakes. I have done things that are wrong and I am being open and honest with Your Lordship about these things.*

It is a sentiment he will repeat again.

> *I have done things that I am ashamed of, M'Lord. That makes me human. It does not make me a lying murderer.*

Anchoring his narrative to some key events – such as the Cranks investigation or his ex-wife's suicide attempt – Carrington presents to the court a parallel story to the one offered by the state. It was 1995, not 1999. It was Mary, not Betty. It was food being stolen from Cranks, not money. It was Candice who conducted the investigation, not him. There were no Hillbrow raids. No extramarital affair with Monique, only an innocent romance after his divorce. No murder that he knew of. No shallow grave. No instructions to dispose of a body years later. The only reason he was on trial, he argues, was because of his feud with Eric Neeteson-Lemkes.

Carrington is not going to budge, no matter how long Broodryk keeps him in the box. So after nine days, feeling he has done enough damage, the prosecutor announces he has no further questions for the witness.

> *I must congratulate you, Mr Laughton, you gave, on the face of it, a very good performance for somebody who is in the witness box for the first time.*
>
> *M'Lord, I never said it was the first time I am in a witness box. I said it is the first time I have been put on trial to this extent.*

And then, he just can't resist it:

But thank you.

70.

Carrington and his team have two expert witnesses lined up. The first is David Swanepoel, who has analysed the DNA results from Bosnia. Swanepoel works at Lancet Laboratories in Johannesburg and this is his first time testifying in a trial. He calls himself a 'Human Identification Specialist', although during cross-examination the state will point out that there is no such title and that he has created it.

Compared to Professor Thomas Parsons, Swanepoel is a lightweight. He has six years' experience and his highest qualification is a BSc Honours in biochemistry, which he obtained in 2009. Parsons, on the other hand, received his PhD in the same subject in 1989, 20 years earlier. Parsons leads a team of dozens of scientists at the ICMP, was involved in the investigation into the 9/11 World Trade Center attacks and has testified at The Hague, whereas Swanepoel is still studying for his master's and has never published a research article. But the defence leads Swanepoel for two full days, during which he makes some serious allegations.

Swanepoel has done his own calculations and has come up with a lower level of probability for the hypothesis that the bone that yielded DNA results belongs to Betty Ketani. He takes a more conservative approach and disregards some of the alleles on which the ICMP has reported. His evidence raises questions about how the bones had been handled and the possibility of a mismatch. Swanepoel testifies that Betty Ketani could still be excluded as the donor of the DNA found and that the statistics are too low to be relied on. He also makes the controversial claim that some of the reagents used at the ICMP had expired.

Broodryk is happy to let Kowlas take the cross-examination. They have consulted Parsons (who took great offence at Swanepoel's claims) and keep the defence witness on the stand for a further two days. The science aside, they force him to admit that he has no qualifications to calculate statistical probabilities (whereas Parsons does) and the oldest sample he has ever worked with was a year old, while the ICMP has successfully processed DNA from the skeletons of Second World War soldiers. They also set out to show that the ICMP is a fully accredited, globally renowned laboratory that undergoes regular inspections and that the chemicals it used were just fine.

Next, the defence calls document examiner Cecil Greenfield to take on Colonel Marco van der Hammen over his handwriting report. Unlike Swanepoel, Greenfield is a veteran of his field with over 50 years' experience and hundreds of cases behind him. He has founded associations and has testified in trials in South Africa and in neighbouring countries. He commands respect from all sides and his credibility is never in question.

Interestingly, Greenfield tells the court that after examining the confession he can find no evidence that it is a forgery. In fact, in his opinion, the signatures have 'all the features of genuineness'. This is an unexpected assessment, given that it aligns with what Van der Hammen has said. Greenfield goes on to testify that the signatures had been created with speed and fluency, which is normally not found in forgeries. He says one of the sure ways to spot a fake is to check whether it is exactly the same as the original, an identical copy, which these signatures are not.

Greenfield speaks of several anomalies, such as the possibility that a different pen had been used, but to a large extent he agrees with the state's expert. He does testify, though, that the document and the ink should have been tested further and disagrees with Van der Hammen about what kind of printer had been used. He pays attention to the differences in the signatures on the first two pages versus the one on the third, which is something Jayne Laughton also mentioned.

The handwriting expert cautions the court about handwriting analysis in general, stating that it is subjective and is not an exact science. Different analysts can interpret the same information in a variety of ways. A glass could be half full or half empty, depending on who is looking at it.

'Our minds are very clever,' Greenfield explains. 'If we want to see similarities, we can find similarities. If we want to find dissimilarities, we will find dissimilarities.'

The words relate to handwriting and signatures, but they seem profound. They speak to what lies at the very heart of the Ketani case: a fundamental difference of interpretation. Those who believe and support Carrington and the Rangers can see nothing but a conspiracy in every piece of evidence. Every discrepancy or misalignment screams out as proof of a set-up. All they can see are the faults in the state's case. They can't imagine how anyone can think it is real.

On the other hand, Broodryk, Kowlas and Van Wyk – and all the investigators before them – see all the pieces that fit. All the similarities and coincidences. All the alignments. In their eyes there can be no other explanation. Broodryk never once thinks that Carrington is innocent. He never thinks the Rangers made a mistake with the year of the hospital trip. There are gaps, yes, but there is just too much evidence for it all to be a mistake.

There is east and there is west, and they are never going to meet.

• • •

Broodryk and his team consulted with Mark Eardley and had even summoned him to court on a few occasions, but in the end never called him to testify. Once the state closed its case, Eardley became available to the defence and Carrington decided to use him as one of his witnesses.

The chef and father of three is able to tell the court about the old railway bus that stood 30 or 40 metres from the main house, explaining that his father had bought it for him when he was about 16. The bus had been towed to the farm and Mark built the concrete blocks on which it was placed. It served as his bedroom until he went to the army in the early nineties.

Mark is asked to describe the easiest routes to and from the farm, and says he was surprised to hear allegations that a woman had been brought to the bus in 1999 and left to die there. In his opinion, it would have been impossible for anyone to visit the farm without him knowing. He justifies this by saying that farm workers would have informed him of any visitors and that there were always dogs on guard. That last part is particularly important to Carrington.

Much of the cross-examination is consumed by the detail of distances, directions and aerial photographs, along with descriptions of the various friendships that existed between Carrington and the others. Despite having said that he always knew what was going on at his farm, Mark concedes he knew nothing about the 1995 visit that Carrington described in his evidence.

Mark struggles with dates and has with him a sheet of paper with some key life events. He tells the court he had had to ask his wife the year in which they were married. His children's birthdays were double-checked against medical-aid cards. There is also a chronology of his jobs and other random facts, such as when the big beer factory had been built near his house.

Mark testifies that he and Sandor had done some work for Carrington, that their task was to sit in a car and watch someone who was under investigation. At one point, he says, Sandor or someone else had parked a caravan on the plot and used it as a field office. During his consultation with the prosecutors, Mark had described Carrington as a *larney* (fancy) man, someone who was 'a bit above everyone else' and who told others what to do. In court, he does not deny having said those things.

Carrington's fourth witness is Leon Rehrl, Jayne's ex-husband, who, over the years, has become a close friend. Like all Carrington's other friends, Leon had worked for him, both in private investigations and on *Naked Motoring*.

A short, skinny man, Leon is brought in primarily to testify about conversations he claimed had taken place in 2004. Leon's story is that after a meal at a Spur restaurant, Dirk had told him that Paul had said that a letter was being created to frame Carrington and make his life difficult. Leon says he communicated this to Carrington by telephone, who was abroad at the time.

Further, Leon claims he had tried to tell all this to Captain Alan Fagan, but had been ignored. Fagan, of course, had committed suicide and wasn't able to deny the accusation. Dirk and Paul both state that the Spur story is a lie.

Unlike his friend Carrington, Leon is a poor witness. He is vague and argumentative and far too often sarcastic. At one point Kowlas asks whether he considers himself a joker, to which he replies, 'Yes, I am.'

Leon had brought Carrington's daughter to visit him in prison several times after he had been arrested, but claims he never discussed the 2004 phone call with him. Then, halfway through the trial and after Paul had testified, he decided to raise it with Carrington and his legal team. This is something the prosecutors have a difficult time believing and cross-examine him about it at length. Surely, they maintain, this crucial bit of information should have been raised right from the start. After all, the existence of the confession letter was already known at the bail stage.

Leon has a history of heavy drug abuse and the state had looked through the SMS messages he had exchanged with Carrington in 2012. Messages such as:

> I just saw the promo and I still have very little memory of last week. I still feel the craving from my little adventure with captain ketamine. Plus the holes in my memory, and when I miss my meds I have other versions of choo running around ...

And:

> No I don't seem to be in a good place. Which is why I am concerned about it affecting you and those around me here at home. I have conversations with people who are not present ...

> Hi, everything is okay. I just had one of those blackout days. I didn't know where I was or who I was. It happens.

In his messages to Carrington, Leon complained about his health. He is a cancer survivor whose drug abuse had caused major damage to his organs. In other messages he spoke about not wanting to let his friend down or made racist comments about hating black people. In one message he told Carrington about a trick he had been shown to alter video footage and insert a driver in a car.

> So Poul [sic] driving becomes you driving.

Leon tries to explain all these messages as two guys joking around. He says that was just the way he communicated. Kowlas is having none of it.

The first day of cross-examination ends with Leon asking the court to allow him to stand down and go home. He complains about not feeling well and of being confused. He is pale and doubled over in the witness box. Broodryk and Kowlas wonder whether he will come back, but he does, some two weeks later.

Kowlas keeps working the SMSs, the Spur conversation that is impossible to prove and the question of why Leon decided to come forward only mid-trial. She also produces a confirmatory affidavit he had signed to help Carrington during his divorce from Jayne, which Kowlas claims shows that Leon had come to his aid before. Leon, however, denies he came to court to lie for Carrington.

71.

David and Carel Ranger take turns to testify, trying to unshackle themselves from the bail statements they had signed back in early 2012. Their stories now align neatly with Carrington's telling of the 1995 hospital trip and both maintain they had run a harmless errand, which David describes as a 'non-event' in his life.

The brothers claim they were too stressed and angry to think clearly during those early days of their bail application and should never have signed their affidavits. They say the translation from Afrikaans to English threw them and they weren't able to fully take in what was happening in court as their statements were read into the record. They say they heard about what happens to policemen in jail and were frightened and frustrated.

'Nice try, Mr Ranger!' Broodryk booms while cross-examining David.

He accuses the policeman of changing his version to fit Carrington's defence, and asks how a policeman with over 15 years' service – who has testified several dozen times and trained other officers – could claim not to have paid attention during his bail application. Especially when the magistrate specifically warned him and his brother that anything they say in their statements would be used against them later.

'I didn't join the police to hurt people,' David tries to fight back. 'I am a person who helps people.'

But Broodryk pushes on. He is feeling stronger now and the Ranger brother is nowhere near as impressive in the witness box as Carrington had been. He questions why David's bail statement made no mention of Godfrey and Shadrack, or the red suitcase. Why had he said nothing about Mary? How tall was she? How many steps did she take at the farm? He feasts on the details Carrington has given, using them against David. The cross-examination lasts two days, during which David also denies he took part in any illegal raids in Hillbrow.

Second in line, Carel speaks about how stressed he had been after his arrest. He says that his son had been diagnosed with meningitis and he had panicked because he had no way of receiving news from his family. He also claims that he had not been paying attention when the statement was read into the record.

As for the Hillbrow abductions, Carel sticks to the same explanation he had given in 1999, claiming he had gone to Themba's flat only once and with legitimate intentions. André Coetzer had confessed that the two of them had lied to Inspector James van Rooyen, carefully coordinating their statements, but Carel still denies it.

He is cross-examined by Namika Kowlas and faces similar questions as his brother. He calls his former mother-in-law to testify about a family holiday, which he claims he had taken over the same period as some of the raids at Aintree Flats. Carel also has to deal with his arrest for armed robbery back in 1999, with his lawyer raising objections about his credibility being tested.

The Ranger brothers may not have been close before their arrest, but now, as the trial nears its end, they are singing in perfect harmony, issuing identical denials, which fit precisely with the version Carrington has dropped during his testimony.

72.

While Herman Broodryk was cross-examining Carrington Laughton, Captain Gerhard van Wyk finds and quietly meets two brand-new witnesses.

It is late in the game, and introducing them into the trial will require special permission from the judge to reopen the state's case, but what these two people are saying is potentially detrimental to Carrington's surprise alibi.

Warren Dawson and Karyn Griffin are old friends. Warren works in IT, rides a big Triumph and is training to become a police reservist. Karyn is arty, loves horses and has come a long way from being the girl who once convinced Mark Lister to sell his CD collection to help her run away from home.

Van Wyk speaks to Warren first. It is just hours after Carrington had pulled him in as an alibi, claiming that he had been training Warren and Mark at the time Betty Ketani was stabbed. Warren knows about the case and has been following it from a distance, but he never expected to become Carrington's alibi.

He last saw Carrington in 1999, and aside from those few months during which they had tried to open a franchise of C&C Commercial Services in the Cape, he has had no dealings with him. He wasn't friends with anyone in that circle and had barely ever thought about those days in Hermanus. He has a happy life now, is a father, and being dragged into a criminal trial with Carrington Laughton in the dock fills him with apprehension. But his sense of duty also prevents him from remaining silent.

Warren doesn't have a lot of memories of Carrington. He recalls that his father had warned him against the business venture, urging him to walk away because he had no clue what he was doing. Warren also found it strange that Carrington so openly boasted about being in army intelligence. As far as he knew, people who were in the intelligence world didn't advertise it. Most importantly, he is absolutely certain that Carrington had spent no more than a day or two with him and Mark in the Cape and that the story about them training together for five weeks cannot possibly be true.

Warren remembers the day they signed their agreement as well as the day they took a drive to the airport. But that is it.

He refers Captain Van Wyk to Karyn, who also has no recollection of Mark Lister being away from Johannesburg during that time. They were a couple for six years – she had even moved to Australia with him for a while (she was there over the 2000 Sydney Olympics) – yet he had said nothing about wanting to move down to Cape Town in 1999. Karyn had met Carrington's first wife, Candice, whom she liked and saw as passionate and a little crazy; she had also met Monique, whom she disliked instantly. She tells Van Wyk that to her it seemed that Carrington and Monique were having an affair and that she wanted to tell Candice, but didn't feel it was her place. Later, when Candice shot herself, she was riddled with guilt.

Karyn has another stirring memory: of Mark returning from a job with Carrington and collapsing into her arms, crying uncontrollably. He was 'hysterical' but would not explain why. This, too, was shortly before Candice's suicide attempt and went against what Mark had told a reporter in Australia, claiming he had stopped working with Carrington by the time the Cranks investigation began.

Karyn says that from that night something about Mark changed. He was never the same again and 'began to act very strangely'. He told her to stay away from Carrington and everyone he knew. She asked, but he never told her what happened. Karyn describes Mark as a sweet person who was easily manipulated. The confession under the carpet appears to implicate him in the abduction of Betty Ketani:

> BETTY KETANI was 'arrested' by Mark and his friend Warren Williams ...

Both Warren Dawson and Karyn knew Warren Williams but have nothing to offer Van Wyk that could be used to persuade Williams to testify. His lawyer stands guard at the door and unless Van Wyk has evidence, he is not getting inside. Dawson and Griffin, however, agree to sign statements and to come to court.

Once Carrington and the Ranger brothers finish testifying, the state reopens its case. Given that Carrington presented his defence so late, Broodryk has no difficulty with the application to summon his two new witnesses. The trial is now set to finish just as it had started, with yet another unexpected twist.

Warren and Karyn are strong witnesses. They have not been accused of any wrongdoing and come to give evidence because they choose to, not because they are forced to. They have had no contact with Carrington for over a decade and have nothing to gain by falsely implicating him. Neither appears to have any grudges or hidden agendas. The best the defence can do is to test their memories to try to soften the impact of their testimony.

In court, Warren confirms that he had spent no more than a day or two with Carrington in May 1999. He doesn't know why Carrington would claim to have spent five weeks with him and Mark Lister. Karyn testifies that Mark had not been away for any extended period of time during 1999 and if he had been in Cape Town for that long, she would have remembered.

Karyn is anxious. Her body is stiff and her voice soft. She leans in to the questions, as though the few extra centimetres can somehow help. She speaks only about aspects of the case of which she has first-hand knowledge and refuses to speculate. Reliving some of those old memories, particularly about how Mark had changed after that strange night when he couldn't stop crying, she appears haunted.

As with so much else, there is no way to prove that what Karyn is describing are the hours immediately after Betty Ketani's kidnapping. It is another piece of circumstantial evidence. The final piece. Because once Karyn is excused, the trial is postponed for closing arguments.

· · ·

For both sides, pulling together all the evidence proves a mammoth task. The court record runs to over 6 000 pages. Including judgment, the trial will have lasted a full two years. In that time, the court sat for almost 100 days – ten times longer than for an average trial. The state has some seven full lever-arch files of exhibits. Of these, 27 exhibits are still in dispute.

The state has led nearly 40 witnesses. There are dossiers of complicated DNA analysis and medical records. There are all the handwriting comparisons. There are 13 days of evidence from Carrington and 17 days' worth from the state's accomplice witnesses. There are exhibits that had been provisionally allowed and judgments that had been delivered but not fully explained. The defence is preparing yet another application to try to have the trial declared unfair, this time by identifying five key 'irregularities'. And, crucially, there is no word yet on whether the court has accepted the confession found at Conway's house as an exhibit and what it makes of it.

For the state, most of the work in preparing closing arguments falls to Namika Kowlas, while Broodryk's health takes another unexpected turn for the worse. During the trial he had undergone an operation to remove cataracts, had taken a nasty fall at home and had suffered with his heart. He then landed up in hospital again, now with a hernia. It wouldn't have been such a big deal, but he caught an infection and was rushed into ICU. He spent three days there, drifting in and out of consciousness. Some days disappeared altogether. His liver was failing and doctors fought to bring him back.

Broodryk pulled through and was eventually discharged. By the time he arrives in court for closing arguments in mid-October 2015, he has lost a lot of weight and has stopped drinking completely. Not even a glass of wine with dinner.

Broodryk had recently had a new waistcoat made for courtroom appearances, but is now back in his old one, and is wearing new shirts because his old ones hung loosely on his frame. He had only started feeling better that August and knows the magnitude of the responsibility that had now befallen Kowlas. He goes over her work and writes up certain parts that relate to Carrington's testimony. He isn't prepared to miss out.

Neither side holds back in their written heads of argument.

The state presents its mosaic of proof. Broodryk and Kowlas argue that once all the evidence is considered holistically only one conclusion is possible. It is the argument of the feathers: each piece of circumstantial evidence is as light as a bird's feather, but a pile of these feathers becomes heavy enough to tip the scale in favour of the state. Another legal analogy is that of a rope, which carries the weight of the 'beyond a reasonable doubt' test, but is made up of many far weaker threads. In other words, not every piece of evidence has to be flawless or beyond a reasonable doubt, but tie them all together into a rope and on it you can confidently hang a conviction.

The prosecutors claim that the state's and the defence's DNA and hand-writing experts have essentially reached the same conclusions and that the evidence of four accomplice witnesses, however shaky, cannot be ignored. It isn't perfect, but the 'essential features' are corroborated.

> There might well be improbabilities, contradictions and inconsisten-cies … but holistically their version remains standing, despite brutal cross-examination.

Out to prove their case, Broodryk and Kowlas also rely on the confession itself and the 1999 victims. Carrington is accused of having no version and of creating one only once the state had finished presenting its evidence.

> Accused 1 [Carrington] challenged the state's case not on the merits but rather on technicalities such as incorrect dates on albums, the absence of a photograph depicting six bones, the manner in which the reference [DNA] samples were taken and submitted to the laboratories. Accused 2 and 3 [the Ranger brothers] merely went along with this approach.

Broodryk calls Carrington 'arrogant' and 'haughty', stating that he had tried to come across as well-spoken and confident. He argues that Carrington's presentation of his evidence was well rehearsed – a bit too well rehearsed – and that it was nothing more than 'veneer' and 'gloss', which was easily penetrated. Instead, Broodryk argues, Carrington was 'evasive', 'argumentative' and told bald-faced lies. He says he was 'manip-ulative in nature and blamed everyone else' while making 'pathetic attempts to claim he had ethics'.

> Some of his references on the stand … were so over-dramatic and exag-gerated that he should be awarded an Oscar.

As for Carel and David Ranger, Broodryk and Kowlas maintain that they have simply gone along with Carrington's version. Their explanations, the prosecutors argue, are 'vague and bizarre'.

Broodryk and his team are feeling good about the way the trial has ended. Finding Warren and Karyn means, in their minds, that Carrington's alibi is gone. Without it, all he has is a conspiracy theory he can't prove. They want to show the court that he has adapted their evidence, shifted the timeline and superimposed the events of 1999 to 1995.

But Laurence Hodes and his team have fought all the way through the trial and are not about to stop now. They prepare a comprehensive, 218-page summary of their case, complete with a chronology of key events and their take on all the witnesses. They argue that the state has failed to push this case over the necessary mark of 'beyond a reasonable doubt'. Their legal metaphor is the chain – not the rope – which is only as strong as its weakest link.

Carrington's lawyers describe him as an 'impressive witness' who has no responsibility – legal onus – to prove why so many of his friends have turned on him, nor to present his version at the outset of the trial. They argue that it is not possible to exclude the possibility that the confession is a freehand forgery and, despite the ICMP findings, the 'origin of the bones remains unknown'. 'The state,' they say, 'has an ethical obligation to pursue truth and not merely secure a conviction or win a case.'

What the defence is essentially saying is: we have heard your case, and our version is that Carrington was not in Johannesburg at the time – now try to prove that he was. As for the hospital trip … well, that happened in 1995 and, again, you can't prove that it didn't. And we can explain why Carrington is being set up for this crime: it's because Eric Neeteson-Lemkes has a vendetta against him. Just look at their history and how Eric had tried to have him thrown in jail unlawfully in 2001.

That is the legal strategy, along with a relentless assault on procedure and the chain of evidence. Technically, the trial has not yet ended, but Hodes and his team make it clear that they will appeal against a conviction and will not stop trying to have the case declared irregular. They give five reasons for this: Teunis Briers was allowed to introduce new evidence during re-examination; Thomas Parsons and his colleague had not submitted statements before they testified; Themba Tshabalala testified about elements that were not in his statements; the judge's decision not to provide a full explanation for his Section 174 ruling; and some irregularities with the transcript, which the defence claims have put them at a disadvantage.

Judge Natvarial Ranchod had settled most of these disputes, but Hodes wants him to know that he will appeal to see if another court would reach a different conclusion. It is unusual to raise all this before a judgment is handed down and Broodryk suspects it is an attempt to put pressure on the judge. Hodes, on the other hand, argues he is simply being open about his legal approach.

Ultimately, the defence's case boils down to the argument that the state has tried but failed to glue together a difficult puzzle with weak forensic evidence and witnesses who, at best, have fading memories and, at worst, are liars out to save themselves.

> *The mosaic the state seeks to create has numerous missing pieces that one cannot merely force together in an endeavour to satisfy the public interest.*

• • •

When Broodryk and Hodes come together to deliver their final arguments, they have to let their papers do the talking. Judge Ranchod does not want them to cover everything again and makes this very clear. He is happy to hear them on a few main points, but is anxious to set a date for judgment and put this case to rest.

Broodryk uses the opportunity to remind the court that while Carrington has offered a theory about being framed by Eric, there has been no evidence to support it. He briefly explains why certain individuals – such as Doc and JB – have not been called and argues that it is impossible for Eric to have orchestrated the discovery of the confession 12 years after his last contact with Carrington, and even more impossible for Betty Ketani's bones to have been planted. He draws a distinction between a contaminated crime scene and a disturbed one and concludes that it is a prosecutor's job to call witnesses who support the state's case. Anything else amounts to playing chess against yourself.

Hodes is in fine form and mocks Broodryk's argument about a scene being disturbed but not contaminated. He says that sounds like something out of a James Bond movie ... 'shaken not stirred'. He also accuses the state of not only playing chess against itself, but of getting itself into a checkmate.

Hodes tells the court that 'every possible contradiction had been made' and that if a court were to give leeway to the accomplice witnesses because of the passage of time, the same should apply to his client. He does not see the discrepancies as simply 'cosmetic', but as fundamental. He calls Broodryk's arguments emotional and ends off with the question of whether the test of reasonable doubt has been passed.

Judge Natvarial Ranchod, who has shown immense patience through-out the trial, declares that he needs time to go through all the evidence. It is October and he wants to go over everything during the next court recess, when it is quiet and he can apply his mind to the case without interruptions.

• • •

In his 2009 'Crime and Punishment' article, Carrington complains that police officers and prosecutors don't take enough risks to catch and convict criminals. They are too scared to 'stick their necks out', he writes, for fear of civil claims.

Broodryk, Kowlas and Van Wyk stand accused of many things by Carrington's legal team, but they cannot be accused of not sticking their necks out. They have secured the best possible local and international expert witnesses, have tried tactics never seen before in South African courts, and arranged for DNA tests in one of the world's finest laboratories. Through the work of the original investigating team, they negotiated deals and saw three men convicted before Carrington and his co-accused even went on trial. They consulted and led dozens of other witnesses, present-ing their case under the scrutiny of the world's media and with Hodes and his team's legal barrels pointed at them at every turn. They never stopped looking for evidence, some of which – such as the Ketani missing persons docket – was found just two days before trial. They fought off repeated attempts for the trial to be stopped and struck off the court roll.

The pressure of the case had landed both Broodryk and his investigating officer in hospital. Van Wyk had a criminal case opened against him by Carrington. Kowlas was insulted in open court. Yet they continued to build their case like a tall, wobbly Jenga tower, never sure whether the defence would finally pull out a piece that would bring it all crashing down. Or, if it stood, what the judge would make of it in the end. It was such a unique case and there was never any certainty. When the Teunis Briers debacle was playing out, Broodryk felt the case slipping through his fingers. But by the time he rose to deliver his closing arguments, he felt more alive than he had in years. It had been a long trial. Now, finally, all that is left is judgment. It is agreed that it will be handed down in four months – on 16 February 2016.

73.

Why was Betty Ketani killed?

The question arose when Jeffrey Marshall lifted that filthy carpet square. Four years later, it remains unanswered.

It is the most frequently asked question and the most persistent of all the mysteries swirling around the cold case. Why would a mother be stolen from her children? Why would a restaurant cook, the owner's favourite and longest-serving member of staff, meet such a brutal end? Was she the target or was it all a terrible mistake?

Conway Brown explained why he hid the confession (his 'insurance policy' against Carrington Laughton) under the carpet. We know he didn't intend to leave it there but forgot to retrieve it when he and his family moved out. He and Dirk Reinecke have clarified how the confession landed up in their hands.

Carrington's history with Eric Neeteson-Lemkes (the 'campaign of terror') sheds enough light on why such a confession may have been written in the first place.

The trial unravelled the various friendships and how each of the characters fits in. The alleged roles played by the policemen – badges for hire – is clear. Through his testimony and the testimony of others, Carrington emerges as a natural leader who was admired, worshipped even, by his friends. He employed most of them. He created alter egos, be it through a murky military past or fake diplomatic number plates. Doc describes him as 'cold steel', a man he would have struggled to work on as a target.

> *I think he would have been any deep-cover agent's worst fucking nightmare. The only tools of your trade – because, let's be honest, criminals have bigger guns and more bullets – so the tools of your trade are deception and manipulation. I don't think any agent would have been able to do that with Carrington. He strikes me as a person who is in control of everything.*

Carrington denies having anything to do with the murder. Not only that, he questions whether it can be proved that Betty Ketani is in fact dead. Those in Australia, New Zealand, Thailand and England remain silent, for now. So all that is left is speculation about what the motive could have been. The fog refuses to lift.

Was Betty killed during a Cranks-related interrogation that went horribly wrong, as Paul Toft-Nielsen claims? Was she silenced for being a troublemaker and rabble-rouser at the restaurant? Did her CCMA case have anything to do with it? Or did she know some other, dark secret about what was going on at Cranks? Was Betty blamed or even framed for the thefts at Eric's restaurant, or was she perhaps taken out as a way for the real thieves to cover up their crimes? Did those who murdered her believe they could act with impunity and that the disappearance of a poor, black woman living in Hillbrow would go unnoticed? Did they think that, with her family so far away, there would be no one to ask questions or demand answers? Did Betty Ketani get caught up in some kind of fantasy game or did she fall into the clutches of a gang of men who afforded her life no value because of her circumstances?

'We have so many theories,' says Namika Kowlas. 'But we still don't know.'

Three men have been convicted and sentenced in connection with the kidnapping and murder. But their confessions only go so far. Broodryk and Kowlas admit that these men held back, not wanting to 'implicate themselves in offences they were not charged for'. And so the delicate vase of truth remains in pieces. Those who have tried to glue it back together have very different ideas about what it looked like back in 1999.

South African law, meanwhile, does not require a motive. Proof that the murder was committed is enough. Well-known Johannesburg lawyer Cliff Alexander sat through most of the trial. He calls it being a spectator to a 'ghoulish' case full of 'intriguing legal complexities' that revealed themselves at every twist and turn. He too wonders about the motive, but his focus is on how the judge will interpret various laws and what precedents will be set:

> The fact that the corpse of Betty Ketani was never discovered compounds the situation to the extent that the state relies on what could be aptly

termed a non-conformist spider web, with a strand branching into the
content of a confession discovered by chance.

Alexander says that the other strands of that web lead to the DNA and handwriting evidence (which he describes as the 'epicentre' of the case) and the Section 105A and Section 204 witnesses.

The case is similar to the Dewani matter in the sense that the state had
to rely, inter alia, on witnesses who themselves were perpetrators to the
crime and who, when being evaluated, would not be described by some as
morally scrupulous individuals.

Alexander says that whichever way the judgment goes, both sides put up a fierce fight. The defence was 'riding a bucking bronco into uncharted territory', while the state displayed a 'robust and at times sanguine attitude'. He adds: 'By the state's own admission, this has been one of the most challenging cases it has ever had to handle.'

74.

Two months before judgment Carrington Laughton's legal team launches another surprise bail application. The papers are served mid-December, well into the festive season. It's another lengthy attack on the state's case, which infuriates Herman Broodryk, who is on holiday with his family in the Kruger National Park. He is convinced Carrington's lawyers have waited for him and Namika Kowlas to go on leave before dropping a 30-page affidavit on them, along with annexures that run into hundreds of pages.

The application needs to be opposed and that job falls, for a second year in a row, to Kowlas, who is with her family in Durban. Once again, she is losing her December leave to fight off an application that has, at best, only a slim chance of ever making it to court.

By January, it becomes clear that – just like that of the previous year – this bail application is going nowhere. Why it was launched in the first place remains unclear, but all Broodryk and Kowlas can do is wait for Judge Natvarial Ranchod to deliver his verdict. It's not long now.

Plans are made for Betty Ketani's brother Mankinki and her eldest daughter, Bulelwa, to get to Johannesburg. Thulani is still too sick, making regular trips to the hospital, and Lusanda is back at school. She's missed a year, but is now hoping to pick up where she left off. Her son is at crèche and she can focus on passing Grade 11. The threat of her dropping out of school for good had troubled Mankinki a great deal and he is relieved to share news that she is back on track.

Judge Ranchod is concerned about how long it will take to read out his judgment and requests that they start a day early, on 15 February 2016. He floats the idea of setting aside a full week, but in the end just three days are rostered for him to unpack his verdict.

That Monday, 15 February, Broodryk arrives in court shortly after 6am. When asked why – given that there are no more arguments to be presented or witnesses to be led – he replies, 'Years of discipline!' His team drives through early to meet him. Their office is empty now, the filing cabinets are gone and the desk has resurfaced from under a blanket of legal papers. The storm of the trial has blown over.

Everyone is on edge. Broodryk and Kowlas have the same answer when asked how they feel: 'Nervous, but cautiously optimistic'. The words feel a little shallow given how much work and emotion have gone into the case. How much of their lives it has consumed and how much turmoil rages inside. Two years of battle and now here they are, with no way to tell whether Judge Ranchod will see a broken chain or a thick, strong rope, woven with all the threads of circumstantial evidence. Will he accept the legal thinking that, individually, the threads may not carry the full weight of the case, but together they are unbreakable?

As they wait for court to start, Broodryk, Kowlas and Van Wyk try to keep the mood light. They joke and make small talk, avoiding looking directly into the eyes of the monster squid sloshing about in the corner of the room: the fear that everything they've done, everything they've been through, will amount to naught.

Inside courtroom 6, the front row of the public gallery fills up with family members and relatives of the three accused. Carrington's wife, Anel, arrives with her mother. It's the first time in a long while that she has come to see him at Palm Ridge. She may have moved on, but Carrington is still the father of her two young sons. The remaining spectators are there to support Carel and David Ranger, some in court for the first time.

Mankinki and Bulelwa slip in at the last minute, and take their seats in the back row. Mankinki flashes a big, warm smile and a thumbs up. Bulelwa is nervous and looks down at the floor, not wanting to make eye contact with the men in the dock. For her and her family, today is about justice, but it is also about slaying the fear that one day, she or her siblings could run into the men who stood trial for murdering their mother. She is scared to think what that confrontation would be like. All this time they've lived with the knowledge that Betty Ketani's alleged killers could be set free, worried they may come after the family.

There's a slight delay in proceedings as police officers in the holding cells hunt down leg irons for Carrington and the Ranger brothers. At 10.30am, Judge Ranchod and his assessors arrive and take their seats. The judge gets straight into it. There are no opening remarks about the case, no comments on its complexity or uniqueness and no words for the legal teams. Just the ruling. As usual, Carrington begins copying it all down in his notebook.

After some legal formalities, Judge Ranchod begins to read out the confession, the single most important piece of evidence without which there would be no trial. After all these years, it's strange to hear it again. The dramatic opening: 'Sandor if you are reading this then I am dead'; the chilling detail around how Ketani had been kidnapped and killed; the plea for revenge; and then those final words: 'Lastly, fuck them all!' Three pieces of paper under a carpet that sent ripples through the universe and changed the fate of so many men and women.

With the confession behind him, the judge presents a narrative of the state's case. He doesn't go into too much detail, but his summary does cover the key witnesses and significant testimony. From the first policeman who presented the yellowing pages of Betty Ketani's missing-persons docket all the way to Karyn Griffin, who, along with Warren Dawson, promises to be the hole in Carrington's apparent alibi.

Judge Ranchod gives little away. He focuses on the quality of work done at the ICMP laboratory in Bosnia and seems impressed with Professor Thomas Parsons's testimony about the DNA match. He covers the handwriting analysis and the evidence of Conway Brown, Paul Toft-Nielsen, Dirk Reinecke and André Coetzer. He makes one small finding by rejecting Themba Tshabalala's diary, but quickly adds that this has no bearing on the statements Tshabalala had made in 1999 relating to his abductions. This hardly surprises anyone.

The court pauses first for tea and then for lunch. At 1.30pm, Judge Ranchod walks in, greets the court and settles down. But something is wrong. Something has happened, possibly in just the last hour. His voice is soft and his eyes are downcast. He announces that he cannot continue. He doesn't explain why, and postpones the case to Wednesday morning, which means a day and a half of judgment lost. The legal teams are stunned. Usually, if there is a problem, they are summoned to chambers. But there had been no warning. None whatsoever. The court rises as Judge Ranchod and his assessors leave. Nobody knows what to make of it all.

. . .

Wednesday is the last day set aside for judgment and if Judge Ranchod doesn't finish delivering it, what will happen is anyone's guess. He is done summarising the state's case, but must still cover what the defence presented and then evaluate the evidence. What he initially wanted to do over a period of a week must now be done in a day and a half.

Paranoia sets in. Herman Broodryk wonders whether the judge has been threatened. In reality, it's probably some kind of family or work emergency, but why such a sudden postponement? Nerves are so frayed that it's easy to tumble down the rabbit hole of conspiracy theories. Broodryk and his team do their best to remain calm, but now there's an extra day of agony, of helpless waiting.

Betty's youngest daughter, Lusanda, is messaging from the Eastern Cape, eager to know what's happening. Mankinki and Bulelwa are stuck in their hotel near Bruma Lake. They can't possibly know, but they are just a kilometre or two from where Doc now lives. He has done a lot of healing since the shooting at Dragon City, but some unfortunate setbacks have left him confined to a wheelchair, spending his days at a home for the disabled. He's joked about not living long enough to hear judgment on the case, but now that it's under way, he is following as best as he can.

His biker friends still come to visit, but Doc's life as an undercover agent for the Scorpions is a distant memory, a faded tattoo on his pale skin. He's all but lost contact with JB and detectives Gerhard Pretorius and Lufuno Sono. The Yeoville team left many mistakes to be mopped up, but they also secured Conway's confession and executed the arrests, setting in motion all the plea-bargain deals that would follow. Sono is still in the police force and JB is still pounding the streets, but Pretorius has left the service and is now conducting polygraph tests. If they are monitoring the outcome of the cold case that they brought back to life, they are doing so in their own private ways, far away from the courtroom.

Conway Brown is also watching from a distance. After his release from prison, he began a new life under house arrest, serving out the remainder of his sentence. His wife has stood by him and he says he has done his best to make his children understand what happened back in 1999. Whether they do, and whether they will ever fully forgive him, he says, only time will tell. Sheldon lives down the road with his own family now and Toni moved out of home just a few days ago.

Conway still lives in Alberton, leaving the house only to go to work or for a few hours on Sundays. Having testified against Carrington and the Rangers, he and Blanche have some new safety routines, such as driving off at the same time each morning and doing their best to make sure he is home by the time she returns. From the moment he was confronted by the police in 2012, he has been obsessed with protecting Blanche and his kids.

A man from his church has helped him find a job in maintenance. It doesn't pay much, but it's honest work and Conway is grateful to have it. Sometime after his release he was hit by a car while on his motorbike – his Fireblade named Eve – and, with his leg smashed, he spent weeks in hospital.

'I have some awesome scars,' he jokes.

Asked whether he still paints, Conway says, 'I haven't done that in a long time.'

Conway spoke in prison about reaching out to Betty's family once he was out. He hasn't done so. He says he wants to stay 'out of sight and out of mind'. It's doubtful he will ever connect with the Ketanis.

Years have passed and he still stands by what he told the police and later a court. His truth remains his truth.

> I haven't changed one bit. I wish I could have said it clearer. Got my point across better than I did. But people talk like they talk. If I said something out of turn, I'm sorry. But the truth did come out.

• • •

The last day of judgment marks two years to the day since the start of the Betty Ketani trial. On 17 February 2014, Carrington Laughton and the

Rangers pleaded not guilty and Herman Broodryk called his first witness. Exactly two years later, the accused will learn their fate.

On that morning, Judge Natvarial Ranchod continues as though nothing has happened, like there has been no unexplained disruption of the court proceedings. It takes him about 20 minutes to traverse the defence's case. He is moving quickly now, compressing Carrington's 13 days on the witness stand into a neat summary.

Then the analysis begins.

The first blow to the defence is dealt straight away. Even though the defence had challenged the very existence of the bones, kicking up a storm about the fact that all six had not been photographed together, Judge Ranchod accepts that the bones were discovered in a shallow grave at Conway's old house. He also finds nothing untoward in the way they were handled and shipped abroad for DNA tests.

The court also accepts the evidence of all of the local police officers and international experts led by the state, particularly Thomas Parsons. Judge Ranchod stresses that the DNA match is being considered with caution, as per the ICMP's own request, but that it remains an important piece of circumstantial evidence. The defence's DNA expert, David Swanepoel, is taken to task for his lack of relevant experience and his 'self-made title' of Human Identification Specialist. Swanepoel is criticised for not running his own, independent DNA tests and for making unfounded allegations, such as his claim that the ICMP used expired reagents.

> *This witness did not conduct a proper inquiry and was willing to comment and provide an opinion without checking his facts. There is simply no scientific basis for his opinion, in contrast to the state's witnesses. The report Mr Swanepoel submitted is considered unreliable. The result of the ICMP is more reliable and is accepted as such.*

It takes Judge Ranchod no more than a minute and a half to throw out Leon Rehrl's evidence, and in doing so deliver the next blow to the defence. Leon had claimed that he had been told about a plot to frame Carrington with a fake letter. His version was that Paul had described this plot to Dirk, Dirk had repeated it to him and he had told Carrington. All this had happened back in 2004, but he only remembered it mid-trial and had no way to prove it, and of course Paul and Dirk both denied it.

The judge finds that since Dirk and Carrington were close friends at the time, if Dirk had become aware of any conspiracy he surely would have alerted Carrington directly, instead of confiding in a stranger. Ranchod dismisses Leon as a 'poor witness' and his evidence as 'highly improbable' and 'inconceivable'.

The handwriting evidence is next. The report compiled by the state's expert, Colonel Marco van der Hammen, sails through with ease. Judge Ranchod notes that the evidence of the defence's handwriting expert, Cecil Greenfield, supports Van der Hammen's findings.

Ranchod then changes direction to deal with the evidence of the state's last two witnesses, Warren Dawson and Karyn Griffin. Both are found to be credible and reliable. Neither, the court finds, has any reason to lie. With their evidence accepted, Carrington Laughton's alibi is in serious trouble.

And it's about to get worse for the defence.

Judge Ranchod lays out Laurence Hodes's application to have the trial declared irregular, the one in which the defence presented grounds ranging from the introduction by Teunis Briers of a real exhibit during re-examination to an issue with the court transcript. Each of the grounds is dissected and dismissed as 'frivolous and vexatious'.

By this point the threads of circumstantial evidence are twirling around each other like a magical beanstalk, spinning faster and faster, fusing together and filling Broodryk and Kowlas with hope. They have won the DNA and handwriting battles. They have damaged, if not destroyed, Carrington's alibi. They have seen off the defence's attempts to find fault with the way the trial was conducted. But they are yet to hear what the court makes of their accomplice witnesses – the 'grin-and-bear-it' crew – and, crucially, of Conway Brown's evidence.

• • •

Conway is driving home from work when he hears the first of the reports on the radio. All of a sudden, Judge Ranchod's voice fills the cabin of the car and his mind rushes back to the court in which he spent almost a week testifying against his friend Carrington Laughton.

He pulls over near the Germiston golf course and tries to catch up on tweets relating to the case. Everything outside the car begins to fade away. The world can go on without him for a bit, Conway thinks, as he tries to process the judgment. He's desperate to understand what's happening, but it's all moving so quickly. Eventually, he decides 'bugger it' and drives home to go over everything at his own pace. His emotions are all over the place.

Carrington had not only dismissed Conway's version of how Betty Ketani was stabbed, but mocked his friend, claiming that Conway's version of events was not worthy of even a really bad movie. But Judge Ranchod's assessment is clear: what Conway's version has that Carrington's doesn't is corroboration.

> *Although he is a single witness and an accomplice in respect of the attempted murder of Ms Betty Ketani, and the cautionary rule would apply, his evidence is corroborated by Exhibit G [the confession]. Brown's evidence of his role after the death of the deceased is corroborated by Exhibit G and other witnesses. Even if I were to apply the cautionary rule, I find his evidence to be clear, frank and reliable on the pertinent issues in this trial.*

For Conway this is a 'personal victory'. Hearing that Betty's family is there to witness it first-hand also makes him happy.

Back in court, Judge Ranchod is working his way through the state witnesses who testified about the bones and the DNA. Claudia Bisso is described as 'erudite, competent and helpful', and while Briers may have caused the prosecutors a great deal of stress, his explanation about the evidence bags is accepted as 'perfectly reasonable', with the court finding that the chain of evidence had not been broken. Leonie Ras is found to be credible and reliable, the ICMP experts 'impressive', and Marco van der Hammen 'objective and fair'. It's a clean sweep for the state. Laurence Hodes had kicked up a great deal of dust, going as far as to point out spelling mistakes on police forms, but the court has refused to be distracted.

Ranchod then arrives at the evidence of Paul Toft-Nielsen, who, on some days, can still be spotted walking a dog past the coffee shops in Westcliff, the leafy suburb where he and Carrington grew up.

> *Mr Nielsen is clearly no angel. However, in respect to the evidence he gave in this matter, this court is satisfied he has told the truth with regard to the exhumation and disposal of the body.*

André Coetzer is also found to be 'no angel', but the court can see no reason for him to implicate his friends. Dirk Reinecke's evidence helps further corroborate the hidden confession. The judge is not prepared to see each piece of evidence in isolation.

> *Although we have mentioned numerous elements, which corroborate the authenticity and authorship of Exhibit G, each one taken on its own may not be sufficient to be conclusive. However, if they are taken all together, then the result is overwhelmingly in favour of Exhibit G being the genuine article and the author thereof being Accused 1.*

Carrington's entire defence is built on the premise that the confession found at Conway's old house is a fake – a well-crafted forgery created as part of a conspiracy against him. By ruling that the confession is real and that Carrington is the man who wrote it, the foundation of his case crumbles. All the accused has left is the evidence he himself gave on the witness stand.

Judge Ranchod foregrounds his analysis of Carrington's testimony by reminding the court that his alibi was given at the last minute and was not put to any of the state's witnesses. He recounts the version Carrington gave about visiting the hospital in 1995, not 1999, to pick up Mary, not Betty, at the request of an employee, not as part of a plot to cover up a botched murder.

The judge states that Carrington has tried to distance himself from all of the crimes and has blamed his legal team for staying silent until the end, while offering no proof of any conspiracy. The accused's strategy has backfired and the guillotine blade finally falls.

> *Accused One was not an impressive witness, although he was confident and easy-going during his evidence-in-chief. He testified in a controlled manner. However, under cross-examination he became evasive and argumentative. As will be apparent by now, his evidence was fraught with inconsistencies and improbabilities. Accused One was a poor witness. His evidence is rejected as false beyond reasonable doubt.*

Carel and David Ranger's hopes of walking free are slashed by the same blade. The court rejects their evidence and finds them to have been poor witnesses.

Judge Ranchod is nearing the end now. From the public gallery, the three accused appear to be motionless, listening. It's hard to tell whether Carrington is still writing or whether he has stopped to absorb the findings against him. His wife, Anel, is crying. The judge explains the legal concept of *dolus eventualis*, finding that Carrington foresaw the possibility that abandoning Betty Ketani in that bus, with the kind of injuries she had, would kill her, and that he reconciled himself to this eventuality.

> *It is trite law that the state must prove its case beyond reasonable doubt. That does not mean proof beyond all shadow of a doubt. The state has presented a formidable case against the three accused ... this court is satisfied that the state has proven its case beyond reasonable doubt.*

For the first time, Judge Ranchod speaks directly to Carrington Laughton, David Ranger and his brother Carel: 'Please stand up, gentlemen.'

. . .

Carrington is convicted on five counts. There's the attempted kidnapping of Ruth Mncube in June 1999; two kidnappings the month before – one from Cranks, the other from the hospital; the attempted murder near the Blockhouse; and the main charge: the murder of Betty Ketani.

Carel and David Ranger escape the murder charge and are instead found guilty of culpable homicide and kidnapping. Their convictions are lighter because they were not involved in the stabbing and there is no evidence to suggest they would have known how serious Betty's injuries were when they picked her up from hospital days later and left her in the bus. The judge does find, though, that they were negligent and failed to act like policemen.

Once Judge Ranchod is finished, Carrington turns to look at Anel. His eyebrows flick up but his lips stay frozen. His jaw is clenched. Moments later, a camera catches him processing the verdict, his eyes shut and his arms folded across his chest.

'Our defence is simple,' he had proclaimed loudly across the courtroom earlier in the trial. 'Prove it!'

The state accepted the challenge and now it was done.

The legal teams discuss sentencing and the prosecutors indicate that they plan to push for life behind bars on the murder charge. But there's no time to deal with that now and a short adjournment is granted so that a new hearing date can be set. Any appeal will have to wait until after sentencing, a process that is due to commence on 3 May 2016.

Captain Gerhard van Wyk struggles to control his emotions. His eyes are red as he walks out of the courtroom. Bulelwa stands in the corridor and cries. Seventeen years after her mother was murdered, she has finally been avenged. There is closure. The men who killed her are going to jail and there is no longer any reason for the family to fear them.

Namika Kowlas and Herman Broodryk walk out to be with Bulelwa and Mankinki. For Broodryk, the most difficult case of his 34-year career is over. There are handshakes and more tears. There are SMSs and phone calls. Towering over Bulelwa, Broodryk gives her an awkward but heartfelt hug.

'It's over now,' he tells her. 'It's all done.'

75.

For Herman Broodryk those brief, emotional moments outside the court-room make everything worthwhile. Walking out into the corridor to see Bulelwa Ketani – whose face so closely resembles her mother's – makes the past four years melt away, giving way to a feeling that if he could, he would do even more. Such as finding Betty's body and returning it to her family. He knows that's not possible, but he can't help the thoughts and tells Bulelwa as much.

Speaking a short while later, Bulelwa says she is overjoyed.

'God has answered our prayers,' she says. 'I think my brother and sister will be happy.'

The family will now meet back in Queenstown to discuss bring-ing her mother's spirit home. Mankinki will have to consult the elders and lead the journey. The family is coming to terms with the fact that even though a small bone remains at the police forensic laboratory in Pretoria, it's unlikely it will be handed over to them. Out of the six bones that emerged from the shallow grave at Conway's house, it is the only one that survives and it may be required in future. Carrington and his co-accused are likely to appeal against their convictions and sentences, while successful extraditions could lead to an entirely new trial.

And so the Ketani family may have to guide Betty's soul for hundreds of kilometres, from Johannesburg to Queenstown, without any of her remains. This will require a special traditional ceremony at the location where she was buried. Mankinki explains that sometimes, in cases like this, a twig from a nearby thorn tree or some other item is used to help shepherd the spirit home.

Bulelwa knows it won't be easy or cheap, but she is pleased that her mother will finally get her own grave. Bulelwa says she, Lusanda and Thulani will be able to visit it on Mother's Day or when they experience problems in their own lives. She wants her daughters to be able to visit their grandmother when they grow up.

. . .

On the evening of the judgment, Conway Brown is on the road again. He's driving towards Kenilworth, navigating familiar routes to reach 21 Leo Street. He hasn't seen Shama Marshall much since he came out of prison. Once or twice perhaps. But now that Carrington and the Rangers have been convicted, he feels a strange desire to see her. He wants to have a quiet cup of coffee with Shama and talk some things through.

As always, it's an impulsive move. He must be home soon to meet his parole curfew. He hasn't worked through his emotions yet and going back to the house is difficult. He's nervous and unsure about what he's doing. But he keeps driving, finding Shama at home.

They talk about Geoffrey Marshall, the man who took Conway under his wing, and about the old days. Conway is in a rush so they don't get through everything that has happened. It's a quick catch-up. Conway has neither the time nor the nerve to explore next door, the side of the house where he and his family lived. Where Betty Ketani's body lay under the concrete and his garden blossomed above her grave. Maybe next time, he thinks.

Shama's son, Jeffrey, isn't there. He's moved out and now lives with his new girlfriend. But he still works at the car workshop and rides his motorbike. Like Conway, he too had an accident, but his was nowhere near as serious as Brown's. The two of them have not seen each other since the confession was found.

In the interim, Shama and Werner also called off their engagement. Werner moved out but continues to work as a chef at a Spar up north. The three of them are friends and there are no hard feelings

Jeffrey says he is both relieved and surprised that the case has ended in convictions. He says that he felt it was falling apart at one stage and he didn't have much faith in the justice system. He and his family, like the Ketanis, lived in fear of those 'seeking vengeance'. He says this fear cast a shadow over what would have otherwise been a moment of victory.

Looking back, Jeffrey gives Werner a lot of the credit. He says he didn't have a clue about what to do with the strange letter he found under the carpet. Those three neatly typed pages, stapled together, folded in half, and then hidden under that dirty old carpet. How easily they could have simply been discarded and thrown away.

76.

'[A] cold and lonely death.' Of all the words Judge Natvarial Ranchod utters while sentencing those responsible for Betty Ketani's murder, these five linger. Like a restless spirit, they refuse to fall onto the pages of the court record or settle down into notebooks. Instead, they continue to conjure images of a dark night, a bus rusting away in the middle of nowhere, a wounded woman locked inside. By morning, she is dead.

For two years, Judge Ranchod has listened patiently and has said little. He has been reluctant to pass unnecessary comment on the torrent of evidence flowing before him. But on the final day of the trial, he makes his impressions clear:

> *The deceased was abandoned carelessly in the middle of winter in an old bus to die a cold and lonely death. No doubt the deceased must have experienced mortal fear, anguish and considerable pain. [These actions] can only be described as heartless and cruel. This was a brutal attack on a defenceless woman for reasons that remain unknown.*

Compared to what came before, sentencing proceedings are wrapped up quickly. They run over the course of four days, starting on 3 May 2016. Carrington Laughton's legal team presents a report compiled by a social worker, which calls on Judge Ranchod to adopt a balanced approach.

The author has interviewed Carrington, his father and several of his close friends. In a comprehensive report, which chronicles Carrington's life and is read into the record, the social worker presents a man who is both caring and intelligent, but also deceitful.

The report speaks of Carrington's happy childhood, festive family Christmases arranged by his mother and his journey from a 'reserved and socially awkward' child to a 'peace maker' amongst friends, a persuasive and confident man and patient father.

It is based almost exclusively on the views of those sympathetic to him, and discusses Carrington's cooking skills and the lessons he taught his children.

'Mr Laughton may have his faults,' the report states. 'Being a father is not one of them.'

It quotes Carrington's third wife, Anel, describing how she missed his support and protection. Had it not been for his arrest and lengthy detention, she speculates, they would still be together.

The report glides over Carrington's previous marriages, his military history and his work experience. It reveals that, while in custody, he has started studying towards a paralegal qualification and even has him expressing empathy for the Ketani family, stating that, as a parent, he can relate to their loss.

The social worker's report covers his previous conviction and the lies that have been exposed; the fake business associates, the Aston Martin insurance claim and the doctored photographs of a made-up murder. It points out that Carrington can be over-confident and stubborn, and that a pattern of him resolving business problems 'in a deceitful manner' has emerged.

It does not argue for anything but direct imprisonment, but draws attention to the other facets of his life and argues that mitigating circumstances exist to deviate from the prescribed minimum sentences.

Brothers Carel and David Ranger also present pre-sentencing reports, compiled by the same social worker. Prosecutors, meanwhile, push hard for Carrington to be sent to jail for life and for the court to consider that the Ranger brothers were both serving policemen at the time of the offence.

Ketani's brother, Mankinki, and her middle child, Bulelwa, take the stand and testify in aggravation of sentence. Bulelwa tells the court she still dreams of her mother as though she will one day return. Prosecutor Herman Broodryk keeps circling back to the argument that, by maintaining their innocence, Carrington and the Rangers are denying the family answers about why Ketani was murdered.

On 6 May 2016, Judge Ranchod sentences the three men in the dock. He appears unmoved by the personal information they have offered and describes Carrington as having 'played a leadership role', while Carel and

David Ranger are, in his opinion, the 'authors of their own misfortune'.

> *In my view, [Laughton] was manipulative and used various persons to do his bidding. However, what cannot be overlooked is that [the Rangers] were experienced police officers who should have known better than to participate in unlawful activities no matter under what influence ...*

Having been convicted of murder, attempted murder, attempted kidnapping and kidnapping, Carrington is handed a 30-year sentence. The Rangers, found guilty of culpable homicide and kidnapping, are sent to serve four years behind bars. All three have already spent four years in custody awaiting trial. Almost three months have passed since the convictions and there is less emotion surrounding the sentencing. The legal fight moves swiftly on to the appeals.

· · ·

Five days after sentencing, on 11 May 2016, the Ketanis are back in Johannesburg. For the first time, all three of Betty's children have made the journey from Queenstown. The eldest, Thulani, had always been too sick to travel, but this time it is different.

It's a sunny but windy afternoon and the white Toyota Avanza pulls its trailer along the R59 highway, pausing briefly at the Blockhouse Engen 1-Stop. It's heading south, down to Eardley's farm, to that empty bus that stands on blocks of concrete just in front of the main house. That cold and lonely place ...

Mankinki has invited two family elders to conduct the ceremony. With the three children, the six passengers are crammed into the Avanza, a hired driver behind the wheel. Their escort is Detective Gerhard van Wyk, who is in his own car up ahead.

When they finally pull up at Eardley's farm, Van Wyk jumps out to speak to tenants who live next to the red-and-white bus. He explains what is about to happen and a noisy dog is pulled inside to give the family some peace.

Mankinki takes the lead as they untie the canvas cover and open the trailer. Inside lies a shiny, empty coffin. Lusanda joins in as a pall bearer, carrying the casket from the trailer to the side of the bus. The youngest child, still a teenager, is wearing a jumper with the words 'I'll think about it' on the front. She and the other children must now confront the scene where their mother died on a day much like this, 17 years previously. The elders believe this is where her spirit is waiting for them.

The old municipal bus, which once served as an outside bedroom, is locked and there is no way to get inside. But some of the top windows are open, which means that if they call out to Ketani's spirit it should hear them and escape its prison. The family prepare the coffin. They fold out a blanket and lay down a blouse and a skirt where a body would otherwise be. They've also brought a leafy branch, broken off a buffalo thorn tree in the Eastern Cape. The thorns tend to face away from each other like the horns of a buffalo, and the belief is that they will help hook the spirit and guide it inside the coffin. A female blood relative must speak to the spirit and plead with it to return. The spirit must be assured that it will be looked after and reunited with other ancestors. If it refuses, the belief goes, it will continue to haunt the place of death.

Thulani hangs back to process his emotions in his own way as the elders begin to knock on the side of the bus. Their chants drown out the hollow gong of the metal. Bulelwa and Lusanda feel the arms of an elder wrap around them as they break down and cry. One by one, the children are introduced to the spirit.

Captain Van Wyk keeps his distance. Being here is important for him; he wants to see his case through to the end. But he is not familiar with Xhosa rituals and wants the family to have privacy. A short while later, as the closed coffin is carried back to the trailer, one of the elders pulls him in for a long, emotional embrace.

The family then drives to Kenilworth, to the house where the confession was found by Jeffrey Marshall and his family in 2012, and where Ketani's body was buried under what is now a garage. A slightly bewildered tenant agrees to remove his car from the garage of the house that Conway and his family once rented to allow the next part of the ceremony to proceed. In what must be a strange spectacle for those unaware of the circumstances, the coffin is carried across Leo Street and opened next to the spot where the shallow grave was once dug.

As handfuls of earth are scattered inside the coffin, Lusanda falls back against the garage wall. She covers her eyes with her sleeve as she sobs for a mother she never knew. For her and the rest of the family, the brutality of the crime is brought home. In court, Mankinki had said that his sister was killed like a dog. This is where she was buried, in a grave that was later robbed. From a distance, Jeffrey's mother, Shama, and her former fiancé, Werner Nortjé, look on. Dark clouds gather overhead and at some point it begins to drizzle.

'Showers of blessing,' Shama says, ever the believer in karma.

The Avanza finally drives off, making its way back down the street. Betty Ketani's spirit is on its way home.

Epilogue

Updated: March 2017

The moment Carrington Laughton and the Ranger brothers were sentenced, their dissatisfaction with Judge Natvarial Ranchod's conclusions was clear. All three immediately applied for leave to appeal against their convictions, while Carrington went further by appealing against his 30-year sentence.

Judge Ranchod heard arguments in this respect, but remained unmoved. He refused all three leave to appeal, finding that there was no prospect of another court reaching a different verdict. Previously, he had described Carrington's attempts to have the trial declared irregular as 'frivolous and vexatious'.

For Carrington and the Rangers the next stop was the Supreme Court of Appeal (SCA) in Bloemfontein. At the SCA, Carrington continued to argue that he had not received a fair trial and that his sentence was 'startlingly inappropriate' and induced 'a sense of shock'.

In court papers that ran to 85 pages, including uncontested explanations for why certain appeal deadlines had been missed, Carrington again attacked the state's case, from beginning to end. He argued the trial was 'plagued by anomalies and inconsistencies' and that he had been prejudiced in the process. Much like the defence he presented during trial, he led a wholesale assault on the DNA results, handwriting analysis, the gathering of evidence, safeguarding of the crime scene and the chain of custody. He continued to claim there was no way to be certain that Betty Ketani was actually dead, given that her body had never been found. Carrington challenged the discovery of six bones, only three of which had been photographed at the excavation. During the trial, the state had led at least five witnesses to prove the additional bones had been found, supplementing their evidence with a crime-scene report.

The former private investigator further claimed that too much weight had been attached to the confession, while his explanations had been rejected. He criticised every aspect of the case against him, from his arrest to the judge's reliance on the evidence of the accomplice witnesses, who were found to be 'no angels'. There was again reference to his access to the court record and questions as to whether Judge Ranchod had properly explained all his decisions.

Carrington questioned the logic of the court in dismissing him as an unreliable witness while relying on his 1999 confession as the 'gospel truth'. He brought up Themba Tshabalala's diary, the fact that Ruth Mncube could not identify him in court and that Dirk Reinecke testified about seeing Ketani after her initial kidnapping and interrogation in a hotel room. Judge Ranchod, he charged, had been 'consumed and swayed by the confession letter'.

What Carrington did concede was that the Ketani trial was remarkable and unique, both because of the nature of the case and the law surrounding it. He called it 'unusual' and 'peculiar', a case covered in the media and discussed in legal circles. Since his arrest in early 2012, he had been downplaying the bizarre circumstances of the Betty Ketani case, denying any involvement and dismissing it as nothing more than a poor attempt to frame him for a murder he did not commit.

Carel and David Ranger did not ask the SCA to review their sentences, which were significantly less than Carrington's, and limited their appeal to the convictions – probably well advised because courts have been known to increase sentences being reviewed under appeal. Their central argument was that the confession could not be used to incriminate them and that they had been 'conned' into making certain admissions in their bail statements. While applying for bail, they spoke of events that had occurred in 1999, but when they testified years later they changed this to 1995. Prosecutors argued that the Rangers had adjusted their evidence to align with Carrington's, but Carel and David maintained they had been pressured into making this mistake by the state, given the weight of the charges they initially faced.

Prosecutors Herman Broodryk and Namika Kowlas answered all of these arguments, maintaining that they had, in the words of the trial court, built a formidable case. They had faced most, if not all of these attacks during the trial. Their argument was that Judge Ranchod could not have covered all of the evidence presented to him in his judgment – given that the trial had run over two years and the court record was over 7 000 pages long – but that this didn't mean he hadn't fairly assessed all of it to reach his findings.

In early November 2016, the SCA ruled on Carrington's application for leave to appeal. The application – which is fought with affidavits from both sides – had been considered by two judges of the court, who were not convinced by Carrington's arguments:

> *The application for leave to appeal is dismissed on the grounds that there are no reasonable prospects of success and there is no other compelling reason why an appeal should be heard.*

A month later, Carrington launched the next offensive. This time, he petitioned the president of the SCA to review the decision of the two judges who had agreed with Judge Ranchod. In another lengthy application, consisting of nearly 70 pages of arguments, Carrington set out to show that he deserved 'another bite at the cherry', failing which an injustice would arise. Once again, he gave the full history of the case and the trial, claiming that the two SCA judges had not properly dealt with certain aspects. Once again, he pointed out what he believed to be the many irregularities that had denied him a fair trial. He spoke of 'human fallibility' and the possibility of judges making mistakes. He acknowledged that he had to demonstrate exceptional circumstances and not merely repeat arguments that had already been rejected.

During the same month, in December 2016, Carel and David Ranger were granted leave to appeal against their conviction by the SCA. When Carrington found out, he submitted a further affidavit claiming that this could be considered as further exceptional circumstances.

For the third consecutive year, Broodryk and Kowlas spent much of their December preparing answering affidavits. They accused Carrington of persisting in giving the appeals court incorrect facts and failing to show any exceptional circumstances.

'This is nothing more than a regurgitation of the applicant's previously rejected arguments,' Broodryk stated. He responded by dismissing

Carrington's claims one by one, paragraph by paragraph.

Broodryk referred the president of the SCA to his previous affidavit and Judge Ranchod's judgment, arguing that all the points being raised had already been dealt with. He also accused Carrington of making 'sweeping statements' without presenting examples.

Broodryk also argued that the Ranger brothers had not been convicted on the same evidence as Carrington and their appeal thus had no effect on his. The brothers were found guilty of culpable homicide, not murder, and were not implicated in the initial attack on Ketani on the side of the R59 highway. Therefore, Broodryk reasoned, while Carrington knew his actions would lead to Ketani's death (the legal principle of *dolus eventualis*), the Rangers would not have known the extent of her injuries while kidnapping her from hospital.

In late February 2017, Carrington's appeal to the president of the SCA was refused. He still has the option of petitioning the Constitutional Court, the highest court in the land, but will need to convince it that a constitutional issue is at play. This application is expected to be made and challenged in coming months.

At the time of going to print with this paperback edition, this is where the appeal battle stands. The Rangers are due to appeal against their convictions before a full bench of judges at the Gauteng Local Division. Each step is bringing all those involved closer to what former deputy chief justice, Dikgang Moseneke, calls 'judicial truth'.

. . .

The weekend after Betty Ketani's family drove home from Johannesburg, they finally held a funeral for her at a cemetery near the Queenstown house where her children live. There is no headstone on the grave yet, and the coffin remains empty, but it offers Thulani, Bulelwa and Lusanda a place to visit on Sunday mornings or on special occasions. What matters is that their mother's spirit has returned.

Thulani is still ill and continues to travel long distances for check-ups at a hospital in East London. Bulelwa is unemployed and spends her days looking after her twins and Lusanda's son, along with running a small spaza shop from the house. Lusanda, the youngest, is in her final year at school. Despite the time she lost during the trial, her uncle, Mankinki, says she is now doing well and her marks are good. He says she tells him she wants to be a social worker.

Mankinki still lives in Barkly East and visits his sister's children about once a month. He still has his little petrol station shop, but doesn't see it lasting too much longer. He's turned much of his attention to another business, which involves towing and repairing broken-down cars.

Mankinki says Captain Gerhard van Wyk phoned him just before Christmas to check how the family was doing. He told him they were doing all right.

Detective Van Wyk has moved on to other cases, as has Kowlas, who spends a lot of time in court. In 2016, her family was struck by a tragedy when her mother suffered a heart attack and collapsed at a seventieth birthday party Kowlas had organised for her. An only child, and having already lost her father, Kowlas spent time in Durban grieving and arranging the funeral.

Broodryk's heart continues to give him problems. On a happier note, he has become a grandfather, an event that has had a profound effect on his life. He's also been put in charge of planning the High Court criminal roll in his division, an important job that keeps trials flowing, but also a stressful task that makes his 'heart creak'. There's a joke going around that the position required someone old and grumpy, and that he fitted the profile. Broodryk is approaching retirement but says he will continue to fight the appeals along with Kowlas.

The two prosecutors have been preparing extradition papers relating to Monique Neeteson-Lemkes and Mark Lister, but the appeals have slowed the process. Broodryk says they have been keeping the Australian attorney-general appraised of developments and will finalise the requests in the course of 2017.

Carrington's legal team was approached to comment for this update, but did not respond. Attempts to interview Carrington for this book began in 2012 and continued throughout the trial. They have all proved unsuccessful. His side of the story, and that of all the accused, is however comprehensively represented through the cases they presented in court. It took four years of patiently following the trial for these versions to emerge.

There has been no word from Conway Brown, Paul Toft-Nielsen and Dirk Reinecke, nor from the original investigating team from Yeoville. None of the characters who remained silent throughout the trial – people such as Sandor Egyed or Carrington's first wife Candice – have broken their silence. Eric Neeteson-Lemkes, who left South Africa before the trial began, has not reappeared. In short, in the year since this book was first published, no new puzzle pieces have fallen into place. But who knows, perhaps some day they will.

Appendix

Sandor if you are reading this then I am ~~either~~ dead. Contained herein is all the information relating to Monique and the investigation that was undertaken, as well as the details of all those concerned and the level of their involvement. Your mission is to bring them all down completely.

1. During the course of the investigation several people were abducted and tortured namely; THEMBA TSHABALALA, BETTY KETANI & NDABA BHEBHE.

2. In the case of THEMBA the people involved in his three abductions were myself, Monique, Mark Lister (and Dirk who must be left out of this). Andre Coetzer and Carel Ranger also picked him up once, but did not harm him. Their involvement is being investigated by Internal Affairs (Hillbrow Office) by an Insp. Van Rooyen. The first time THEMBA was abducted was from his home, where he was taken to the place where we played the night paint ball game. We slapped him around for a while and eventually released him – involved were me, Mark, Monique and Dirk. The second time was from his work at the Carnivore restaurant where Mark and I posed as army officers and took him to the broken house near Eardley's place in the bush (the one closest to Eardley and not the one that we first walked to when we checked out that area of bush for the night game). Again the same four of us were involved. I can't remember the details of the third. Insp. Van Rooyen will be most interested to know that Monique, Carel and Andre know each other.

3. BETTY KETANI was "arrested" by Mark and his friend Warren Williams (0836002130) in Rosebank. Mark was in army uniform. She was taken to the same little house where she was slapped around for a few hours. After this Monique, Mark and Warren left her in my care at the house where Conway met me, we drove her about 10 minutes further down the highway and "killed" her, this was I think on 25 May 1999. However we did not do a brilliant job and three weeks later she surfaced and regained conciousness in the Kopanong Hospital in Vereeniging suffering from mild brain damage and severe mental trauma. Dave Ranger (0828981718), Carel Ranger (0828241808) and myself posing as medical transfer service staff uplifted her for the hospital and using a hired Kombi took her to the bus on Eardley's farm where we locked her up for the night. Dave pushed the wheelchair out of the hospital. Mark and Monique followed in my car. However during the night she died (I think from shock). On the morning that Candice shot herself (12 June 1999?) Mark, Monique and Conway fetched the body and buried it in about a cubic metre of cement in Conway's garden behind his garage. For obvious reasons Conway cannot be involved in this. Her clothing and other shit was burned by Mark, Monique & I next to Alexander. For this we hired a wheel chair from a medical supply company off Louis Botha Ave in Corlett City. This was done in the name of C. Anderson, 25 Rathmines Road. Both Dave and Carel Ranger are policemen (sergeants) who are based at Douglasdale station.

4. NDABA BHEBHE who is related to THEMBA somehow was picked up from his home (1906 Aintree Place, cnr Tudhope & O' Reilly Streets, Berea) and taken by Mark to Randburg Police Station where we slapped him around for a while with Carel & Monique in attendance. Thereafter we took him to a section of bush near to where Poul (0823225074) used to live in Fourways. Mark, Monique and I did this.

5. Anyway another victim was MALEMLELI MPOFU who lives in 901 Britton Manor, Cnr Kaptein & Klein Streets, Hillbrow. He was "arrested" by Monique and I posing as policemen, I was D/Sgt Richard Wessels (see fake ID) and she was D/Sge Louise Brenner. We took him to the Sandton Hotel Formule One and kept him there for the night, thereafter we took him to the Sandton Park Hotel, where we were staying (room 002), under the name Mac Intosh or Mac Donald. Included in the tin is an 8mm video tape of his questioning. He was kept by us for 3 days and eventually released. Involved were me, Monique, Mark & Douglas. Dirk guarded him once for about 3 hours at Sandton Park. MALAMLELI was one of the people who deposited one of Monique's stolen cheques in his account.

6. Included in the tin are some photos of Monique and I, a letter she wrote me, a video of us screwing and other interesting bits and pieces. All of these should be copied and copies given to her father (Eric) who is on (011) 880-3442, as well as a copy of this letter. Use your discression to censor this letter to protect those who need protecting, a black marker pen should do the trick. The large professionally taken photo could also be used by THEMBA to identify me as one of his abductors, as well as to tie me in with Monique. As you know there are more such photos on my desk as well as several cards from her and the A4 "I Love You" certificate on the notice board, which may or may not still be there. Our sexual relationship began 4 weeks after meeting (29 April 1999) each other and started in the Protea Gardens Hotel in Hillbrow. From there we went to the Chamberry Hotel (room 8) in Randburg (Main Road) where we booked in under the name of Louise Crawford, and from there to Sandton Park Hotel.

7. Included is a 1.44 MB stiffy with wav files of telephone conversations as well as copies of all letters that I wrote Monique (in Word 97) plus all invoices, etc (including this letter).

8. In the box is also a black hood, which Insp. Van Rooyen would be most interested to see, as he has about 4 already from various abductions.

9. During the investigation Monique told her father all sorts of stories about a woman called RUTH MNCUBE, whom he believes is dead. RUTH is very much alive and well and all photos to prove this are in an envelope marked "Ruth". Also at no stage whatsoever did we ever manage to capture or detain RUTH, only once did I grab her in town, but she escaped as a large crowd helped her. I think Eric should know the truth as to how dishonest and deceitful his daughter really is! She lied to him every step of the way regarding every stage of the investigation.

10. In my cupboard are some of Monique's clothes that she left here, which also may or may not be there, as well as cosmetics and toiletries.

11. At her house in the cottage is a wooden single door cupboard in which all letters, gifts, etc that I gave her are kept. Tell her father this too.

12. In my gun safe (copy of key included) is an ABSA bank bag belonging to Monique in it is some personal paperwork as well as money in white envelopes, happy birthday Sandor the money is yours, use it to help me. Please note that Monique has a copy of the safe key so I will insert a lock block, the key should also be included. Last count about US$ 3000 and R 10000. There may also be some Australian Dollar travellers cheques which she stole from her father.

13. Monique opened a Nedbank account at the Hyde Park Branch, using Commercial Services as a front for employment, etc. Let dad know this too.

14. Her full names are Monique Naiyana Neeteson-Lemkes, ID number (770326 0788 080).

15. Inside the box is the Cranks investigation file, which contains lots of information, which you should find useful.

16. Also included is a strange photo of lots of little photos, this can prove a connection between everyone involved. It was taken at a group dinner. - *(handwritten annotation)*

17. Sandor please do everything you can to avenge me.

18. Speak to Candice, she will also be able to help (if she wants to) and speak to Dirk (0823746905), he definitely can help.

19. Luigi (Tanfoglio 9mm), the shotgun, 22 pistol, and AMT 9mm short are yours as well as my Astina. Enjoy! Also if you want it C&C Commercial Services cc. is yours too.

20. Lastly – fuck them all!!!!!

Regards, best wishes and see you sometime. Alex & I are waiting patiently.

30 September 1999

(handwritten) ALSO IN THE VOICE FILES ARE 3 CONVERSATION WITH A DET/SGT ERWIN HYDE (RANDBURG) - 2 OF THEM ARE BETWEEN HIM & MONIQUE ! HYDE DID NOT DO ANYTHING BUT KNEW ABOUT THE CASE.

Acknowledgements

Writing this book required an extraordinary amount of patience and no one showed greater patience than my wife, Kay. Thank you for giving me the space to work on this project and for all your love, support and guidance. The seed to write *Cold Case Confession* was sowed before our son was born, and seeing it through has had a profound impact on our family. The Russian author Mikhail Bulgakov once wrote: 'The silent writer doesn't exist. If he has fallen silent, that means he's not a real writer. And if a real writer has fallen silent, he will perish.' You, Kay, helped me through those dark times when I risked falling silent. I couldn't have done this without you. Two against the world.

My gratitude goes, too, to my parents, Anatoly and Irina, the bravest people I know. Thank you for inspiring me and for being my teachers. Everything I achieve in life is a ripple across a pond you created. You showed me a world filled with art and literature, not walls and boundaries. And thanks to my sister, Anastasya, who not only designed this book cover but continues to fill my heart with pride each and every day. You have won some mighty battles; please continue to paint the world in bright colours, like only a real artist can.

To my family scattered across the globe – Ian, Margaret, Bronwen and your wonderful family: I know the distance doesn't make it easy, but we are never too far apart. Thank you for your support.

To my friends Jess, Alicia, Justin, Steve and Kelly, thank you for being excited for me. Here's a toast to our group!

Thank you to the team at Pan Macmillan and specifically to Andrea Nattrass, Terry Morris and Laura Goldsworthy. For more than three years you refused to give up on this project and accepted me into your family. You have helped me achieve a lifelong dream and showed me that a business can indeed have a warm heart and a gentle soul. I am enormously grateful and can't help but feel that the adventure is only beginning.

To my Eyewitness News family ... Katy Katopodis, thank you for realising the potential of this story – remember how I burst into your office to tell you about it straight after meeting my source? – and allowing me to devote so much time to it. You are a true leader, an inspiring mentor and a great friend. This book would not have been possible without you and I am proud, every day, to be part of your team. Mandy Wiener, you showed us the way. Thank you for your friendship and for the role you played in making this book a reality. Whatever the future holds, we will always have those coffee chats on the newsroom couch. Camilla Bath, Barry Bateman, Stephen Grootes, Benita Levin, Sheldon Morais, Gia Nicolaides and everyone else in the EWN team and at Primedia, it is an honour and a privilege to work with you and to count you as my friends.

This book required me to work closely with many reporters, some based in Australia. Thank you to Ross Coulthart, Ean Higgins and Peter Munro for helping me obtain information that would otherwise remain out of reach, and for telling the story in different ways.

As part of my research, I conducted dozens of interviews (over 60 at last count), travelled to the Eastern Cape, trawled through archives and read books such as *Bosnia's Million Bones: Solving the World's Greatest Forensic Puzzle* by Christian Jennings, which details the work of the International Commission on Missing Persons. Over the past four years, I have met a great number of people and worked with some trusted old sources. I wish I could thank by name everyone who helped me, but I can't. You know who you are, so please accept my gratitude and know that no journalist can exist without his sources.

To the people who kindly gave up their time to read through the manuscript – Jonathan Ancer, Lesley Cowling, James Grant and Peter James – I am in your debt. Jonathan, I have always admired your writing and your input has been invaluable. James, you have an incredible legal mind and some of your explanations here led to significant breakthroughs in understanding the law around the Betty Ketani trial. Lesley, your kind words gave me the confidence to trust my writing, and your direction helped shape the manuscript. Peter, having met me once on a trip to South Africa, you were very kind to read the book and give me a shout quote. I hope I can repay the favour some day.

To my editor on this project, Sean Fraser, it's been an absolute pleasure. You led me through a tricky part of the forest, and had it not been for you, this book might still contain long, philosophical chapters deconstructing the literature of Dostoyevsky. Thank you for wielding the axe and helping me stay on the path.

I have also been incredibly fortunate to work with photographer Alon Skuy, who has had an interest in the Betty Ketani story from the very start. Alon and I were colleagues at the *Star* and remain friends. He is, without a doubt, one of the finest photographers in this country and his images in this book have captured some powerful moments.

A word of gratitude also to Anton Harber, the Wits journalism department and the Taco Kuiper Fund. Aside from the grant, which helped with some of the investigation that was conducted, just being associated with such a prestigious fund is an honour.

To my friend Branko Brkic, thank you for letting me aboard your pirate ship. You and your team at *Daily Maverick* restore my faith in our profession.

To the team over at *Carte Blanche*, thank you for handling this story with such care and for sharing it with your audience. And I gratefully acknowledge all the other television programmes and publications that picked up on it, from the *Daily Dispatch* in the Eastern Cape to the *Toronto Star* in Canada.

Jenny Crwys-Williams, thank you for your interest, interviews and invitations to all the events. I must still be the only author in history to do the circuit two years in a row without an actual book. I am deeply grateful for the opportunities you have given me.

I am always in gratitude to the editors at the *Sandton Chronicle* who, for some reason, decided to take a chance on a 19-year-old kid with dyed red hair and far too many misguided metaphors. Thank you, Ellen Raubenheimer, Olivia Schaffer, Jacci Babich, Mary Mulke and everyone else.

Finally, and very importantly, to the Ketani family: Thulani, Lusanda and Bulelwa, thank you for trusting me with your story and for opening up your lives to me. Mankinki, your smile cut through so much of the pain we were dealing with during all our interviews. I know it couldn't have been easy. Betty, we never met but you have occupied my life for four years. Your brother gave me a photograph of you, the one where you are casually leaning back against the boot of an old yellow Chevrolet. It must have been taken in Johannesburg during a happier time. I put this photograph up on the wall of my office and every time I wrote or did research, it caught my eye. Some days I just sat there and looked at it. I tried to imagine life through your eyes and agonised over all the mysteries surrounding your death. Whenever I felt weak or wanted to quit, this photo brought me back and reminded me why I had to finish telling your story.

Alex Eliseev
March 2016

For further information and details about this case, visit the website

www.alexeliseev.co.za

and follow Alex Eliseev on Twitter at @alexeliseev